THE FRANCIS PARKMAN PRIZE

The Society of American Historians was founded in 1939 by Allan Nevins and others to stimulate literary distinction in historical writing. In its early years, the Society sought to create a magazine for popular history; this effort culminated in the establishment of *American Heritage* in the early 1950s. The Society then resolved to advance its mission by offering an annual prize for the best-written book in American history. To name the prize after Francis Parkman seemed nearly a foregone conclusion.

Parkman was born in 1823, the grandson of one of Boston's wealthiest merchants. Throughout his life, Parkman was plagued with nervous disorders and problems with his eyes. Yet he loved the outdoors and exulted in sojourns into the wild. "I was haunted with wilderness images day and night," he recalled, one reason why his evocations of frontier life were so powerful.

But he also was drawn to history. As a sophomore at Harvard he resolved on his life's work—a history of the struggle between France and Britain for mastery of North America. But first he trekked to the West and wrote *The Oregon Trail* (1849), a youthful work that exhibited the masterful writing that became his hallmark. The first volume of *France and England in North America* was published in 1865, the ninth and final volume in 1892.

Some of Parkman's judgments have been superseded by modern scholarship, and, in matters of style, he overused the concept of opposition (the most significant being the contrast between authoritarian and Catholic France, and democratic and Protestant Britain). Henry Adams was a more sophisticated thinker, and perhaps a more profound writer, but Parkman was the great American historian of the nineteenth century.

The first Parkman Prize was awarded in 1958 to Arthur M. Schlesinger, Jr., for his *Crisis of the Old Order*, published the previous year. And now the Society of American Historians is pleased to be working together with History Book Club to develop their exclusive new editions of Parkman Prize winners from the past— allowing readers to rediscover what many consider to be some of the best writing on the American story.

Mark C. Carnes
Executive Secretary
The Society of American Historians

AMERICAN SLAVERY, AMERICAN FREEDOM

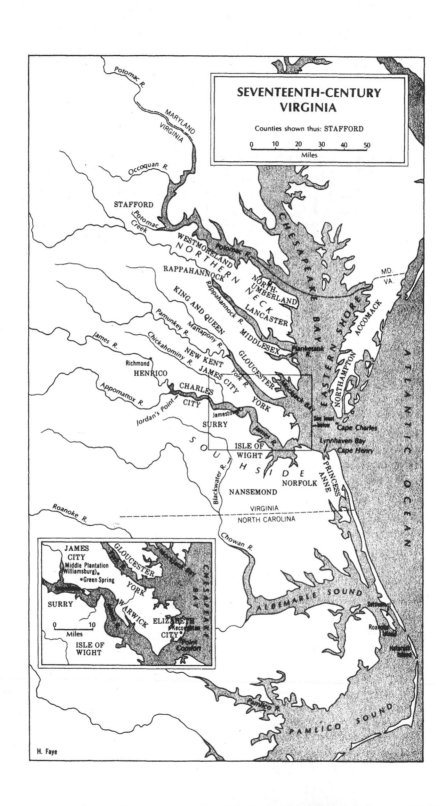

SEVENTEENTH-CENTURY
VIRGINIA

Counties shown thus: STAFFORD

0   10   20   30   40   50
Miles

Potomac R.

MARYLAND
VIRGINIA

Occoquan R.

STAFFORD

Potomac
Creek

CHESAPEAKE BAY

MD.
VA.

WESTMORELAND
NORTHERN
RAPPAHANNOCK
NORTH
UMBERLAND
N E C K
LANCASTER

EASTERN SHORE

ACCOMACK

KING AND QUEEN
MIDDLESEX

Rappahannock R.

Pamunkey R.

Mattapony R.

NEW KENT
GLOUCESTER

James R.

Chickahominy R.

Richmond

HENRICO
JAMES CITY
YORK R.

YORK

Piankatank
R.

Mobjack Bay

NORTHAMPTON

Appomattox R.

CHARLES
CITY

Jordan's Point

Jamestown

SURRY

S O U

Cape Charles
Old Point
Comfort

ISLE OF
WIGHT

Lynnhaven Bay
Cape Henry

T H S I D E

NORFOLK

PRINCESS
ANNE

Blackwater R.

NANSEMOND

ATLANTIC OCEAN

Roanoke R.

VIRGINIA
NORTH CAROLINA

Chowan R.

ALBEMARLE SOUND

JAMES
CITY
Middle Plantation
(Williamsburg)
Green Spring

GLOUCESTER

YORK

WARWICK

SURRY

ELIZABETH
CITY
Kecoughtan
Point
Comfort

CHESAPEAKE BAY

ISLE OF
WIGHT

0   10
Miles

Roanoke I.

Hatteras I.

Pamlico R.

PAMLICO SOUND

H. Faye

AMERICAN SLAVERY, AMERICAN FREEDOM

THE ORDEAL OF COLONIAL VIRGINIA

Edmund S. Morgan

With a New Introduction by the Author

FRANCIS PARKMAN PRIZE EDITION
HISTORY BOOK CLUB
NEW YORK

For Helen

As Always

Contents

Acknowledgments

This book has been a good many years in the making, and many people have helped me to write it. Helen M. Morgan, as always, has helped much more than anyone else. She has worked with me from the beginning, and every draft of every chapter has had the benefit of her critical scrutiny. If the final result has any clarity of thought or expression, it is because of her patience and perception.

Parts of the book, in a different form, were delivered as the Commonwealth Lectures at the University of London in 1970. Part of chapter 3 appeared in the *American Historical Review* in 1971 as "The Labor Problem at Jamestown, 1607–18"; parts of chapters 5 and 6 appeared in the same year in the *William and Mary Quarterly* as "The First American Boom, Virginia 1618 to 1630"; and I tried out some of the ideas in chapter 18 in "Slavery and Freedom: The American Paradox," in the *Journal of American History* in 1972. In these preliminary formulations I was able to benefit from the criticism of several colleagues and friends. F. J. Fisher, Jack Hexter, Peter Laslett, Lawrence Stone, and Joan Thirsk helped me to avoid some errors in what I have to say about English history. And I have profited in a variety of ways from discussions with Charles Boxer, John M. Blum, David B. Davis, William N. Parker, the late David Potter, and C. Vann Woodward.

For help in avoiding some of the pitfalls in compiling the statistical tables (I surely have not avoided all of them), I am grateful to a number of people: to John McCarthy and to Robert Luft for programming information for computer analysis, and to Lois Carr, Gloria Main, and Russell Menard, who read the first draft of the Appendix and gave valuable advice about it. I also wish to thank

E. J. Hundert, John McCusker, and Robert V. Wells for suggestions offered by correspondence on matters of common interest. At W. W. Norton and Company, James L. Mairs and George Brockway have given the kind of editorial assistance that every author hopes for.

I owe many institutional debts. Initial research for the book was begun during a sabbatical leave from Yale University in the year 1962–63, with assistance from the Social Science Research Council and the American Council of Learned Societies. Subsequently Yale's policy of triennial leaves of absence gave me two more semesters of leave, and I enjoyed a third as Johnson Research Professor at the University of Wisconsin.

Many libraries and many librarians have helped me. The Virginia State Library not only made their collections of manuscripts available but provided microfilms of the most valuable county court records. At Colonial Williamsburg Edward Riley has made the Research Library the most effective working library of Virginia history that I know of. His hospitality went far beyond the call of duty. The staff of the Virginia Historical Society in Richmond and of the Alderman Library in Charlottesville were uniformly helpful. But most of the research and writing were done in the Yale Library and the Henry E. Huntington Library in San Marino, California, which has become a home away from home for many scholars besides myself. It would be hard to measure the benefits of conversations there with old friends and new. A historian could scarcely ask for better places to work than I have enjoyed, and I am deeply grateful to those who have made them so.

January, 1975   E. S. M.

Introduction to the
Francis Parkman Prize Edition

In recent years the study of slavery in the United States has concentrated on the independent culture that men and women from Africa were able to preserve or create in America, in spite of their forcible dislocation and subjection. Studies have shown their success in a variety of ways: maintaining family ties that could be dissolved at the whim of their owners; African styles of dancing, singing, and bodily adornment; the creation of new and of hybrid forms of music; the building of a pan-African culture or cultures from the many disparate people thrown together in a strange land. The success of Afro-Americans in maintaining a life of their own has dictated a recognition that slavery is always a negotiated relationship. Human beings find ways of asserting their humanity despite all efforts to reduce them to beasts of burden. Slavery can never be as absolute as slave-owners might claim it to be and wish it to be and legislate it to be.

While studies of slavery have thus disclosed the history of a rich black culture in America, dating back to the first settlements, other studies of American separation from Great Britain have shown the development of expanded ideas of freedom among the free. For more than a century and a half after the English stepped ashore at Jamestown, the free men and women of England's American colonies had acknowledged their subordination to the mother country. During that time they thrived under the restrictions that such a status imposed on them. But when England began an active interference in their internal affairs after 1763, they soon repudiated any subordination beyond what other Englishmen owed to their common king. Americans, they now insisted, were legally and constitutionally the equals of the King's subjects in England and entitled to the same liberties, rights, and privileges. In 1776 when they declared all men to be created equal and recited the ways they were not being treated equally by England, the immediate purpose may have been to assert the equality of free Americans with free Englishmen. But the words said much more than that. The words committed the country to a human equality more dramatically violated by the subjection of slaves than it ever was by any British infringements on the rights of the free. Many Americans recognized the contradiction and took immediate steps to resolve it through laws and constitutions that ended slavery in the northern States. In the end, of course, it required a Civil War.

It required a civil war because slavery and freedom are irreconcilable opposites. The negotiated relationship between master and slave never approached a negotiation between equals. The slave might be able to wrest privileges from a master by behavior beyond the master's control that would reduce work done and profit gained: feigned (or real) sickness, running away for a time, deliberate clumsiness, what today would be called sabotage. Some slaves won eventual freedom in return for an agreed number of years of conscientious labor. There could be grades of status within slavery, some slaves winning more privileges than others. But there was no halfway house between slavery and freedom, no set of steps that led progressively from one to the other.

Within the ranks of the free there could be much wider variation of status. The early colonists could admit their subordination to the English. The rich could always command the services of the poor. Freedom might be the only thing they had in common. But whatever powers the rich might exercise, however dependent the poor might become upon them, no one mistook mere poverty or dependence for slavery. There were, as we shall see, proposals for enslaving the poor, but the proposals themselves were a recognition that the poor were not slaves, in fact or in law. In rebelling against English rule, Americans might complain that taxation by Parliament was an attempt to enslave them, but they knew at first hand that slavery was really something else.

What, then, was the relationship between American slavery and American freedom? Our own society demonstrates that there need be no relationship. The gradations among us include the presence of the extremely rich alongside the extremely poor. We have no slavery recognized by law. But we once did, as the dominant role of Virginians in our early history attests. In the American Revolution Virginians were the most eloquent spokesmen for freedom and equality. George Washington led Americans in battle against British denial of American equality. Thomas Jefferson led them in declaring independence. Virginians drafted not only the Declaration but also the Constitution and the Bill of Rights; they were elected to the presidency of the United States under that Constitution for thirty-two of the first thirty-six years of its existence. Thus four out of five of our first presidents were slaveholders.

Human relations among us still suffer from the former enslavement of a large portion of our predecessors. Indeed the freedom of the free, the growth of freedom experienced in the American Revolution, depended more than we like to admit on the enslavement of more than 20 percent of us at that time. How republican freedom came to be supported, at least in large part, by its opposite, slavery, is the subject of this book.

—Edmund S. Morgan

Book I

THE PROMISED LAND

1

DREAMS
OF LIBERATION

I n 1756 the people of Virginia lived in fear. A year earlier General Edward Braddock had marched against the French and Indians on the colony's western frontier. Braddock had been overwhelmed, and now Virginians faced invasion. The Reverend Samuel Davies summoned them to battle, lest "Indian savages and French Papists, infamous all the World over for Treachery and Tyranny, should rule Protestants and Britons with a Rod of iron." Virginians, Davies was sure, would never give up their freedom. "Can you bear the Thought," he asked them, "that Slavery should clank her Chain in this Land of Liberty?" [1] British troops turned back the French, and Virginia was spared enslavement to papists and savages. Yet in that "Land of Liberty" even as Davies spoke, two-fifths of all the people were in fact already enslaved, under the iron rule of masters who were "Protestants and Britons."

Twenty years later the people of Virginia were again in peril. The mother country, having saved them from the French, now herself threatened to reduce them to slavery through the devious method of Parliamentary taxation. With the other English colonies in America they sprang to arms, to determine, as Edmund Pendleton put it, "whether we shall be slaves." [2] George Washington, who had helped to fight off enslavement to papists, prepared to fight again and grieved that "the once happy and peaceful plains of America are either to be drenched with Blood, or inhabited by Slaves." It was, he thought, a sad alternative. But, he asked, "Can a virtuous

[1] Samuel Davies, *Virginia's Danger and Remedy* (Williamsburg, 1756), 45.
[2] Edmund Pendleton, *Letters and Papers, 1734-1803*, David J. Mays, ed. (Charlottesville, 1967), I, 110.

3

Man hesitate in his choice?"[3] Washington led his countrymen in arms, while another Virginian led them in a Declaration of Independence that founded the American republic. The starting point of that document, the premise on which it rested, was that all men are created equal and endowed by their Creator with inalienable rights to life, liberty, and the pursuit of happiness. At the time when Thomas Jefferson wrote those words, he was personally depriving nearly two hundred men, women, and children of their liberty. When he died, on the fiftieth anniversary of his great Declaration, he still owned slaves, probably more than two hundred. When Washington faced his sad alternative, the happy and peaceful plains of Virginia had been inhabited by slaves for more than a century, and 135 of them belonged to him. When he died, he was master of 277.[4]

The seeming inconsistency, not to say hypocrisy, of slaveholders devoting themselves to freedom was not peculiar to Davies or to Jefferson or Washington. Nor was it peculiar to Virginia. The men who came together to found the independent United States, dedicated to freedom and equality, either held slaves or were willing to join hands with those who did. None of them felt entirely comfortable about the fact, but neither did they feel responsible for it. Most of them had inherited both their slaves and their attachment to freedom from an earlier generation, and they knew that the two were not unconnected. The rise of liberty and equality in America had been accompanied by the rise of slavery.

That two such seemingly contradictory developments were taking place simultaneously over a long period of time, from the seventeenth century to the nineteenth, is the central paradox of American history. For the historian it poses a challenge to probe the connection: to explain how a people could have developed the dedi-

[3] George Washington, *Writings*, John C. Fitzpatrick, ed. (Washington, 1931–44), III, 292.

[4] Jefferson had more than 185 slaves in 1774; in 1781, in spite of losing some thirty in the British raid on Monticello, he had more than 200. Dumas Malone, *Jefferson the Virginian* (Boston, 1948), 163, 391; Edwin M. Betts, ed., *Thomas Jefferson's Farm Book* (Princeton, 1953), 5. I have been unable to determine the exact number of his slaves at the time of his death. William Cohen, "Thomas Jefferson and the Problem of Slavery," *Journal of American History*, LXVI (1969–70), 503–26, at p. 519 says that he willed over 260 to his heirs, but citations do not reveal the source of the statement. On Washington's slaves see his *Writings*, XXXVII, 268, and James Flexner, *George Washington: Anguish and Farewell, 1793–1799* (Boston, 1972), 432–48.

cation to human liberty and dignity exhibited by the leaders of the American Revolution and at the same time have developed and maintained a system of labor that denied human liberty and dignity every hour of the day.

The connection between American slavery and freedom is evident at many levels if we care to see it. Think, for a moment, of the traditional American insistence on freedom of the seas. "Free ships make free goods" was the cardinal doctrine of American foreign policy in the revolutionary era. But the goods for which the United States demanded freedom were produced in very large measure by slave labor. The irony is more than semantic. American reliance on slave labor must be viewed in the context of the American struggle for a separate and equal station among the nations of the earth. At the time the colonists announced their claim to that station, they had neither the arms nor the ships to make the claim good. They desperately needed the assistance of other countries, especially France, and their single most valuable product with which to purchase assistance was tobacco, produced mainly by slave labor. So largely did tobacco figure in American foreign relations that one historian has referred to the activities of France in supporting the Americans as "King Tobacco Diplomacy," a reminder that the position of the United States in the world depended not only in 1776 but during the span of a long lifetime thereafter on slave labor.[5] To a large degree it may be said that Americans bought their independence with slave labor.

The paradox is American, and it behooves Americans to understand it if they would understand themselves. But the key to the puzzle, historically, does lie in Virginia. Virginia was the largest of the new United States, in territory, in population, in influence—and in slaveholding. Virginians owned more than 40 percent of all the slaves in the new nation.[6] It was Virginia slaves who grew most of

[5] Curtis P. Nettels, *The Emergence of a National Economy, 1775–1815* (New York, 1962), 19. See also Merrill Jensen, "The American Revolution and American Agriculture," *Agricultural History*, XLIII (1969), 107–24.

[6] U.S. Bureau of the Census, *Historical Statistics of the United States, Colonial Times to 1957* (Washington, D.C., 1960), 756. Virginia's black population is given as 187,605 for 1770 and 220,582 for 1780. The preciseness of the figures is misleading, for they are estimates, and the estimates are probably low. The census of 1790 placed Virginia's slave population at 292,717 out of a total of 697,681 for the United States. See Evarts B. Greene and Virginia D. Harrington, *American Population before the Federal Census of 1790* (New York, 1932), 155; *Historical Statistics of the United States,* 11–13.

the tobacco that helped to buy American independence. And Virginia furnished the country's most eloquent spokesmen for freedom and equality. Virginia adopted the first state constitution with a bill of rights. A Virginian commanded the Continental Army that won independence. Virginians drafted not only the Declaration of Independence but also the United States Constitution of 1787 and the first ten amendments to it. And Americans elected Virginians to the presidency of the United States under that constitution for thirty-two out of the first thirty-six years of its existence. They were all slaveholders. If it is possible to understand the American paradox, the marriage of slavery and freedom, Virginia is surely the place to begin.

This book tries to make such a beginning. It may be read as a history of early Virginia, but it is intended to be both more and less than that. It is the story of how one set of Americans arrived at the American paradox, an attempt to see how slavery and freedom made their way to England's first American colony and grew there together, the one supporting the other.

Virginia gained its name in 1585 when Sir Walter Raleigh sponsored an attempt by Englishmen to settle in America. Raleigh's colony, the famous lost colony of Roanoke, was the starting point of Virginia's history. It was a false start, and the next attempt, at Jamestown in 1607, was made under different auspices, by men who had learned something from Raleigh's failure. But Raleigh's venture was an end as well as a beginning, and its failure was a greater failure than can be found in the romantic story of the band of colonists who disappeared. Roanoke was the failure of a dream; a dream on the verge of becoming reality, a dream in which slavery and freedom were not yet married, a dream in which Protestant Britons liberated the oppressed people of the New World from the slavery that the papist Spaniard had imposed on them.

Perhaps it was no more than a dream. Perhaps it could never have come to pass, and perhaps no one really intended that it should. No one spelled it out, and only the outlines can be recovered today. But we may understand a little better what Virginians did after 1607 if we know what their predecessors thought of doing in the New World but failed to accomplish.

What they thought of doing was to save themselves and the rest of mankind from the tyrannous Spaniard. And no people were more in need of saving than those in the New World. For by the time

Englishmen began to think about their own role in America, half a century after Columbus, Spain had overrun the Caribbean, Central America, Mexico, and much of South America. The story of the Spanish conquest had been widely told, and even in the Spaniards' own accounts it was a horror story.[7] They had found in the New World, they said, the most loving and lovable human beings ever seen. They had also, to be sure, found some cannibals, who met them with showers of poisoned arrows. But it was not the cannibals whom the Spaniards first enslaved and destroyed; it was the kindly Arawaks whom Columbus found on Hispaniola. There were great numbers of them (the most recent modern estimate places the population of the island at about eight million at the time of discovery); and the Spanish, while admiring their simplicity and generosity, put them to work with a ruthlessness that (along with European diseases) eventuated in their virtual extermination. A half century after Columbus there were no more than two hundred Arawaks left on Hispaniola.[8]

In the rest of Spanish America the story was much the same: the natives were reduced to a species of slavery or serfdom and declined in numbers catastrophically. In their place the Spanish brought in slaves of other regions, especially Africa. As the story spread through Europe in the wondering pages of the Spanish chronicler Peter Martyr and in the withering pages of the Dominican friar Bartolomé de Las Casas, it added new dimensions to the traditional European image of Spanish cruelty.

Midcentury Englishmen were already experiencing what they took to be a taste of that cruelty at home. In 1553 the Protestant boy king Edward VI had died and was succeeded by his Catholic sister

---

[7] The Spanish account most readily available to Englishmen was Peter Martyr's *De Orbo Novo*, a running account by decades, which began to appear in print in 1511. The completed Eight Decades appeared in 1530. In 1555 Richard Eden published in London an English translation of the first half of the work under the title *The Decades of the Newe Worlde or West India*, which was reprinted with continuations and additional material under the same and other titles in subsequent years. The most sensational description of Spanish tyranny was by Bartolomé de Las Casas, who wrote from his own experience in Hispaniola. Las Casas' major work, *Historia de las Indias*, remained in manuscript until 1875, but his *Brevissima relacion de la destrucción de las Indias* was translated into English and published in London in 1583 as *The Spanish Colonie; or, Briefe Chronicle of the Acts and Gestes of the Spaniardes in the West Indies*.

[8] Sherburne F. Cook and Woodrow Borah, *Essays in Population History: Mexico and the Caribbean*, I (Berkeley, Calif., 1971), 376–410.

Mary, who promptly married Philip, the future king of Spain. There followed the series of martyrdoms and exiles that gave to English Protestants their undying hatred of Mary and of everything Spanish. From exile on the Continent Protestant spokesmen called for the queen's head and expounded radical theories of the right of a people to judge their rulers. One of the most forceful expositories made the connection between what was happening to Englishmen at home and what was happening to the Indians in the New World.

John Ponet, who had once been bishop of Winchester, offered his countrymen a multitude of examples from the Bible and from ancient history of people who had rightly resisted wicked rulers. But he also interspersed a few pointed modern references, as of the wicked, idolatrous Prince Eglon, who brought in as his advisers many Ammonites and Amalekites, "two kinds of people in beggerly pride and filthiness of life much like to the common nature of Italians and Spaniardes." And when Ponet needed an example of the woeful consequences of monarchs who treated their subjects as slaves, he found it in Spain's New World empire. Borrowing from Peter Martyr, he told how the natives of the West Indies, when the Spaniards came, "were simple and plaine men, and lived without great labour." The Spaniards in their lust for gold "forced the people (that were not used to labour) to stande all the daie in the hotte sunne gathering golde in the sande of the rivers. By this meanes a great nombre of them (not used to such paines) died, and a great numbre of them (seeing themselves brought from so quiet a life to such miserie and slaverie) of desperacion killed them selves. And many wolde not mary, bicause they wolde not have their children slaves to the Spaniardes." Englishmen, Ponet suggested, would not be so patient. Mary Tudor should remember that she ruled over "a bodie of free men and not of bondemen" and that she could not "geve or sell them as slaves and bondemen." [9] England held no slaves.

After Elizabeth succeeded Mary on the English throne in 1558, English Protestants no longer felt it necessary or politic to direct such warnings to their monarch. But they retained a sympathy for the American victims of Spanish oppression. The riches that Spain drew from slave labor in the New World had helped to make her the greatest power in the Old World, strong enough perhaps to overrun Europe and saddle people there with the same slavery that

[9] John Ponet, *A Shorte Treatise of Politike Power* (n.p., 1556), 69, 93, 94, 122.

the Indians were suffering. In addition, Spain's aggressive Catholicism posed a challenge to all Protestants. Any blow struck against her in the New World could be viewed as a blow for truth as well as freedom.

The situation invited men to think of a strategy that might bring freedom to the New World and at the same time relieve the Old World of the Spanish threat. Such a strategy did develop. And as has often been the case in the history of freedom, it took its rise almost accidentally out of a shady enterprise for private profit. It began with the activities of John Hawkins of Plymouth, a man of doubtful righteousness but undoubted daring, who had learned of the demand for African slaves in Spanish America. Although the Portuguese forbade English trade in Africa and the Spanish forbade it in the New World, Hawkins in three separate voyages bought, stole, and captured slaves from the coast of Guinea and carried them to the Spanish Main, where he was able to frighten the authorities into letting him sell them. During the last voyage, on which he was accompanied by Francis Drake, the Spanish made a surprise attack on his fleet of six ships, lying at anchor in the port of San Juan de Ulúa in Mexico. After a fiery battle in the harbor, he and Drake were able to make their escape in separate ships, but with the loss of the other ships and of three hundred of the four hundred men. Hawkins regarded the attack as treachery, coming as it did after a solemn agreement, with hostages given on both sides. If English seamen had needed an excuse for piracy against Spain, they now had it. And foremost of those who seized the excuse was Francis Drake.[10]

There is no denying that Francis Drake was a pirate and that the enterprise he conducted four years later in Panama was highway robbery, or at best, highjacking. But it was on the scale that transforms crime into politics. Nearly half a century later, Drake's friend Walter Raleigh, waiting trial in the Tower of London, put the case with his usual succinctness. Raleigh had admitted to the Lord Chan-

[10] James A. Williamson, *Hawkins of Plymouth* (2nd ed., London, 1969), is the best general account of Hawkins' voyages, though modified by Antonio Rumeu de Armas, *Los Viajes de John Hawkins a America* (Seville, 1947). Contemporary English accounts are in Clements R. Markham, ed., *The Hawkins Voyages*, Works issued by the Hakluyt Society, 1st ser., LVII (London, 1878). The Spanish accounts of Hawkins' activities have been translated and published in Irene A. Wright, ed., *Spanish Documents concerning English Voyages to the Caribbean, 1527–1568*, Works issued by the Hakluyt Society, 2nd ser., LXII (London, 1929), 60–162.

cellor of England that he would have taken the whole Spanish treasure fleet on the high seas in a recent voyage, if he could only have found it. "Why then," said the Chancellor, "you would have ben a pyrate." "Oh," replied Raleigh, still regretting the lost opportunity, "did you ever knowe of any that were pyratts for millions? They that risk for small things are pyratts." [11] If a man can steal an empire, he becomes, not a thief, but an emperor. If a pirate captures a large enough prize, he may be transformed into a statesman. Francis Drake was not above taking small prizes, but in 1572 he was after a large one, the Spanish treasure from Peru that was carried by mule train across the Isthmus of Panama to the town of Nombre de Dios on the Caribbean side. The surprising thing is not that he got it, or as much of it as he could carry away, but the method by which he succeeded, a method that made him, perhaps not a statesman, but something close to a revolutionary.[12]

Drake had apparently been to the coast of Panama before 1572 and knew his way around. He also knew that the Spanish fleet loaded the treasure of Peru for the last leg of the voyage to Spain at Nombre de Dios. But he evidently did not know at what time of year the shipments were made, for when he arrived the gold was not there. After holding the town for a few hours, he was forced back to his ships, leaving the governor with a message advising him "to hold open his eyes, for before hee departed, if God lent him life and leave, hee meant to reape some of their Harvest, which they get out of the Earth, and send into *Spaine* to trouble all the Earth." [13] The exaltation of large-scale theft is already evident in the message. And while he waited for the treasure to arrive, engaging in petty piracy of coastal vessels, Drake added a new, political dimension to his enterprise. Going ashore, he made contact with an extraordinary group of men, the Cimarrons, described as "certaine valiant Negros fled from their cruel masters the Spaniards." [14]

Now, Drake had been a slaver. He and John Hawkins had had

---

[11] V. T. Harlow, ed., *Ralegh's Last Voyage* (London, 1932), 279.

[12] All the documents on which the following account of Drake's voyage is based are in Irene A. Wright's extraordinary collection from Spanish archives, *Documents concerning English Voyages to the Spanish Main, 1569–1580*, Works issued by the Hakluyt Society, 2nd ser., LXXI (London, 1932). Unless otherwise indicated, page references are to this volume, which also reprints the anonymous English account, *Sir Francis Drake Revived* (London, 1628).

[13] P. 268.   [14] P. 336.

no scruples about carrying on the trade and had even managed a
certain amount of righteous indignation at Portugese and Spanish
efforts to bar them from it. It seems unlikely that an alliance with
the Cimarrons had been a part of Drake's original plan in going to
Panama or that it derived from any moral or philosophical objection
to slavery. If his first attack on Nombre de Dios had netted him the
treasure he was seeking, he would have had no occasion to linger in
the country. But Drake had time on his hands, and he and the Cimarrons evidently took to one another or recognized that they had
common or complementary interests.

The Cimarrons were no fearful little band of fugitives. The
officials at Nombre de Dios estimated their numbers at more than
3,000.[15] From their principal settlement at Vallano, thirty leagues
below Nombre de Dios, they organized periodic raids on the Spanish settlements, carrying off more of their people. They had already
threatened to burn both Nombre de Dios and Panama. And when
the Spanish prepared to send an expedition against them, they constructed a gallows on the road to Vallano and sent messages saying
that "on that gallows they were going to hang the captain and cut
off the heads of all who accompanied him,"[16] an undertaking in
which, however, they were unsuccessful. The Cimarrons evidently
welcomed Drake as an ally and agreed to assist him in waylaying the
pack train that carried the treasure from the Pacific to Nombre de
Dios. Cimarrons infiltrated the town of Panama and learned the
time of departure; then a picked force of Cimarrons and English,
along with some French Huguenot pirates, waited in ambush.
Though the first attempt failed, when the allies attacked the van-
guard of the train too soon (allowing the main body to retreat to
Panama city), on the second try they succeeded and came off with
a small fortune in gold and silver.

Just how far Drake intended to go with the alliance is impossible to say, for he never said himself. The Spanish authorities in Panama, however, had no doubt. "We hold it certain," they reported,
"that the principal design of these English is to explore and study
this land, and what strength there is in it, in order to come from
England with more people to plunder and occupy it."[17] Drake and
his lieutenant, John Oxenham, may not have been so ambitious, but
they certainly did not mean to leave the Spanish in unmolested possession. In the days while they waited for the passage of the pack

[15] P. 72.   [16] P. 10.   [17] Pp. 49–50.

train, their Cimarron friends had taken them to a lookout atop a tree on a high ridge that overlooked both the Atlantic and the Pacific. It was Drake's first sight of the Pacific, and "hee besought Almightie God of his goodnesse to give him life and leave to sayle once in an English Ship in that sea." Oxenham vowed that "he would follow him by Gods grace." [18]

The Spanish had already envisaged that the English with the help of the Cimarrons would reach the Pacific and prey on the unprotected ships that carried the treasure from Peru to Panama.[19] But this, as the Spanish saw it, was only the beginning. Nombre de Dios, one official announced "is as good as lost." [20] And a prisoner taken by the Spanish assured them that the pirates had promised the Cimarrons to sack the city "and deliver to them what Spanish inhabitants, men and women, it may have, to be their slaves." [21]

The Spanish were more fearful than they need have been. When Drake departed, loaded with gold and silver, he had made no further attack on Nombre de Dios. But neither had he closed the books on his alliance with the Cimarrons. Three years later John Oxenham was back on the isthmus with fifty men. On the Atlantic side he unloaded a cargo of supplies for the Cimarrons, then stripped the rigging from his ship and beached and burned her to extract the hardware. He and his men with the help of the Cimarrons carried everything to Vallano and there, close to the Pacific, built and rigged a ship forty-five feet long in the keel. By February, 1577, guided by the Cimarrons, Oxenham was raiding Spanish shipping from Peru and Spanish settlements on the Pearl Islands. The raiders collected all the gold, silver, and jewels they could lay their hands on, liberated seventy slaves, who were turned over to the Cimarrons, and took pains to desecrate the papist churches, smashing images, altars, and crucifixes.[22]

The English, it seems, had now begun to indoctrinate the Cimarrons with a hatred of Catholicism that added yet another dimension to the alliance. The Spanish reported that the Cimarrons had become as ardent "Lutherans" (the Spanish word for all Protestants) as the English.[23] They joined with delight in the destruction of Catholic insignia, crying, "I, English; pure Lutheran," and even exhorted their victims "not to believe in the Holy Trinity nor in Our Lady, Holy Mary, declaring that there was only one God." [24]

[18] P. 300.   [20] Pp. 46–47.   [22] Pp. 109–13.   [24] P. 120.

[19] P. 52.   [21] P. 69.   [23] Pp. 113–16.

Once again the Spanish feared the worst. Oxenham, they were sure, had been sent by his queen and planned to "make himself master of all this realm." [25] With Cimarron support there would be no stopping him. But if Oxenham had any such plans, they came to an end when a Spanish force captured him and carried him to Lima. There he was hanged, and every known Englishman in his expedition was eventually hunted down and killed or captured. The Spanish breathed a sigh of relief, convinced that if the English had escaped "they would have returned in such strength that, aided by the negroes, they would have become masters of the Pacific, which God forbid, for this is the key to all Peru." [26]

Whether the English, with the assistance of the Cimarrons, could have ousted the Spanish from the isthmus is open to doubt. What gives the Cimarron alliance significance is not its success or failure but the light it sheds on the English view of themselves and of their role in the New World. In spite of the fact that Drake had engaged in the slave trade, in spite of the fact that the English in Ireland were at that very moment subjecting the natives to a treatment not much different from what the Indians of Hispaniola received from Columbus, the English in Panama had cast themselves as liberators and had allied with blacks against whites. They had taught the Cimarrons their own religious views and engaged them in piracy and pillage flavored with righteousness and revolution. The alliance seems to have been untroubled by racial prejudice. To be sure, the English were scarcely in a position to assume airs of superiority, but the accounts suggest a camaraderie that went beyond the mutual benefits of the alliance. When the Spanish caught up with them, they were camped together on a riverbank where they had stretched a canvas awning for shade and "were cooking a quantity of pork in kettles and amusing themselves together." [27]

The Spanish were far from amused by the combination. They knew there was no reason why the English should confine their appeal to blacks. The Cimarrons were not the only oppressed peoples in the Spanish dominions who might become willing allies. Indeed, Drake was already making contact with some. While Oxenham was launching his English ship in the Pacific, Drake was preparing for his voyage around the world, and by early in 1578 was cruising down the east coast of South America. There at every pause his chaplain, Francis Fletcher, recorded the good nature of the natives

[25] P. 113.   [26] P. 142.   [27] Pp. 132–33.

and the sadness of their subjugation. Whenever the expedition met with hostile reactions, he interpreted these as a result of the Indians' assumption that all white men were Spaniards or Portuguese. Where it was possible to strike up relations with the natives he found them charming. "How grievous a thing it is," he exclaimed, "that they should by any meanes be so abused as all those are, whom the Spaniards have any command or power over." [28]

Drake's voyage round the world was partly a pirate cruise, but it was almost on the scale of piracy for millions. Drake brought back perhaps half a million; and if he had reached Peru before Oxenham was captured, he might conceivably have stolen part of an empire as well, for he had a Cimarron aboard and may have planned to join forces with Oxenham at Panama. [29] The queen of England refrained from outright endorsement of Drake's depredations and sequestered most of the loot he brought back. But even though Spain loudly demanded the return of the stolen goods, Elizabeth hung on to them and rewarded Drake with a knighthood. His success had transformed him automatically into something of a statesman. While Elizabeth could not yet risk outright war with Spain, Drake had made himself England's unofficial ambassador to Spain's most formidable New World enemies, the Cimarrons, and he stood publicly as the friend of all who suffered under Spanish rule. We may ask how sincere his friendship could be or how genuine could be an alliance with rebels that aimed at large-scale theft. But alliances dignified under solemn treaties have often had no larger aim; and friendships between different peoples have seldom extended beyond mutual interest. The real question was whether the English could have or would have offered the Cimarrons and other victims of Spanish masters the kind of freedom that Englishmen at home were beginning to pride themselves on.

In revulsion from their oppression under Mary and in the glow of their enthusiasm for Elizabeth, some Englishmen were ready to think of English freedom in global terms. Two in particular, who both bore the name of Richard Hakluyt, had begun to urge their countrymen to bring the blessings of English rule overseas and to bring to England the riches that could be found not only in New Spain but elsewhere in the wide world. Neither of the Hakluyts

---

[28] W. S. Vaux, ed., *The World Encompassed by Sir Francis Drake*, Works issued by the Hakluyt Society, 1st ser., XVI (London, 1854), 100.
[29] Kenneth R. Andrews, *Drake's Voyages* (New York, 1967), 42.

ever took an ocean voyage. One was an undistinguished lawyer; the other, his younger cousin and protégé, was an undistinguished clergyman, who devoted his days more to geography than to God.[30] Neither stood close to the centers of power. But both were sure that England needed more of the world and that the world needed England. The younger Hakluyt was the more ardent of the two, and his great achievement was a monumental collection of narratives describing English voyages throughout the world, *The Principal Navigations of the English Nation*.[31] Though the first edition was not published until 1589 and the much enlarged second edition not until 1600, the compilation reveals the direction in which the exploits of a Drake and an Oxenham were turning the thoughts of the Hakluyts and other Englishmen by the 1570s and 1580s.

The *Principal Navigations* was in fact a triumph of creative editing, a polemic in the form of a collection of documents. By his massive accumulation of texts, Hakluyt was able to present his countrymen with a record of persistent and pervasive overseas accomplishments that had taken place during years when the English had been in fact running considerably behind the Spanish and the Portuguese. The object was not so much to give the English pride in their past as to spur them to greater ventures overseas. Hakluyt's effort was comparable to what English parliamentarians were at the same time doing on behalf of political liberty. Modern freedom may be considered in large measure an English invention, and some of the principal inventors were scholars who scoured the past for precedents to magnify the power of the House of Commons. The precedents that they found were often of dubious historical validity, but Parliament's insistence on them turned them into bulwarks of Parliamentary privilege and popular rights and made the arbitrary rule of an absolute monarch impossible in England. Similarly Hakluyt—in order to magnify England's global power—drew precedents from the past, some of which were of equally doubtful validity. He did not resort to doctoring his texts to suit his intentions. He maintained standards of editorial accuracy far above those that prevailed at the time. Nor did he exclude narratives that shed no glory on his countrymen. He never lost the scholar's passion for inclusiveness, but he

[30] The best study is George B. Parks, *Richard Hakluyt and the English Voyages*, American Geographical Society, Special Publication No. 10 (New York, 1928).

[31] I have used the twelve-volume edition published at Glasgow, 1903. Volume and page numbers refer to this edition.

could use inclusiveness to his own purposes. By adopting generous criteria of relevance, he was able to present documents which imparted to the whole book a powerful suggestion that Englishmen ought to rule the world they had discovered.

Although Hakluyt devoted the great bulk of the book to the spectacular voyages that had taken place in his own lifetime, he put the reader in a receptive frame of mind by leading him first through the semi-mythical exploits of earlier Englishmen in subduing a large part of the narrower world known to earlier generations. In the opening pages was the inspiring example of King Arthur, for whom "This kingdome was too little . . . and his minde was not contented with it," wherefore he had taken over Norway, Iceland, Greenland, and other northern countries where the people "were wild and savage, and had not in them the love of God nor of their neighbors." [32] And then there was King Edgar, who had yearly sailed with a navy of 4,000 ships round an empire (the boundaries not specified) which Englishmen might yet be able to "recover and enjoy." [33] The famous 1436 poem on sea power, *The Libelle of Englyshe Policye*, which Hakluyt included in full, showed how to go about the recovery by urging Englishmen "to make this land have lordship of the sea." [34] There were precedents for expansion too in Chaucer's description of the knights who "were wont in his time to travaile into Prussia and Lettowe [Latvia], and other heathen lands, to advance the Christian faith against Infidels and miscreants, and to seeke honour by feats of arms." [35] And there was perhaps a lesson to be learned even in the chronicle of John de Plano Carpini concerning the savage tyranny of the Tartars over the barbarous people of northern Asia, so unlike the free and Christian governance of England's kings.[36]

Like other imperialists, Hakluyt was convinced that the world would be better off under his country's dominion, and indeed that all good people would welcome it. Who would not gladly abandon the tyranny of Spain for the benevolence, the freedom of English rule? The thought occurred to Hakluyt when he heard of Drake's alliance with the Cimarrons, and it prompted his first plans for an English colony overseas. In 1579 or 1580, while Drake was completing his circumnavigation, Hakluyt proposed that the English seize the Straits of Magellan, the gateway to the Pacific, and plant a

---

[32] I, 6.   [34] II, 131.   [36] I, 55–179.
[33] I, 16–24.   [35] I, 307.

colony there. Empire was clearly the object, but the means lay in the freedom from tyranny and slavery that England's brand of government would offer to the colonists, who were to be principally Cimarrons. The Cimarrons, Hakluyt said, were "a people detesting the prowde governance of the Spanyards." Because of their trust in Drake, they would gladly move to the straits, by the hundreds or thousands. There they would "easily be induced to live subject to the gentle government of the English." The colony would be easy to sustain because the Spaniard was too effeminate to endure the harsh climate of the straits, whereas the Cimarron, bred "in all toyle farre from delicacie," would think himself happy there "when as by good provision he shal find himselfe plentifully fed, warmly clothed, and well lodged and by our nation made free from the tyrannous Spanyard, and quietly and courteously governed by our nation." With the assistance of the Cimarrons, who would be led by English captains, and with a good navy, England could roll up the Pacific coast of South America and "make subjecte to England all the golden mines of Peru." [37]

The Cimarrons need not be the only people to benefit from settlement in the straits colony. Hakluyt thought it might also include "condemned Englise men and women, in whom there may be founde hope of amendement." [38] Emigration would provide a second chance for these unfortunates. Hakluyt's scheme, like Drake's actual alliance with the Cimarrons, shows no sign of racial prejudice, unless in this assignment of English criminals to a place alongside the Cimarrons. That the colonists would enjoy the freedom of Englishmen is suggested in Hakluyt's admission that they might ultimately become independent. "Admit," he said, ". . . that the English there would aspire to governement of themselves, yet were it better that it sholde be soe then that the Spanyard shold with the treasure of that countrey torment all the contries of Europe." [39] He did not say that the Cimarrons would share in the aspiration for self-government, but neither did he suggest that they would be held in any kind of bondage. And indeed the voluntary immigration he envisaged for them would seem to preclude any such intention.

England did not pursue Hakluyt's proposal, but by the time he made it, in 1579 or 1580, colonization was in the air. And Raleigh's

[37] E. G. R. Taylor, ed., *The Original Writings and Correspondence of the Two Richard Hakluyts,* Works issued by the Hakluyt Society, 2nd ser., LXXVI, LXXVII (London, 1935), 142–43.

[38] *Ibid.*   [39] *Ibid.*

Roanoke colony was only five years off. In that venture Drake and Hakluyt were both to be closely involved. Some of the preconceptions they brought to the enterprise should by now be evident. But the experience gained by Drake and other corsairs in the Caribbean was not the only experience available to guide the Roanoke colonists. While Drake and Oxenham were probing the Spanish empire close to its center, another set of Englishmen farther north in the New World had been serving a somewhat different apprenticeship for colonization.

If the Spanish had thought the continent north of Florida worth having, they would probably have taken it. They traveled through it to see what was there, on expeditions that measured their own endurance as much as the resources of the continent. What they saw did not tempt them; and though they worried about other European countries gaining a foothold in the area, they left it unoccupied north of Florida. Englishmen, partly because they had sponsored John Cabot's voyage to North America in 1497, partly because of their own northern location, and partly because the Spanish were not there, came to think of the northern continent as their part of the New World.[40] They wanted to find a passage to the Pacific through it or above it, but by the 1570s they also thought of occupying it. To do so, they would have to establish some sort of relations with the natives. Since the northern Indians had not suffered at the hands of the Spaniard, they would not require liberation and might not even welcome English dominion. How then to approach them?

In the pages of Peter Martyr, Englishmen read how the Spanish had done it in the south. It was apparent in Peter Martyr's account that the New World contained two kinds of Indians. There were the friendly, tractable peoples like the Arawaks whom Columbus had found on Hispaniola; and there were hostile, unlovely peoples like the Cannibals (a variation of "Carib") whom Columbus had found on several other Caribbean islands, and whose name was

[40] In the first edition of the *Decades of the Newe Worlde*, Richard Eden followed his translation of Peter Martyr with various accounts of the northern regions that urged their exploration and colonization. See ff. 253, 263–76, 318. See also Roger Barlow. *A Briefe Summe of Geographie*, E. G. R. Taylor, ed., Works issued by the Hakluyt Society, 2nd ser., LXIX (London, 1932), 180–82.

given by subsequent explorers to virtually every unfriendly tribe, whether on the islands or the mainland. The good Indians, by definition, hated the Cannibals and welcomed the assistance of the Spaniards against them. And with the assistance of the good Indians a handful of Spaniards had taken over the populous empires of Montezuma and of the Incas.[41]

Supposedly the principal characteristic of the Cannibals was the one to which the western world has ever since applied their name. But their most visible characteristic was hostility to invaders. In the Spanish accounts there are scarcely any eyewitness reports of someone actually eating human flesh, but there are numerous accounts of hostile tribes, whom the invaders immediately identify as Cannibals. When Englishmen thought about occupying North America, they expected that they would find both kinds of Indians there too and that the good ones would welcome assistance against the bad. English assistance would, of course, bring them gentle English government and would, of course, be preferable to the tyranny of the bad tribes.

The first large-scale English attempt to establish a colony in North America took place in an area so bleak that it supported few native inhabitants at all, and what few there were seemed to be of the wrong kind. Martin Frobisher, in search of a northwest passage to the Pacific, found on an island near Baffin Land a quantity of ore that assayers in England pronounced to be gold. He also found a people who failed to welcome him with the cordiality proper to good Indians. Moreover, five of his men disappeared among them, presumably down their throats. When Frobisher returned to Baffin Land with a large-scale expedition of eleven ships, he did not count on friendly relations with the natives, nor did he count on their labor to help him load his ships with ore. Instead, he came provided with soldiers and settlers to seize the land, dig out the ore, and establish a permanent gold-mining colony. Frobisher's plans for a colony expired when the two hundred tons of ore he brought back to England turned out to be fool's gold. He never indicated what place the Indians would have had in his settlement if he had been successful; but he gave a hint of how gentle his government might have been when on his first voyage he enticed one man in a kayak close to his ship

---

[41] For a succinct, though later, English reading of the lesson to be learned from the Spanish conquest, see *RVC*, III, 558.

and then, seizing him by the arm, pulled him aboard, kayak and all, and carried him home to show the queen. This was hardly the way that Drake had dealt with the Cimarrons.[42]

It was, however, akin to the way Englishmen had behaved in another land where the natives proved unfriendly.[43] The wild Irish had no poisoned arrows and could not put up an effective resistance against invaders. Perhaps for that reason the English who subdued them in the sixteenth century did not generally call them cannibals.[44] But the Irish, like the Eskimos, were clearly the wrong kind of people. In the English view they were barbarous, only nominally Christian, and generally intractable. The English therefore made no attempt to find a good set of them to ally with. The Irish could become good, that is, civil and Christian, only by submission. Those who chose not to submit could be exterminated and replaced by more deserving settlers from England. Sir Humphrey Gilbert, who won his knighthood by subduing the Irish, himself proposed a colony that would bring peace and prosperity to Ireland by replacing rebellious Irish with Englishmen.[45] It did not augur well for English relations with the Indians of North America that Gilbert was to transfer his interest from Ireland to the New World.

When he did, after Frobisher's failure, he had in view a location

[42] R. Collinson, ed., *The Three Voyages of Martin Frobisher*, Works issued by the Hakluyt Society, 1st ser., XXXVIII (London, 1867). For a lively and authoritative account of the voyages of Frobisher and of other English explorers see Samuel Eliot Morison's incomparable *The European Discovery of America: The Northern Voyages. A.D. 500–1600* (New York, 1971).

[43] The significance of the English experience in Ireland for later experience in America has been extensively discussed by Howard M. Jones in *O Strange New World* (New York, 1964), 167–79; by David B. Quinn in a number of works, especially "Ireland and Sixteenth-Century European Expansion," *Historical Studies*, I (1958), 20–32; and most recently by Nicholas P. Canny, "The Ideology of English Colonization: From Ireland to America," *WMQ*, 3rd ser., XXX (1973), 575–98. [Footnote Abbreviations will be found on pp. 383–93.]

[44] But there were English reports of the Irish eating dead bodies and of old women eating little children (Jones, *Strange New World*, 169), and Sir Henry Sidney, the Lord Deputy of Ireland, referred to the rebel leader Shane O'Neill as "that canyball" (Canny, "Ideology of English Colonization," 587).

[45] David B. Quinn, ed., *The Voyages and Colonizing Enterprises of Sir Humphrey Gilbert*, Works issued by the Hakluyt Society, 2nd ser., LXXXIII, LXXXIV (London, 1938), I, 12–16, 118–28; II, 490–97.

well to the south of the area abandoned by Frobisher. Gilbert had in mind a permanent settlement of Englishmen that would serve many different purposes, among them a base for piracy against the Spanish. Gilbert, by promising investors princely domains in the New World, was able to gather about him a group of associates to finance the immigration of English laborers and beggars. These poor wretches, like the felons in Hakluyt's proposed straits colony, might be redeemed by the economic opportunities available in the new land, and at the same time their labor in the colony would enrich the gentlemen who backed them.[46]

Although Queen Elizabeth granted Gilbert a charter that allowed him to hand out American land to investors, he had to consider the question of how to deal with the current owners or occupiers of it. There was no reason to suppose that the temperate regions of North America were less densely populated than the tropics. And to achieve a military conquest of the natives as he had done in Ireland might require more men and longer supply lines than he could manage without government financing. It would be wiser and safer to follow the Spanish practice of alliance with good Indians against bad. Such was the advice that the elder Hakluyt gave Gilbert. Nothing was more important, he said, than to get on good terms with the Indians of the area where the settlement was made. In this way the English would learn "all their wantes, all their strengthes, all their weakenesse, and with whome they are in warre, and with whome confiderate in peace and amitie." [47] If the Indians on the coast were hostile, this need not impair the strategy. The first settlement should be at the mouth of a river, preferably on an island, which could be fortified. Then if the neighboring Indians proved to be of the cannibal type, the English could send an expedition up the river or along the coast to make contact with the right kind.[48]

Gilbert confirmed the desirability of this strategy by questioning David Ingram, an Englishman who had survived the battle at San Juan de Ulúa. He had been put ashore near there and, so he claimed at least, had walked through the continent to Nova Scotia, where he picked up a ride home in a fishing boat. According to Ingram, North America was full of Indians at war with one another, and the most feared were the Cannibals, "whose foode is mans flesh, and have teeth like dogges, and doo pursue them with ravenous myndes

[46] *Ibid.*, II, 245–78. [47] *Ibid.*, I, 182.
[48] *Ibid.*, I, 185; cf. Taylor, *Writings of the Hakluyts*, II, 342.

to eate theyr flesh, and devoure them." It was not to be doubted that good Indians pursued by Cannibals would welcome the protection of the English and gratefully give up to them "such competent quantity of Lande, as every way shall be correspondent to the Christians expectation, and contentation." [49]

Nor was it to be doubted that the good Indians would work for the English in producing whatever commodities the country afforded. Drake, confining himself to pillage, had not been obliged to think about getting work out of anybody other than the men who manned his ships, and the compulsion available to a captain aboard ship has always been extraordinary. Hakluyt had not really confronted the question of work in the colony he proposed for the Straits of Magellan. Frobisher had brought along paid English labor, and his colony had not lasted long enough to establish relations with the natives. In planning for labor, therefore, Gilbert had little to go on except the Spanish example, and that he rejected. Gilbert did not count on discovering gold or silver. Though he naturally hoped for treasure, and hoped also to find a northwest passage, he envisaged a settlement in which men would "manure," that is, cultivate the soil and engage in the production of ordinary commodities, either those that the country afforded naturally or those that human ingenuity could extract from it: furs, fish, dyestuffs, lumber, and who knew what else. Hakluyt had assured him that however barren the land might appear, "every soyle of the world by arte may be made to yeelde things to feede and to cloth men." [50] In thinking about the labor needed to make the earth yield its fruits, Gilbert and his associates had decided to employ both Englishmen and Indians. In both cases, they reasoned, all the inducement needed was the comfort that well-directed work would purchase.

Christopher Carleill, an enthusiastic supporter, reported how good-for-nothing English beggars had become new men when given a job to do in the English army in the Netherlands. [51] If such paupers were shipped to North America, they would surely have more to do and a better life than in the army. Similarly the Indians, who now eked out a savage existence without proper clothing or housing, would be transformed by the material comforts of civilization and the spiritual comforts of Christianity. Sir George Peckham, who intended to sponsor a special community within the colony,

[49] Quinn, *Voyages of Gilbert*, II, 452.
[50] *Ibid.*, I, 185.   [51] *Ibid.*, II, 361.

believed that the Indians "so soone as they shall begin but a little to taste of civillitie, will take mervailous delight in any garment be it never so simple." [52] And the demand for the trappings of civility would turn them from the indolent manner of living in which they allegedly gathered from the land only what "the ground of itself· dooth naturally yeelde." [53] When instructed by the English, they would understand "how the tenth part of their land may be so manured and emploied, as it may yeeld more commodities to the necessary use of mans life, then the whole now dooth." [54] As a result they would "by little and little forsake their barbarous and savage living, and growe to such order and civilitie with us, as there may be well expected from thence no lesse quantitie and diversitie of merchandize then is now had out of Dutchland, Italie, France or Spaine." [55]

It was a blueprint for Utopia: English benefactors living side by side with Indian beneficiaries, both enjoying new comforts in peace and prosperity, with the Cannibals expelled to some outer region. Indeed, if we turn to Utopia itself, we find that Sir Thomas More had envisaged nothing better in his ideal state, when he described the Utopian manner of colonization:

> . . . they enroll citizens out of every city [in Utopia] and, on the mainland nearest them, wherever the natives have much unoccupied and uncultivated land, they found a colony under their own laws. They join with themselves the natives if they are willing to dwell with them. When such a union takes place, the two parties gradually and easily merge and together absorb the same way of life and the same customs, much to the great advantage of both peoples. By their procedures they make the land sufficient for both, which previously seemed poor and barren to the natives. The inhabitants who refuse to live according to their laws, they drive from the territory which they carve out for themselves. If they resist, they wage war against them. They consider it a most just cause for war when a people which does not use its soil but keeps it idle and waste nevertheless forbids the use and possession of it to others who by the rule of nature ought to be maintained by it.[56]

Gilbert, like the Utopians, was probably prepared to expel uncooperative savages from unworked land that they would not part with. Sir George Peckham ventured his own opinion: "I doo verily

[52] *Ibid.*, II, 461. [54] *Ibid.*, II, 468.
[53] *Ibid.*, II, 452–53. [55] *Ibid.*, II, 357.
[56] Thomas More, *Utopia*, Edward Surtz ed. (New Haven, 1964), 76.

think that God did create lande, to the end that it shold by Culture and husbandrie, yeeld things necessary for mans lyfe." [57] The Indians, then, were expected to give their land willingly and willingly to work under English guidance. But land could rightly be taken, even in Utopia, from those who did not work it.

Work came first, property rights second. And where did freedom come? What if the Indians refused the enticements of civility and refused to work for what they did not want? The Spanish on Hispaniola had considered and answered the question. In 1517 a team of Jeronymite friars had investigated the treatment of the remaining Indians there and concluded that it was justified because they would not work unless forced to.[58] They must be made to work for Spain, as the Spanish government proclaimed in 1513, "to prevent their living in idleness." [59] In Hispaniola work took precedence over freedom as well as property. Neither Gilbert nor More reached such a conclusion. More would simply have driven out the lazy natives. Gilbert and his friends probably would have taken the same course, but were never faced with the decision. After a preliminary reconnaissance of Newfoundland and the Gulf of Maine, Gilbert was lost at sea on the way home. His colony never got on the ground.

The Englishmen who finally settled North America would have to face the problem of unwilling workers, not only with regard to the natives but also with regard to the needy laborers they brought with them. But by 1583, when Gilbert's ship went down, English plans for the New World did not include slavery or forced labor of any kind. The Cannibals, to be sure, would receive rough treatment; but those who would join with the English, whether the Cimarrons of the south or the good Indians of the north, would enjoy gentle government, civility, Christianity, superior technology, and abundance. This was the point at which English experience and thinking about America had arrived when Walter Raleigh brought to convergence at Roanoke the southern experience of Drake, the northern plans of Gilbert, and the skilled guidance of the Hakluyts.

[57] Quinn, *Voyages of Gilbert*, II, 468.

[58] Lewis Hanke, *The First Social Experiments in America* (Cambridge, Mass., 1935), 26–39.

[59] Lewis Hanke, *The Spanish Struggle for Justice in the Conquest of America* (Philadelphia, 1949), 25.

2

THE LOST COLONY

WALTER Raleigh was Humphrey Gilbert's half brother. Though Raleigh was the younger by about fifteen years, the two men had been close. Like Gilbert, Raleigh had served an apprenticeship with the queen's forces in Ireland and had then become interested in America. He had invested in Gilbert's proposed colony and might have gone along on the exploratory expedition had he not been tied to England by a queen who liked to have her favorites close at hand. Raleigh, for the moment at least, was one of her favorites. She had endowed him with sinecures, monopolies, and pensions that transformed him rapidly from a poor young gentleman into a rich young courtier. Tall and handsome, looking like a costume actor ready for the stage, he had at the same time the vision, the brilliance of mind, and the daring that England nourished in such abundance during those years. When Gilbert vanished at sea, Raleigh had no difficulty in getting the queen to issue him a patent like Gilbert's, conveying dominion over any part of the American coast where he could establish a colony (and everything six hundred miles north and south of it) within the ensuing six years.[1]

Raleigh may have toyed with the idea of fixing his settlement in the northern area that Gilbert had investigated, but by the time he received his patent, on March 25, 1584, he had his eye on territory farther south, closer to the Spanish. He had already begun to fit out

[1] David B. Quinn, *The Roanoke Voyages, 1584–1590*, Works issued by the Hakluyt Society, 2nd ser., CIV, CV (London, 1955), I, 82–89. This chapter is based primarily on the documents contained in this superb collection.

two small ships to reconnoiter the region; and on April 27 they were off, commanded by two young men from the large household he had gathered around him, Philip Amadas and Arthur Barlowe. With them as pilot went Simon Fernandez, a naturalized Portuguese who had sailed with Gilbert. Raleigh himself was not aboard. The queen would let him found a colony, but she was not likely to let him go to it himself.

Amadas and Barlowe took the southern route to America, the one initiated by Columbus. Leaving Plymouth on April 27, they picked up the trade winds at the Canaries, and raised the Windward Islands by June 10. By July 13 they had passed up the east coast of Florida and made their way along the Carolina Outer Banks to an inlet just above Hatarask Island. After passing into Pamlico Sound, they went ashore first at Hatarask and later at nearby Roanoke Island, the home of the Roanoke Indians. How long they stayed is not clear, but they were back in England by mid-September with two Indians, a bag of pearls, and stories to assure their sponsors that this part of America was the way America was supposed to be, worthy indeed to be distinguished by the name that Raleigh now gave it, Virginia, after England's virgin queen.

Arthur Barlowe wrote up the episode, emphasizing what was evidently expected of him.[2] The Roanoke Indians were Peter Martyr's Indians: "most gentle, loving, and faithfull, void of all guile, and treason, and such as lived after the manner of the golden age. . . . a more kinde and loving people, there can not be found in the world, as farre as we have hitherto had triall."[3] Seemingly belying this judgment was his report that in trading deerskins to the English they were most eager for hatchets, axes, and knives, "and would have given any thing for swordes."[4] Moreover, the wars they waged with one another were "very cruell, and bloodie, by reason whereof, and of their civill dissentions, which have happened of late yeeres amongest them, the people are marvelously wasted, and in some places, the Countrey left desolate."[5] But this contradiction was inherent in the expectation. Good Indians were supposed to live in terror of bad Indians, against whom they would welcome the assistance of the English. The good Indians of Roanoke were governed by a king who would, no doubt, become the willing ally, not to say

---

[2] Quinn, *Roanoke Voyages*, I, 91–115.   [4] *Ibid.*, I, 101.
[3] *Ibid.*, I, 108, 110.   [5] *Ibid.*, I, 113.

the vassal, of so great a friend as Raleigh would be to them. Amadas and Barlowe had not met the king, Wingina, because he was recovering from wounds suffered in war. But they had met his brother, Granginemeo, whose friendliness and hospitality were a sufficient sign that Wingina would behave in the proper manner.

The land, too, came up to expectations: "The earth bringeth foorth all things in aboundance, as in the first creation, without toile or labour." [6] With labor added, of course, it would bring much more. The soil was "the most plentifull, sweete, fruitfull, and wholsome of all the world." [7] The expedition had sown English peas that were fourteen inches high in ten days' time. Wildfowl, deer, and other game were everywhere. Cedars grew higher than in the Azores, and grapevines flourished so profusely that "in all the world the like abundance is not to be founde." [8] The new Eden would not lack for wine.

Even the location that the explorers had happened on seemed to be ideal. Roanoke Island was inside the barrier beaches of the Carolina Outer Banks and thus appeared to offer a snug harbor, safe from Atlantic gales. And nearby was seemingly the great river Hakluyt had prescribed for access to interior kingdoms in case the coastal kings should prove recalcitrant: "Beyond this Islande there is the maine lande, and over against this Islande falleth into this spatious water, the great river called Occam." [9]

The only apparent drawback to the site was at the same time one of its advantages: its close proximity to Spanish outposts in Florida at San Agustin (St. Augustine) and Santa Elena (St. Helena, South Carolina). Although the Spanish had little interest in the Atlantic coast of North America, they did not care to have any other European country plant a colony on it. They feared, rightly, that the purpose of such a colony would be to facilitate raids on the Spanish treasure fleets, which followed the same route out of the Caribbean that Amadas and Barlowe had taken, up the east coast of Florida. Because of prevailing winds and currents, this was the only effective route, and the Spanish had always kept a jealous eye on Florida in order to protect it. When the French tried a colony there, they wiped it out and planted one of their own. The French in turn wiped out the Spanish colony, but the Spanish returned. If only to

[6] *Ibid.*, I, 108.   [7] *Ibid.*, I, 106.   [8] *Ibid.*, I, 95.
[9] *Ibid.*, I, 110. Actually this was not a river but part of Croatan Sound.

keep others out, they needed a foothold in Florida. An English colony at Roanoke, so close by, would be in grave danger of Spanish attack.

That Raleigh intended his colony as a base for action against Spain is scarcely to be doubted. The queen had surely known of the intention when she granted him the patent. The only question was how far she would let him go, for in 1584 she was still wary of any move that would provoke a full-scale Spanish attack on England. Raleigh, on the other hand, like Drake and Hawkins, preferred to take the initiative; and he hoped to persuade the queen to follow up the patent with direct assistance in planting the colony and in mounting an assault from it on Spain's American empire. To this end, while Amadas and Barlowe were reconnoitering, he had summoned the younger Richard Hakluyt, who was then serving as a minor functionary in the English embassy in Paris. Hakluyt hurried home and prepared a paper, for the queen's eyes, that detailed the advantages of colonizing the southern part of North America, advantages so compelling that the queen should not merely allow the enterprise but should also contribute to the large initial outlay it would entail.[10]

Hakluyt's argument centered on the need and opportunity to deal a crippling blow to Spain. The need was urgent, for Spain threatened not only England but all Europe, "afflictinge and oppressinge of moste of the greatest estates of Christendome." [11] How had Spain become so powerful and so dangerous? Hakluyt was certain that the danger lay in its immense wealth. "Riches," he told the queen, "are the fittest instrumentes of conqueste." [12] With its riches Spain would subvert the whole of Europe. And the riches of Spain, he was equally sure, came from its New World empire. The colony that Raleigh proposed would, at the very least, enable English seamen to cut off the flow of gold and silver by intercepting the annual treasure fleets. "Touching the fleete," he pointed out, "no man (that knoweth the course thereof comyinge oute betwene Cuba, and the Cape of Florida along the gulfe or straite of Bahama) can denye that it is caried by the currant northe and northeaste towardes the coaste which wee purpose God willinge to inhabite." [13]

But Hakluyt (and presumably Raleigh) had more in mind than raids on Spanish shipping. Hakluyt had not forgotten Francis Drake

---

[10] Taylor, *Writings of the Hakluyts*, II, 211–326.
[11] *Ibid.*, II, 244.
[12] *Ibid.*, II, 245.
[13] *Ibid.*, II, 240.

and the Cimarrons, and he had since learned of other rebels against Spanish tyranny. Miles Phillips, an Englishman who had been stranded in Mexico with David Ingram after the battle at San Juan de Ulúa, had stayed there fourteen years and only recently returned. Phillips was full of tales of the Chichimici, a nation of Indians in the north of Mexico. They had disrupted Spanish rule there, led by a Negro who had "fledd from his cruel spanishe Master." [14] Hakluyt had assurance that the Spanish were much more thinly planted in America than anyone realized, and everywhere the natives and the imported slaves were ready to revolt against them. Now was the time for England to strike. If the Chichimici, with the aid of one Negro, could force the Spaniards to abandon their mines in northern Mexico, as Phillips said, think what damage they might do with the help of "divers hundreds of englishe men . . . being growen once into familiaritie with the valiaunte nation." [15]

The Cimarrons and the Chichimicis would be only a beginning. Hakluyt wanted nothing less for the king of Spain than to see "the people revolte in every forrein territorie of his, and cutt the throates of the proude hatefull Spaniardes their governours." [16] That the subjects of Spain had every reason to revolt Hakluyt demonstrated by reciting the atrocities recounted by Las Casas. That Spain had no right to rule the New World he demonstrated by refuting the right of the Pope (who had divided the New World between Spain and Portugal in 1493) to assign dominion over any land.[17] (He even tried to cast doubt on the validity of the Spanish claim that derived from the discoveries of Columbus: Columbus had sought the support of Henry VII of England before turning to Ferdinand and Isabella, and had dealt falsely with Henry by not waiting long enough for Henry's answer.)

What Hakluyt and Raleigh were affirming was not quite a right of self-determination for the nations held in Spanish bondage. They were clearly bent on substituting English rule for Spanish. It had seemed obvious to the Spanish in Panama that Drake and Oxenham were trying to take over part of Spain's empire by promoting the revolt of her subjects. It seemed equally obvious to Hakluyt and Raleigh that this was precisely what England ought to do. Raleigh's colony could furnish not only a base from which to prey on Spanish shipping, but a rallying point for the oppressed natives of New

---

[14] *Ibid.*, II, 241.   [16] *Ibid.*, II, 246.
[15] *Ibid.*, II, 241.   [17] *Ibid.*, II, 296–313.

Spain. Hakluyt assured Elizabeth that "whensoever the Queene of England, a prince of such clemencie, shall seate upon that firme [i.e., mainland, continent] of America, and shalbe reported throughoute all that tracte to use the naturall people there with all humanitie, curtesie, and freedome, they will yelde themselves to her governement and revolte cleane from the Spaniarde." [18]

While the colony would thus enable the queen to win the oppressed peoples of the New World, it would also enable her to rescue those Englishmen at home who suffered want and oppression. Like Thomas More, Hakluyt was troubled by the growing number of men and women for whom England could afford neither food nor shelter nor even the opportunity to work for their bread. They drifted from place to place by the hundred, begging and thieving until the gallows claimed them. The prisons of the land were "daily pestered and stuffed full of them." [19]

Hakluyt was not exaggerating. England's population, for reasons that still mystify demographers, had begun to rise rapidly in the early sixteenth century and continued to do so until the middle of the seventeenth century, so that the island's numbers rose from under three million in 1500 to more than five million by the middle of the next century.[20] England's economy did not expand correspondingly, to furnish work for the new millions. Prices rose steadily, followed at some distance by a rise in rents and a much smaller rise in wages. The price of provisions used by a laborer's family rose twice as fast as wages. From a quarter to a half of the population lived below the level recognized at the time to constitute poverty. Few of them could count on regular meals at home, and more and more were forced to the road, where, as Hakluyt said, they fell "to pilferinge and thevinge and other lewdnes." [21]

To plant a colony in America, Hakluyt argued, would furnish a twofold remedy to the problem of the unemployed poor. Not only the colonists but their Indian friends would need English goods,

---

[18] *Ibid.*, II, 318.   [19] *Ibid.*, II, 234.
[20] E. A. Wrigley, *Population and History* (London, 1969), 78–80.
[21] Taylor, *Writings of the Hakluyts*, II, 234; E. H. Phelps Brown and Sheila V. Hopkins, "Seven Centuries of Building Wages," *Economica*, 2nd ser., XXII (1955), 95–206; "Seven Centuries of the Prices of Consumables, Compared with Builders' Wage-Rates," *ibid.*, XXIII (1956), 296–314; "Wage Rates and Prices: Evidence for Population Pressure in the Sixteenth Century," *ibid.*, XXIV (1957), 289–306; H. P. R. Finberg, ed., *The Agrarian History of England and Wales*, IV, *1500–1640*, Joan Thirsk, ed. (Cambridge, 1967), 435–57, 531, 583–695.

especially English cloth. In order to supply them, shuttles would fly in England's looms and the poor would be able to earn a decent living. Those not employed in supplying the colonies would themselves become colonists and enjoy the manifold opportunities of the New World.

Hakluyt was a compassionate man. He wanted to save those who "for trifles may otherwise be devoured by the gallowes." [22] The idleness, poverty, and corruption of the English poor did not seem to him to be the result of any unworthiness of character. Desperation, not depravity, drove them to crime. The problem was that England had more people than jobs. The cure was to find more jobs, whether in England or in America. Hakluyt's feeling for the English poor was of a piece with his feeling for the oppressed Indians and blacks in America. Both were good people, suffering through no fault of their own. As England was "swarminge at this day with valiant youthes rusting and hurtfull by lacke of employement," [23] so New Spain was filled with "valiant" people like the Cimarrons and the Chichimici, suffering by Spanish oppression. The two must be brought together, under England's benevolent rule, in a new English empire on American soil.

The argument was persuasive, and the queen was persuaded, but only to the extent of lending a ship of the royal navy, the *Tyger*, as the flagship of the expedition that Raleigh gathered during the next year to start his colony. She was also persuaded, either by Hakluyt's argument or by others, once more to unleash Sir Francis Drake. As Raleigh was gathering the ships and men for his colony, Drake was gathering ships and men for a raid on the Caribbean, a raid that was designed to be more than a raid. For obvious reasons, neither Drake nor Raleigh sought publicity for what he was doing. Hakluyt's discourse was not published, and the coordination of plans for the raid and for the colonizing expedition can only be surmised from events and, once again, from the testimony offered by Drake's Spanish victims. [24] But given Raleigh's objectives, as expounded in Hakluyt's discourse, the two enterprises had to be connected. While

---

[22] Taylor, *Writings of the Hakluyts*, II, 319.   [23] *Ibid.*, II, 315.

[24] The only evidence of coordination in the English archives consists of the fact that the two ventures were linked in some of the few surviving documents that mention them, as when Hakluyt wrote to Sir Francis Walsingham, one of Elizabeth's principal advisers, that the Spanish were worried by rumors of the two, or when Lord Burghley, in drafting an authorization for Raleigh to impress men and shipping, added "the like to Sir Francis Drake." Quinn, *Roanoke Voyages*, I, 155, 157.

Raleigh was establishing a permanent base just north of Florida, Drake would be harassing the Spanish in the Caribbean, and perhaps, with the aid of the Cimarrons, liberating a portion of the Spanish empire. Drake knew from past experience in the Caribbean that the Spanish defended their coastal cities only with galleys, vessels rowed by "galley slaves," another emblem of Spanish tyranny. Galleys had once been effective in Mediterranean warfare, but they were no match in the ocean for the swift sailing ships that Drake and Hawkins had developed for the English.[25] By September, 1585, when he set off, Drake had a fleet of twenty-five of them, including two lent by the queen. Martin Frobisher was his vice admiral, and Christopher Carleill, who had backed Gilbert, was his general, in command of 2,300 soldiers.[26]

Drake's expedition was naval and military, and unfortunately Raleigh allowed his also to take on a strong military character. Part of the reason was that the queen had not been sufficiently generous and probably could not have been. Neither Raleigh nor his backers had the money to risk for a long-term investment in getting the colony going. They all, including the queen, wanted every voyage to pay, and the only way to make it pay was to pick up Spanish prizes en route. But by giving the expedition a military organization, as Raleigh did, he was placing the government of his colony, which was supposed to win the natives by its gentleness and courtesy, in the hands of men whose business was war. The hot-tempered Sir Richard Grenville was the general in charge; below him Thomas Cavendish (who later sailed round the world) was marshal; and Ralph Lane, on whom the command at Roanoke finally devolved, was lieutenant. Little is known about Lane other than the fact that he had been serving in Ireland, where he had distinguished himself for rapacity, and that he was released especially for the voyage.[27] These men were in charge of about six hundred others, of whom probably half were sailors to man the five ships. Most of the rest must have been soldiers. Only 108 were designated as colonists, and even they may have been expected to serve as soldiers if necessary.[28]

Probably a large percentage of the soldiers and settlers as well

[25] Julian S. Corbett, *Drake and the Tudor Navy* (New York, 1899); Williamson, *Hawkins of Plymouth*, passim.

[26] The voyage can best be followed in Irene A. Wright, *Further English Voyages to Spanish America, 1583-1594*, Works issued by the Hakluyt Society, 2nd ser., XCIX (London, 1951).

[27] Quinn, *Roanoke Voyages*, I, 149-50.   [28] *Ibid.*, I, 173.

as the seamen had been impressed for the voyage. Impressment was England's way of recruiting for military expeditions across the Channel or overseas. The casualty rate on such expeditions was notorious, and the communities that furnished men for them deliberately selected their most undesirable inhabitants.[29] Those who returned were likely to be found among the beggars who wandered England's roads. Hakluyt had, in fact, included these veterans among the persons whom England might send to the colony. If any of the Roanoke colonists were obtained in this way, they fulfilled Hakluyt's plan for snatching men from the gallows, but they were scarcely the most promising material for starting a new biracial community in combination with the "kind and loving people" of Roanoke. The thought apparently occurred to someone else who was in on planning the colony. An anonymous document spells out the need for strict discipline and includes a brief set of proposed regulations with specific injunctions against any soldier striking an Indian or entering an Indian's house without leave. The same document also contains the provision, in keeping with the colony's purpose, "That no Indian be forced to labor unwillyngly." [30]

The author of this document, like the Hakluyts, advised Raleigh to bring his own labor, at least skilled labor, to assure that the community would be economically viable and productive from the start. But it is not clear that Raleigh succeeded in securing skilled artisans. He would almost certainly not have been able to impress them, and the men he did send certainly showed no great capacity for work. Raleigh did, however, persuade John White, a painter, to go along and make a visual record of the new land; and Thomas Hariot, a mathematician of no small competence, accompanied the expedition to make scientific observations that might reveal the country's natural resources. Hariot had spent the winter with Manteo and Wanchese, the two Indians brought back by Barlowe. He had

[29] The casualties came from disease rather than battle. The expedition of the Earl of Essex in 1591 to assist Henry IV of France met with only a few skirmishes, but only 800 men out of 3,400 returned. Gladys S. Thompson, *Lords Lieutenants in the Sixteenth Century* (London, 1923), 111. Even naval forces mustered to meet the Spanish Armada in 1588 suffered appalling losses from disease. In ten of the largest ships, in spite of heavy replacements, only 2,195 out of the original complement of 3,325 men were on the payroll by September. The total loss was probably equal to the entire original number. Lawrence Stone, "The Armada Campaign of 1588," *History*, XXIX (1944), 120–43, esp. 137–41.

[30] Quinn, *Roanoke Voyages*, I, 138.

taught them English and they had taught him their language and filled him with anticipation of the good things he would find. They returned with the expedition, so that there were at least three members who could serve as interpreters.

Grenville got the expedition off in April, 1585, proceeding by way of the West Indies. At Puerto Rico he landed, built a fort, and cut trees for the construction of a pinnace (to replace one lost in a storm). There and at Hispaniola he also gathered livestock and tropical plants, including bananas and sugar cane, so that the colonists could try growing these profitable Spanish commodities in Virginia. In the last two weeks of June the vessels straggled into various inlets of the Carolina Banks. Simon Fernandez, piloting the *Tyger*, ran her aground crossing the bar. For two hours she lay there, and by the time they got her off, many of the provisions intended to sustain the colony during its first year were awash in the hold and ruined. Grenville established headquarters on Roanoke Island, from which he explored the mainland below the island, while another party examined the country bordering Albemarle Sound. But Grenville apparently did not intend to stay permanently with the colony. He, and presumably Cavendish too, departed at the end of August, leaving Lane in command.[31]

As Grenville sailed toward England, picking up a valuable prize off Bermuda, Drake was on his way to the West Indies with his armada. Failing to intercept the treasure fleets, which got out just before he arrived, he pounced on Santo Domingo, the oldest bastion of Spain's New World empire. Almost before the Spaniards knew what was happening, their city was in flames, the slaves rowing the galleys that were supposed to defend it were freed, and the churches were desecrated in the manner the Spanish had learned to expect from this "Lutheran." After a month of occupation Drake returned the shell of the city to its Spanish inhabitants for 25,000 ducats, raised from the personal belongings of those who had managed to hide in the bushes. Taking along four or five Spanish ships from the harbor and hundreds of liberated slaves, he sailed away on February 9. Two weeks later the audiencia of the city reported to the king, "we have understood both from these evil people and also from others that this and other fleets which cleared from England will meet at Cape Canaveral, where they have made a settlement." [32]

But Drake was not ready to move north yet. On Ash Wednes-

31 *Ibid.*, I, 178–242.   32 Wright, *Further Voyages*, 34–37.

day, February 19, he appeared off Cartagena and by Friday had captured it, burned its defending galleys, and again liberated the slaves. Negro slaves from surrounding plantations also joined him, and in negotiating with the city fathers to ransom the city, he made it clear that he would return no slaves, "except when the slaves themselves desired to go." [33] It was said at Cartagena that Drake's next stop would be Panama, that he carried clothing and other gifts for the Cimarrons there and "pinnaces made in sections so that the soldiers can carry them on their backs and so enter the Pacific." [34] If Drake did intend to stop at Panama, he changed his mind. On April 10, when he left Cartagena (much of it in ashes) with a ransom of 107,000 ducats, he headed for the Florida channel, taking with him three hundred Indians ("mostly women") and two hundred Negroes, Turks, and Moors.[35]

When he showed up off San Agustin, Florida, he demonstrated once again the vulnerability of Spanish dominion. As soon as the English attacked the fort, the local Indians began to burn the town. The Spanish women and children, who had been evacuated to the interior to escape the English, were now more in danger of an Indian attack. So the Spanish commander abandoned his fort and hastened inland to protect them. "If our people escape from the English," the commander reported to his superiors in Spain, "the Indians will fall upon them or both will attack together." For the future, he advised, it would be necessary to have sufficient strength to resist both the Indians and outside enemies, "for when the crisis arrives both are foes to the death." [36]

Drake apparently raided San Agustin not for the sake of plunder, for Florida was no source of treasure, but as part of the larger strategy of the expedition. In one stroke he reduced the threat that the garrison at San Agustin posed to Roanoke and at the same time promoted Anglo-Indian solidarity against the Spaniard. The authorities at San Agustin wrote home that "although he had burned this city and fort he did no damage at all to an Indian village which is a cannon's shot from here." They also reported that Drake sent a party ashore at Santa Elena and "greatly flattered the Indians of that district, assuring them that in the spring the English would return and that they had a settlement on the coast near." [37]

---

[33] Ibid., 54, 159.   [36] Ibid., 180–86.
[34] Ibid., 55, 195.   [37] Ibid., 205.
[35] Ibid., 173.

The existence of the Roanoke settlement seems to have been widely known among Spanish officials in the Caribbean, probably as a result of Grenville's call at Puerto Rico. One report even had it that Grenville was operating under Drake's orders.[38] And it seems to have been common knowledge, after Drake left Cartagena, that he was headed for the English colony. Otherwise, it was pointed out, "there would be no sense in his taking the pains he took to carry off launches and frigates, implements, locks and all sorts of hardware and negro labourers who in his country are free." [39] Three Negroes left behind at San Agustin confirmed this reasoning, saying, "He meant to leave all the negroes he had in a fort and settlement established at Jacan by the English who went there a year ago." [40]

The various reports of Drake's activities in the Caribbean suggest that liberating victims of Spanish oppression was part of the plan. With Drake's help, it seems, the vision of Hakluyt and Raleigh was beginning to materialize: England was bringing freedom to the New World. To be sure, it was coming as a means to an end; Drake and Raleigh were both interested in power, profit, and plunder. But freedom has frequently had to make its way in the world by serving as a means to an end, and it has often proved a powerful means. At Roanoke we look for it now to show its power. But by the time Drake arrived there in triumph, in June, 1586, something had gone awry.

The colony had begun auspiciously, with the leaders as confident as Barlowe had been. On August 12 Lane had written to Sir Francis Walsingham that even the barrenest regions yielded "sumwhat that ether for knowen Vertue ys of pryce in Chrystendom, or sumwhat at leeste to the smelle pleasing." They had not, he said, found "one stynckinge weede growynge in thys lande." [41] Three weeks later he wrote to the elder Hakluyt in even more extravagant terms: Virginia not only smelled good, it was "the goodliest and most pleasing territorie of the world," and once inhabited by Englishmen it would yield every commodity of Spain, France, Italy, and the East. It was already "very wel peopled and towned, though savagelie," but these savages were "naturally most curteous, and very desirous to have clothes." [42]

Lane was perhaps telling Hakluyt what he knew Hakluyt

[38] *Ibid.*, 172.
[39] *Ibid.*, 188–89.
[40] *Ibid.*, 204.
[41] Quinn, *Roanoke Voyages*, I, 200.
[42] *Ibid.*, I, 208–9.

wanted to hear and what he himself wanted to believe. But Thomas
Hariot, who spent the ensuing months in a careful investigation of
Virginia's native commodities, was also optimistic about the future
productivity of the country. By 1587, when Hariot wrote his sober
and detailed appraisal of Virginia,[43] he knew that the Indians were not
as numerous or as courteous or as fond of clothes as Lane supposed in
1585. But he still thought that "in respect of troubling our inhabiting
and planting, [they] are not to be feared, but that they shall have
cause both to feare and love us, that shall inhabite with them."[44] A
few years later, he wrote of them, "to confesse a truthe I cannot remember, that ever I saw better or quietter people than they."[45]

Hariot wrote sympathetically of the Indians. He probably
knew them better than the other settlers did, because of his months
of teaching and being taught by Manteo and Wanchese. John White,
the artist of the expedition, also knew them and recorded his respect
for them in the way he painted them. White enjoys a distinction
among artists of his time because of the spontaneous naturalism of
his drawings, a quality not to be found in other English painters for
another half century. John White's Indians are his own, not Peter
Martyr's paragons, and yet there is a dignity in them that conforms
to what civil men have liked to call the myth of the noble savage.[46]
That myth has been expressed as often by men who knew the Indian
at first hand as by those who idealized him from the distance. It has
survived massacre, murder, and war, perhaps because the Indian himself believed it. Although he probably did not share the European's
dream of a primitive but perfect golden age, the Indian's view of
himself evidently included an element of pride that gave him, especially in relations with other men, an extraordinary dignity. It is
impossible to read the first-hand accounts of Indians, from widely
separated regions and of widely divergent cultures, without being impressed by this quality, as Arthur Barlowe and John White and
Thomas Hariot were impressed by it at Roanoke. Unfortunately,
there as in Hispaniola, it led the white man to expect more of the
Indian than the Indian expected of himself.

At the same time, both Indians and Englishmen expected more

[43] *A Briefe and True Report of the New Found Land of Virginia*
(London, 1588), in Quinn, *Roanoke Voyages*, I, 317–87.
[44] Quinn, *Roanoke Voyages*, I, 368.   [45] *Ibid.*, I, 443.
[46] The best reproductions are in Paul Hulton and David B. Quinn,
The American Drawings of John White (London and Chapel Hill, N.C.,
1964).

of Englishmen than Englishmen were able to fulfill. The myth of the noble savage was matched by the equally tenacious myth of the godlike white man. Hariot, after describing the Indians' admiration for English weapons, books, clocks, and deadly diseases (which seemed like magic weapons the English could direct at will), explained that "some people could not tel whether to thinke us gods or men, and the rather because that all the space of their sicknesse, there was no man of ours knowne to die." [47] The fact that there were no women in the expedition and that the men showed no interest in Indian women (if we may believe Hariot) led some Indians to the opinion "that wee were not borne of women, and therefore not mortall, but that wee were men of an old generation many yeeres past then risen againe to immortalitie." [48]

The English could not quite accept this view of themselves and explained to the Indians about the Almighty God whom they worshiped. But the Indians whom they persuaded of this being's existence were not slow to recognize his special favors to the English. If the invaders did not have superhuman power at their command, they had something close to it, Hariot admitted, in "the speciall woorke of God for our sakes, as wee our selves have cause in some sorte to thinke no lesse, whatsoever some doe or may imagine to the contrarie. . . ." [49] The humility enjoined on men by the Christian God has seldom prevented the assimiliation of a share of divinity by the successful, and especially by those in a position to command others. English technical superiority—together with the vulnerability of Indians to English diseases—encouraged the settlers at Roanoke to assume something of the stature that the Indians were all too ready at first to assign them. They had come with the expectation sooner or later of ruling the land, and it was easy to attach the sanction of divine right to their expectations. The attitude toward the English that Hariot evidently sought from the Indians was "that they shall have cause both to feare and love us," the proper attitude of man toward God and of subjects toward godlike rulers.

What went wrong at Roanoke was that the Indians did not show the nobility or the English the divinity that was expected of them. The trouble began even before Grenville departed. In July, during his exploration of the mainland, at the Indian village of Aquascogoc on a branch of the Pamlico River, an Indian allegedly stole a silver cup. Three days later, as the party was returning down the Pamlico, Grenville sent Philip Amadas to recover it. When he

[47] Quinn, *Roanoke Voyages*, I, 379.   [48] *Ibid.*, I, 380.   [49] *Ibid.*

failed to get it, the record says, "we burnt, and spoyled their corne, and Towne, all the people beeing fledde." [50] If the theft was ignoble, the English reaction was scarcely godlike.

At Roanoke itself things went smoothly for a time. Wingina, recovered from his wounds, welcomed the visitors, and the Indians gave freely of their supplies to the English, who had lost most of their own when the *Tyger* grounded. By the time the colonists were settled, it was too late to plant corn, and they seem to have been helpless when it came to living off the land. They did not know the herbs and roots and berries of the country. They could not or would not catch fish in any quantity, because they did not know how to make weirs. And when the Indians showed them, they were slow learners: they were unable even to repair those that the Indians made for them. Nor did they show any disposition for agriculture. Hariot admired the yields that the Indians got in growing maize; but the English, for lack of seed, lack of skill, or lack of will, grew nothing for themselves, even when the new planting season came round again. Superior English technology appeared, for the moment at least, to be no technology at all, as far as food production was concerned.

The English refusal or inability to help themselves live from the land is a little surprising in the light of the sponsors' interest in making their colony yield marketable commodities. In England there had been talk of getting ten times as much from the land as the Indians did. Grenville had taken pains to collect plants from the West Indies to try out at Roanoke; and Hariot occupied himself almost entirely in ascertaining what grew and what might be made to grow. The difficulty may have lain in the military character of the settlers. Soldiers expected to go hungry often, but they did not expect to grow their own food. It was up to their commanders to see that they were fed; and on overseas expeditions commanders usually bought or seized supplies from the people of the country. Lane may, in fact, have considered it more practicable to get food from the Indians than to turn his troops into farmers. He evidently had his hands full maintaining discipline without putting the men to unexpected tasks. He had, he complained to his friend Sir Philip Sidney, "emungst savages, the chardege of wylde menn of myne owene nacione, Whose unrulynes ys suche as not to gyve leasure to the goovernour to bee all most at any tyme from them." [51]

Unfortunately, the Indians, though hospitable, were not pre-

[50] *Ibid.*, I, 191.   [51] *Ibid.*, I, 204.

pared for company that came to stay. They had no great stores to draw upon when faced with the English demands for corn. Whatever the English may have offered in exchange, the extra labor of feeding so many extra mouths must have imposed a severe strain on them, for sustained work was not a normal part of Indian life. The Roanokes, like most other North American Indians, grew corn (maize) in quantities barely adequate to their survival from harvest to harvest, relying on roots and berries and on hunting and fishing to get them through when the corn ran out. They had no extra fields or seed prepared for guests. If the English continued to demand food from them, the Indians, in order to supply it, would have to clear more land, plant more corn, and beg, borrow, or steal seed from other Indians.

The situation was hardly conducive to good relations between the newcomers and the natives. No records tell us how the two groups got along during the winter, but it seems unlikely that the wild men of England displayed the attributes that the Indians expected of gods. And it seems certain that everybody was on short rations. By the time spring came, Wingina had had enough of his grasshopper guests.

If we may believe Ralph Lane, Wingina arranged a conspiracy of the nearby mainland tribes to wipe out the English. Feigning friendship, Wingina warned Lane of the hostile intentions of the mainland Indians, apparently suggesting the need to chastise them; and as bait he hinted of mines and of a westward passage up the Chowan or Roanoke rivers. Sometime in March Lane took the bait; but coming by surprise on the Indians whom Wingina had alerted to trap him, he succeeded in overawing them, put the principal chief, Menatonon, in chains, and took his son Skiko as a hostage. From Menatonon he learned of Wingina's alleged treachery. After exploring the mainland without finding mines or a westward passage, Lane returned to Roanoke, where he found the Indians on the point of deserting the island for the purpose of starving the English.[52]

The fact that the Indians, by Lane's own account, could have done the English in simply by deserting them, renders the story of the conspiracy not altogether credible. According to Lane, Wingina was so taken aback by his safe return that he agreed to sow enough corn to feed the English the following year and to construct weirs for them and also to give them some land for themselves. (The English

[52] *Ibid.*, I, 246–48, 275–81.

still, apparently, recognized Roanoke as belonging to Wingina and his people.) But as the spring progressed and the winter stores dwindled (the corn, sown in April, would not ripen for several months), Wingina's people refused to trade any more supplies. And Wingina himself retired to the mainland, partly, Lane believed, to evade Lane's daily demand for provisions and partly to prepare another conspiracy to wipe out the English. Lane learned of the plot through the hostage, Skiko, and proceeded to nip it in the bud. Surprising Wingina at his headquarters on the mainland, he killed him and his principal advisers.[53] This was the first of June, and on the eighth Francis Drake arrived with his load of Indians and Negroes freed from their Spanish oppressors.

It was the age of Shakespeare and Marlowe, the age of Elizabeth, the age of Drake and Raleigh, when Englishmen were filled with heady visions of their country's glory. Roanoke might have become the scene of another English triumph. But by the time Drake came onstage, the supporting cast had long since forgotten their lines and spoiled the play. Lane, with only six weeks or so to go before corn harvest, had murdered his host and alienated the people on whom he depended for survival, and his opinion of the territory that he had described as the "goodliest and most pleasing" in the world had, not surprisingly, been revised. He now thought that unless they could find good mineral deposits or a passage to the Pacific, nothing could "bring this country in request to be inhabited by our nation." [54] It would also be necessary to find a decent harbor, for it had become clear that all the sheltered areas around Roanoke were too shallow. Nevertheless, when Drake offered him a bark of shallow draft, two pinnaces, four boats, and four months' supply for a hundred men, Lane agreed to stick it out. With the new vessels he would explore the Chesapeake region for a suitable harbor and then report back to England. But the next day, June 13, 1586, a storm broke out and scattered Drake's fleet, which was riding outside the Banks. Lane's bark of 70 tons with provisions aboard headed for the high seas and did not return. Drake offered him another ship and more provisions, but the only ship available now was a bark of 170 tons, too large to cross the shoals, and Lane suddenly gave up. Instead of waiting for the supply ships from England that had been promised him and that were actually on their way, he put his whole expedition aboard Drake's fleet, and headed home.[55]

[53] *Ibid.*, I, 248–49, 282–88.   [55] *Ibid.*, I, 253–54, 288–94.
[54] *Ibid.*, I, 273.

What, then, of the liberated slaves and Indians? The saddest part of the story and perhaps the most revealing is that no one bothered to say. None of the accounts either of Drake's voyage or of the Roanoke colony mentions what became of them. Thus casually and ignominiously ended the first attempt to join the planting of English gentle government in North America with the liberation of the Caribbean and South America from Spanish tyranny.

Raleigh himself did not give up and later tried again in Guiana. But at Roanoke what followed was anticlimax. Grenville returned there with seven or eight ships and three or four hundred men a few weeks after Lane's departure. Finding the place deserted, he left only fifteen or eighteen men to hold the fort and hurried on to the South Atlantic in quest of Spanish prizes. The following July, when John White arrived with 110 settlers, Grenville's small force was not to be found. White's party included his daughter and her husband and again Manteo. They had intended to settle on the Chesapeake but never got that far, apparently because their pilot (Simon Fernandez again) was too eager to get at the business of privateering and refused to take them. Instead, they settled again at Roanoke, where they baptized Manteo and declared him, as vassal of Raleigh, the lord of the island, a ceremony designed to carry out the original strategy of allying with the local Indians. Having killed the king of the Roanokes, the English were installing a puppet of their own. Manteo, however, was probably the only Indian prepared to recognize the authority with which the English invested him. He could not, at any rate, command from his countrymen the supplies of corn that the colony still needed for survival. In order to speed the flow of provisions from England, White decided to go back with the returning ships. He sailed in late August, 1587, leaving behind his daughter and her newborn child.[56] Because of the Spanish Armada and other difficulties, he did not get back to Roanoke until 1590, and he found the Island again deserted.[57]

John White's colony was lost and what became of the settlers will probably never be known.[58] But something more had been lost before White's settlers even landed. At Roanoke in the winter of 1585–86, English plans and hopes for America had come up against their first serious encounter with the continent and its people. In that

[56] *Ibid.*, II, 515–38.   [57] *Ibid.*, II, 598–622.
[58] The most informed discussion of the question is David B. Quinn, *England and the Discovery of America, 1481–1620* (New York, 1974), 432–81.

encounter neither Englishmen nor native Americans lived up to expectations. Doubtless the expectations had been too high, but it is always a little sad to watch men lower their sights. And Roanoke was only the beginning.

3

IDLE INDIAN AND LAZY ENGLISHMAN

Roanoke dispelled some illusions, both among the Indians and among the English. The Indians of the Virginia region would not be likely again to mistake the English for gods. The English, on the other hand, would be wary of expecting to find America divided into good Indians and cannibals, with the good Indians eagerly awaiting English help. From this point we can perhaps date the beginnings of the English disposition to regard all Indians as alike. As yet, however, it did not follow that the only good Indian was a dead one. When the first permanent English settlers arrived in America in 1607, their sponsors had not given up hope of an integrated biracial community, in which indigent Englishmen would work side by side with willing natives, under gentle English government.

The sponsors were closely linked to the Roanoke venture. The Virginia Company of London came into existence in 1606, created by a charter from the king to Richard Hakluyt and "divers others," including one of London's leading merchants, Sir Thomas Smith.[1] Smith, the son of one of Raleigh's backers, became the treasurer of the new company, its principal officer and its moving force. It was a joint-stock company, and its members hoped for a profit, just as Raleigh's backers had. But they were barred, ostensibly at least, from the one source of wealth that had paid off for Raleigh: his only re-

[1] Philip L. Barbour, ed., *The Jamestown Voyages under the First Charter, 1606–1609*, Works issued by the Hakluyt Society, 2nd ser., CXXXVI, CXXXVII (Cambridge, 1969), I, 24–34; Alexander Brown, *The Genesis of the United States* (Boston, 1890), 46–63.

turns had come from the Spanish prizes that Grenville and Fernandez took on their voyages to and from the colony. England's new king, James I, had made peace with Spain, and he did not countenance freebooting expeditions against England's old enemy. It seems clear that some of the investors in the Virginia Company expected to use an American colony as a base from which to continue their depredations, far from the king's watchful eye. But the company could not officially engage in such exploits or even condone them, nor could it serve as a cover for schemes to subvert the Spanish empire.[2]

Probably the majority of investors looked toward legitimate profits. They invested their money in hopes of finding precious metals or minerals, of discovering valuable plants for dyestuffs and medicines, and perhaps of opening a northwest passage to the Pacific. But they were prepared to settle for less spectacular goods like glass, iron, furs, potash, pitch, and tar, things that England needed and mostly had to import from other countries. After the Roanoke experience they must have known that it might take time to develop a trade in any product. Of all the natural treasures mentioned in Barlowe's and Hariot's glowing accounts of Virginia, only sassafras (thought to be a cure for syphilis) had yet a ready market in the Old World. Though the promoters of the company still hoped for instant success, they had to stress the country's future promise, the great multitude of good things it was going to yield.

The plan was to send settlers who would pool their labors to produce whatever proved feasible. After the cargoes of riches, whatever they might be, began pouring into England, the company would pay out dividends to all members in proportion to the number of shares they owned. Men could "adventure" in the company by buying shares (at a rate fixed two years later at £12.10.0 per share). But a man could also get a share simply by going to Virginia at his own expense. With the money from sales of shares the company would send over shiploads of England's unemployed laborers as well as skilled specialists. Such men would be servants of the company and not entitled to a share in the proceeds. They would work for the

[2] The authoritative work on the Virginia Company is W. F. Craven, *The Dissolution of the Virginia Company* (New York, 1932). A briefer treatment with more attention to the company's early years is his *The Virginia Company of London, 1606–1624*, Jamestown 350th Anniversary Historical Booklet No. 5 (Williamsburg, 1957). See also his *Southern Colonies in the Seventeenth Century* (Baton Rouge, La., 1949), 82–92.

company for seven years in return for their transportation and then be free to work as they chose, taking advantage of the limitless opportunities of the New World to create new lives for themselves.[3]

It was the intention of the sponsors of the colony that benefits for the settlers and their backers would march hand in hand with beneficence toward the natives. While reaping the good things of the new land, the colony would "bring the infidels and salvages lyving in those partes to humane civilitie and to a setled and quiet govermente." [4] The Spanish had planted their false religion and their tyrannical government in the south, but God had reserved the northern parts of the New World for English freedom and true religion. King James himself retained ultimate control of the colony's government, which he exercised through a council in England, giving orders to a president and council in Virginia. And at the outset the king gave instructions that everyone in the colony must "well entreate" the Indians and that "all just, kind and charitable courses shall be holden with such of them, as shall conforme themselves to any good and sociable traffique and dealing with the subjects of us, . . . whereby they may be the sooner drawne to the true knowledge of God, and the Obedience of us." [5]

More specific instructions given by the company to the first settlers showed some of the disillusionment toward the Indians derived from the Roanoke experience. The colony was to be planted well to the north of Roanoke in the Chesapeake region, where Raleigh himself had planned to move his settlement. Apart from the superior harbors that this area afforded within Cape Charles and Cape Henry, Ralph Lane had suggested that the Indians to the north were more reliable than those at Roanoke (at least Lane had not yet estranged them).[6] But even so, the company was wary of counting on their friendship. The settlers were still to follow the strategy devised by Hakluyt: find a navigable river and settle some distance up it, for defense against European enemies, and for access to different groups of Indians, so that they could play off one against another. They were to allow no Indians in the area between them and the sea-

---

[3] The details of the enterprise were not set down and perhaps not fully worked out until 1609, when the company received a new charter (see below). It is not clear who or how many were the initial investors, apart from those named in the charter. It was probably not until 1609 that the company began selling shares to the public.

[4] Barbour, *Jamestown Voyages*, I, 25.   [5] *Ibid.*, I, 43.

[6] Quinn, *Roanoke Voyages*, I, 272–75, 284; II, 523.

coast, "for you Cannot Carry Your Selves so towards them but they will Grow Discontented with Your habitation and be ready to Guide and assist any Nation that Shall Come to invade You."[7] And who more likely to come than the Spanish? Already the shoe seems to be on the other foot: Spanish adventurers may take advantage of natives discontented with English rule.

In spite of its distrust, the Virginia Company was eager to affirm its good will. Its aim for the Indians, as explained a little later, was only to bring them the gospel, and "to cover their naked miserie, with civill use of foode, and cloathing, and to traine them by gentle meanes, to those manuall artes and skill, which they so much affect, and doe admire to see in us." In return for these blessings, the English would require nothing of them "but a quiet residence to us and ours, that by our owne labour and toyle, we may worke this good unto them and recompence our owne adventures, costs and travells." They were still expected to become a part of the English community, where they would be "most friendly welcome to conjoyne their labours with ours, and shall enjoy equall priviledges with us." Virginia Indians would experience none of the "stormes of raging cruelties" perpetrated by the Spanish in the West Indies, but only "faire and loving meanes suting to our English Natures."[8]

The Virginia Company thought of the enterprise as something like the conversion of the primitive Britons by the Romans. Without the civilizing influence of the Romans, England itself would still be populated by heathen savages just as America still was.[9] The members who stayed in London clung to this vision for most of the company's life. Their company, they believed, was not like other joint-stock companies, "the ends for which it is established beinge not simply matter of Trade, butt of a higher Nature."[10] Although they hoped for profits, theirs was a patriotic enterprise that would bring civility and Christianity to the savages of North America and redemption from idleness and crime to the unemployed masses of England.

[7] Barbour, *Jamestown Voyages*, I, 50.

[8] [Robert Johnson], *Nova Britannia: Offering Most Excellent Fruits by Planting in Virginia* (London, 1609; New York, 1867), sig. C, fols. 1–2.

[9] *Ibid.*; Alexander Whitaker, *Good Newes from Virginia* (London, 1613), 24; William Strachey, *The Historie of Travell into Virginia Britania*, L. B. Wright and Virginia Freund, eds., Works issued by the Hakluyt Society, 2nd ser., CIII (London, 1953), 24.

[10] *RVC*, II, 527.

The colony did not work out as the company envisaged it. The adventurers who ventured their capital lost it. Most of the settlers who ventured their lives lost them. And so did most of the Indians who came near them. Measured by any of the objectives announced for it, the colony failed. And it failed, as Roanoke failed, because neither the Indians nor the English lived up to expectations.

At this remove the expectations, considerably reduced from those that preceded Roanoke, do not appear to have been unrealistic. The company wanted the settlers to go at their jobs with a will and make the new land grow the good things that everyone was sure it could grow and that it has since proved entirely capable of growing. They did not have their hearts set on gold and silver and jewels or on any single preconceived product. They were willing to experiment with a variety of prosaic staples. And they did not expect the Indians to fall down before them and do their bidding. The Indians would be welcome to "conjoin their labors with ours," but only insofar as the Indians saw how advantageous it would be to adopt English civility and civilized techniques.

Nevertheless, the expectations that seem reasonable to us were not fulfilled. Indian and Englishman in Virginia seem to have had different expectations of themselves than the company had. And before examining the disasters that befell them together, it will be necessary to look more closely at the kind of life each had led and the expectations that life engendered in them before they encountered one another on the banks of the James River.

Most Indians of North America felt the force of government in their lives far less than men in England did. If we may believe the testimony of Englishmen who later lived among different Indian tribes in the eastern part of the continent, the power of the chiefs, or kings, or werowances, as they were variously called, rested mainly on personal dignity and prestige. James Adair, a trader among the southeastern tribes, wrote that "the power of their chiefs is an empty sound. They can only persuade or dissuade the people, either by the force of good-nature and clear reasoning, or colouring things, so as to suit their prevailing passions. It is reputed merit alone, that gives them any titles of distinction above the meanest of the people." [11] Henry Timberlake, a soldier who spent some time with the Chero-

[11] James Adair, *The History of the American Indians* (London, 1775), 428.

kee, reported, "Their government, if I may call it government, which has neither laws nor power to support it, is a mixed aristocracy and democracy, the chiefs being chose according to their merit in war, or policy at home." [12] And numerous observers among other tribes gave similar reports of Indian freedom.[13]

It did not appear to the English who first came to Virginia that the Indians who lived along its great rivers had much freedom. One tribe, the Pamunkeys, under the leadership of a single chief, Powhatan, had reduced about thirty other tribes, constituting perhaps 8,000 persons, into a primitive empire, occupying precisely the area where the English settled, from the James to the Potomac.[14] As the English

[12] Henry Timberlake, *The Memoirs of Lieut. Henry Timberlake* (London, 1765), 70.

[13] For example, Robert Rogers on the Iroquois: ". . . the great and fundamental principles of their policy are, that every man is naturally free and independent, that no one . . . on earth has any right to deprive him of his freedom and independency, and that nothing can be a compensation for the loss of it." Robert Rogers, *A Concise Account of North America* (London, 1765), 233. For other examples see E. S. Morgan, "The American Indian: Incorrigible Individualist," in *The Mirror of the Indian* (Providence, R.I., 1958), 5–19.

[14] Maurice A. Mook, "The Aboriginal Population of Tidewater Virginia," *American Anthropologist*, n.s., XLVI (1944), 193–208; Nancy O. Lurie, "Indian Cultural Adjustment to European Civilization," in James M. Smith, ed., *Seventeenth-Century America: Essays in Colonial History* (Chapel Hill, N.C., 1959), 33–60. Virtually everything now known about the Indians of the Virginia region, apart from the meager archeological evidence, is derived from five accounts: Captain John Smith's writings in *Travels and Works*, Edward Arber, ed. (Edinburgh, 1910), (Smith's early writings, in a more reliable transcript, are in Barbour, *Jamestown Voyages*); a brief account by Henry Spelman, printed in the introduction to Smith, *Travels and Works*, I, ci–cxiv; William Strachey, *Historie of Travell*; Thomas Hariot's *Briefe and True Report of the New Found Land of Virginia* (Quinn, *Roanoke Voyages*, I, 314–87); and Robert Beverley, *The History and Present State of Virginia*, Louis B. Wright, ed. (Chapel Hill, N.C., 1947). Beverley wrote in 1705 and thus knew the Indians only after they had had generations of contact with the English. Hariot, of course, was familiar only with the Indians south of the Chesapeake, and therefore not all of what he says is applicable. Strachey copied large sections of his work from Smith, but added details of his own (some of which do not appear wholly plausible). There are also a few useful observations in a letter of the Reverend John Clayton, printed in David I. Bushnell, "Virginia from Early Records," *American Anthropologist*, IX (1907), 41–44, and in an anonymous "Account of the Indians in Virginia," dated 1689, Stanley Pargellis, ed., *WMQ*, 3rd ser., XVI (1959), 228–43.

saw it, Powhatan, "a tall well proportioned man, with a sower looke," was able to rule with a rod of iron. His word was law, and there seems to be no doubt that he exercised powers of life and death over his subjects.[15]

It is likely, nevertheless, that his subjects had more freedom than was apparent to the English and that his dominion differed from that of other Indian rulers mainly in its ruthless enforcement of customary practices. The English who commented on it found it neither capricious nor arbitrary. The most astute English observer, Captain John Smith, whose ways with Indians we will examine later, noted that "the lawes whereby he [Powhatan] ruleth is custome."[16] But custom can be a powerful form of law, restraining rulers as well as sheltering liberty within its dictates. And though Powhatan himself may have seemed strong enough to ignore it if he chose ("When he listeth his will is a law"), the inferior chieftains of the tribes that he had subdued, who continued to govern their peoples under him, were, according to Smith, "tyed to rule by customes."[17] Smith acknowledged that the magistrates of Indian Virginia (presumably both Powhatan and the subchiefs) "for good commanding, and their people for due subjection, and obeying, excell many places that would be counted very civill."[18] But the obedience of the subjects may well have depended on the goodness of the commanding and on its conformity to customary expectations.

Powhatan exacted a tribute from each of his subject tribes, payable in "skinnes, beades, copper, pearle, deare, turkies, wild beasts, and corne."[19] We are even told what cannot be taken seriously, that he took eight parts in ten of everything they produced, and that he had a storehouse fifty or sixty yards long in which he hoarded his alleged treasure.[20] He may have had such a storehouse, but the reports doubtless exaggerated his splendor to conform to European views of how an emperor ought to live. If Powhatan actually did have such an acquisitive instinct, he was an unusual Indian and probably unlike the people over whom he exercised dominion. Robert Beverley, writing at the end of the century, tells us that the Virginia Indians

[15] Barbour, *Jamestown Voyages*, II, 369–72; Smith, *Travels and Works*, I, cx–cxi, 79–82, 375–78.

[16] Barbour, *Jamestown Voyages*, II, 371; Arber has garbled this passage (Smith, *Travels and Works*, I, 81).

[17] Barbour, *Jamestown Voyages*, II, 371.

[18] *Ibid.*, II, 369.   [19] *Ibid.*, II, 371.

[20] Strachey, *Historie of Travell*, 62, 87.

"had nothing which they reckoned Riches, before the English went among them, except Peak, Roenoke, and such like trifles made out of the Cunk shell." [21] Indians did not vie with one another in conspicuous consumption. And indeed there would seem to be little likelihood of anyone storing up treasures among a people who valued leisure above worldly goods. The Indian way of life was of the kind that still generates, among those who practice it, a minimum of worldly goods and a maximum of leisure time.[22]

Indians did not, for example, devote much attention to housing. Powhatan, to be sure, was enchanted by the relative sturdiness of the flimsy houses that the English threw up and persuaded them to build him one.[23] But other Indians showed no interest in anything so solid. Although they lived during most of the year in permanent towns or villages, their houses were simple affairs, constructed by inserting saplings in the ground and bending the tops together to make a frame like an arbor. Large frames were rectangular or oval in ground plan, small ones circular. On the frame they placed bark, hides, or mats to keep out the weather, leaving a hole at the top to release smoke and one next to the ground for an entrance. Large or small, the houses were all of a piece and offered little opportunity for display of status: "who knoweth one of them knoweth them all, even the Chief kings house yt self." And the furniture was as simple as the house. The ground served for a floor. There were no chairs or tables, and platforms raised from the ground on forked sticks served as beds. House and furniture alike could be put together without heavy labor. Building them was women's work.[24]

Men provided clothing in the form of skins taken in the hunt. But Indians, like well-to-do Englishmen, apparently regarded hunting as sport. Hunting grounds might be some distance from the village; and when hunting season came round, the whole tribe picked up and

[21] Beverley, *History and Present State of Virginia*, 227. Beverley refers to the beads, used as a medium of exchange, made from clamshells.

[22] See in general Marshall Sahlins, *Stone Age Economics* (Chicago, 1972). On the lack of acquisitiveness of Indians, see Morgan, "American Indian," 16–17.

[23] Smith, *Travels and Works*, I, 130; Barbour, *Jamestown Voyages*, II, 421. It appears from a later account that Powhatan's brother and successor, Opechancanough, was also entranced with English houses and that George Thorpe had one built for him. *RVC*, III, 552.

[24] Smith, *Travels and Works*, 67, 362; Barbour, *Jamestown Voyages*, II, 356; Strachey, *Historie of Travell*, 78–79; Beverley, *History and Present State*, 174–77; Quinn, *Roanoke Voyages*, I, 370.

moved, the women preceding the men in order to build temporary housing. The hunt itself was a cooperative venture among the men, in which they set fire to an area, enclosing a group of deer or driving them into the water, where they could be killed from canoes.[25] The men were also in charge of fishing, which they did with weirs and nets, as well as with spears and hooks.[26] But the Virginia Indians did not rely on hunting or fishing for most of their food. They relied principally on the nuts and fruits they gathered and on the corn, beans, and squashes or melons that they grew. Tending the crops was also women's work.

Indeed, nearly any activity that could be designated as work at all was left to the women. They were the principal means of production in Indian Virginia. Having acquired a wife (for whom he may have had to pay a bride price), a man counted on her to support him.[27] He could make canoes, weapons, and weirs without losing his dignity, but the only other labor he ordinarily engaged in was clearing fields for planting, and the method employed made this less than arduous. Clearing consisted merely of girdling the trees and burning brush around them to hasten their death. The next year the women worked the ground between the trees, using a crooked stick as a hoe and planting corn, beans, squash, and melons all together in little hills.[28]

[25] Smith, *Travels and Works*, cvi–cvii, 69–70, 365–66; Barbour, *Jamestown Voyages*, II, 359; Strachey, *Historie of Travell*, 82–84; Beverley, *History and Present State*, 154–56. The Indians on the Eastern Shore were evidently still hunting in this manner in 1655, when a settler collected damages from the king of the Machepungo for burning part of a fence "in his hunting Exercyse." Northampton V, 151.

[26] Smith, *Travels and Works*, 69, 365; Barbour, *Jamestown Voyages*, II, 358; Strachey, *Historie of Travell*, 75, 82; Beverley, *History and Present State*, 148–49.

[27] The Virginia Indians were polygamous, but it would appear that few men other than chiefs managed to obtain more than one wife. On marriage customs Smith tells us little. See Strachey, *Historie of Travell*, 112; Beverley, *History and Present State*, 170.

[28] Smith, *Travels and Works*, cxi–cxii, 61–62, 357–58; Barbour, *Jamestown Voyages*, II, 351; Strachey, *Historie of Travell*, 118; Quinn, *Roanoke Voyages*, I, 337–43. Indian agriculture is discussed, largely on the basis of these sources, in John R. Swanton, *The Indians of the Southeastern United States*, Smithsonian Institution Bureau of American Ethnology, Bulletin 137 (Washington, D.C., 1946), 304–10; and in Charles C. Willoughby, "The Virginia Indians of the Seventeenth Century," *American Anthropologist*, n.s., IX (1907), 82–84.

Although we do not know how long the Indians used a field before allowing it to return to forest, it seems likely that they did not have to move whenever they depleted the soil they were cultivating. The English had the impression that their villages were permanently located. Given the probable acreage under cultivation, it would have been possible to use a field for several years and then to leave it fallow for thirty or forty and still not have to move the village to find fresh land.[29] It required less than an acre to grow in Indian fashion enough food to feed a person in Indian fashion for a year. Indian corn gave a yield several times greater than English wheat; and according to modern authorities "one acre in mixed planting of maize, beans, and squash, perhaps with sunflower or *Chenopodium* added, would indeed sustain a person for a year."[30] John Smith found the fields adjoining the villages to vary from 20 to 200 acres, which was probably roughly the size of their populations.[31] At that rate, most villages could stay in one place on a tract of, say, 500 or 600 acres with a cycle of using a field for five or ten years and then leaving it for thirty or forty. Thus the labor of building permanent new houses would come only seldom, as the old ones fell down.

This form of agriculture is common among pre-industrial populations all over the world and has generally been regarded as wasteful and primitive. Recent investigators have shown, however, that it can produce more food per man-hour (or woman-hour) of labor than any other form. Growing a mixture of crops in the same field tends to prolong its fertility, and the long fallow period, allowing trees and shrubs to spring up, restores the fertility of the soil by bringing up

[29] The evidence of Indians abandoning fields after a time is mostly indirect. The observers cited in the preceding note describe the process of clearing new fields, which probably implies the abandonment of old ones. John Pory, writing in 1619, noted that there were "many grounds here cleared by the Indians to our handes, which being much worne out, will beare no more of their corne." L. G. Tyler, ed., *Narratives of Early Virginia, 1606-1625* (New York, 1907), 283-84. The Indians' loose attachment to particular plots is suggested also by the episode (see below, chap. 4) in which one Indian warned John Smith that the Indians could plant anywhere and could do away with the English simply by abandoning their fields and moving to new ones in the interior.

[30] Quinn, *Roanoke Voyages*, I, 343; Carl O. Sauer, *Sixteenth Century North America: The Land and People as Seen by the Europeans* (Berkeley, Calif., 1971), 295.

[31] Smith, *Travels and Works*, I, 67, 363; Barbour, *Jamestown Voyages*, II, 356.

nutrients from well below the root level of crop plants and spreading them on the surface in the form of litter.[32] The system requires no manure and no animals to furnish manure. It requires no plows and no draft animals to feed and care for. It requires virtually no work on the land other than clearing, planting, and harvesting. Even weeding is minimized, because few weed seeds are present in the newly cleared land. Only when an increasing population demands a larger total product and furnishes a larger labor force to grow it do peoples turn to more intensive but more labor-consuming forms of agriculture.[33]

The Indians had more than enough land for their shifting agriculture: and in the course of the centuries they had lived in Virginia, they had shaped the land to their purposes, so that it also yielded foods other than those which they planted. In particular they had achieved great tracts of meadow. Their fires for turning woodland into cornfield must often have escaped; and the same was true of their fires for hunting, which were apparently set in grassy areas. The periodic large-scale incineration of young shrubs and trees tended in the long run to produce and preserve grasslands. As a result, there was probably more open land in Indian Virginia than there is in Virginia today.[34] At the same time there were great and unusual forests. When the English arrived, they described the country as

[32] Carl O. Sauer, "The Agency of Man on the Earth," in W. L. Thomas, ed., *Man's Role in Changing the Face of the Earth* (Chicago, 1955), 49–69, esp. 56–67.

[33] Ester Boserup, *The Conditions of Agricultural Growth: The Economics of Agrarian Change under Population Pressure* (Chicago, 1965); Brian Spooner, ed., *Population Growth: Anthropological Implications* (Cambridge, Mass., 1972); Harold E. Conklin, *The Study of Shifting Cultivation*, Pan American Union, Studies and Monographs, VI (Washington, D.C., 1963).

[34] For examples of contemporary observations of open land: Smith, *Travels and Works*, I, li, cvi, 18, 32; Barbour, *Jamestown Voyages*, I, 85; Brown, *Genesis*, I, 156, 157, 164, 409; Ralph Hamor, *A True Discourse of the Present Estate of Virginia* (London, 1615), 32; Louis B. Wright, ed., *A Voyage to Virginia in 1609* (Charlottesville, 1964), 68; Edward Williams, *Virginia: More Especially the South Part Thereof, Richly and Truly Valued* (London, 1650), in Peter Force, ed., *Tracts and Other Papers Relating Principally to the Origin, Settlement, and Progress of the Colonies in North America* (Washington, D.C., 1836–46), III, No. 11, p. 13. A perceptive discussion, which assembles much of the evidence, is Hu Maxwell, "The Use and Abuse of Forests by the Virginia Indians," *WMQ*, 1st ser., XIX (1910), 73–103.

almost entirely wooded, and so did travelers who came there for the next two hundred years.[35] But the woods, as the English found them in 1607, consisted mainly of trees too large or thick-barked to be affected by fire, and they were generally free of undergrowth. The repeated burnings prevented the forest from renewing itself, so that the large trees became widely spaced, with room for light to penetrate between them. The English noted that you could see for more than a mile through the woods, that you could ride a horse through them at a gallop, or that you could drive a coach through them.[36]

The effect was not only to give the landscape a more open appearance than it has today, but to make room for a much greater variety of plants and animals. The grasslands supported not only deer but also elk and buffalo, which had made their way from pasturelands similarly cleared by Indian burnings beyond the mountains. And the open glades supported fruit and nut trees that cannot be found in the dense second-growth pine forests that have replaced the Indian landscape. Hickory and black walnut were both plentiful and highly valued. Mulberries, plums, and persimmons abounded, as did wild grapes and wild strawberries.[37] None of these would have grown or produced fruit in deep woods. The Indians, though without domestic animals, had by their burnings turned the country into a veritable park, abounding in game and in natural fruits, berries, and nuts, not to mention flowers. One Englishman walking out for four miles from Jamestown found his promenade the whole way "all flowing over with fair flowers of sundry colors and kinds, as though it had been in any garden or orchard in England." [38] During a large part of the year, especially during the early summer, before their corn ripened, the Indians relied heavily on this natural orchard. Since early summer was the time when Arthur Barlowe made his reconnaissance of Roanoke, he was perhaps not wholly fanciful in insisting

[35] Brown, *Genesis*, I, 164, 335; Force, *Tracts*, II, No. 8, pp. 10, 14; Sloane Mss. 1008, ff.334-35, British Museum; J. F. D. Smyth, *A Tour in the United States of America* (London, 1784), I, 15.

[36] Smith, *Travels and Works*, I, 34; Barbour, *Jamestown Voyages*, II, 356; Clayton C. Hall, ed., *Narratives of Early Maryland* (New York, 1910), 40; William Bullock, *Virginia Impartially Examined* (London, 1649), 3.

[37] Smith, *Travels and Works*, I, 56-59, 352-55; Barbour, *Jamestown Voyages*, II, 101, 345-47; Strachey, *Historie of Travell*, 119-23; Hamor, *True Discourse*, 22-23; George Percy, *Observations Gathered out of a Discourse of the Plantation of the Southern Colony in Virginia by the English, 1606*, David B. Quinn, ed. (Charlottesville, 1967), 19-20.

[38] Percy, *Observations*, 17.

that the earth brought forth all things in abundance without toil or labor.

Barlowe may not have realized that the abundance was not entirely natural. It did require the clearing and burning that the Indians had been carrying on for centuries. But even if Barlowe had spent longer in Virginia, he might still have been impressed by the absence of toil. In order to stay alive the Indian needed to do very little work. His women needed to do more. Smith noted how the male scorned doing anything that could be considered women's work, with the result "that the women be verie painefull [industrious] and the men often idle." [39] But even the women may have had less to do than we might expect. Studies of modern hunting and food-gathering societies and of societies practicing long-fallow agriculture show that the amount of time spent in productive work is considerably below what is required of most people in industrial societies, averaging from two to six hours a day. [40] Thomas Hariot at Roanoke estimated that the work of growing corn required no more than about twenty-four hours a year, all told, for enough to feed one person. [41] There were surely plenty of other jobs for the women to do: making baskets and pots, fashioning furs and skins into clothing, pounding corn into meal, cooking, making houses, tending children. But they may have had more leisure than women in European peasant societies and a good deal more than most women in early industrial societies. No landlord or employer collected a toll from their labor. The tribute their tribe owed to Powhatan was the only drain on their efforts. They may therefore have had a good many idle hours too.

While the Indians had worked out a way of life that required a minimum of labor, especially for men, they did interrupt their leisure with lengthy ceremonies that we can now view only dimly through the eyes of their unsympathetic English observers. According to the English, Indian religion was focused on an evil deity, whom the English identified at once as the devil. This devil the people were obliged to propitiate in a variety of ceremonies, conducted by priests who served as his emissaries. The most formidable ceremony, seen in the context of other primitive cultures, appears to have been a puberty rite, in which young men were beaten and then

[39] Smith, *Travels and Works*, I, 67; Barbour, *Jamestown Voyages*, II, 357.

[40] Boserup, *Conditions of Agricultural Growth*, 44–48; Sahlins, *Stone Age Economics*, 14–28.

[41] Quinn, *Roanoke Voyages*, I, 343.

taken to live in isolation for several months. To the English, insofar as they were allowed to observe it, this looked like human sacrifice. It is not clear that they actually saw a sacrifice performed, but they were persuaded that it took place, perhaps because they assumed that the devil would demand it. Whatever the ceremony, it seems to have occupied an important place in Indian life, as apparently did the deity who presided over it.[42]

The English were persuaded that the Indian deity was also, at least in some instances, behind another activity that interrupted and perhaps relieved the Indians' habitual idleness, namely war. It is not known how extensive or frequent warfare may have been before the English came or whether the Indian god actually demanded it from time to time, as civilized deities so often did.[43] The English assumed that the devil and his priests would incite people to war especially against those who were bringing the gospel. But the Indians had certainly made war among themselves before the English arrived. Powhatan apparently obtained his hegemony over the Virginia region by force of arms; and Amadas and Barlowe noted that the Indians in the Roanoke region had been wasted by warfare.[44]

What the actual purpose of Indian warfare may have been must remain speculative. Smith reported that "They seldome make warre for lands or goods, but for women and children, and principally for revenge."[45] It does seem unlikely that booty or plunder was a common war aim; but land may have been more involved than Smith realized. Any increase in a tribe's population (natural or acquired) might have necessitated an increase in land, for the Indian economy required large amounts of it. Although a given tribe might have only a small acreage under cultivation at a given time, a substantial acreage had to be left in long-term fallow to renew its fertility. And much

[42] Smith, *Travels and Works*, I, civ–cv, 74–79, 370–75; Barbour, *Jamestown Voyages*, II, 364–69; Strachey, *Historie of Travell*, 88–103; Quinn, *Roanoke Voyages*, I, 372–75; Pargellis, "Account of the Indians," 234–35.

[43] Arthur Barlowe had reported of the Roanoke Indians that "when they go to warres, they carry with them their Idoll, of whome they aske counsell, as the Romanes were woont of the Oracle of Apollo" (Quinn, *Roanoke Voyages*, I, 112). Smith says that in preparing for war, "the Werowances usually have the advice of their Priests and Conjurers, and their Allies and ancient friends, but chiefly the Priestes determine their resolution" (*Travels and Works*, I, 71; Barbour, *Jamestown Voyages*, II, 360).

[44] Quinn, *Roanoke Voyages*, I, 113.

[45] *Travels and Works*, I, 71; Barbour, *Jamestown Voyages*, II, 360.

more was needed for hunting and fishing and for the gathering of nuts and fruits. What looked like unused empty forest to the English did not necessarily look that way to the Indians. Each tribe had recognized boundaries within which it carried on its activities, and any expansion of hunting or gathering activities by one tribe might bring it into conflict with another.

Warfare played a large role in Indian men's sense of masculinity. Although Indian warriors seem to have felt it no shame to retreat in the face of superior force, they took inordinate pride in suffering torture and death without flinching if captured. And they took pleasure in inflicting pain and death on their own captives. On the other hand, they did not undertake war with the systematic rigor and discipline or even the lasting hostility that Europeans brought to it. They did not put to death the women, children, or chieftains whom they captured, but probably adopted them into the tribe, as the Iroquois did. War seems to have been in some measure ritualized, an occasion for the display of masculine virtues. Indians did not have the patience or even the desire to conduct a siege or a prolonged campaign. When they had shown how horrendous they could be in chopping a few people to bits, they were ready to call it a day and return to the easy life.[46]

Such were the people who awaited the English in Virginia. To the first settlers, aboard the *Susan Constant*, the *Godspeed*, and the *Discovery*, they must have looked as outlandish and strange as Englishmen expected non-Englishmen to be. They wore skins instead of clothes; they lived in oddly made flimsy shacks; they were armed only with hatchets and bows; they had no ships; they were covered with paint. The differences between the English and the Indian were not small, but it would be easy to exaggerate them and to overlook some similarities in their ways of life that boded no good for the colony's future.

England, like Virginia, was ruled by a monarch who had subdued the lesser potentates of the country to his dominion. In the

---

[46] Although Smith has a great deal to say about his own exploits in defeating Indian attacks or planned attacks, he tells us surprisingly little about Indian methods of warfare. Barbour, *Jamestown Voyages*, II, 360–62. The fullest account I know of warfare among the Indians of the southeast, from a later period, is Adair, *History of the American Indians*, 378–99. On Iroquois adoption, see Cadwallader Colden, *The History of the Five Indian Nations* (Ithaca, N.Y., 1958), 8.

fabric of English life these potentates, the nobility, occupied a far stronger place than the subsidiary werowances did under Powhatan in Virginia. And the character of English government depended heavily on the curbs they placed on the king. Part of their strength lay in their private armies of "retainers," and they often demonstrated their contempt for the king's peace by brawling with one another in what might today be called gang wars. The king was kept uneasy by the magnitude of their powers, which he sought steadily to reduce. In order to tame them he tried to keep them as close to him as possible at his court, where he could keep an eye on them and where they could vie with one another in the richness of their clothing rather than the fierceness of their arms. Englishmen, being civil, were more fond of clothing than Indians were, and the king was able to keep many of his nobles engaged in a kind of continuous fancy dress ball at court.[47]

The king was not, however, strong enough to get along without them. The nobility and their retainers were, in fact, his army or the nucleus from which he built one when it was needed. And he often needed it, in order to sustain the independence of his island in a world dominated by the larger powers of the European continent. Even in peacetime he needed their help, for England, though not a large country, was too big for him to manage by himself. To rule it he relied heavily on his Parliament, an assemblage of the nobles, to which had been added a group of representatives elected by the landholders of the country. Parliament not only assisted the king by making laws, but also levied taxes for him and enabled him to collect them.

Although in England, as in Indian Virginia, custom was the principal law, with its highest embodiment in the set of judicial precedents known as common law, the king in Parliament could override custom and enact laws for the whole country. For the king to do so by himself, however, as Powhatan apparently could do in Virginia, would have been dangerous. One of the prices he had to pay for Parliament's help in running England was to forgo any attempt to make laws or levy taxes by himself. Two kings during the seventeenth century did make the attempt; but neither got away with it: one lost only his throne, the other his head. Most kings

[47] Lawrence Stone, *The Crisis of the Aristocracy, 1558–1641* (New York, 1965), 199–270; W. H. Dunham, *Lord Hastings' Indentured Retainers, 1461–1483*, Connecticut Academy of Arts and Sciences, *Transactions*, XXXIX (New Haven, 1955).

recognized the limits of their power; they could not act upon their subjects or even tax them (except for some customary duties) with- out the consent of Parliament. This was the source of English liberty, of English "gentle government." And Englishmen were proud of it.

Not many Englishmen had a hand in that government. The nobility, who sat in Parliament by virtue of their birth, amounted to only a tiny fraction of the population. There were 55 of them in 1603. By 1628 the number had increased to 126, but they were never significant by their numbers.[48] A somewhat larger group of digni- taries, the gentry, also had a hand in government. Less exalted and less powerful than the nobles, they were distinguished by a variety of titles and commanded the respect of their neighbors by their wealth, especially wealth in land. They amounted to perhaps 5 per- cent of the adult male population. Along with the other landowners of the country, amounting to perhaps another 10 percent, they elected representatives to Parliament, the members of the House of Commons, which belied its name by the rank of those who sat in it. English gentle government was government by gentlemen.[49]

It was the gentry who saw that the laws of Parliament were en- forced in their neighborhoods. England was divided into counties, each of which, like the tribes of Virginia, had its definite geographi- cal boundaries. In each county the king appointed a number of gentlemen as justices of the peace to settle minor disputes among neighbors. Sitting together in county courts, the justices tried more serious cases, including criminal cases. If anyone was dissatisfied with their decision, he could appeal to a higher court, presided over by men of greater dignity, directly under the king.

Although ordinary people had no voice at all in the English government, the system gave them a security of which they could well be proud. Not only were they ruled under established laws, which not even the king could break, but in any cases involving loss of life or limb the court had to put the question of guilt to a jury composed of their peers, that is, persons from roughly the same rank

[48] Stone, *Crisis of the Aristocracy*, 758.

[49] Any estimate of the percentage of landowners at the end of the sixteenth century must remain rough. Of those qualified to vote by posses- sion of a "forty-shilling freehold," a total of 15 percent of adult males is probably generous. See J. H. Plumb, "The Growth of the Electorate in England from 1600 to 1715," *Past and Present*, No. 45 (Nov., 1969), 90–116; J. P. Cooper, "The Social Distribution of Land and Men in England, 1436– 1700," *Economic History Review*, XX (1967), 419–40.

in life and from the same neighborhood as the accused. Trial by jury was one of the emblems of English freedom, which Englishmen took pride in contrasting with the more authoritarian legal procedures of other countries.

In the eyes of Englishmen the superiority of their civil government was matched by the superiority of their religion and by the church in which it was embodied. England's monarchs had broken from what they considered the tyranny of the Roman church and had established what they liked to think of as the true church of Christ on earth. At its head stood the king; and he ruled his church as he ruled his state, through a set of spiritual nobles, the bishops and archbishops, who sat in Parliament as well as in a Convocation of their own. Below them were their priests, who presided over the local units of their government, the parishes. There were several parishes in each county, and each parish church was equipped with a set of local officers, vestrymen and churchwardens, who looked after the church building and helped the priest to supervise the daily lives of his parishioners.

Churchwardens were supposed to report every breach of morals, especially sexual morals, and every sign of heresy. Church courts presided over by bishops could then reprimand or excommunicate offenders, cutting them off from all contact with their neighbors until they repented and made amends. Although neither churchwardens nor church courts were always zealous in performing their duties, they could, if they pleased, impose strict standards of belief and behavior at every turn of an Englishman's life.[50]

Between the surveillance in his parish and the regular enactments of Parliament that affected him, the Englishman probably felt the force of government in his daily life far more than the Indians who endured Powhatan's dominion. And English government, both civil and ecclesiastical, exerted itself with particular force in an area where Indians scarcely knew control. Most Englishmen worked for other Englishmen. It was a major concern not only of their employers but also of the government to keep them working.

To judge from what churchmen had to say about the matter, the harder all men worked and the harder they had to work the better. Idleness, a masculine virtue among the Indians, had always

---

[50] On local institutions and daily life see Wallace Notestein, *The English People on the Eve of Colonization, 1603–1630* (New York, 1954), and Carl Bridenbaugh, *Vexed and Troubled Englishmen* (New York, 1968).

been a vice in Christian teaching. The Reformers who denounced Catholicism had been particularly emphatic on this point and had condemned as idle the lives of prayer and contemplation sanctioned by the Roman church in its monasteries and convents. God called men to work by the sweat of their brows, the Reformers believed, and a man who worked hard at the job to which God called him, however humble, was honorable in the sight of God. His disposition for hard work might even be a sign that God had singled him out for the saint's everlasting rest in heaven (where work was apparently no longer required).[51]

Preachers intoned these ideas from English pulpits; and though the church courts did not ordinarily attempt to excommunicate men for not working hard enough, the members of Parliament prescribed hours of work by law that would seemingly have left little opportunity for idleness. The Statute of Artificers of 1563 (reenacting similar provisions from the Statute of Laborers of 1495) required all laborers to work from five in the morning to seven or eight at night from mid-March to mid-September, and during the remaining months of the year from daybreak to night. Time out for eating, drinking, and rest was not to exceed two and a half hours a day.[52]

As with all legislation, we may ask whether the provisions of this act were a description of prevailing practices or an attempt to change them. The Statute of Laborers answers the question by telling us in the preamble that laborers "waste much part of the day . . . in late coming unto their work, early departing therefrom, long sitting at their breakfast, at their dinner and noon-meat, and long time of sleeping after noon."[53] Whether this statute or that of 1563 (still in effect when Virginia was founded) altered the situation is not easy to determine. The records of the county courts show varying efforts to enforce other provisions of the statute of 1563, but they are almost wholly silent about this one. That their silence was a product of

[51] The classic statements are Max Weber, *The Protestant Ethic and the Spirit of Capitalism* (London, 1930), and R. H. Tawney, *Religion and the Rise of Capitalism* (London, 1926). Some of the discussion of English working habits that follows is taken from my article, "The Labor Problem at Jamestown, 1607-18," *American Historical Review*, LXXVI (June, 1971), 595-611.

[52] R. H. Tawney and Eileen Power, eds., *Tudor Economic Documents* (London, 1924), I, 342.

[53] 11 Henry VII, c. 22, sec. 4; Douglas Knoop and G. P. Jones, *The Medieval Mason* (Manchester, 1933), 117.

general compliance with the act seems unlikely for a number of reasons, reasons that may shed some light on the behavior of the first Englishmen in Virginia.

One part of the adult male population of England was not even expected to comply: gentlemen, including those who passed the act in Parliament, were not affected, except as employers, by the injunctions contained in it. The attitude of gentlemen toward work betrayed the same inconsistency that is suggested in the preachers' praise of work as a virtue while excluding it from among the joys to be found in paradise. As far as work was concerned, gentlemen had already reached paradise. They expected those who had not yet arrived to work, but to do so themselves would have been to stop being gentlemen. A gentleman, by contemporary standards, was one who could "live idly and without manuall labour, and will beare the port, charge and countenance of a gentleman." [54] The port, charge, and countenance of a gentleman meant not merely fancy clothing and spacious housing but an entourage of servants who added to the dignity of their employer's idleness by being as conspicuously idle as possible themselves. According to the leading authority on the English aristocracy of the period, not only were the rich and well-born "idle almost by definition" but they kept "a huge labour force . . . in slothful and parasitic personal service." [55] When the members of Parliament enjoined work without respite, it was a case of "Do as I say, not as I do."

Even for anyone inclined to obey the precept rather than the example, it was not possible to keep at work without work to do. In what are today called modern or developed countries unemployment is scarcely unknown. In underdeveloped countries both unemployment and underemployment are persistent facts of life. And England in the seventeenth century, like Virginia, was an underdeveloped country.[56] Its people, that is, produced far less in the way of material goods than they were capable of producing if they had been organized and motivated for the purpose. The great majority of them, as in all underdeveloped countries, were still engaged in agriculture; and agriculture, in spite of the myths of dawn-to-dusk toil that sur-

[54] Sir Thomas Smith, *De Republica Anglorum*, L. Alston, ed. (Cambridge, 1906), 40.

[55] Stone, *Crisis of the Aristocracy*, 331.

[56] F. J. Fisher, "The Sixteenth and Seventeenth Centuries: The Dark Ages in English Economic History," *Economica*, 2nd ser., XXIV (1957), 2–18.

round it, could not employ men the year round, continuously, or usefully, at the hours prescribed in the Statute of Artificers.

In large parts of the south and east of England farmers engaged in a much more intensive kind of agriculture than the Indians of Virginia.[57] They plowed and planted their land every year with wheat, rye, barley, and a variety of other crops, allowing only occasional fallow periods and maintaining fertility by the dung from their cattle and sheep. They worked hard and expected their servants to work hard whenever there was work to do, especially when planting time or harvest time came round. But even with milking cows, hedging, ditching, thatching, and a hundred other tasks, there were times when the most industrious farmer could find no good way to keep himself and the men he might employ continuously busy. Bad weather could halt most farm work. You could not plow frozen ground and should not plow if it was soggy. John Law, writing in 1705 and hypothesizing a model economy that might be established on a newly discovered island, took it for granted that the persons engaged in agriculture would be idle, for one reason or another, half the time.[58] Such may have been the case in the parts of England where farmers grew grain and practiced the most intensive husbandry.

In the greater part of England and Wales, in most of the north and west and in the hilly parts of the south and east, where lands were only marginally fertile, men lived from a way of farming that occupied a good deal less than half their time. In the midst of moors and pastures and woodland they tended little gardens of an acre or two and supplemented their diets, as the Indians did, by gathering roots and nuts and berries from the wilds. In some places they shifted their gardens from time to time, like the Indians, allowing the land to return to forest or waste for a long fallow period. They did not grow enough grain even for their own bread. Their only advantage over the Indians in food production came from the domestic animals (cattle, swine, and sheep) which they kept. Turned into the woods or pastures to forage for themselves in the warmer months, the animals required only a little more care than it took to hunt deer in Virginia (hunting in England was reserved to the gentry). This was a way of life that resembled the Indians' way more than it resembled the one prescribed in the Statute of Artificers. It offered

[57] My discussion of English farming practices is based primarily on Thirsk, ed., *The Agrarian History of England and Wales, 1500–1640.*

[58] D. C. Coleman, "Labour in the English Economy of the Seventeenth Century," *Economic History Review*, 2nd ser., VIII (1956), 280–95.

only a hand-to-mouth existence. It meant frequent hunger and regular malnutrition. But it did not require much work.[59]

People who lived in this manner, though they may have constituted half the population or more, were not in good repute with their countrymen. Grain-growing farmers in the "champion" country of the south and east thought that the woodland and pasture people were no farmers at all. Precisely because their way of life required so little work, it seemed not a proper way for a farmer or a Christian or a good subject of the king. The government worried too about the unruliness of people who had too much time on their hands and too little meat in their bellies. The devil finds work for idle hands, and some of his work might threaten the state as well as the church. It was observed that "the people bred amongst woods are naturally more stubborn and uncivil than in the champion countries." They were said to "live lawless, nobody to govern them, they care for nobody, having no dependence on anybody." [60]

The problem was magnified by the explosion of England's population. As we have seen, the numbers were growing faster than the country could find jobs for them.[61] Hungry and boisterous, they swarmed the roads, looking for enough work to buy them bread but ready to steal if they could not find it. They wound up not only in jail and on the gallows but in the woodlands, eking out a living like other woodland and pasture people. In its efforts to cope with the situation the government was torn between the wish to make people work as hard as possible and the need to supply jobs for them to work at. The latter seemed the more urgent. The government could not contemplate without alarm the rising numbers of hungry, masterless men. They must be found jobs and masters to keep them under control.

The gentlemen in Parliament, considering the situation, adopted a policy that may be called the conservation of employment. They seem to have assumed that their society could pay for only a fixed amount of work. Work must therefore be rationed, so that everyone could have a little, and those with family responsibilities could have a little more.[62] So that youngsters should not take work away from

[59] Thirsk, *Agrarian History*, 1–112, 396–465; Eric Kerridge, *The Agricultural Revolution* (New York, 1968), 24–27, 39, 106–7, 155–60.

[60] Thirsk, *Agrarian History*, 111.

[61] In general prices of provisions rose much more rapidly than wages. See chap. 2, note 21.

[62] Compare Bert F. Hoselitz, *Sociological Aspects of Economic Growth* (Glencoe, Ill., 1960), 33–34.

their elders, the Statute of Artificers made it illegal for a man to practice a trade until he had become a master through seven years of apprenticeship. Even then, until he was thirty years old or married, he was supposed to serve some other master of the trade. And the courts did enforce these provisions. In a typical example, John Pikeman of Barking, Essex, a tailor, was brought to court because he "being a singleman and not above 25 years of age, does take in work of tailoring and works by himself to the hindrance of other poor occupiers, contrary to the law." [63]

The policy expanded employment by fostering underemployment. Employers in most trades were required to hire labor only by the year, not by the day or hour.[64] The intention was not only to see that a man's master would have control of him throughout the year but to see that more men had masters, that more men had jobs. As the justices of Essex County observed, hiring labor by the day caused "the great depauperization of other labourers." [65] But hiring by the year meant that a laborer did not have to work as hard or as long at any task as he would otherwise have had to. Work could be strung out to occupy needless amounts of time, because whether or not a master had work to occupy his servants, they had to stay with him and he had to keep them. The records show many instances of masters attempting to turn away a servant or apprentice before the stipulated term was up, only to have him sent back by the courts with orders that the master "entertain" him for the full period. We even have the extraordinary spectacle of the runaway master, the man who illegally fled from his servants and thus evaded his responsibility to employ and support them.[66]

---

[63] April, 1594. Calendar of Essex Quarter Sessions Rolls (microfilmed typescript, in Yale University Library) XVI, 165. See also the indictment (1589) of four bachelors for taking up the trade of poulterer, which "hindreth other powre men." *Ibid.*, XV, 54. While the statute seems to allow single men and women under thirty to set up in trade provided their services are not demanded by a master, the courts, in Essex County at least (where the earliest and most extensive records are preserved), required such persons to find themselves a master.

[64] Tawney and Power, *Tudor Economic Documents*, I, 335.

[65] Calendar of Essex Quarter Sessions Rolls, IV, 128.

[66] William LeHardy, ed., *Hertfordshire County Records*, V (Hertford, 1928), 191–92, 376, 451; E. H. Bates, ed., *Quarter Sessions Records for the County of Somerset*, I, Somerset Record Society, XXIII (London, 1907), 11–12, 21, 97, 193, 258, 325; B. C. Redwood, ed., *Quarter Sessions Order Book, 1642–1649*, Sussex Record Society, LIV (1954), 34, 44, 46, 128, 145–46, 188, 190.

In pursuit of its policy of fostering employment in the face of an expanding population, the government often had to create jobs in cases where society offered none. Sometimes men were obliged to take on a poor boy as a servant whether they needed one or not. The parish might lighten the burden of the appointed master by paying a fee, but it might also fine a man who refused to take a boy assigned to him.[67] To provide for men and women who could not be foisted off on unwilling employers, the government established houses of correction in every county, where the inmates toiled at turning wool, flax, and hemp into thread or yarn, receiving nothing but their food and lodging for their efforts. By all these means the government probably did succeed in spreading employment, but they spread it thin. In the long run their policies tended to depress wages and to diminish the amount of work expected from any one man. The division of labor, which economists have customarily regarded as a means of increasing productivity, could be instead a source of idleness. A man was supposed to have only one skill and was not supposed to impinge on the jobs of others by undertaking any task outside his province. Farmers with time on their hands were not to take up handicrafts on the side (though some did) because "for one man to be both an husbandman and an Artificer is a gatheringe of divers mens livinges into one mans hand."[68] And even on the farm different tasks became the special province of men claiming a special skill in them. Such specialization increased the number of jobs; but unless an employer could time his jobs carefully, he might have some of his laborers idle, waiting for others to perform an operation necessary to their continued work. Plowing, for example, seems to have been a special skill—a plowman was paid at a higher rate than ordinary farm workers. But the ordinary laborer's work might have to wait upon the plowing of a field, and a whole crew of men might be kept idle by a plowman's failure to get his job done at the right time. For an ordinary laborer to have attempted the job himself would have been presumptuous and antisocial if not illegal.

Laborers who learned to work under these conditions learned to work not very hard. On top of everything else, they were underpaid and underfed, caught in the vicious circle frequently found in underdeveloped countries, whereby low wages beget low productivity

---

[67] Bates, *Quarter Sessions for Somerset,* 114, 300; Redwood, *Order Book* (Sussex), 96, 146, 194; W. L. Sachse, ed., *Minutes of the Norwich Court of Mayoralty,* Norfolk Record Society, XV (Norwich, 1942), 78, 216.
[68] Tawney and Power, *Tudor Economic Documents,* I, 353. The statute of 37 Edward III, c. 6, forbade artisans to practice more than one craft.

which in turn justifies low wages.[69] Laborers were the despair of everyone who employed them, large or small. Robert Loder, an ambitious yeoman farmer in Berkshire, striving to expand his income, kept close track of the labor costs on his farm year by year and always found reason to bewail the shiftlessness of the men who worked for him. There was no telling how much or how little to expect of them. One year two men in fifteen days threshed more barley than they did in twenty-four days the year before, which led Loder to observe that "men can worke yf they list and soe they can loyter." But on the whole he found that they much preferred to loiter and to "play legerdemaine with theyr masters and favour themselves." [70] Besides loafing and sleeping on the job, laborers were notorious for spending their small wages on drink and failing to show up for work at all. Since the Reformation had done away with the celebration of the traditional saints' days, they took off frequent "Saint Mondays" to nurse their hangovers.[71] Some, especially those who worked in coal mines, simply refused to recognize the Protestant calendar and every year continued to take more than a month's worth of the old holidays, in addition to the irregular ones they took when the spirits moved them.[72]

Rather than hire such help, men with capital preferred to invest in enterprises that required a minimum of labor. Large landowners, including the nobility, avoided the labor problem by renting out their land in small parcels instead of hiring men to work it for them.[73] Or they turned their arable land into pasture and enclosed it with fences where sheep could graze unattended. The result was fewer jobs, contrary to the aims of the government—and there were complaints that sheep were eating up the livelihood of men. But sheep at least went about cropping grass and growing wool more dependably than hired men would plow and plant.

Manufactures in this economy remained what the word itself

[69] W. F. Moore, *Industrialization and Labor* (Ithaca, N.Y., 1951), 106–13, 308.

[70] G. E. Fussell, ed., *Robert Loder's Farm Accounts, 1610–1620*, Camden Society, 3rd ser., LIII (London, 1936), 25, 59.

[71] Edgar S. Furniss, *The Position of the Laborer in a System of Nationalism: A Study in the Labor Theories of the Later English Mercantilists* (Boston, 1920), 117–34; E. P. Thompson, "Time, Work-Discipline, and Industrial Capitalism," *Past and Present*, no. 38 (1967), 56–97.

[72] Lawrence Stone, "An Elizabethan Coal Mine," *Economic History Review*, 2nd ser., III (1950), 97–106.

[73] Stone, *Crisis of the Aristocracy*, 295–97; Thirsk, *Agrarian History*, 198.

implies: things made by hand. Labor was the principal cost in nearly every manufactured article. Employers engaged in manufacturing countered the shiftlessness of their workmen by paying starvation wages. They could get the cheapest labor in the woodland and pasture areas where the country's hungry drifters trended. Here too was the wood needed for such varied enterprises as smelting and shipbuilding, the bark for tanning, and the cattle for hides to tan. Hence industries, such as they were, grew up mainly in the areas where cheap, irresponsible, hungry (and thirsty) labor guaranteed a low level of productivity.[74]

A possible exception was the woolen industry, the only industry that England supported on a large scale and the only one that furnished her with exports sizable enough to pay for the things like oil and pitch that she had to buy from other countries. Wool was spun and woven everywhere, perhaps more in the woodlands and pasture lands than elsewhere, but also in large-scale establishments in cities and towns. But the finer, more exacting processes of finishing and dyeing the cloth were beyond the skill of England's listless laborers. Most English cloth was shipped abroad in an unfinished state, leaving the last, most lucrative stages of the business to foreigners.[75]

England's mercantile dependence on this single export product had made her peculiarly vulnerable to economic depression. During the last half of the sixteenth century farsighted men had begun to see that one way to overcome the problem and to increase the number of jobs available for the growing population would be to increase the variety of the country's exports. They introduced (with the assistance of Flemish artisans) new, lighter kinds of cloth for sale in warmer countries. They tried, not very successfully at first, to teach their laborers to finish the cloth. They expanded the production of coal and iron. They began to make glass, paper, brass, and gunpowder on a large scale. They brought in skilled foreigners to make things that Englishmen did not know how to make.[76] And they

[74] Thirsk, *Agrarian History*, 417–29; Joan Thirsk, "Industries in the Countryside," in F. J. Fisher, ed., *Essays in the Economic and Social History of Tudor and Stuart England* (London, 1961), 70–88; E. L. Jones, "Agricultural Origins of Industry," *Past and Present*, No. 40 (1968), 58–71.

[75] Lawrence Stone, "Elizabethan Overseas Trade," *Economic History Review*, 2nd ser., II (1949), 30–58.

[76] John Nef, *The Conquest of the Material World* (Chicago, 1964), 121–212; D. C. Coleman, "An Innovation and Its Diffusions: The New Draperies," *Economic History Review*, 2nd ser., XXII (1969), 417–29.

thought about acquiring colonies in America filled with loving native peoples and abounding in exotic natural products that all the world would crave as well as less exotic ones that England could not do without. In 1607 the Virginia Company was intent on presenting such a colony to England.

Under the spur of imaginative patriots like the Hakluyts, men with capital had already for several decades been investing in overseas trading ventures, to the Levant, to the East Indies, to Russia (above which they had hoped to find a shorter route to the East); and many of the same men joined in the Virginia Company, which was also a trading venture. But in order to produce profits, Virginia could not be a mere trading post, like those which Englishmen were establishing in other parts of the world, where it was necessary only to unload English goods and take on native ones. Virginia would have to be an expansion of England itself, but with improvements. Englishmen would have to live there and themselves produce articles of trade that they could not or would not produce at home. The natives were expected to help, but first they would have to be shown how.

The men, then, who sailed up the James River in the spring of 1607 bore a heavy burden of expectation. They were to create a biracial society that would remedy England's deficiencies. In Virginia they faced a people who had some of the same shortcomings, as well as—from the English point of view at least—a few of their own. The Virginia Company had sent the idle to teach the idle. And they had sent, as it turned out, a quarrelsome band of gentlemen and servants to bring freedom to the free. It was a formula for disaster.

4

THE JAMESTOWN
FIASCO

THE first wave of Englishmen reached Virginia at Cape Henry, the southern headland at the opening of Chesapeake Bay, on April 26, 1607. The same day their troubles began. The Indians of the Cape Henry region (the Chesapeakes), when they found a party of twenty or thirty strangers walking about on their territory, drove them back to the ships they came on. It was not the last Indian victory, but it was no more effective than later ones. In spite of troubles, the English were there to stay. They spent until May 14 exploring Virginia's broad waters and then chose a site that fitted the formula Hakluyt had prescribed. The place which they named Jamestown, on the James (formerly Powhatan) River, was inland from the capes about sixty miles, ample distance for warning of a Spanish invasion by sea. It was situated on a peninsula, making it easily defensible by land; and the river was navigable by oceangoing ships for another seventy-five miles into the interior, thus giving access to other tribes in case the local Indians should prove as unfriendly as the Chesapeakes.[1]

Captain Christopher Newport had landed the settlers in time to plant something for a harvest that year if they put their minds to it. After a week, in which they built a fort for protection, Newport and twenty-one others took a small boat and headed up the river on a diplomatic and reconnoitering mission, while the settlers behind set about the crucial business of planting corn. Newport paused at various Indian villages along the way and assured the people, as best

[1] Smith, *Travels and Works*, I, 5–6, 91; Barbour, *Jamestown Voyages*, I, 168–70; II, 378–80.

he could, of the friendship of the English and of his readiness to assist them against their enemies. Newport gathered correctly from his attempted conversations that one man, Powhatan, ruled the whole area above Jamestown, as far as the falls at the present site of Richmond. His enemies, the Monacans, lived above the falls (where they might be difficult to reach if Powhatan proved unfriendly). Newport also surmised, incorrectly, that the Chesapeake Indians who had attacked him at Cape Henry were not under Powhatan's dominion. He accordingly tried to make an alliance against the Chesapeakes and Monacans with a local chief whom he mistook for Powhatan. At the same time, he planted a cross with the name of King James on it (to establish English dominion) and tried to explain to the somewhat bewildered and justifiably suspicious owners of the country that one arm of the cross was Powhatan, the other himself, and that the fastening of them together signified the league between them.[2]

If the Indians understood, they were apparently unimpressed, for three days later, returning to Jamestown, Newport found that two hundred of Powhatan's warriors[3] had attacked the fort the day before and had only been prevented from destroying it by fire from the ships. The settlers had been engaged in planting and had not yet unpacked their guns from the cases in which they were shipped. That was a mistake they were not likely to repeat. But for the next ten years they seem to have made nearly every possible mistake and some that seem almost impossible. It would take a book longer than this to recount them all, and the story has already been told many times. But if we are to understand the heritage of these ten disastrous years for later Virginia history, we should look at a few of the more puzzling episodes and then try to fathom the forces behind them.

Skip over the first couple of years, when it was easy for Englishmen to make mistakes in the strange new world to which they had come, and look at Jamestown in the winter of 1609–10. It is three planting seasons since the colony began. The settlers have fallen into an uneasy truce with the Indians, punctuated by guerrilla raids on both sides, but they have had plenty of time in which they could have grown crops. They have obtained corn from the Indians

[2] Smith, *Travels and Works*, I, xl–lv, 6–7, 91–92; Barbour, *Jamestown Voyages*, I, 80–95, 170–72; II, 380.

[3] Smith says 400, but Gabriel Archer, who says 200, gives a much more detailed account of these days than Smith. Barbour, *Jamestown Voyages*, I, 95.

and supplies from England. They have firearms. Game abounds in the woods; and Virginia's rivers are filled with sturgeon in the summer and covered with geese and ducks in the winter. There are five hundred people in the colony now. And they are starving. They scour the woods listlessly for nuts, roots, and berries. And they offer the only authentic examples of cannibalism witnessed in Virginia. One provident man chops up his wife and salts down the pieces. Others dig up graves to eat the corpses. By spring only sixty are left alive.[4]

Another scene, a year later, in the spring of 1611. The settlers have been reinforced with more men and supplies from England. The preceding winter has not been as gruesome as the one before, thanks in part to corn obtained from the Indians.[5] But the colony still is not growing its own corn. The governor, Lord De la Warr, weakened by the winter, has returned to England for his health. His replacement, Sir Thomas Dale, reaches Jamestown in May, a time when all hands could have been used in planting. Dale finds nothing planted except "some few seeds put into a private garden or two."[6] And the people he finds at "their daily and usuall workes, bowling in the streetes."[7]

It is evident that the settlers, failing to plant for themselves, depend heavily on the Indians for food. The Indians can finish them off at any time simply by leaving the area. And the Indians know it. One of them tells the English flatly that "we can plant any where . . . and we know that you cannot live if you want [i.e., lack] our harvest, and that reliefe we bring you."[8] If the English drive out the Indians, they will starve.

With that in mind, we look back a year on a scene in the summer following the starving, cannibal winter. It is August, when corn is ripening. The governor has been negotiating with Powhatan about some runaway Englishmen he is thought to be harboring. Powhatan

[4] Smith, *Travels and Works*, I, 170; II, 498-99; Barbour, *Jamestown Voyages*, II, 460-61; George Percy, "A Trewe Relacyon of the Procedeinges and Occurrentes of Momente which have hapned in Virginia from the Tyme Sir Thomas Gates was shippwrackte uppon the Bermudes anno 1609 until my departure outt of the Country which was anno Domini 1612," *Tyler's Quarterly Historical and Genealogical Magazine*, III (1922), 260-82, at 266-69.

[5] Smith, *Travels and Works*, II, 503.   [6] Brown, *Genesis*, I, 491.

[7] Hamor, *True Discourse*, 26.

[8] Smith, *Travels and Works*, I, 152; Barbour, *Jamestown Voyages*, II, 444.

returns "noe other then prowde and disdaynefull Answers," and so the governor sends George Percy "to take Revendge upon the Paspeheans and Chiconamians [Chickahominies]," the tribes closest to Jamestown. Percy, the brother of the Earl of Northumberland and the perennial second in command at Jamestown, takes a group of soldiers up the James a few miles by boat and then marches inland three miles to the principal town of the Paspaheghs. They fall upon the town, kill fifteen or sixteen Indians, and capture the queen of the tribe and her children.[9]

Percy then has his men burn the houses and "cutt downe their Corne groweinge about the Towne." He takes the queen and her children back to his boats and embarks for Jamestown, but his men "begin to murmur becawse the quene and her Children weare spared." Percy therefore obliges them by throwing the children overboard "and shoteinge owtt their Braynes in the water." Meanwhile he sends another party under Captain James Davis to attack another Indian town (presumably a Chickahominy town), where again they cut down the corn and burn the houses. Upon returning to Jamestown, Percy hears that the governor is displeased that the queen of the Paspaheghs has been spared. Davis wants to burn her, but Percy, "haveinge seene so mutche Bloodshedd that day," insists that she merely be put to the sword. So she is led away and stabbed.[10]

Thus the English, unable or unwilling to feed themselves, continually demanding corn from the Indians, take pains to destroy both the Indians and their corn.

One final scene. It is the spring of 1612, and Governor Dale is supervising the building of a fort at Henrico, near the present site of Richmond. He pauses to deal with some of his men, Englishmen, who have committed a serious crime. In the words of George Percy, "Some he apointed to be hanged Some burned Some to be broken upon wheles, others to be staked and some to be shott to death." The reason for such extremities was the seriousness of the crime and the need to deter others from it: "all theis extreme and crewell tortures he used and inflicted upon them to terrify the reste for Attempting the Lyke." What, then, was the crime these men had committed? They had run away to live with the Indians and had been recaptured.[11]

---

[9] Percy, "Trewe Relacyon," 271.   [11] Ibid., 280.
[10] Ibid., 272–73.

It is not easy to make sense out of the behavior displayed in these episodes. How to explain the suicidal impulse that led the hungry English to destroy the corn that might have fed them and to commit atrocities upon the people who grew it? And how to account for the seeming unwillingness or incapacity of the English to feed themselves? Although they had invaded Indian territory and quarreled with the owners, the difficulty of obtaining land was not great. The Indians were no match for English weapons. Moreover, since the Indians could afford to give up the land around Jamestown as well as Henrico without seriously endangering their own economy, they made no concerted effort to drive the English out. Although Indian attacks may have prevented the English from getting a crop into the ground in time for a harvest in the fall of 1607,[12] the occasional Indian raids thereafter cannot explain the English failure to grow food in succeeding years. How, then, can we account for it?

The answer that comes first to mind is the poor organization and direction of the colony. The government prescribed by the charter placed full powers in a council appointed by the king, with a president elected by the other members. The president had virtually no authority of his own; and while the council lasted, the members spent most of their time bickering and intriguing against one another and especially against the one man who had the experience and the assurance to take command. The names of the councillors had been kept secret (even from themselves) in a locked box, until the ships carrying the first settlers arrived in Virginia. By that time a bumptious young man named John Smith had made himself unpopular with Captain Christopher Newport (in command until their arrival) and with most of the other gentlemen of consequence aboard. When they opened the box, they were appalled to find Smith's name on the list of councillors. But during the next two years Smith's confidence in himself and his willingness to act while others talked overcame most of the handicaps imposed by the feeble frame of government. It was Smith who kept the colony going during those years. But in doing so he dealt more decisively with the Indians than with his own quarreling countrymen, and he gave an

[12] They did report that they had sown "good store of wheat." Brown, *Genesis*, I, 107, 165; Percy, *Observations*, 22; Smith, *Travels and Works*, I; lxx.

initial turn to the colony's Indian relations that was not quite what the company had intended.[13]

Smith, the son of a yeoman, was a rare combination of actor and man of action. He had already won his spurs fighting against the Turks in Hungary, where, as he tells it, he won all the battles except the last, in which he was captured, enslaved, and then rescued by a fair princess. With her assistance he made his escape, then trekked across Europe and was back in England to join the Jamestown expedition at the age of twenty-seven.[14] In spite of his youth, he may have had more experience than anyone else at Jamestown in making war, in living off the land, and in communicating with people whose language he did not know. Certainly he showed more aptitude than anyone else in all these matters. And it was probably his ability to deal with the Indians that prevented them from destroying or starving the settlement.

When the supplies ran out in the first autumn, Smith succeeded in trading with the Indians for corn. Then, on an exploring expedition up the Chickahominy River, he was made a prisoner and brought before Powhatan. This was the point at which another fair princess, Pocahontas, stepped in to save his life—or so Smith later told it; and in spite of the skepticism engendered by the larger-than-life view of himself that Smith always affected, there seems to be no good reason to doubt him.[15] In any case, he returned unharmed; and while he remained in Virginia (until the fall of 1609), he conducted most of the colony's relations both with Powhatan and with the tribes under Powhatan's dominion.

Smith took a keener interest in the Indians than anyone else in

[13] The most thorough modern treatment of Smith is Philip L. Barbour, *The Three Worlds of Captain John Smith* (Boston, 1964). A perceptive brief study is Alden T. Vaughan, *American Genesis: Captain John Smith and the Founding of Virginia* (Boston, 1975).

[14] The veracity of Smith's account of his Hungarian adventures, long held in doubt, has been effectively defended by Barbour and by Laura Polanyi Striker in "Captain John Smith's Hungary and Transylvania," in Bradford Smith, *Captain John Smith: His Life and Legend* (Philadelphia, 1953), and "The Hungarian Historian, Lewis L. Kropf, on Captain John Smith's True Travels: A Reappraisal," *VMHB*, LXVI (1958), 22–43.

[15] The Pocahontas story does not appear in Smith's first accounts of his experience (*Travels and Works*, I, 14–20, 98; Barbour, *Jamestown Voyages*, I, 181–87; II, 387–88) but in his later and larger *Generall Historie of Virginia, New England, and the Summer Isles* (*Travels and Works*, II, 400, 531. See also *ibid.*, I, cxv–cxviii).

Virginia for a century to come. The astonishingly accurate map he made of the country shows the locations of the different tribes, and his writings give us most of the information we will ever have about them. But his interest in them was neither philanthropic nor philosophic. As he came to know them, he was convinced that they could be incorporated into the English settlement, but he scorned the notion that gentleness was the way to do it. Although Smith looks a little like a latter-day Drake or Hawkins, he did not see the Indians as Drake saw the Cimarrons. His own model seems to have been Hernando Cortez, and he would gladly have made Powhatan his Montezuma. He was disgusted when orders came from the company requiring that the settlers give the old chief a formal coronation, designed to make him a proper king, ally, and in some sense a vassal of King James. Smith witnessed the ceremony with undisguised contempt. Powhatan himself submitted with ill grace to the dignity thus thrust upon him and made it plain that he did not consider himself anybody's vassal and that he needed none of the proffered English assistance against his enemies.[16]

Smith was sure that kindness was wasted on savages, and within weeks he was successfully bullying and browbeating Powhatan out of hundreds of bushels of corn. Years later, as he reflected in England on the frustrations that continued to beset Virginia, he was sure he had been right, that the Spanish had shown the way to deal with Indians. The English should have learned the lesson of how the Spanish "forced the treacherous and rebellious Infidels to doe all manner of drudgery worke and slavery for them, themselves living like Souldiers upon the fruits of their labours." [17] John Smith's idea of the proper role of the Virginia Indians in English Virginia was something close to slavery. Given the superiority of English arms, he had no doubt of his ability to conquer the lot of them with a handful of men, just as Cortez had conquered the much more populous and formidable Aztecs. Once conquered, they could forthwith be put to work for their conquerors.[18]

[16] Smith, *Travels and Works*, I, 125; II, 437, 443; Barbour, *Jamestown Voyages*, II, 414.

[17] *Travels and Works*, II, 579. In his *Generall Historie* and, to a lesser extent, in his earlier works, Smith appropriated extensive passages from other authors. Here he is paraphrasing and commenting on Edward Waterhouse, *A Declaration of the State of the Colony and . . . a Relation of the Barbarous Massacre* (London, 1622), reprinted in *RVC*, III, 541–79.

[18] *Travels and Works*, II, 564, 578–82, 600–603, 955–56.

Smith was not afraid of work himself; and in the absence of Indian slaves he bent his efforts as much toward getting work out of Englishmen as he did toward supplying their deficiencies from Indian larders. In these first years many Englishmen perceived that the Indians had a satisfactory way of living without much work, and they slipped away "to live Idle among the Salvages." [19] Those who remained were so averse to any kind of labor, Smith reported, "that had they not beene forced nolens volens perforce to gather and prepare their victuall they would all have starved, and have eaten one another." [20] While the governing council ruled, under the presidency of men of greater social prestige than Smith, he could make little headway against the jealousies and intrigues that greeted all his efforts to organize the people either for planting or for gathering food. But month by month other members of the council died or returned to England; and by the end of 1608 Smith was left in complete control. He divided the remaining settlers into work gangs and made them a little speech, in which he told them they could either work or starve: "Howsoever you have bin heretofore tolerated by the authoritie of the Councell from that I have often commanded you, yet seeing nowe the authoritie resteth wholly in my selfe; you must obay this for a law, that he that will not worke, shall not eate (except by sicknesse he be disabled)." [21] He did not except himself from the rule and assured them that "every one that gathereth not every day as much as I doe, the next daie shall be set beyond the river, and for ever bee banished from the fort, and live there or starve." [22] And lest this only produce a general exodus to the Indians, Smith used his influence with the neighboring tribes to apply the same discipline to any settler who dared choose that course. As a result, in the winter of 1608–9 he lost only seven or eight men.[23]

Had Smith been left in charge, it is not impossible that he would have achieved a society which, in one way or another, would have included the Indians. They might have had a role not much better than the Spanish assigned them, and they might have died as rapidly as the Arawaks from disease and overwork. But it is unlikely that the grisly scenes already described would have taken place (they all occurred after his departure). In spite of his eagerness to

---

[19] *Travels and Works*, I, 157; Barbour, *Jamestown Voyages*, II, 448.
[20] *Travels and Works*, I, 155; Barbour, *Jamestown Voyages*, II, 446–47.
[21] *Travels and Works*, I, 149; Barbour, *Jamestown Voyages*, II, 441.
[22] *Travels and Works*, I, 156–57; Barbour, *Jamestown Voyages*, II, 448.
[23] *Travels and Works*, I, 157; Barbour, *Jamestown Voyages*, II, 448.

subdue the Indians, Smith was in continual contact and communication with them. He bullied and threatened and browbeat them, but we do not read of any atrocities committed upon them under his direction, nor did he feel obliged to hang, break, or burn any Englishman who went off to live with them.

But the Virginia Company in 1609 was not yet ready to abandon its goal of making its own way in Virginia and sharing the country with the Indians on more favorable terms than Smith would have allowed them. The members of the council who returned to England complained of Smith's overbearing ways, with Englishmen as well as Indians. So the company decided not to leave the colony in the hands of so pushy a young man. At the same time, however, they recognized that the conciliar form of government was ineffective, and that a firmer authority was necessary to put their lazy colonists to work. They accordingly asked, and were given, a new charter, in which the king relinquished his government of the colony. Henceforth the company would have full control and would rule through a governor who would exercise absolute powers in the colony. He would be assisted by a council, but their advice would not be binding on him. In fact, he would be as much a military commander as a governor, and the whole enterprise would take on a more military character.[24]

For the next eight or nine years whatever evils befell the colony were not the result of any diffusion of authority except when the appointed governor was absent—as happened when the first governor, Lord De la Warr, delayed his departure from England and his deputy, Sir Thomas Gates, was shipwrecked en route at Bermuda. The starving winter of 1609–10 occurred during this interval; but Gates arrived in May, 1610, followed by De la Warr himself in June. Thereafter Virginia was firmly governed under a clear set of laws, drafted by Gates and by De la Warr's subsequent deputy, Sir Thomas Dale. The so-called *Lawes Divine, Morall and Martiall* were mostly martial, and they set the colonists to work with military discipline and no pretense of gentle government.[25] They pre-

---

[24] Brown, *Genesis*, I, 206–37; Barbour, *Jamestown Voyages*, II, 263–64. On the military character now given the colony see Darrett B. Rutman, "The Virginia Company and its Military Regime," in Rutman, ed., *The Old Dominion: Essays for Thomas Perkins Abernethy* (Charlottesville, 1964), 11–20.

[25] William Strachey, *For the Colony in Virginea Britannia: Lawes Divine, Morall and Martiall*, David H. Flaherty, ed. (Charlottesville, 1969).

scribed that the settlers be divided into work gangs, much as Smith had divided them, each of which would proceed to its assigned tasks at regular hours. At the beating of a drum, the master of each gang would set them to work and "not suffer any of his company to be negligent, and idle, or depart from his worke" until another beat of the drums allowed it.[26]

The *Laws* prescribed death for a variety of crimes, including rape, adultery, theft, lying, sacrilege, blasphemy, or doing or saying anything that might "tend to the derision" of the Bible.[27] On a more practical level, in order to increase the livestock which had by this time been brought over, the *Laws* made it death to kill any domestic animal, even a chicken.[28] It was also death, in weeding a garden, to take an ear of corn or a bunch of grapes from it, death too to trade privately with anyone on the ships that came to the colony.[29] And the punishments were inflicted with an arbitrary rigor that became a scandal. For stealing two or three pints of oatmeal a man had a needle thrust through his tongue and was then chained to a tree until he starved.[30]

The *Laws* did not even contemplate that the Indians would become a part of the English settlement. Though the company had frowned on Smith's swashbuckling way with Indians, it was disenchanted with Powhatan and convinced that he and those under his dominion did need to be dealt with more sternly. Sir Thomas Gates was instructed to get some Indian children to bring up in the English manner, free of their parents' evil influence. And he was also told to subjugate the neighboring tribes, to make them pay tribute, and to seize the chiefs of any that refused. If he wanted to make friends with any Indians, they must be "those that are farthest from you and enemies unto those amonge whom you dwell." [31] The company's new attitude was incorporated in several provisions of the *Laws.* When Indians came to Jamestown to trade or visit, they were to be placed under guard to prevent them from stealing anything; no inhabitant was to speak to them without the governor's permission; and the settlers were forbidden on pain of death to "runne away from the Colonie, to Powhathan, or any savage Werowance else whatsoever." [32] The company's desire to bring the Indians into the

---

[26] P. 66.   [27] Pp. 11–13.   [28] P. 18.   [29] Pp. 21, 23.

[30] L. G. Tyler, ed., *Narratives of Early Virginia*, 423.

[31] Barbour, *Jamestown Voyages*, II, 266; *RVC*, III, 18–19.

[32] Strachey, *Laws*, 20.

community had given way to an effort to keep settlers and Indians apart.

In their relations to the Indians, as in their rule of the settlers, the new governing officers of the colony were ruthless. The guerrilla raids that the two races conducted against each other became increasingly hideous, especially on the part of the English. Indians coming to Jamestown with food were treated as spies. Gates had them seized and killed "for a Terrour to the Reste to cawse them to desiste from their subtell practyses." [33] Gates showed his own subtle practices by enticing the Indians at Kecoughtan (Point Comfort) to watch a display of dancing and drumming by one of his men and then "espyeinge a fitteinge oportunety fell in upon them putt fyve to the sworde wownded many others some of them beinge after fownde in the woods with Sutche extreordinary Lardge and mortall wownds that itt seemed strange they Cold flye so far." [34] It is possible that the rank and file of settlers aggravated the bad relations with the Indians by unauthorized attacks, but unauthorized fraternization seems to have bothered the governors more. The atrocities committed against the queen of the Paspaheghs, though apparently demanded by the men, were the work of the governing officers, as were the atrocities committed against the Englishmen who fled to live with the Indians.

John Smith had not had his way in wishing to reduce the Indians to slavery, or something like it, on the Spanish model. But the policy of his successors, though perhaps not with company approval, made Virginia look far more like the Hispaniola of Las Casas than it did when Smith was in charge. And the company and the colony had few benefits to show for all the rigor. At the end of ten years, in spite of the military discipline of work gangs, the colonists were still not growing enough to feed themselves and were still begging, bullying, and buying corn from the Indians whose lands they scorched so deliberately. We cannot, it seems, blame the colony's failures on lax discipline and diffusion of authority. Failures continued and atrocities multiplied after authority was made absolute and concentrated in one man.

Another explanation, often advanced, for Virginia's early troubles, and especially for its failure to feed itself, is the collective organization of labor in the colony. All the settlers were expected to work together in a single community effort, to produce both their

[33] Percy, "Trewe Relacyon," 281.   [34] *Ibid.*, 270.

food and the exports that would make the company rich. Those who held shares would ultimately get part of the profits, but meanwhile the incentives of private enterprise were lacking. The work a man did bore no direct relation to his reward. The laggard would receive as large a share in the end as the man who worked hard.

The communal production of food seems to have been somewhat modified after the reorganization of 1609 by the assignment of small amounts of land to individuals for private gardens.[35] It is not clear who received such allotments, perhaps only those who came at their own expense. Men who came at company expense may have been expected to continue working exclusively for the common stock until their seven-year terms expired. At any rate, in 1614, the year when the first shipment of company men concluded their service, Governor Dale apparently assigned private allotments to them and to other independent "farmers." Each man got three acres, or twelve acres if he had a family. He was responsible for growing his own food plus two and a half barrels of corn annually for the company as a supply for newcomers to tide them over the first year. And henceforth each "farmer" would work for the company only one month a year.[36]

By this time Gates and Dale had succeeded in planting settlements at several points along the James as high up as Henrico, just below the falls. The many close-spaced tributary rivers and creeks made it possible to throw up a palisade between two of them to make a small fortified peninsula. Within the space thus enclosed by water on three sides and palisaded on the fourth, the settlers could build their houses, dig their gardens, and pasture their cattle. It was within these enclaves that Dale parceled out private allotments. Dignified by hopeful names like "Rochdale Hundred" or "Bermuda City," they were affirmations of an expectation that would linger for a century, that Virginia was about to become the site of thriving cities and towns. In point of fact, the new "cities" scarcely matched in size the tiny villages from which Powhatan's people threatened

[35] For the evidence of private allotments as early as 1609 see Brown, *Genesis*, I, 248-49, 252-53. See also Dale's reference to private gardens in 1611, *ibid.*, I, 491; Robert Johnson, *The New Life of Virginea*, Force, *Tracts*, I, No. 7, pp. 14, 18.

[36] Hamor, *True Discourse*, 17-19; John Rolfe, "Virginia in 1616," *Virginia Historical Register and Literary Advertiser*, I (July, 1848), 101-13, at 107.

them. And the "farmers" who huddled together on the allotments assigned to them proved incapable of supporting themselves or the colony with adequate supplies of food.

At first it seemed to sympathetic observers that they would. Ralph Hamor, in an account of the colony published in 1615, wrote, "When our people were fedde out of the common store and laboured jointly in the manuring of the ground and planting corne, glad was that man that could slippe from his labour, nay the most honest of them in a generall businesse, would not take so much faithfull and true paines in a weeke, as now he will doe in a day, neither cared they for the increase, presuming that howsoever their harvest prospered, the generall store must maintain them, by which meanes we reaped not so much corne from the labours of 30 men, as three men have done for themselves." [37]

According to John Rolfe, a settler who had married John Smith's fair Pocahontas, the switch to private enterprise transformed the colony's food deficit instantly to a surplus: instead of the settlers seeking corn from the Indians, the Indians sought it from them.[38] If so, the situation did not last long. Governor Samuel Argall, who took charge at the end of May, 1617, bought 600 bushels from the Indians that fall, "which did greatly relieve the whole Colonie." [39] And when Governor George Yeardley relieved Argall in April, 1619, he found the colony "in a great scarcity for want of corn" and made immediate preparations to seek it from the Indians.[40] If, then, the colony's failure to grow food arose from its communal organization of production, the failure was not overcome by the switch to private enterprise.

Still another explanation for the improvidence of Virginia's pioneers is one that John Smith often emphasized, namely, the character of the immigrants. They were certainly an odd assortment, for the most conspicuous group among them was an extraordinary number of gentlemen. Virginia, as a patriotic enterprise, had excited the imagination of England's nobility and gentry. The shareholders included 32 present or future earls, 4 countesses, and 3 viscounts (all members of the nobility) as well as hundreds of lesser gentlemen,

---

[37] Hamor, *True Discourse*, 17.   [38] Rolfe, "Virginia in 1616," 106.

[39] Smith, *Travels and Works*, II, 536.

[40] *RVC*, III, 118-22; Alexander Brown, *The First Republic in America* (Boston, 1898), 257, 308.

some of them perhaps retainers of the larger men.[41] Not all were content to risk only their money. Of the 105 settlers who started the colony, 36 could be classified as gentlemen. In the first "supply" of 120 additional settlers, 28 were gentlemen, and in the second supply of 70, again 28 were gentlemen.[42] These numbers gave Virginia's population about six times as large a proportion of gentlemen as England had.

Gentlemen, by definition, had no manual skill, nor could they be expected to work at ordinary labor. They were supposed to be useful for "the force of knowledge, the exercise of counsell"; [43] but to have ninety-odd wise men offering advice while a couple of hundred did the work was inauspicious, especially when the wise men included "many unruly gallants packed thether by their friends to escape il destinies" at home.[44]

What was worse, the gentlemen were apparently accompanied by the personal attendants that gentlemen thought necessary to make life bearable even in England. The colony's laborers "were for most part footmen, and such as they that were Adventurers brought to attend them, or such as they could perswade to goe with them, that never did know what a dayes worke was." [45] Smith complained that he could never get any real work from more than thirty out of two hundred, and he later argued that of all the people sent to Virginia, a hundred good laborers "would have done more than a thousand of those that went." [46] Samuel Argall and John Rolfe also argued that while a few gentlemen would have been useful to serve as military leaders, "to have more to wait and play than worke, or more commanders and officers than industrious labourers was not so necessarie." [47]

The company may actually have had little choice in allowing

[41] Stone, *Crisis of the Aristocracy*, 372. About half of the members were either gentry or nobility. See Theodore K. Rabb, *Enterprise and Empire: Merchant and Gentry Investment in the Expansion of England, 1575–1630* (Cambridge, Mass., 1967).

[42] Smith, Travels and Works, I, 93–94, 107–8, 129; Barbour, *Jamestown Voyages*, II, 382–83, 397–99, 418–20.

[43] Smith, *Travels and Works*, II, 502; Brown, *Genesis*, I, 411–12.

[44] Smith, *Travels and Works*, I, 162; Barbour, *Jamestown Voyages*, II, 452.

[45] Smith, *Travels and Works*, II, 486–87.

[46] Smith, *Travels and Works*, I, 84; II, 616; Barbour, *Jamestown Voyages*, II, 374.

[47] Smith, *Travels and Works*, II, 537.

gentlemen and their servants to make so large a number of their settlers. The gentlemen were paying their own way, and the company perhaps could not afford to deny them. But even if unencumbered by these volunteers, the colony might have foundered on the kind of settlers that the company itself did want to send. What the company wanted for Virginia was a variety of craftsmen. Richard Hakluyt had made up a list for Walter Raleigh that suggests the degree of specialization contemplated in an infant settlement: Hakluyt wanted both carpenters and joiners, tallow chandlers and wax chandlers, bowstave preparers and bowyers, fletchers and arrowhead makers, men to rough-hew pikestaffs and other men to finish them.[48] In 1610 and again in 1611 the Virginia Company published lists of the kind of workers it wanted.[49] Some were for building, making tools, and other jobs needed to keep the settlers alive, but the purpose of staying alive would be to see just what Virginia was good for and then start sending the goods back to England. Everybody hoped for gold and silver and jewels, so the colony needed refiners and mineral men. But they might have to settle for iron, so send men with all the skills needed to smelt it. The silk grass that Hariot described might produce something like silk, and there were native mulberry trees for growing worms, so send silk dressers. Sturgeon swam in the rivers, so send men who knew how to make caviar. And so on. Since not all the needed skills for Virginia's potential products were to be found in England, the company sought them abroad: glassmakers from Italy, millwrights from Holland, pitch boilers from Poland, vine dressers and saltmakers from France.[50] The settlers of Virginia were expected to create a more complex, more varied economy than England itself possessed. As an extension of England, the colony would impart its variety and health to the mother country.

If the company had succeeded in filling the early ships for Virginia with as great a variety of specialized craftsmen as it wanted, the results might conceivably have been worse than they were. We have already noticed the effect of specialization in England itself, where the division of labor had become a source not of efficiency but of idleness. In Virginia the effect was magnified. Among the skilled men who started the settlement in 1607 were four carpenters,

[48] Taylor, *Writings of the Hakluyts*, II, 322–23, 337.
[49] Brown, *Genesis*, I, 352–53, 469–70.
[50] Barbour, *Jamestown Voyages*, II, 420; Brown, *Genesis*, I, 203, 268; Wright, *Voyage to Virginia*, 89; *RVC*, III, 240, 477; Force, *Tracts*, III, No. 1, p. 20.

two bricklayers, one mason (apparently a higher skill than brick-laying), a blacksmith, a tailor, and a barber.[51] The first "supply" in 1608 had six tailors, two goldsmiths, two refiners, two apothecaries, a blacksmith, a gunner (i.e., gunsmith?), a cooper, a tobacco pipe maker, a jeweler, and a perfumer.[52] There were doubtless others, and being skilled they expected to be paid and fed for doing the kind of work for which they had been hired. Some were obviously useful. But others may have found themselves without means to use their special talents. If they were conscientious, the jeweler may have spent some time looking for jewels, the goldsmiths for gold, the perfumer for something to make perfume with. But when the search proved futile, it did not follow that they should or would exercise their skilled hands at any other tasks. It was not suitable for a per-fumer or a jeweler or a goldsmith to put his hand to the hoe. Rather, they could join the gentlemen in genteel loafing while a handful of ordinary laborers worked at the ordinary labor of growing and gathering food.

The laborers could be required to work at whatever they were told to; but they were, by all accounts, too few and too feeble. The company may have rounded them up as it did in 1609 when it ap-pealed to the mayor of London to rid the city of its "swarme of un-necessary inmates" by sending to Virginia any who were destitute and lying in the streets.[53]

The company, then, partly by choice, partly by necessity, sent to the colony an oversupply of men who were not prepared to tackle the work essential to settling in a wilderness. In choosing pro-spective Virginians, the company did not look for men who would be particularly qualified to keep themselves alive in a new land. The company never considered the problem of staying alive in Virginia to be a serious one. And why should they have? England's swarming population had had ample experience in moving to new areas and staying alive. The people who drifted north and west into the pasture-farming areas got along, and the lands there were marginal, far poorer than those that awaited the settlers of tidewater Virginia. Though there may have been some farmers among the early set-tlers, no one for whom an occupation is given was listed as a hus-

51 Smith, *Travels and Works*, I, 93–94; Barbour, *Jamestown Voyages*, II, 382–83.
52 Smith, *Travels and Works*, I, 107–8; Barbour, *Jamestown Voyages*, II, 397–99.
53 Brown, *Genesis*, I, 252–53.

bandman or yeoman. And though thirty husbandmen were included in the 1611 list of men wanted, few came. As late as 1620 the colony reported "a great scarcity, or none at all" of "husbandmen truely bred," by which was meant farmers from the arable regions.[54] In spite of the experience at Roanoke and in spite of the repeated starving times at Jamestown, the company simply did not envisage the provision of food as a serious problem. They sent some food supplies with every ship but never enough to last more than a few months. After that people should be able to do for themselves.

The colonists were apparently expected to live from the land like England's woodland and pasture people, who gave only small amounts of time to their small garden plots, cattle, and sheep and spent the rest in spinning, weaving, mining, handicrafts, and loafing. Virginians would spend their time on the more varied commodities of the New World. To enable them to live in this manner, the company sent cattle, swine, and sheep: and when Dale assigned them private plots of land, the plots were small, in keeping with the expectation that they would not spend much time at farming. The company never intended the colony to supply England with grain and did not even expect that agricultural products might be its principal exports. They did want to give sugar, silk, and wine a try, but most of the skills they sought showed an expectation of setting up extractive industries such as iron mining, smelting, saltmaking, pitch making, and glassmaking. The major part of the colonists' work time was supposed to be devoted to processing the promised riches of the land for export; and with the establishment of martial law the company had the means of seeing that they put their shoulders to the task.

Unfortunately, the persons charged with directing the motley work force had a problem, quite apart from the overload of gentlemen and specialized craftsmen they had to contend with. During the early years of the colony they could find no riches to extract. They sent back some cedar wood, but lumber was too bulky a product to bear the cost of such long transportation to market. Sassafras was available in such quantities that the market for it quickly collapsed. The refiners found no gold or silver or even enough iron to be worth mining. Silk grass and silk proved to be a will-o'-the-wisp.

The result was a situation that taxed the patience both of the leaders and of the men they supervised. They had all come to Vir-

[54] *RVC*, III, 256.

ginia with high expectations. Those who came as servants of the company had seven years in which to make their employers rich. After that they would be free to make themselves rich. But with no prospect of riches in sight for anybody, it was difficult to keep them even at the simple tasks required for staying alive or to find anything else for them to do.

The predicament of those in charge is reflected in the hours of work they prescribed for the colonists, which contrast sharply with those specified in the English Statute of Artificers. There was no point in demanding dawn-to-dusk toil unless there was work worth doing. When John Smith demanded that men work or starve, how much work did he demand? By his own account, "4 hours each day was spent in worke, the rest in pastimes and merry exercise." [55] The governors who took charge after the reorganization of 1609 were equally modest in their demands. William Strachey, who was present, described the work program under Gates and De la Warr in the summer of 1610:

> It is to be understood that such as labor are not yet so taxed but that easily they perform the same and ever by ten of the clock they have done their morning's work: at what time they have their allowances [of food] set out ready for them, and until it be three of the clock again they take their own pleasure, and afterward, with the sunset, their day's labor is finished.[56]

The Virginia Company offered much the same account of this period. According to a tract issued late in 1610, "the setled times of working (to effect all themselves, or the Adventurers neede desire) [require] no more pains then from sixe of clocke in the morning untill ten, and from two of the clocke in the afternoone till foure." [57] The long lunch period described here was spelled out in

---

[55] Smith, *Travels and Works*, I, 149; Barbour, *Jamestown Voyages*, II, 440. Twelve years later Smith rewrote this statement and changed the figure of four hours to six hours. *Travels and Works*, II, 466. Even so, what are we to make of a six-hour day in a colony teetering on the verge of extinction?

[56] Wright, *Voyage to Virginia*, 69–70.

[57] *A True Declaration of the Estate of the Colonie in Virginia* (London, 1610), in Force, *Tracts*, III, No. 1, p. 20; Smith, *Travels and Works*, II, 502. Captain Daniel Tucker maintained a similar program in Bermuda in 1616: "according to the Virginia order, hee set every one [that] was with him at Saint Georges, to his taske, to cleere grounds, fell trees, set corne, square timber, plant vines and other fruits brought out of England. These

the *Lawes Divine, Morall and Martiall.* If we calculate the total hours demanded of the work gangs between the various beatings of the drum, they come to roughly five to eight hours a day in summer and three to six hours in winter.[58] And it is not to be supposed that these hours refer only to work done in the fields and that the men were expected to work at other tasks like building houses during the remainder of the day. The *Laws* indicate that at the appointed hours every laborer was to repair to his work "and every crafts man to his occupation, Smiths, Joyners, Carpenters, Brick makers, etc." [59] Nor did military training occupy the time not spent in working. The *Laws* provided for different groups to train at different times and to be exempt from work during the training days.[60] Although colonists and historians alike have condemned the *Laws* as harsh, and with reason, the working hours that the code prescribed sound astonishingly short to modern ears. They certainly fell way below those demanded at the time in English law; and they seem utterly irrational in a chronically starving community.

To have grown enough corn to feed the colony would have required only a fraction of the brief working time specified,[61] yet it was not grown. Even in their free time men shunned the simple planting tasks that sufficed for the Indians. And the very fact that the Indians did grow corn may be one more reason why the colonists did not. For the Indians presented a challenge that Englishmen were not prepared to meet, a challenge to their image of themselves, to their self-esteem, to their conviction of their own superiority over foreigners, and especially over barbarous foreigners like the Irish and the Indians.

---

by their taske—Masters by breake a day repaired to the wharfe, from thence to be imployed to the place of their imployment, till nine of the clocke, and then in the after-noone from three till Sunneset" (*ibid.*, II, 653).

[58] *Laws*, 61–62.   [59] *Ibid.*, 59.   [60] *Ibid.*, 44–45.

[61] Although Thomas Hariot's estimate of a day a year among the Roanoke Indians is doubtless too small, the cultivation of a couple of acres per person would have occupied only a part of the work force for a small part of the year. The quota expected of English husbandmen was about thirty acres per man (Thirsk, *Agrarian History*, 652). Alexander Whitaker, a minister who came to the colony in 1611, wrote in 1613 that "in the idle hours of one weeke" he and three others had set enough corn to last for a quarter of the year. Whitaker, *Good Newes from Virginia*, 43. Edward Williams (*Virginia Richly Valued*, Force, *Tracts*, III, No. 11, p. 12) says that "one man in 48 hours may prepare as much ground, & set such a quantity of Corne, that he may be secure from want of Bread all the yeere following."

If you were a colonist, you knew that your technology was superior to the Indians'. You knew that you were civilized, and they were savages. It was evident in your firearms, your clothing, your housing, your government, your religion. The Indians were supposed to be overcome with admiration and to join you in extracting riches from the country. But your superior technology had proved insufficient to extract anything. The Indians, keeping to themselves, laughed at your superior methods and lived from the land more abundantly and with less labor than you did. They even furnished you with the food that you somehow did not get around to growing enough of yourselves. To be thus condescended to by heathen savages was intolerable. And when your own people started deserting in order to live with them, it was too much. If it came to that, the whole enterprise of Virginia would be over. So you killed the Indians, tortured them, burned their villages, burned their cornfields. It proved your superiority in spite of your failures. And you gave similar treatment to any of your own people who succumbed to the savage way of life. But you still did not grow much corn. That was not what you had come to Virginia for.

By the time the colony was ten years old and an almost total loss to the men who had invested their lives and fortunes in it, only one ray of hope had appeared. It had been known, from the Roanoke experience, that the Indians grew and smoked a kind of tobacco; and tobacco grown in the Spanish West Indies was already being imported into England, where it sold at eighteen shillings a pound. Virginia tobacco had proved, like everything else, a disappointment; but one of the settlers, John Rolfe, tried some seeds of the West Indian variety, and the result was much better. The colonists stopped bowling in the streets and planted tobacco in them—and everywhere else that they could find open land. In 1617, ten years after the first landing at Jamestown, they shipped their first cargo to England. It was not up to Spanish tobacco, but it sold at three shillings a pound.[62]

To the members of the company it was proof that they had been right in their estimate of the colony's potential. But the proof was bitter. Tobacco had at first been accepted as a medicine, good for a great variety of ailments. But what gave it its high price was the fact that people had started smoking it for fun. Used this way it

[62] Smith, *Travels and Works*, II, 536.

was considered harmful and faintly immoral. People smoked it in taverns and brothels. Was Virginia to supplement England's economy and redeem her rogues by pandering to a new vice? The answer, of course, was yes. But the men who ran the Virginia Company, still aiming at ends of a higher nature, were not yet ready to take yes for an answer.

5

THE PERSISTENT VISION

THE Englishmen who invested their money in the Virginia Company's high purpose were naturally disappointed in the colony's failure to live up to expectations. But they were not sure what, if anything, to do about it. By 1618 they were divided into factions. One group, led by Sir Thomas Smith, was composed of big merchants, for whom Virginia was only one of many ongoing enterprises. These men, who had dominated the company's counsels hitherto, could afford to regard Virginia as a long-term investment in which one need not look for immediate success. They were disappointed with the results thus far achieved and with the settlers' new addiction to tobacco, but they were willing to wait for Smith, who had been highly successful in other ventures, to bring this one to fruition.[1]

Another group of members, led by Lord Robert Rich and his son, the future Earl of Warwick, were also willing to wait for returns on their investment. Their immediate interest in the colony lay less in direct profits from the settlers there than in the protection the colony could afford their ships. In spite of James I's policy of peace with Spain, Rich and his associates were continuing the lucrative war of attrition begun by Hawkins and Drake. By obtaining privateering commissions from petty principalities like Savoy, they gave a color of legality to piratical cruises against Spanish shipping. But it was difficult to conduct such voyages from England without running into trouble with the king. Rich saw in Virginia a convenient

---

[1] My account of the divisions in the company rests heavily on W. F. Craven, *Dissolution of the Virginia Company.*

base from which to strike the Caribbean. Bermuda, where the Virginia Company had planted another small settlement (on the grounds that Bermuda fell within the boundaries of the company's charter), could serve the same purpose. As long as Virginia and Bermuda furnished a haven for their ships, Rich and his friends were not overly troubled by the failure to produce iron or silk or glass or any other commodity.

A third group of company members consisted of smaller men for whom the investment probably represented a larger share of their working capital than was the case with the Smith or Warwick factions. After ten years of waiting they were dissatisfied with the management of the big men. They wanted to see some action, and the production of a disreputable weed was not what they had in mind. Their leader, Sir Edwin Sandys, son of the Archbishop of York, had become famous for his opposition to the policies of James I in the House of Commons. In the minds of other Englishmen, and doubtless in his own mind, he was one of the country's outstanding defenders of freedom, a fact that probably helped to win him his following in the company.

It may also have won him, at least initially, the good will of the other factions. Neither merchants like Smith nor noblemen like Rich were notably fond of their king's pretensions to divine right or less devoted than Sandys to the liberties that flowed from the power of Parliament. Nor were they any more content than Sandys to see their colony devote itself to the mere production of smoke. In 1618 all parties in the company agreed on a reorganization of the colony's government and a rededication of its purposes. Most of the directives aimed at carrying out these objectives were adopted while Sir Thomas Smith was still treasurer of the company. But the man who carried them out or tried to carry them out, and who has been associated with them ever since, was Sir Edwin Sandys, whose following had grown large enough by 1619 to place him in the treasurer's seat.

The new program involved a variety of measures, many of which were to have lasting effects on the colony's history and on the pattern of human relations in it. Most of them derived from a recognition that the company must furnish greater incentives to individuals, both investors and settlers. Military organization and martial law had enabled the colony to survive, but they had not done much more than that. Men needed a larger stake in the country if they were to make it flourish. Governor Dale had recognized the need when he began assigning land to individuals as early as 1614, but he did it only in small amounts and without passing permanent title to the property. The first step in the new program was to grant some of Virginia's land to the people who had chosen to live there. "Old Planters," defined as those who had arrived before the spring of 1616, were to get a hundred acres apiece whenever their terms of service were up, or at once if they had come on their own. If they were also shareholders in the company by purchase, they got an additional hundred acres for every share. Settlers who had come after 1616 would get fifty acres. Henceforth anyone who came on his own or who paid for the transportation of someone else would be entitled to a "headright" of fifty acres.[2]

The company reserved a "quitrent" of a shilling a year on every fifty acres granted. The amount was small—a shilling was roughly the value of an ordinary day's labor in England at the time and less than half that generally given in Virginia—but land was abundant. Though conveyed to individuals, it would yield a small annual income in quitrents to the company, increasing with the arrival of every new settler. Sandys was eager to use whatever funds he could raise for getting more people to the colony. In order to make settlement more attractive to England's impoverished laborers, he offered an alternative to servitude: persons sent at company expense would be assigned land to work as sharecropping tenants under the direction of a company agent. They would turn over half of their earnings to the company for seven years, and then each would get fifty acres of his own.[3]

Sandys managed to send several hundred such tenants to work lands set aside for the company. And in order to speed up settlement, he induced various members of the company to join in sub-corporations or associations to found "particular plantations" peopled by tenants on the same terms. Investors in these associations obtained a hundred acres for every share of stock in the company plus fifty acres for every tenant they sent to occupy their lands. The lands of each association would form a separate little community within the colony.

Company members thus acquired a special interest in the colony,

[2] *RVC*, III, 100–101, 107.

[3] *RVC*, III, 99–100. Though the records do not say how the tenants were to be supported until they were able to raise a crop for themselves, the company evidently expected to furnish them with provisions for the first months.

beyond the mere holding of stock. In other ways, too, the company encouraged the formation of special-interest groups within itself. It had already given up in 1616 the attempt to serve as the source of supplies for the colony and had turned this function over to a sub-corporation known as the "magazine," in charge of an agent in the colony known as the "cape merchant." The magazine, which was given exclusive rights for four years, expected to make a profit by selling English goods to the settlers, taking their produce in exchange. When the four years were up, in January, 1620, and the magazine showed no profit, the trade was thrown open to other associations, usually formed to support a single voyage at a time. Sandys was somehow able to persuade investors, for patriotism or profit, to keep risking their money on such magazines, on particular plantations, and on a variety of other projects to benefit the colony, such as the shipment of a hundred willing maids, to be sold to planters who could afford to buy a wife.

Sandys gave particular encouragement to the production of commodities, other than tobacco, for export to England. He proposed to set up three separate iron foundries and sent 150 men with experience in the business to man them, even though the colonists had not yet located an adequate source of ore.[4] He made the sponsors of particular plantations agree to direct their tenants to "staple and solide Commodities . . . and not onely or chiefly to Tobacco."[5] And he gave specific instructions to the men in charge of the company tenants to see to it that they were employed in producing cordage (from silk grass), pitch, tar, potash, lumber (he sent materials for setting up sawmills and German millwrights to supervise the job), silk (King James, a silk enthusiast, furnished the cocoons), wine, salt, and fish. These, together with glass (the next year he sent some Italian glassmakers), were the commodities he wanted the colony to concentrate on, adding parenthetically, "Corne and Cattell we passe over, being only for sustenance of the People."[6] Sandys took for granted that the settlers by this time could provide themselves with plenty of corn and cattle while devoting their major attention to the commodities named. Tobacco was not one of them, and Sandys had made it plain that he wanted the company tenants to plant none of it. The following year, 1621, the company ordered that the colony grow no more than 100 pounds per person annually,

[4] *RVC*, III, 309. [6] *RVC*, III, 275–80, 489.
[5] *RVC*, III, 360, 628.

a restriction that applied to everyone in the colony, including tenants on particular plantations.[7]

It was easier to make these orders than to enforce them, and a principal reason for the difficulty grew out of another element in the company's new program. In its effort to make the colony attractive to settlers, the company had decided not only to give out land to settlers but also to furnish them with a more liberal, more English frame of government than the semi-military dictatorship that had prevailed for the preceding eight or ten years. The governor and council of the colony, appointed by the company, remained as before the principal governing officers, charged to carry out the instructions of the company. But their powers were henceforth to be limited in a way that would give the settlers on the spot a much greater degree of control over their lives. The *Lawes Divine, Morall and Martiall* were junked, and the company prepared to draft a new code based on English common law.[8] In addition, the first governor under the new regime, Sir George Yeardley, was instructed to call annually an assembly, consisting of his council and of two "burgesses" from every settlement in the colony, including the particular plantations and the four centers of settlement where the company was placing its own tenants: Jamestown, Charles City, Henrico, and Kecoughtan (later Elizabeth City). The burgesses were to be elected by the "inhabitants," but the instructions said nothing about who was to be included under this term, nor does any surviving record tell us who actually was included. The assembly had the power to make laws, which became valid when approved by the company; and the company declared its intention ultimately to make its own regulations depend on approval by the assembly.[9] Although its authority was thus limited, at least on paper, this was the first representative legislative assembly in English America and it would eventually expand its authority in the manner that other representative assemblies, including Parliament, have done.

In the eyes of the company at the time, however, the assembly was probably not the most important element in the plans to make Virginia politically attractive. The most conspicuous burden that every government imposes on its subjects is the cost of supporting it. At some point it occurred to the leaders of the company that they had a way of giving their settlers a unique freedom from this age-old

[7] *RVC*, III, 473; Smith, *Travels and Works*, II, 565.
[8] *RVC*, I, 333, 394–95. [9] *RVC*, III, 483–84.

burden of taxation. The lands that the king had granted the company in Virginia were abundant beyond measure, and England was filled with men who needed land and would work as sharecropping tenants for seven years in order to get it. The company would therefore assign to every office of government a portion of land and would undertake to furnish the initial tenants for it on the same seven-year fifty-fifty basis prescribed for the tenants sent to occupy the company lands. The purpose was plainly stated: "because our intent is to Ease all the Inhabitants of Virginia forever of all taxes and public burthens as much as may be and to take away all occasion of oppression and corruption." [10]

The amounts were generous. The governor got 3,000 acres and 100 tenants.[11] The treasurer (of the colony as distinct from the treasurer of the company), charged with over-all supervision of the production of new commodities, got 1,500 acres and 50 tenants.[12] The marshal, an officer created in anticipation of the need to defend the colony against invaders, also got 1,500 acres and 50 tenants.[13] The vice admiral, who had no ship, got 300 acres and 12 tenants.[14] Ministers got 100 acres and 6 tenants.[15] When the secretary of the colony was found to be taking high fees for issuing land grants, he was forbidden to do so and given land and tenants instead.[16] It seemed an ideal arrangement. A government whose officers "should not need to prey upon the people"[17] should be a gentle government indeed. When the settlers heard of it, one of them observed that if it were carried out, "then we may truly say in Virginia, we are the most happy people in the world."[18]

In the effort to recover its original purpose and direction, the company did not forget the Indians. The new program coincided with the death of Powhatan and the succession of his brother Opechancanough, who at first showed as much coolness to the English as Powhatan ever had. Sandys secured £550 from an anonymous donor to pay for bringing up Indian children in English houses and teaching them English skills, but the Indians were fond of their children and unwilling to part with them. Governor Yeardley accordingly proposed, and Opechancanough agreed, to take whole families of Indians to live in the English settlements and provide them

[10] RVC, III, 99.
[11] RVC, I, 256, 268; III, 99.
[12] RVC, I, 454.
[13] RVC, I, 454.
[14] RVC, I, 549.
[15] RVC, III, 277.
[16] RVC, I, 332–33; II, 94–95, 109.
[17] RVC, IV, 523.
[18] Smith, Travels and Works, II, 543.

with houses of their own.[19] By supporting Opechancanough in a quarrel with an interior tribe, Yeardley won a seeming support from the new monarch of Indian Virginia.[20] The company also revived an earlier project for which funds had been donated, the establishment of a college where Indian youth would become acquainted with the more sophisticated aspects of Christianity and civility. Ten thousand acres had been set aside at Henrico for its endowment, and Sandys sent a hundred tenants to begin producing for it.[21] To take charge of them in 1621 went George Thorpe, a former member of Parliament, now a member of the governor's council and an ardent advocate of the biracial settlement that had thus far eluded realization. Thorpe, acting for a new governor, Sir Francis Wyatt, proved a more congenial negotiator than Yeardley, who had demonstrated his opinion of Indians too often in the past with gunfire. On a visit to the Indians Thorpe found that Opechancanough "had more motiones of religione in him then Coulde be ymmagined," and the two of them projected an exchange whereby some Indian families would live among the English and some English families among the Indians.[22]

Meanwhile Sandys was rounding up settlers at a great rate. He pressed every English parish to ship off its poor.[23] He got the City of London to send a hundred destitute boys to serve as apprentices.[24] He got forty-four individuals and groups to take out patents for particular plantations.[25] One way or another he managed within three years of becoming treasurer to get more than 3,500 persons to the colony, probably twice as many as had come in the preceding ten years.[26] If all had gone as planned, Virginia should have presented an idyllic scene: tenants producing new commodities for the English market, enriching their sponsors while they laid up a nest egg for themselves, Indians learning English technology and religion in the bosom of the English settlement, the two races blending in a new community of good will. Instead, once again, good intentions paved the way to race war, famine, disease, death, and tobacco.

The most dramatic catastrophe came on March 22, 1622, when

---

[19] *RVC*, I, 307–8, 585–89; III, 128–29.
[20] *RVC, III*, 228.
[21] *RVC*, III, 102, 115.
[22] *RVC*, III, 446, 584.
[23] *RVC*, I, 411–12, 479–80, 489.
[24] *RVC*, I, 304–7.
[25] Craven, *Dissolution of the Virginia Company*, 59.
[26] A tally of the number sent from the beginning to May, 1616, comes to 1,650. Brown, *Genesis*, II, 782.

the Indians demonstrated that they did not share the hopes of men like Thorpe and Sandys for an integrated community. Thorpe had already observed that most of the English settlers did not share them either. "There is scarce any man amongest us," he reported, "that doth soe much as afforde them [the Indians] a good thought in his hart and most men with their mouthes give them nothinge but maledictions and bitter execrations."[27] The Indians seemed to swallow the insults and moved freely among the settlers. And the settlers, relieved of the terrors of guerrilla warfare, spread out along the river, taking up lands wherever the location looked promising, with little heed for Indian ownership. But Indians were notoriously proud, their empty lands were not "unused," and their seeming subservience might have signaled a warning. Opechancanough, spurred not only by the arrogance of the English but by their alarming growth in numbers, apparently decided on a concerted effort to wipe them out in a surprise attack. One of his subjects who had been converted to Christianity and to working for an English master revealed the plan in the nick of time. Even so, warnings could not be spread fast enough through the straggling settlements to prevent the massacre of 347 men, women, and children, including George Thorpe.[28]

The massacre released all restraints that the company had hitherto imposed on those who thirsted for the destruction or enslavement of the Indians. There was some disagreement as to whether they should be exterminated or put to work in some way. Captain John Martin, the leader of a particular plantation notorious for harboring debtors and dubious characters, argued against extirpation, not only because it seemed to him unchristian, but because the Indians kept down the woods (by firing), reduced the number of wolves and bear by their hunting, and because they were actually "apter for worke then yet our English are," being able "to worke in the heate of the day." They would be "fitt to rowe in Gallies and friggetts and many other pregnant uses too tedious to sett downe."[29] The secretary of the company, who reported the details of the massacre in a lengthy pamphlet, dwelt upon the Spanish example, dear to John Smith, and rejoiced that Virginia would now be free to follow it. He suggested that the Indians might "now most justly be compelled to servitude and drudgery, and supply the roome of men that labour, whereby even the meanest of the Plantation may imploy

---

[27] *RVC*, III, 446.   [28] *RVC*, III, 541–79.   [29] *RVC*, III, 706.

themselves more entirely in their Arts and Occupations, which are more generous whilest Savages performe their inferiour workes of digging in mynes, and the like, ..." [30]

But Virginia had neither mines nor galleys, and though the settlers yearned for men who would be "apter for worke" than those they were getting from England, they bent their efforts more to exterminating than to enslaving the Indians. Since the Indians were better woodsmen than the English and virtually impossible to track down, the method was to feign peaceful intentions, let them settle down and plant their corn wherever they chose, and then, just before harvest, fall upon them, killing as many as possible and burning the corn. [31] When the company advised the governor and council to observe rules of justice in their campaign, they replied that "wee hold nothinge injuste, that may tend to their ruine, (except breach of faith)." [32] But the exception in this case proved to be the rule. The English made treaties with the avowed intention of lulling the Indians into security, the better to surprise them. [33] One negotiator carried a butt of poisoned sack to a peace parley on the Potomac and, after concluding a treaty, persuaded his hosts to drink to it. He could not be sure afterwards of the exact number he netted this way, but he estimated two hundred, besides fifty that he and his men killed with more solid weapons afterwards. [34]

Within two or three years of the massacre the English had avenged the deaths of that day many times over. They had also put an end to Sandys' plans for an integrated community of which the Indians would be a part. Though a few remained among them as servants or slaves (there is no way to be sure of their status), there was no longer any pretense of carrying on with the pious intentions that were still expressed from time to time in England.

The massacre was a setback to the company's plans. Glassworking was halted. The ironworks, located far up the river, and still without a worthwhile source of ore, had to be abandoned, along with many of the particular plantations, as the settlers pulled together around Jamestown for safety. [35] But the Indians, however frightening, were less effective at killing Englishmen than other causes that came to light after the massacre. By the time the massacre

[30] *RVC*, III, 558–59.
[31] *RVC*, IV, 9–10, 507–8, 569.
[32] *RVC*, IV, 451.

[33] *RVC*, IV, 98–99, 102.
[34] *RVC*, IV, 220–22.
[35] *RVC*, III, 612–13; IV, 11–12, 23.

occurred, Sandys had succeeded in alienating the other factions in the company beyond recall. He insulted Sir Thomas Smith by demanding a more detailed accounting of his treasurership (hinting at embezzlement of company funds), and he made enemies of the Rich faction by ordering Governor Yeardley to clamp down on piracy. After the massacre, when his enemies began to close in on him, they discovered that the company was virtually bankrupt and that its colony, long before the Indians raised their hands, had become a charnel house. The story is succinctly told in some notes made by Samuel Wrote, a disgruntled and disillusioned investor. After finding that the company records showed 3,570 persons sent to the colony in three years under the Sandys program and that 700 had been already there, for a total of 4,270, he discovered that only 1,240 were alive at the time of the massacre. "It Consequentlie followes," he noted, "that wee had then lost 3000 persons within those 3 yeares." The Indians had killed 347, but something else had killed 3,000, the great majority of the persons sent.[36]

The figures seem incredible, but if they erred it was only in perhaps underestimating the number of people present at the time Sandys took over. The death rate may have been even worse than Wrote supposed, and it continued at least as high after the massacre as before. The only question is how it could have happened. The Smith and Rich factions in the company knew that whoever else might be to blame, Sir Edwin Sandys was. Unable to challenge him successfully in the company itself, they turned to the king and called for an official investigation. To the commission the king appointed they presented the shocking facts, together with letters from the colony describing the arrival of masses of immigrants without adequate supplies. Handicapped by an empty treasury, Sandys had been able to find men but not supplies. And ship captains, interested only in the fee received for transporting them, overloaded their ships with passengers and dumped the survivors ashore in Virginia half dead with scurvy. When the king's commission found out what was happening, they had little choice but to call for an end to the Virginia Company. In 1624 the king dissolved the company and placed Virginia under his own control.

Because the Stuart kings became symbols of arbitrary government and because Sir Edwin Sandys was a champion of Parlia-

[36] *RVC*, III, 536–37; IV, 158–59.

mentary power and was even accused at the time of being a republican, historians for long interpreted the dissolution of the Virginia Company as a blow dealt to democracy by tyranny. Modern scholarship has altered the verdict and shown that any responsible monarch would have been obliged to stop the reckless shipment of his subjects to their deaths.[37] There can be no doubt that Sandys and the members of the company who backed him must bear the blame for sending so many ill-equipped settlers to a colony that was unprepared to receive them. But when we pause to consider the dimensions of his responsibility, we are faced by the same enigma with which we started. In 1619, when Sandys started to pour in settlers, the colony had been in existence for twelve years. Giving all due consideration to the conditioned laziness of English labor and to the disastrous alienation of the Indians, we may still ask how it could be that a colony which had lasted for a dozen years in a country where a minimum of labor would sustain life was nevertheless unable to provide for so many helping hands. Since question and answer center on the lack of food supplies, it will be appropriate to examine what people in Virginia during the Sandys administration said about the scarcity of provisions, considering their statements from the harvest of one year to the harvest of the next.

1619–20. When George Yeardley arrived as governor in April, 1619, to inaugurate the company's new program, he took over a colony in which the supplies of cattle and corn were, as usual, low. Yeardley reported that he would devote himself in the coming year to getting a good crop of corn.[38] On June 25 the arrival of the *Trial,* loaded with corn and cattle, "tooke from us cleerely all feare of famine." In spite of an epidemic that weakened and killed large numbers, the colony reaped unprecedented harvests that summer, and by the end of September the settlers enjoyed, according to John Pory (no friend of Yeardley) "a marvelous plenty, suche as hath not bene seen since our first coming into the lande." [39] In January, 1620, John Rolfe too reported the abundance of corn, and of fish brought from Newfoundland and sturgeon caught in Virginia.[40] According to these leaders of the settlement, Virginians were apparently well fed in the winter of 1619–20.

[37] Craven, *Dissolution of the Virginia Company,* esp. 1–23.
[38] *RVC,* III, 118–22.
[39] Smith, *Travels and Works,* II, 541; *RVC,* III, 220; I, 310.
[40] *RVC,* III, 241–48.

1620–21. There are no surviving reports about the amount of corn grown in the summer of 1620, but in November Sir Edwin Sandys informed the company that the settlers no longer wanted English meal sent them. Instead, they preferred beads for trade with the Indians.[41] It is evident from other sources too that the colonists were getting corn from the Indians. In December, long after harvest time, George Thorpe observed that "this countrey meandes [i.e., mends, improves] in plentie of victuall everie daie," and he probably meant in supplies obtained from the Indians.[42] By May, 1621, Captain Thomas Nuce, a newcomer, observed that the men sent under his charge lived "very barely for the most part: haveinge no other foode but bread and water and such manner of meate as they make of the Mayze: which I would to God I Could say they had in any reasonable plenty." They would have been distressed, he said, if one of their ships had not brought in corn from Chesapeake Bay, where the colony now had "good and free trade" (with the Indians).[43] The winter of 1620–21 was apparently not a plentiful one, but there was no talk of starvation. In June George Thorpe reported that people were blessed with good health and good hope of a plentiful harvest of all kinds.[44]

1621–22. Again there is no specific report of the harvest. On December 15 ,1621, Peter Arondelle, another newcomer, complained of his family's lean diet of one and a half pints of musty meal a day per man.[45] But the governor and council reported in January that in the nine ships which had arrived during the autumn, none of the passengers died on the way and all continued in health.[46] A ship from Ireland in November came "soe well furnished with all sortes of provisione, aswell as with Cattle, as wee could wishe all men would follow theire example." [47] If Arondelle's complaint represents a general scarcity in the colony, it was not serious enough to lower his enthusiasm for Virginia, because just two weeks later he was writing home about the abundance of cattle and hogs both wild and domestic and observing that "any laborious honest man may in a shorte time become ritche in this Country." [48] The winter of 1621–22 produced no other surviving complaints of scarcity. There was even some boasting that new immigrants no longer need fear

[41] *RVC*, I, 423.
[42] *RVC*, III, 417.
[43] *RVC*, III, 455–56.

[44] *RVC*, III, 462.
[45] *RVC*, III, 534–35.
[46] *RVC*, III, 582.

[47] *RVC*, III, 587.
[48] *RVC*, III, 589.

danger from "wars, or famine, or want of convenient lodging and looking to." [49]

Then, on March 22, the Indians struck, killing not only settlers but also much needed cattle. Planting operations had to be curtailed, for corn furnished shelter to lurking Indians.[50] There was no choice but to seek relief from the Indians themselves, not those who had participated in the massacre, but those to the north or south. Various captains were commissioned to get corn from them, by trade if they could, by force if they could not. There was not even a remote possibility that the harvest might be sufficient.

1622–23. The corn obtained from the Indians and from the settlers' meager crops fell far short of the need, and most Virginians went hungry, as prices skyrocketed for whatever provisions there were.[51] On July 2, 1623, Delphebus Canne, recently arrived from England, regretted not having brought more meal, oatmeal, and peas for sale to the settlers, because "now the land is destitute of food." But he noted that the weather had been good and that people expected a large harvest of both corn and tobacco. Canne also remarked on another source of food. Long before Virginia was thought of, fishermen of all nations had discovered the Grand Banks and swarmed there every summer. By this time the ships that carried settlers to the colony sometimes made a shuttle voyage to the Banks after they arrived or traded there on the way. According to Canne, ships were expected daily from Canada and Newfoundland with enough fish for the whole ensuing year.[52]

1623–24. Whether the corn crop and the awaited cargoes from the north fulfilled expectations is not clear. In January the governor and council reported that "the scarsitie this foreruninge yeere hath been greate, and who could expect less, after such a massacre, yett none to our knowledg hath Perished through wante, many seasoned

---

[49] Brown, *First Republic in America*, 465.

[50] Edward D. Neill, *Virginia Carolorum* (Albany, N.Y., 1886), 53; *RVC*, III, 613–14; IV, 186, 234.

[51] *RVC*, IV, 41–42, 58–62, 89, 231–35. Cf. P. A. Bruce, *Economic History of Virginia in the Seventeenth Century* (2 vols., New York, 1895), II, 6–8.

[52] *VMHB*, VI (1898–99), 373–74. On voyages to Canada see *RVC*, IV, 96, 221, 253, 272, 461, 477, 513. Lawrence Leigh wrote to Nicholas Ferrar from London, September 18, 1623, that someone who left Virginia the last of May in that year had reported that "the people stood well at helth" and were "in great hope of a verye good Croppe of Corne." Ferrar Papers, Box VII, No. 726, Magdalene College, Cambridge.

men goinge through theire labours, beside hard marches, which endured the same Comone scarsitie."[53] By April enough provisions had been obtained from the Indians to end the crisis.[54]

The reports all reflect some scarcity of food between 1618 and 1624. But only during the year following the massacre was the scarcity acute, and in the winter and spring after the bumper harvest of 1619 there seems to have been no scarcity at all. Yet it is precisely from this winter and spring that we have the most explicit complaints from Virginia about people arriving without adequate provisions. On November 4, 1619, when a hundred company tenants arrived "lusty and well" on the *Bona Nova*, the governor and council calculated that the 544 bushels of meal sent with them would last only five and a half months at two pounds a man per day. Fifty men were therefore parceled out for a year to private planters.[55] Yet two or three months earlier, when a Dutch ship put in at the colony, the governor and cape merchant bartered Virginia provisions for twenty-odd Negroes (the first known Negroes to enter the colony), who certainly came ashore unsupplied with anything.[56] It is not recorded that the Negroes were put to work for the company. The following June, after some four hundred more settlers arrived, Governor Yeardley wrote plaintively to the company, urging them to send subsequent ships with more provisions, adding that "yf such nombers of people come upon me unexpected, and that at an unhealthfull season and to late to sett Corne I cannott then be able to feed them owt of others labors." In the future, he begged them, they should send men before Christmas (by November 4 perhaps?) with six months' provisions (instead of five and a half?).[57]

Yeardley's complaints, his purchase of the Negroes, and his disposal of the company tenants from the *Bona Nova*, at a time when the colony was reporting an unprecedented abundance, suggest that the problem was not altogether one of whether supplies existed. It was a question of who had them and of who could pay for them. In

[53] *RVC*, IV, 452.
[54] *RVC*, IV, 475. The harvest in the summer of 1624 was plentiful. *Calendar of State Papers, Colonial: America and West Indies*, I, 70–71 (C.O. 1/3, f.102).
[55] *RVC*, III, 226, 246; Smith, *Travels and Works*, II, 542.
[56] *RVC*, III, 243. It is perhaps no coincidence that in 1625 Yeardley (governor in 1619) and Abraham Peirsey (cape merchant in 1619) held 15 of the 23 Negroes then in the colony.
[57] *RVC*, III, 299.

a year of plenty the governor and council were unable or unwilling to make use of fifty men with allegedly inadequate supplies when other Virginians *were* able and willing to do so. The great shortage of supplies, to which we attribute the failure of the Sandys program, was not an absolute shortage in which all Virginians shared and suffered alike. It was a shortage that severely afflicted the company and its dependents, but it furnished large opportunities for private entrepreneurs, and larger ones for company officials who knew how to turn public distress to private profit.

Thoughout the period when too many men were arriving with too few supplies, the established settlers were so eager for more workers that they paid premium wages for them, even when they had to feed as well as pay them. In 1621 the governor and council set maximum wage rates at three shillings a day for ordinary laborers and four shillings for most skilled craftsmen (joiners got five). If the workman was furnished with food for the day, the rate was only a shilling a day less.[58] These figures amount to three or four times the maximum wages of day labor established by county justices in England, where a man who was fed by his employer generally received about half the wage of one who furnished his own food.[59] Food was comparatively less valuable in Virginia than in England.

Daily-wage earners were only a small part of Virginia's labor force. Most workers were either tenants or servants bound for a period of years. Servants were what the planters most wanted. It had been common in England for farmers to hire servants by the year; and as we have seen, employers in many trades were required by law to hire their labor by the year.[60] But servants who wanted to go to Virginia were willing to pledge several years' work, usually four to seven years, in return for transportation and maintenance. If a Virginia planter could import a man from England, the cost of his passage to the colony was about six pounds sterling; his provisions and clothes for the voyage and to start him out in the New World

[58] *WMQ*, 2nd ser., VII (1927), 246; *RVC*, III, 590. Cf. the similar rates set in tobacco in Bermuda in 1623 and 1627. J. H. Lefroy, *Memorials of the Discovery and Early Settlement of the Bermudas or Somers Islands, 1515–1685* (2 vols., London, 1877–79), I, 305.

[59] J. E. T. Rogers, *A History of Agriculture and Prices in England* (6 vols., Oxford, 1866–1900), VI, 632–33, 692–95; S. A. H. Burne, ed., *The Staffordshire Quarter Sessions Rolls*, V (Collections for a History of Staffordshire edited by the Staffordshire Record Society, Kendal, 1940), 259–61, 324–26.

[60] 25 Edward III, c. 2; 3 Edward VI, c. 22; 5 Elizabeth I, c. 4.

might run another four to six pounds.[61] At this rate the cost per year for a servant in Virginia was not much more, and might be less, than in England; for in England, too, masters had to provide food and shelter and sometimes clothing for their bound servants, and a year's pay for an agricultural worker ran from thirty to fifty shillings (there were 20 shillings to the pound) in the first decades of the seventeenth century.[62]

Although the planter or entrepreneur who brought a servant to the New World ran the risk of losing his investment through death, Virginia planters evidently shared Edwin Sandys' belief that the rewards outweighed the risks. Despite the fact that bound servants had to be fed, clothed, and housed, Virginians could not get enough of them. Everybody wanted servants. Even tenants who had been unable to pay their own passage to the colony wanted servants. Richard Berkeley and John Smyth (of Nibley) received from the tenants at their particular plantation a request for two servants apiece "for their owne pryvate benefit and imploymentes." [63] Indeed, as John Pory put it, "our principall wealth . . . consisteth in servants." [64] And after the Virginia Company had been dissolved, former Governor Yeardley, now representing the interests of the colonists, urged the royal commission in charge of the colony "to advance the Plantation for the future by sending great numbers of people." [65]

It would seem, then, that the failure of the Virginia Company should not be blamed entirely on its transportation of too many unequipped settlers. The demise of the company came at a time when the men on the spot were crying for more settlers. If the Virginia Company was a failure, some at least of its colonists were succeeding. And the way they succeeded will bear looking into.

[61] *RVC*, III, 499–500; Neill, *Virginia Carolorum*, 109–11; *VMHB*, XIII (1905–6), 387; Bruce, *Economic History*, I, 629; Bullock, *Virginia Impartially Examined*, 49.

[62] See references in note 59 and Calendar of Essex Quarter Sessions Rolls, XVII, 116.

[63] *RVC*, III, 399. At least two company tenants, Francis Fowler and Thomas Dunthorne, held servants in 1626. See H. R. McIlwaine, ed., *Minutes of the Council and General Court of Colonial Virginia* (Richmond, 1924), 96, 108, 136, 137.

[64] *RVC*, III, 221. It follows that the rising demand ran up the price of servants in Virginia to an amount well above the mere cost of transportation and maintenance.

[65] C.O. 1/3, ff.227–28; *WMQ*, 2nd ser., VIII (1928), 162.

6

BOOM

From what little can be discovered about the value of a man's labor in Virginia in the 1620s, it is not hard to see why the demand for servants was high, even in the face of a food scarcity. At the time when Sandys took over the company and began pouring men into the colony, Virginia had just begun to ship tobacco in quantity to the English market. The prices it brought were considerably lower than those for Spanish tobacco, but high enough to excite the cupidity of every settler. In the colony in 1619 the best grade sold for export at three shillings a pound.[1] In 1623 what reached England was worth no more than half that, and in bartering within the colony (where it had already become the principal medium of exchange) it was said to be valued at less than a shilling a pound.[2] In a lawsuit recorded in 1624 it was reckoned at two shillings a pound, and in 1625 at three shillings again.[3] The boom lasted until 1629 or 1630, when the price tumbled to a penny a pound.[4] Though it recovered somewhat in ensuing years, it never again reached the dizzy heights of the 1620s. During that decade the profits from tobacco were enough to keep all the colonists growing

[1] RVC, III, 162. The figure 3d. given here is an obvious misprint for 3s.

[2] RVC, IV, 264; H. R. McIlwaine, ed., Journals of the House of Burgesses of Virginia, 1619–1658/59 (Richmond, 1915), 24.

[3] Minutes of Council, 33, 43.

[4] Evidence about the exact time of the collapse is scanty, but see VMHB, VII (1899–1900), 382; C.O. 1/8, ff.17–18; C.O. 1/9, ff.248–49; C.O. 1/10, ff.14–17; Lefroy, Memorials of the Discovery and Early Settlement of the Bermudas, I, 479.

as much of it as they could, in spite of every effort to turn them to other products.

By order of the company Virginians were forbidden to raise more than 100 pounds of tobacco apiece, but they paid scant attention to the prohibition and less attention still to producing the silk and potash and other staples that the company had demanded. None of Virginia's prospective commodities stood a chance in competition with the sure thing that the settlers knew tobacco to be. Under its spell Englishmen found that they could work much harder than they had been accustomed to doing and that they could make their servants work even harder. They still would not grow enough corn to feed themselves, but they grew tobacco as though their lives depended on that. As a result, all of Sandys' projects faded away, even when the men sent to conduct them managed to stay alive. Before the massacre put an end to the ironworks, the men sent to run them had already "turned good honest Tobaccoe mongers." [5] The tenants on both the public lands and the particular plantations scorned the various projects assigned them, so that by 1623 it was reported that "nothinge is done in anie one of them but all is vanished into smoke (that is to say into Tobaccoe)." [6]

Without regard to the limitation imposed by the company (which apparently no one did regard), the amount of tobacco one man could produce in a year by his own labor varied from place to place, from year to year, and from man to man. In 1619 John Rolfe, who introduced tobacco cultivation in Virginia, estimated that a man could tend four acres of corn and 1,000 plants of tobacco.[7] Four years later William Capps, an "old planter," said that a man could tend 2,000 plants and that this would make 500 "weight" (presumably 500 pounds) of tobacco. He also maintained that in 1623 three of his boys, whom he calculated as equal to a man and a half, had produced 3,000 weight of tobacco and 110 barrels (550 bushels) of corn.[8] Richard Brewster working with three men was said to have grown 2,800 weight of tobacco and 100 bushels of corn.[9] In 1626 William Spencer testified in court that in 1620 he had overseen the labor of six or seven men who had produced 3,000 or 4,000 weight.[10] The figures differ, perhaps because some of the authors were boasting, because some men worked harder than

---

[5] *RVC*, IV, 141.   [7] Smith, *Travels and Works*, II, 541.
[6] *RVC*, IV, 145.   [8] *RVC*, II, 524; IV, 38.
[9] *Ibid.*   [10] *Minutes of Council*, 99; *RVC*, I, 256, 268.

others, and because tobacco harvests varied sharply from year to year for reasons beyond human control.[11] The amounts are actually much lower than would be normal a few years later, when more experience with the crop had raised Virginians' expectations of the number of plants a man could tend. But by any calculation the financial returns from labor invested in growing tobacco were high. John Pory, after the exceptionally good harvest of 1619, said that one man had cleared £200 sterling by his own labor and another with six servants had cleared £1,000 sterling. These, he admitted, were "rare examples, yet possible to be done by others." [12]

Because of the chances for such profits Virginia in the last years of the company, while a charnel house, was also the first American boom country. There was no gold or silver. A man could not make a fortune by himself. But if he could stay alive and somehow get control of a few servants and keep them alive, he could make more in a year than he was likely to make in several in England. And if he could get a large number of servants, he might indeed make a fortune.

In boom country not everyone strikes it rich; and even those who come in from the hills with a pocketful of gold generally give it up in a hurry—for drink, for women, even for food and clothing at bonanza prices. Life is cheap, but nothing else is. Those who have what gold will buy get the gold a good deal easier and faster than the miners who dig it. And the pleasures and comforts of normal human relationships, the things that gold will not buy, are not to be had at all. Men have come there not to settle down but to make their pile and move on. But the easy-come, easy-go miner generally carries away as little as he carries in.

So it was in Virginia, where tobacco took the place of gold. Virginia's counterpart of the easy-come, easy-go miner was the

---

[11] If we may judge from the English customs records of tobacco imported from Virginia, Bermuda, and Maryland, a good year often produced twice the amount of a poor year and sometimes almost three times the amount. See figures in Neville Williams, "England's Tobacco Trade in the Reign of Charles I," *VMHB*, LXV (1957), 403–49; Stanley Gray and V. J. Wyckoff, "The International Tobacco Trade in the Seventeenth Century," *Southern Economic Journal*, VII (1940), 16–25; *American Historical Review*, XXVII (1921–22), 526; and Elizabeth B. Schumpeter, *English Overseas Trade Statistics, 1697–1808* (Oxford, 1960), 52–55.

[12] *RVC*, III, 221. By the 1640s it was expected that one man's crop might amount to 1,500 or 2,000 pounds, which at 1619 prices would have brought from £225 to £300 per man. See chap. 7, note 40.

small planter who squandered his small crop on the liquor and luxuries that show up in boom towns. "Our Cowe-keeper here of James Citty," wrote John Pory in 1618, "on Sundayes goes acowterd all in fresh flaming silkes and a wife of one that in England had professed the black arte not of a scholler but of a collier of Croydon, weares her rough bever hatt with a faire perle hattband, and a silken suite therto correspondent." [13] The first legislative assembly in Virginia in 1619 felt obliged to pass acts against excess in apparel and also against drunkenness.[14] For it was drink more than clothes that the planters craved. The thirst of Virginians became notorious in England, and the ships that sailed up the James River were heavily freighted with sack and strong waters, even if they neglected to bring more solid fare.[15]

Virginians needed drink, if for nothing else, to solace them for losing the comforts of a settled life. Few were able, like the collier from Croydon, to enjoy the company of a wife. Women were scarcer than corn or liquor in Virginia and fetched a higher price. Seeking to overcome the shortage, the company dispatched shiploads of maids (for whom prospective husbands were expected to pay), but the numbers were not large enough to alter the atmosphere of transience that pervaded the boom country.[16] The lonely men who pressed aboard every ship in the James to drown their cares in drink looked on Virginia "not as a place of Habitacion but onely of a short sojourninge." [17] They would marry and settle down later, somewhere else.

The whole appearance of the settlements, a mere collection of ramshackle hovels, argued that this was only a stopping place. It was a time when Englishmen of all classes were putting up larger and more substantial buildings throughout their own country; [18] and an Englishman's idea of a house was something solid, preferably of brick or stone. If it had to be made of wood, the walls at least should

[13] *RVC*, III, 221.   [14] *RVC*, III, 165.

[15] *RVC*, III, 658, 666; IV, 11, 14, 23, 271–73; *WMQ*, 2nd ser., VII (1927), 247.

[16] *RVC*, I, 256, 269, 566; III, 493; IV, 231. By 1624 the total female population by count, including children, was 244 out of 1,292. In 1625 it was 276 out of 1,210. There are 58 living persons of indeterminable sex in the 1624 list and 14 in the 1625 list. Most of these are children, but some are persons with names like Francis. See Appendix.

[17] *RVC*, I, 566.

[18] W. G. Hoskins, "The Rebuilding of Rural England, 1570–1640," *Past and Present*, No. 4 (1953), 44–59.

be plastered. Visitors to Virginia rightly judged the intentions of the settlers from the way they were content to live: "Their houses standes scattered one from another, and are onlie made of wood, few or none of them beeing framed houses but punches [posts] sett into the Ground And covered with Boardes so as a firebrand is sufficient to consume them all." [19] In fact, it did not even take a firebrand. Virginia "houses" could be kept standing only with difficulty. At Charles City, where the settlers had considered themselves fortunate to be released earlier than others from the company's service, they went on building "such houses as before and in them lived with continual repairs, and buildinge new where the old failed." [20] There was no point in putting up more than a temporary shelter if you did not intend to stay; and as late as 1626 the governing council admitted that what people looked for in Virginia was only "a present Cropp, and their hastie retourne." [21]

The present crop stood in the way of everything else. Although the government required everyone to plant a certain amount of corn, men would risk both prosecution and hunger in order to put their time into tobacco. Even self-preservation came second. After the massacre, when the government adopted a policy of continuous attack against the Indians, it was difficult to get men to leave their crops in order to carry on the war for a few days. When the governor commanded them to go, they would "Crye out of the loss of Tyme," and when a campaign lasted as long as two weeks, they would demand "that they might have leave to retourne, lest it should prove theire utter undoinge." [22] When William Capps, who had had some experience in Indian fighting, volunteered to lead an expedition of forty men, he found that even the governing council was unwilling to spare them. Capps, whose speech comes through vividly in

[19] *RVC*, IV, 259.

[20] *Journals of the House of Burgesses*, 33. Planters who had built houses at Kecoughtan on land later claimed by the company were paid from 70 to 100 pounds of tobacco for them in 1625. At the maximum valuation of 3s. a pound this would make the best house worth £15 (*Minutes of Council*, 41). In spite of the high wages of carpenters in Virginia, this was probably no more than half what an English husbandman's house might be worth. As late as 1642 Governor Berkeley was ordered by the Privy Council to require everyone with 500 acres to build a brick house "and also not suffer men to build slight cottages as heretofore hath been there used. And to remove from place to place, only to plant Tobacco." *VMHB*, II (1894-95), 284, 287.

[21] *RVC*, IV, 572.   [22] *RVC*, IV, 451.

his letters, had his own explanation of the reasons for the council's refusal: "take away one of my men," he pictures them saying to themselves, "there's 2000 Plantes gone, thates 500 waight of Tobacco, yea and what shall this man doe, runne after the Indians? soft, I have perhaps 10, perhaps 15, perhaps 20 men and am able to secure my owne Plantacion; how will they doe that are fewer? let them first be Crusht alitle, and then perhaps they will themselves make up the Nomber for their owne safetie. Theis I doubt are the Cogitacions of some of our worthier men." [23]

As in other booms, a large share of the winnings was carried away by those who supplied the flaming silks and strong waters, by men who had even less intention of settling down than the planters. The ships that anchored in Virginia's great rivers every summer were, as one settler observed, moving taverns,[24] whose masters, usually private traders, got the greater part of the tobacco that should have been enriching the colonists and the shareholders of the company. Since the company had never been able to satisfy the needs of the colonists, it was helpless to prevent them from trading with outsiders, and by 1620 it gave up trying to.[25] Thereafter, the most it could do was to invest its dwindling funds in the magazines, through which still hopeful members tried to recoup some of their losses.

A magazine was supposed to turn a profit by exchanging supplies for tobacco or other commodities, but it became the practice in Virginia to sell for the promise of tobacco when the next crop was in; and somehow the promises were not kept. The floating taverns got the tobacco before it could reach the cape merchant in charge of the magazine, and all magazines seem to have ended with a loss to the investors in England.[26] There were sometimes as many as seventeen sail of ships to be seen at one time in the James River, and the Virginians crowded aboard and drank away their promises and their profits. Anything that smelled of alcohol would sell, and the governor and council complained bitterly of the "rates which unconscionable marchantes and maryners doe impose uppon our necessities . . . especyally of rotten Wynes which destroy our bodies and empty our purses." [27] One trader even "boasted that the only sale of fower buttes of wyne would be Sufficyent to clere the whole Vioage." [28]

---

[23] *RVC*, IV, 38.   [24] Smith, *Travels and Works*, I, 103–4.
[25] *RVC*, I, 303; III, 362.
[26] *RVC*, II, 52, 218–19; III, 502–5; IV, 14, 23.
[27] *RVC*, IV, 453.   [28] *Ibid.*; cf. III, 528, 658–59; IV, 11.

The private traders from abroad were not the only ones who seized the commercial opportunities of the boom. Complaints reached England against Virginians who got to the ships first and engrossed the commodities most in demand, to sell at monopoly prices.[29] And after the massacre, when corn was at its scarcest, those who had boats and could get a commission from the governor were able to bring back hundreds of bushels from the Chesapeake region, some of it bought, some of it stolen, some of it taken by force from the Indians there. At the price of corn then prevailing in Jamestown, these voyages to the Chesapeake must have been highly profitable, and there were charges that the chief men of the colony were only too willing to prolong the scarcity by discouraging or forbidding the planting of corn. As long as the shortage lasted, "they onely haveing the means in these extremities to Trade for Corne with the Natives doe hereby engrosse all into their hands and soe sell itt abroad att their owne prizes. . . ."[30]

In the winter of 1622–23 English meal was selling at thirty shillings the bushel and Indian corn at ten to fifteen shillings. By April even Indian corn was at twenty to thirty shillings "and non to bee had but with great men."[31] The officers of the colony claimed that corn actually sold at only ten pounds of tobacco a bushel.[32] But even at that rate a man who accumulated a thousand bushels of corn on a short trip to the Chesapeake region would be able to trade it for 10,000 pounds of tobacco, worth from £500 to £1,000 sterling.

Although Sir Edwin Sandys had been bent on profit for the company's investors, profiteering, whether by residents or transients, had been no part of his plans for Virginia. He had hoped to build a community without want and without oppression. Ironically, his concentration on getting men across the water played into the hands of local profiteers who engrossed not only goods but men. Virginia differed from later American boom areas in that success depended not on acquiring the right piece of land, but on acquiring men. Land that would grow tobacco was everywhere, so abundant that people frequently did not bother at first to secure patents for the amounts they were entitled to.[33] Instead, men rushed to stake out claims to

---

[29] *RVC*, III, 504, 703–4; IV, 261.   [30] *RVC*, II, 375; IV, 186, 234.

[31] *RVC*, IV, 89, 231, 234.

[32] *Journals of the House of Burgesses*, 24.

[33] This is evident from any comparison of the dates of patents with the dates of transportation of persons for which headrights were claimed. When Abraham Peirsey made his will in March, 1626/7, he had not yet

men, stole them, lured them, fought over them—and bought and sold them, bidding up the prices to four, five, and six times the initial cost.[34] The company's program obligingly poured men into Virginia for the scramble.

Since the number of older, seasoned servants was limited not only by the high death rate but also by completion of their terms of servitude, it was mainly the newcomers under the Sandys program whose labor enriched the aggressive and enterprising traders and planters. At first sight it might seem that the death rate among the new arrivals (even higher than among men who had survived their first year in the country) was so great as to nullify any advantages to those who sought to exploit them. But the records show that enough of them survived to make up almost the whole labor force and also the vast majority of the population of Virginia by 1625. The muster of inhabitants taken in January and February of that year gives the date of arrival in the colony for 740 of the 1,210 living persons listed.[35] Of the 740, only 110 had come to Virginia before 1618.[36] The muster list also reveals that among the fifteen planters who held ten or more servants, or "men," in 1625, only two servants out of 199 whose arrival dates are known had come before 1618.[37]

The bondage of the men sent under the Sandys program was

---

taken up land for the servants he had transported since 1620. Neill, *Virginia Carolorum*, 404.

[34] Smith, *Travels and Works*, II, 618; *RVC*, IV, 235.

[35] A convenient breakdown of the information in the muster about numbers of cattle and supplies listed for each household is in *VMHB*, VII (1899–1900), 364-67, but this does not analyze dates of arrival or ages, and some of the figures are incorrect. A more detailed analysis is Irene W. D. Hecht, "The Virginia Muster of 1624/5 as a Source for Demographic History," *WMQ*, 3rd ser., XXX (1973), 65-92. My own analysis, which was made before this appeared, differs slightly from hers. See Appendix, note 3. The muster was evidently taken by various people who did not all put down the same kinds of information. The dates of arrival are complete for some plantations; others show no dates at all; and still others show dates for some names but not for others. It seems safe to assume that the 740 are roughly typical of the remaining 470, who include, however, a number of children born in the colony.

[36] The rest had come as follows: 1618, 59; 1619, 78; 1620, 124; 1621, 114; 1622, 95; 1623, 117; 1624, 43.

[37] I have not counted the few children of servants, but I have included the few wives, and I have assumed that "men," presumably tenants, were under the control of the person under whose name they are listed.

of several kinds. Seemingly the most advantageous status was that of tenant. Although tenants were under the supervision of agents sent by the company or by the association that founded a particular plantation, they were entitled to returns on half of what they earned. Ordinary bond servants, on the other hand, belonged completely to their master: he got everything they earned and had only to supply them with food, clothing, and shelter during their term of service. The least attractive form of servitude was apprenticeship. Apprentices, often known as "Duty Boys" from the name of the ship (the *Duty*) on which some of them were transported, were bound as servants for seven years under any planters who would pay ten pounds apiece for them. After their seven years' service, they were to be tenants for another seven years. If, however, a Duty Boy committed a crime at any time during the first seven years, his term as a servant was to begin again for another seven years.[38]

Probably the majority of men sent under the Sandys program were tenants. The particular plantations were supposed to be manned by tenants, as were the company lands. And the men sent to support the various offices of government were also tenants. But the difference between a tenant and a servant in boom-time Virginia was not easy to discern. The company's generosity to its officers combined with the high death rate to lay open every surviving tenant sent by the company to exploitation by any officer who claimed him as part of his quota of tenants. And if an officer did not commandeer him, someone else would. Whether a man came as a servant, as an apprentice, as a tenant, or on his own he was vulnerable. If death disposed of the master who could rightly claim his labor, an heir, real or fraudulent, would quickly lay hold of him. Or if, having paid his own transportation, he arrived in Virginia without a master but also without enough provisions, he was easy prey for anyone who could feed and shelter him. Even if he came with enough to set himself up independently, a bad harvest, insurmountable debts, or Indian depredations might force him into the service of a bigger operator. This was particularly true after the massacre, when it was reported that ordinary men who had made a start on their own were obliged, for fear of the Indians, "to forsake their houses (which were very farre scattered) and to joyne themselves to some great mans plantation."[39]

[38] *RVC*, I, 270–71, 293, 304–7, 411–12, 424, 520; III, 259; *Minutes of Council*, 117.

[39] *VMHB*, LXXI (1963), 410.

Some planters were not above ransoming captives from the Indians in order to claim their labor. Jane Dickenson and her husband, Ralph, were tenants of Nicholas Hide, when Ralph was killed in the massacre of 1622 and Jane carried into captivity. After some time Dr. John Pott, the physician who had been sent to Virginia at company expense, ransomed Jane for two pounds of glass beads. Ten months after her deliverance she complained to the governor and council that she was held in a servitude that "differeth not from her slavery with the Indians," Dr. Pott alleging that she was "linked to his servitude with a towefold Chaine the one for her late husbands obligation [to Hide] and thother for her ransome, of both which shee hopeth that in Conscience shee ought to be discharged, of the first by her widdowhood, of the second by the law of nations, Considering shee hath already served teen months, tow much for two pound of beades." [40] Other complaints reached London that "divers old Planters and others did allure and beguile divers younge persons and others (ignorant and unskillfull in such matters) to serve them upon intollerable and unchristianlike conditions upon promises of such rewardes and recompence, as they were no wayes able to performe nor ever meant." [41]

Among the worst offenders were the company's own officials in the colony. In Sandys' shipments of men bound to the company, they had perceived an opportunity for exploiting not only the tenants but the company itself. The fact that the men arrived without adequate provisions furnished an excuse for treating tenants as servants.[42] Instead of being seated on company lands where they were supposed to clear, fence, plant, and build, the tenants were hired out to private planters, like the fifty men who arrived "lusty and well" on the *Bona Nova*.[43] Although the officers reported that they hired out the sickly rather than the able-bodied, the company got word that it was the other way round: the strongest men, who might have benefited the company most, were put to work on private plantations. And "where it is pretended this placinge them with old planters is for theire health, they are so unmercifully used that it is the

[40] *RVC*, IV, 473.   [41] *RVC*, II, 113; cf. II, 442.

[42] The officers also cited the lack of housing. But the company had repeatedly ordered the construction of guesthouses to quarter newcomers until they could build houses of their own. The officers in the colony regularly found excuses to evade the orders. *RVC*, III, 489, 493, 532.

[43] *RVC*, III, 479, 489. The same hiring out of tenants by those to whom they were entrusted apparently also occurred in Bermuda. Lefroy, *Memorials*, I, 165.

greatest cause of our Tenntes discontent. . . ." [44] Thus while company men labored on the lands of private planters, company land went uncleared, unfenced, and unplanted. It would be difficult to believe that the company officials perceived no personal advantage in this situation.

The hiring out of some tenants should have meant more food for those who remained in the company's care. Apparently, however, the hired men's share of provisions was converted to private uses; [45] and the men who continued as company tenants were deprived even of the supplies intended for them. Whatever the company sent the officers appropriated, and gave the tenants only Indian corn and water,[46] a diet not calculated to speed the recovery of men weakened by a long voyage. But malnutrition and the diseases consequent upon it were not the only reasons for the low productivity of the company men. According to one dissatisfied London investor, the reason the company tenants accomplished so little was that "the officers Tenantes were cheifely reguarded and the generall Companies Tenantes the more neglected," [47] by which he probably meant that the officers made it their business to get a day's work out of their own assigned tenants but not out of the rest. Moreover, John Pory reported to the company in 1624, the officers were seating the men assigned to their offices "on their private Lands, not upon that [that] belongeth to their office," so that the crop produced on these private lands of the officers "alwaies exceeds yours"; and since the land set aside for officers lay "unmanured [48] to any purpose" it would yield little profit to the succeeding officers. The existing ones, Pory added, used the company's tenants "to row them up and downe, whereby both you and they lose more then halfe." [49]

It is only fair to add that what the company wanted for Virginia probably could not have been achieved by even the most faithful and assiduous of officers. The company wanted a stable, diversified society, where men would make reasonable profits and live ordinary, reasonable lives. It was Virginia's misfortune in the last years of the company to offer opportunities for profit that were much more than reasonable.

The men who seized the opportunities and captured the labor of Virginia's perishing immigrants are not difficult to identify. In Janu-

---

[44] *RVC*, III, 489.   [47] *RVC*, I, 456–57.
[45] *Ibid.*   [48] I.e., uncultivated.
[46] *RVC*, IV, 175.
[49] Smith, *Travels and Works*, II, 571; cf. *RVC*, III, 479.

ary and February, 1625, a muster of the inhabitants indicated the names and numbers of every man's "men," or servants, including both tenants and genuine servants.[50] The fifteen who had ten or more may be taken as the winners in the servant sweepstakes:

Ralph Hamor	10
John Pott	12
Edward Bennett	12
William Epps	13
Roger Smith	14
William Barry	15
Edward Blaney	17
William Peirce	17
Francis Wyatt	17
William Tucker	17
Daniel Gookin	20
Samuel Mathews	23
George Sandys	37
George Yeardley	39
Abraham Peirsey	39

Some of these men may have won fair and square; about several of them we know very little.[51] But the careers of the others make it a

[50] See note 35 and Appendix. The number of persons employing ten or more servants in Virginia, with a living population of a little over 1,200 in 1625, was almost as large as in the English county of Gloucestershire in 1608, where the total population was probably more than 50,000 (men aged 20 to 60 amounted to 19,402). See A. J. and R. H. Tawney, "An Occupational Census of the Seventeenth Century," *Economic History Review*, V (1934–35), 25–64.

[51] Wyatt, who served as governor, 1621–26, and Peirce seem to have made their way without eliciting complaints. Bennett, a Puritan merchant of London and Amsterdam, came to Virginia only after the dissolution of the company and did not remain. His estate was built up through the efforts of his brother Robert, who sold provisions at prices that drew protests (J. B. Boddie, *Seventeenth-Century Isle of Wight County* [Chicago, 1938], 34–53; *RVC*, IV, 453). Gookin too was in Virginia only briefly, though his sons and overseers seem to have done very well for him (F. W. Gookin, *Daniel Gookin, 1612–1687* [Chicago, 1912], 38–48). Barry and Smith were agents of the company, and most of the men listed under their names were probably company tenants and not appropriated to private profit (*RVC*, I, 433; *Minutes of Council*, 78, 90). Samuel Mathews was to play a prominent role in the colony in the 1630s and 1640s. He married Peirsey's widow and by 1638 boasted the best estate in the country (Massachusetts Historical Society, *Collections*, 4th ser., IX [1871], 136n; *VMHB*, I [1893–94], 187–88; XI [1903–4], 170–82). Epps, described both as "a mad ranting fellow" and as "a proper yong man," killed another man in a drunken brawl in 1619 and was charged with adultery in 1627. He became a leading figure on the

question whether we should call them labor barons or robber barons. It would be tedious to pile up the evidence about each of them, but a few simple facts may be suggestive.

The front-runner, Abraham Peirsey, with thirty-nine servants, though probably from a high-ranking English family, had been "a verie poore man" when he came to Virginia in 1616 as the cape merchant in charge of the company's magazine. Although he sold goods at two or three times the prices set by the investors, the magazine, under his direction, showed a loss, and in 1626 he had not yet paid the investors for the goods sold. But when he died two years later, he "left the best Estate that was ever yett knowen in Virginia." [52] Edward Blaney succeeded Peirsey as cape merchant in 1620. At his death in 1626 he too had not paid for the goods he sold, but he had acquired seventeen servants. He had also succeeded in embezzling a fair amount by marrying a widow and successfully claiming an estate left by a man with the same surname as his wife's first husband, a trick played by a number of quick-witted Virginians at the death of a stranger who happened to bear the same surname. [53] George Sandys, treasurer of the colony, having failed to receive the full quota of tenants assigned to his office, simply appropriated sixteen company tenants as his servants. Although for some time before his departure for England in 1625 he refused to execute his

---

Eastern Shore, but by 1633 he had moved to St. Christopher (*VMHB*, LXV [1957], 313–27; *RVC*, III, 121, 242; *Minutes of Council*, 48, 50, 91, 140, 148; Northampton I, 9, 21, 67, 116, 163–64).

[52] *Minutes of Council*, 118; *RVC*, I, 333; II, 219; *VMHB*, I (1893–94), 187; XI (1903–4), 175–82; C.O. 1/8, ff.15–18. In spite of his initial poverty, Peirsey was evidently well connected, perhaps with the Earl of Northumberland, whose brother, George Percy, has already figured in these pages. It was probably through this connection that Abraham Peirsey got the job as cape merchant. His social standing is suggested by the fact that he was able to marry in 1625 the widow of Captain Nathaniel West, brother of Lord De la Warr (who married a first cousin of Queen Elizabeth). The Virginia estate left by Peirsey was appraised at only 60,000 pounds of tobacco, but it is likely that his widow's jointure was not included in this.

[53] *RVC*, III, 449, 503–4, 526; IV, 106–7, 111, 263–65; *Minutes of Council*, 93, 121. Blaney evidently married the widow of William Powell. The widow brought with her an estate of which her husband had taken possession on the basis of his name, after the owner, Captain Nathaniel Powell, died in the massacre of 1622. Captain Nathaniel Powell was actually no relation to William Powell, and Nathaniel Powell's surviving brother, Thomas Powell, was trying to recover the estate from Blaney at the time of the latter's death (*VMHB*, XVI [1907–8], 30–31; C.O. 1/4, f.36).

office (the commission having expired), he continued to hold the tenants in bondage. One of them, listed in the muster as a freeman, wrote to a friend, "he maketh us serve him whether wee will or noe and how to helpe yt we doe not knowe for hee beareth all the sway." [54]

William Tucker, who may originally have been a ship captain, probably came to Virginia between 1617 and 1619.[55] Sometime before 1622 he was entrusted by John Ferrar and associates with £900 worth of goods to sell in Virginia, for which, like other Virginia factors, he failed to deliver either cash or accounts.[56] He was one of the men commissioned to trade with the Indians for corn in 1622–23 and was also empowered to negotiate peace with the Pamunkeys of the Potomac River area. His methods of dealing we have already noted in his poisoning of two hundred Pamunkeys with wine brought for that purpose, which he gave them to drink in celebration of the peace treaty he pretended to conclude with them.[57] By 1632 the assembly was finding his attitude toward his fellow Virginians unsatisfactory and objected to the Privy Council about merchants "who have by needlesse and unprofitable Commodities . . . ingaged the inhabitants in debts of Tobacco, to the value almost of theire ensuinge croppe . . . amonge whome we have good cause to complayne of Captayne *Tucker*, who hath farr exceeded all other marchaunts in the prizes of theire goods . . ." [58]

Ralph Hamor, though he wrote one of the most effective pamphlets in praise of Virginia, got off to a slow start or else lost heavily in the massacre. In 1623, when other men were already getting rich, George Sandys observed that "Captain Hamor is miserablie poore and necessitie will inforce him to shiftes." [59] The shifts to which he resorted included trading with the Indians and selling English goods

[54] Lefroy, *Memorials*, I, 264; *VMHB*, VII (1899–1900), 259; C.O. 1/4, f.111. See in general R. B. Davis, *George Sandys, Poet-Adventurer* (New York, 1955).

[55] He invested in the company in 1617, and in 1619 he represented Kecoughtan in the House of Burgesses, *RVC*, III, 58, 154, 535.

[56] *RVC*, II, 104.

[57] *RVC*, IV, 221–22; *WMQ*, 2nd ser., VII (1927), 206–7.

[58] *Journals of the House of Burgesses*, 55–56. See also Governor Harvey's complaints against him, *VMHB*, VIII (1900–1901), 149–50. Tucker was not slow to perceive the danger of Dutch competition to his high profits. He did his best to secure from the government in England a prohibition of Dutch trading in Virginia (*ibid.*, 154; C.O. 1/6, ff.135, 207–12).

[59] *RVC*, IV, 110–11.

at prices that brought accusations of extortion.[60] By 1625, with ten men growing tobacco for him, he was far from poor.

Dr. John Pott seems to have been more assiduous in pursuit of cattle and servants than of his duties as physican. In 1623 George Sandys dismissed him as a mere cipher,[61] but by 1628 he was acting governor. According to his successor, Governor Harvey, he took advantage of the position to advance his private interest "by foule and coveteous ways," in particular "by cuting out the markes of other mens neate cattell and markinge them for himselfe with his owne handes, whereby he hath gotten into a greate stock of cattell." Harvey pardoned him because of the colony's need for his services as a physician and because Harvey found his delinquencies to have been in imitation of "the example of a former governor who passed unquestioned for many notable oppressions." [62]

The former governor to whom Harvey referred was probably George Yeardley, who had found Virginia a rewarding environment from the beginning. According to John Pory, when Yeardley arrived there in 1610, he carried with him nothing more valuable than a sword.[63] But when he visited London in 1617, after his first term as governor of Virginia, he was able "out of his meer gettings here" to spend "very near three thousand poundes." Before returning to the colony he got himself knighted, and Londoners observed that "he flaunts yt up and downe the streets in extraordinarie braverie, with fowreteen or fifteen fayre liveries after him." [64]

Yeardley, when appointed governor in 1618, was assigned 3,000 acres of land and 100 tenants plus 30 more in 1620 to make up for deaths among the first group.[65] When Yeardley gave up the governorship in 1621, he turned over only 46 tenants. The governor's council, which now included Yeardley, wrote to the company in London that "as for the rest of the Tenantes Sir George yardley denieth to make them good, And sayeth that havinge made noe

---

[60] *WMQ*, 2nd ser., VII (1927), 204–5, 212, 254; *Minutes of Council*, 48, 132, 135.

[61] *RVC*, IV, 110.

[62] Hening, I, 145–46; C.O. 1/6, ff.36–43; *VMHB*, VII (1899–1900), 378, 381, 382–85; VIII (1900–1901), 33–35; Massachusetts Historical Society, *Collections*, 4th ser., IX (1871), 143n–144n.

[63] *RVC*, III, 221.

[64] John Chamberlain to Sir Dudley Carleton, Nov. 28, 1618. SP 14/103 (Public Record Office); *New England Historic Genealogical Register*, XXXVIII (1884), 70.

[65] *RVC*, I, 268, 332; III, 471.

strong Agrement with you at any tyme he holdeth nott him selfe tyed unto yt, And therfore should take it for a matter of great Injustice to bee Compelled therunto." [66] Yeardley, whom William Capps characterized as a "right worthie Statesman, for his owne profit," [67] did not give up his tenants, and the records contain accusations against him of appropriating servants belonging to other planters and of keeping as a servant a young man whose relatives had paid his way.[68] He remained nevertheless a member of the council and was again serving as governor when he died in 1627. He was one of those commissioned to trade for corn after the massacre of 1622 and was accused by one settler of discouraging the planting of corn, the word being "that Sir G. Yardlie should provide them Corne if they would provide Tobacco." [69] He did, in fact, provide the corn, 1,000 bushels in January, 1623, alone.[70] At his death Yeardley's estate was apparently valued at only about £10,000.[71] But it is not unlikely that he had already transferred much of what he owned to his wife and children in order to circumvent the litigation that a substantial will often produced.[72]

It seems evident that while the Virginia Company was failing in London, a number of its officers in the colony were growing rich. In order to do so, they not only rendered less than faithful service to their employers; they also reduced other Virginians to a condition which, while short of slavery, was also some distance from the freedom that Englishmen liked to consider as their birthright. The company in 1618 had inaugurated a popularly elected representative assembly, but the effective power remained in the governor and his council.[73] By no coincidence, the council consisted almost entirely

[66] *RVC*, III, 584-85.

[67] *RVC*, IV, 37. Capps's opinion was shared by the Earl of Dorset, who blamed the ruin of Southampton Hundred to Yeardley's "being a man wholy adicted to his private." Dorset to Governor John Harvey, Aug., 1629. Sackville Mss., Library of Congress microfilm (British Manuscripts Project, reel K334).

[68] *RVC*, II, 113, 119; IV, 510-14.

[69] *RVC*, IV, 186.   [70] *RVC*, IV, 9-10.

[71] *Tyler's Quarterly Historical and Genealogical Magazine*, II (1921), 121.

[72] His sons Francis and Argall later cut a large figure in Norfolk and Northampton counties.

[73] Even the assembly showed itself to be a meeting of masters, when the first session, in 1619, adopted measures to secure every man's right to

of the men holding large numbers of servants. Between 1619 and 1627 Hamor, Pott, Peirsey, Sandys, Tucker, Mathews, and Yeardley sat on it, while Wyatt and Yeardley took turns in the governor's chair. These men, with a more than average interest in controlling the labor force, were thus enabled to maintain their personal ascendancy not only over their servants but over all lesser men. Whether operating under the company or, after 1625, under the king, they met every challenge to their authority with a rigor not exceeded by what we know of the earlier absolute government of John Smith or Thomas Dale.

In May, 1624, when they discovered that Richard Barnes had uttered "base and detracting" speeches against the governor, they ordered that he "be disarmed, and have his armes broken and his tongue bored through with a awl. shall pass through a guard of 40 men and shalbe butted by every one of them, and att the head of the troope kicked downe and footed out of the fort: that he shalbe banished out of *James Cittye* and the Iland, that he shall not be capable of any priviledge of freedome of the countery, and that (before he goe out of the Iland) he shall put in suretyes of £200 bond for the good behaviour."[74] When John Heny was reprimanded by Captain Tucker for going aboard a ship contrary to the governor's command, Heny made the mistake of saying, after Tucker had left, that Tucker "would be the death of him as he was of *Robert leyster.*" For these words, reported to the council, Heny got sixty stripes and had to beg forgiveness of Tucker, pay him 100 pounds of tobacco, and be imprisoned until he could give bond for good behaviour.[75]

Heny's offense came at a time when the council had also heard of murmurs against their execution of Richard Cornish, a shipmaster, for sodomy. There is no record of the execution, but some of the testimony in the case was recorded, and there can be no doubt that the execution took place.[76] Afterwards, on a voyage to Canada, one

his servants. As protection against servants' fraudulently claiming freedom, it ordered the establishment of a registry of all servants in the colony and of all that should come in the future, with the dates of expiration of their terms. It also decreed that if a servant, before leaving England, contracted to serve one master in Virginia and then contracted to serve another (who perhaps made a more attractive offer), he should serve two full terms, one with each master (*RVC*, III, 167, 171, 174).

[74] *Minutes of Council*, 14.   [75] *Ibid.*, 85.
[76] See references to case, *ibid.*, 34, 42, 47, 81, 83, 85.

Edward Nevell met up with Cornish's brother, and upon the latter's inquiry as to how the execution came about, Nevell replied, "he was put to death through a scurvie boys meanes, and no other came against him." For this statement, made aboard ship off Canada where the governing council of Virginia could scarcely claim jurisdiction, Nevell upon his return to Virginia was required to "stand one the pillory with a paper one his head shewinge the cause of his offence in the markett place, and to loose both his Ears and to serve the Colony for A yeere, And forever to be incapable to be A ffreeman of the Countrey." [77] A month later Thomas Hatch was heard to say in a private house in James City "that in his consyence he thought the said Cornishe was put to death wrongfully." Hatch had the misfortune to be a Duty Boy, and his seven-year period of service was nearly up. The court therefore ordered "that *Thomas Hatch* for his offence shalbe whipt from the forte to the gallows and from thence be whipt back againe, and be sett uppon the Pillory and there to loose one of his eares, And that his service to Sir *George Yardley* for seaven years Shalbegain [again] from the present dye." [78]

The councillors not only guarded their authority jealously, and perhaps unconstitutionally, but not infrequently they wielded it on their own behalf, participating in decisions that favored their interests. Sandys sat at a meeting in which Luke Eden was seeking payment of twenty bushels of corn due him from Sandys. Whether Eden got the corn is not recorded, but he did get himself fined 200 pounds of tobacco and laid neck and heels "for his lewd behavior and unreverent speche" toward Sandys in the council chamber.[79] Wyatt participated in a judgment that awarded him a Negro servant "notwithstanding, any sale by Capt. *Jonnes* to Capt. *Bass,* or any other chaleng by the ships company" (Captain Jones had brought a privateer into the James for provisions and apparently considered the servant part of the ship's booty).[80] Abraham Peirsey sat at a meeting that had Richard Crocker put in the pillory with his ears nailed for saying that Peirsey and Hamor were not fit to sit on the council because "they deale uppon nothing but extortion." [81] Yeardley sat at a meeting that ordered the execution of a man for killing a calf of Yeardley's and at another meeting that awarded him as tenants all the Duty Boys who had finished their terms as servants.[82] He also participated in sentencing John Radish to lie neck

[77] *Ibid.*, 85. [79] *Ibid.*, 57. [81] *Ibid.*, 135–36.
[78] *Ibid.*, 93. [80] *Ibid.*, 66–68, 73. [82] *Ibid.*, 4–5, 154.

and heels, because Radish "Caryed over Sir *George Yardley* his servants to his house at unsesonable tyme of the night and there gave them Entertainment and made them drunke." [83]

It was apparently not without reason that ordinary men grumbled at the government. In the words of William Tyler, "nether the Governor nor Counsell could or would doe any poore men right, but that they would shew favor to great men and wronge the poore." [84]

It may be contended that severe discipline was necessary in a colony consisting predominantly of lusty young men who had just shaken loose the fetters of home and country. And it must be acknowledged that the men entrusted with government did protect some of the rights of servants. When a master failed to teach an indentured apprentice his trade or when he sought to hold a servant beyond the term of his indenture, the council might interfere. Dr. Pott was ordered by a meeting at which he was himself present either to teach his apprentice the art of an apothecary (which he was neglecting to do) or else pay him wages. [85]

Nevertheless, serious differences made servitude in Virginia more onerous than servitude in England. The ordinary term of service that a man agreed to work in Virginia was not a year but several years; and the wages to which he was entitled had been paid in advance in the form of transportation across the ocean. Almost all servants were therefore in a condition resembling that of the least privileged type of English servant, the parish apprentice, a child who (to relieve the community of supporting him) was bound to service by court order, until he was twenty-one or twenty-four, with no obligation on his appointed master's part to teach him a trade or pay him. In Virginia a master had little reason to treat his servant well in order to obtain a renewal of his services at the expiration of his term; and a servant had little reason to work hard in order to assure being rehired, because men would not bind themselves out for a second long term when they could make more by working for themselves. There was accordingly the more reason for a master to assert his authority in order to get what he considered a full quota of work from his servants. Not surprisingly, it was reported in England that Virginians "abuse their servantes there with intollerable oppression and hard usage." [86]

Hard usage for a servant in Virginia doubtless included working harder and more continuously than Englishmen were used to

[83] *Ibid.*, 58.   [84] *Ibid.*, 19.   [85] *Ibid.*, 117.   [86] *RVC*, II, 442.

working. Although later generations of servants would be made to tend five or six times the number of tobacco plants that the servants of the 1620s tended, the work seemed more onerous and more unrelenting than the intermittent labor of the English farmer; and masters bent on profit "corrected" their laggard, hungry, and diseased servants with barbarous punishments.

The records are not sufficiently complete to show how extensive the abuse may have been, but the council in Virginia (until 1634 the only court) supported masters in severities that would not have been allowed in England. The most extreme example is the case of John and Alice Proctor and their servants Elizabeth Abbott and Elias Hinton, both of whom died after a series of beatings inflicted by the Proctors and by other servants acting under orders from the Proctors.[87] Thomas Gates testified that he counted five hundred lashes inflicted on the girl at one time and warned Proctor that he might as well kill her and be done with it. Alice Bennett, who examined her, "fownd she had been sore beaten and her body full of sores and holes very dangerously raunckled and putrified both above her wast and uppon her hips and thighes." Other witnesses testified that Proctor beat Hinton with a rake. Yet there is no indication that the Proctors were punished. Even the compassionate witnesses who testified against them indicated that when the maid came to them for shelter they had instead returned her to her master and mistress in her half-dead condition, with entreaties that they pardon her! By contrast, we find English courts undertaking the work of correcting unruly servants themselves (as the statutes required) and even on occasion forbidding masters to do it.[88]

Whether physically abused or not, Englishmen found servitude in Virginia more degrading than servitude in England. In England the hiring of workers was dignified by laws and customs that gave a servant some control over his own life. He had to give his master three months' notice if he intended to leave at the end of his term; and in order to move from one place to another he must have a testimonial that his term of service was finished. But by the same token, a master could not turn away a servant before his term was up and must give him three months' advance notice that his contract would not be renewed.[89] Once a year, in the petty sessions held by the constables, servants could renew their contracts or make new ones, with

---

[87] *Minutes of Council,* 22–24.
[88] Sachse, *Minutes of the Norwich Court of Mayoralty, XV,* 90.
[89] 5 Elizabeth I, c. 4, par. 4, 7.

the constables recording the transaction. These sessions, usually held in a churchyard, came to be known as hiring fairs and constituted a kind of open labor market, where workmen sold their annual services.[90] But in Virginia it was the masters who sold the workmen, and there was no annual hiring fair. Masters bought and sold servants at any time for any period of years covered by their transportation contracts; and during that period a servant might find himself sold without his own consent from one master to another. In 1633 a Dutch sea captain found the planters gambling at cards with their servants as stakes.[91] Virginians dealt in servants the way Englishmen dealt in land or chattels.

This development was a simple outgrowth of the extreme demand for labor in combination with the long terms of service that were exacted for transportation to Virginia. In England itself, after labor became more valuable, the demand produced a certain amount of buying and selling of industrial apprentices. When a man had more apprentices than he needed, he might with the permission of his guild sell an apprentice to another master of the guild.[92] But industrial apprentices were a special case, and the idea of a large-scale market in men, or at least in English men, was shocking to Englishmen. "My Master Atkins," wrote Thomas Best from Virginia in 1623, "hath sold me for a £150 sterling like a damnd slave."[93] This "buying and selling men and boies" had already become a scandal by 1619, when John Rolfe noted that it "was held in *England* a thing most intolerable."[94] Captain John Smith denounced the "pride, covetousnesse, extortion, and oppression" of men who sold "even men, women and children for who will give most." It would be better, he said, that these profiteers be "made such merchandize themselves,

[90] M. G. Davies, *The Enforcement of English Apprenticeship* (Cambridge, Mass., 1962), 191, 196–97, 233. There are records of some of these petty sessions in the typescript Calendar of Essex Quarter Sessions Rolls. A good contemporary description is in Henry Best, *Rural Economy in Yorkshire in 1641*, Surtees Society, *Publications*, XXXIII (1857), 134–36.

[91] New-York Historical Society, *Collections*, 2nd ser., III (1857), 36.

[92] O. G. Dunlop, *English Apprenticeship and Child Labor* (London, 1912), 57–58, 127–29.

[93] *RVC*, IV, 235. If the figure is correct and Atkins bore the initial expense of transportation and support, he must have made a profit of several hundred percent on the transaction. The original letter does not survive. The quotation is from a contemporary transcript in the Manchester Papers (P.R.O.), in which it is likely that the scribe erred.

[94] Smith, *Travels and Works*, II, 542.

then suffered any longer to use that trade." [95] And in 1625 Thomas Weston refused to carry servants in his ship from Canada to Virginia, because "servants were sold heere upp and downe like horses, and therfore he held it not lawfull to carie any." [96]

Other shipmasters were not so scrupulous, and the dissolution of the Virginia Company brought no end to the market in men or to their importation. So much did the planters count on continued importations that the council during the 1620s awarded as yet unarrived, unknown, and unnamed servants to the victors in lawsuits.[97] A servant, by going to Virginia, became for a number of years a thing, a commodity with a price. Although the government might protect him against continuation in this status beyond the time agreed upon, it was not likely to shorten his term or give him his freedom, even if his master's crimes against him were serious enough to warrant the death penalty. The servant who was the victim of Richard Cornish's homosexual attack did not win his freedom by his master's execution. Even though no other man had a legal claim to his service, the court decreed that he must choose another master, who in return was to compensate the government for the costs of prosecuting Cornish.[98] A servant in Virginia, as long as his term had not expired, was a machine to make tobacco for somebody else.

In boom-time Virginia, then, we can see not only the fleeting ugliness of private enterprise operating temporarily without check, not only greed magnified by opportunity, producing fortunes for a few and misery for many. We may also see Virginians beginning to move toward a system of labor that treated men as things. In order to make the most out of the high price of tobacco it was necessary to get hard work out of Englishmen who were not used to giving it. The boom produced, and in some measure depended upon, a tightening of labor discipline beyond what had been known in England and probably beyond what had been formerly known in Virginia.

That the masters of Virginia could maintain such power over the colony's work force was due not only to their magisterial backing but to the difficulty of escape from the colony. The nearest European settlements were those of the Dutch hundreds of miles to the north at New Amsterdam and of the Spanish hundreds of miles to the south in Florida. After 1620 there was a small English colony in New England and after 1630 a larger one, but these lay even more

[95] *Ibid.*, 618.
[96] *Minutes of Council*, 82.
[97] *Ibid.*, 181.
[98] *Ibid.*, 47.

perilous miles away. When Maryland was founded in 1633 at a less terrifying distance for a small stolen boat, it did become a refuge of sorts for discontented Virginians. But in the 1620s a servant's choice was work or flight to a wilderness populated by savages. After the abrogation of the *Lawes Divine, Morall and Martiall* in 1618, a man no longer invited the death penalty by going native. And doubtless some did just that. But the growth of a special feeling about Indians gave men pause and made this avenue of escape less feasible and less and less attractive.

It is difficult to identify the first stirrings of racial hatred in Virginia. Englishmen had always had their share of xenophobia, and national consciousness shades easily into racial consciousness. But something more than nationalism or xenophobia seems to have affected English relations with the Indians from the beginning. When Englishmen at Roanoke react to the alleged theft of a silver cup by burning a village, we suspect that more than meets the eye is involved. And when Englishmen at Jamestown throw Indian children in the water and shoot out their brains, we suspect that they might not have done the same with French or Spanish children. George Thorpe was disturbed by the scorn in which his fellow white Virginians held the Indians, a scorn that also sounds like racism. After the massacre of 1622 the government's policy of extermination and the continuing guerrilla warfare between natives and settlers combined to encourage race hatred in both.

Hatred of the Indians, fed on fear, probably affected all white Virginians; and the more it grew the less likely it became that servants would wish to leave their servitude, however severe, for freedom among the Indians. Moreover, the policy of extermination made life among the Indians far more arduous and more dangerous than formerly. Some servants still thought it worth the risk, but most were caught in Virginia's tightening labor discipline, to be bought and sold as their masters pleased and to hoe tobacco as long as they were likely to live.

"Like a damnd slave," said Thomas Best. To buy and sell servants for a period of years was not the same as buying and selling men and women for life and their unborn children with them. And the servitude of Thomas Best and his contemporaries was not a function of their race or nationality. Nevertheless, in the treatment of labor in boom-time Virginia and in the rising hatred of Indians, we can begin to discern some of the forces that would later link slavery to freedom.

Book II

A NEW DEAL

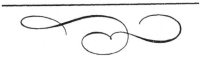

7

SETTLING DOWN

IT would not have been surprising if slavery had developed swiftly in Virginia during the booming 1620s, when tobacco prices were high enough to inspire the same overpowering greed that moved the Spaniards on Hispaniola. Two decades later Englishmen in Barbados turned to slavery in as short a time, in order to exploit the island's newly discovered capacity for producing sugar. But in Virginia, although the tobacco barons of the 1620s bought and sold and beat their servants in a manner that shocked other Englishmen, they did not reduce them to slavery, as we understand the term. And Virginians did not import shiploads of African slaves to solve their labor problem until half a century more had passed. Perhaps if the boom had continued, they would have; but when it collapsed, they relaxed a little in their pursuit of riches and began to think about making the best of life in the new land.

Making the best of life in America meant making their part of America as English as possible, and in the decades after 1630 they worked at it. Although they did not share the broad vision of freedom that had moved Raleigh and Hakluyt and other backers of Virginia, they did want the liberty and security that went with "the rights of Englishmen." From the time of Sir Thomas Dale and the *Lawes Divine, Morall and Martiall* through the subversion of Sir Edwin Sandys' good intentions during the boom years, most Virginians had enjoyed fewer civil and political rights than they would have had in England. Now, for a period of thirty years or more, they busied themselves with building a society that would give them a greater freedom than most could have hoped for in their native land. It was a crude society, peopled by crude men, but it was less crude and less cruel than that presided over by the labor barons of the 1620s. Only by taking a close look at it can we perceive how much like England the Virginians made it—and how unlike it nevertheless remained. Only so will we perceive how it could nurture freedom and yet invite slavery, as new forces emerged to exert new pressures toward the paradoxical union.

It took more than a decade for Virginians to admit to themselves that the boom was indeed over. Tobacco prices, after ranging from one to three shillings a pound during most of the 1620s, fell to as little as a penny a pound in 1630.[1] The reaction of Virginians was to order that the boom return. The legislative assembly, composed of the governor's council and the popularly elected House of Burgesses, continued to meet, albeit unrecognized by the king, after the shift to royal government. In 1629 it tried, ineffectually, to raise prices by limiting tobacco production. In 1632 it took a simpler course and simply forbade anyone to buy English goods at a rate of less than one pound of tobacco for every sixpence that the goods cost in England.[2] Although the order was renewed the following year (and the price raised) such an edict could not have been widely enforced.[3] During the decade tobacco did recover, at least to sixpence a pound, but not for long. When it hit threepence in 1638 and stayed there the next year, the planters again called for controls.

By this time they had divided their settlements into counties, each presided over by a commander, with whom a group of commissioners sat in a county court that exercised extensive jurisdiction, civil and criminal.[4] Equipped with this new arm of government, the assembly tried once again to legislate the boom back into existence. The king had been demanding a limitation of the tobacco crop ever since he had taken over direction of the colony from the company. Like Sir Edwin Sandys, he thought that Virginia should be able to produce something more than smoke, and that the way to achieve

[1] On tobacco prices in the 1630s see the article by Russell R. Menard cited in note 7.

[2] Hening, I, 141–42, 152, 162–64, 188–89.   [3] *Ibid.*, 203–7, 209–12.

[4] *Ibid.*, 224; W. F. Craven, *The Southern Colonies in the Seventeenth Century* (Baton Rouge, La., 1949), 166–72. The only counties for which continuous records survive for the period before 1660 are Lower Norfolk and Northampton. Hence this chapter depends heavily on information derived from these two counties.

the goal was to restrict tobacco production. The king wanted to confine production to an amount that he would undertake to market through a royal commission (thus collecting profits as well as customs duties from the undesirable weed). In 1638 his commissioners offered to take 1,600,000 pounds at sixpence a pound. On behalf of the planters, the assembly declined the offer, but the next year ordered on its own initiative a more drastic limitation, 170 pounds per person, which was calculated to produce only 1,300,000 pounds. At the same time the assembly decreed that it should be sold at no less than a shilling a pound.[5]

This was the last serious effort to recover the boom. For two years the county courts tried conscientiously to enforce the law, but by June, 1642, the scheme had to be abandoned, partly because the authorities in England had disapproved, but also because the planters themselves had seen that it was not working.[6] That summer everyone planted tobacco freely, and the next year it sold at 2.4 pence per pound (20 shillings the hundredweight). It never rose much above that during the rest of the century.[7] The days of getting-rich-quick by growing tobacco were over.

[5] George L. Beer, *The Origins of the British Colonial System, 1578–1660* (New York, 1908), 117–75; Hening, I, 224–26; *WMQ*, 2nd ser., IV (1924), 17–31, 146–47. The act also provided for improving quality: all inferior tobacco and half the good produced in 1639 were to be burned, and henceforth all tobacco was to be stripped of stems and smoothed before it was sold. The price was supposed to rise to 2 shillings a pound in 1641, but this provision was given up before it went into effect (Northampton II, 125). The assembly in 1641 also changed the limitation from 170 pounds to 1,000 plants. But 1,000 plants, stripped of stems, would probably have made no more than 170 pounds. In the eighteenth century the ordinary calculation was six or eight plants to the pound. See Journal of William Hugh Grove, 1732, Alderman Library, Charlottesville.

[6] *VMHB*, II (1894–95), 287. For examples of enforcement in 1640 see Norfolk I, 47, 53, 74. By May, 1641, the court in Northampton County was settling cases at the rate of 16 shillings for 30 pounds (Northampton I, 86). And the Norfolk court in January, 1642, ordered payment of a debt at the rate of eightpence a pound with the stipulation that if the tobacco paid could not be sold in England for that much, the debtor was to satisfy the deficiency at the next return of shipping with 8 percent interest (Norfolk I, 115). Later there were charges that the act was passed by debtors to defraud creditors. Bullock, *Virginia Impartially Examined*, 10.

[7] Norfolk I, 203. The price had dropped to a penny a pound in 1644, according to a letter from the assembly to the king (Ms. Clarendon 24, f.52, Bodleian Library, Oxford). But this was probably because of a temporary lack of shipping, brought on by the Civil Wars in England. That 20 shil-

Yet Englishmen deprived of the dream of easy riches in Virginia continued to come there. From about 1,300 people in 1625 the colony grew to about 2,600 in 1629 and to roughly 8,000 in 1640. For the first four or five years of the 1640s as the Civil Wars in England began and the so-called Great Migration ended, the Virginia population remained about level and may have dropped a little as a result of an Indian massacre in 1644 and of migration to Maryland. But by 1653 the colony held more than 14,000 and continued to grow rapidly, reaching about 25,000 by 1660.[8]

How was the country able to sustain this rapidly expanding population when for so many years a much smaller number had lived so close to starvation? Virginia's newcomers were no more assiduous about planting corn than their predecessors had been, and no less addicted to growing tobacco despite the low price it fetched. Although there were no more famines, scarcity several times drove up the cost of a barrel of corn (5 bushels) to over 100 pounds of tobacco, a figure that Virginians came to regard as a maximum.[9] A law requiring every man to plant two acres of corn had to be reenacted several times before 1660, and during the 1650s people were still being presented to the courts for delinquency either in planting or tending corn.[10] Nevertheless, increased corn production was undoubtedly a factor in Virginia's ability to feed her growing population. Equally important, however, was the fact that the pasture farming introduced by earlier immigrants had at last begun to pay off.

It had occurred to the settlers at least as early as 1624 that they might protect their domestic animals from Indians and wolves by erecting a six-mile palisade between the headwaters of two creeks

---

lings per 100 pounds was the usual rate for most of the 1640s and 1650s appears from various transactions in county court records: Norfolk III, 128–30a, 206; Northampton II, 387–88; IV, 50, 62; V, 143a. After 1655 prices began to drop: Norfolk III, 222; IV, 66, 234. It should be understood that no reliable or regular series of annual prices current can be constructed for seventeenth-century Virginia. But Russell R. Menard has assembled much of the available data in "A Note on Chesapeake Tobacco Prices, 1618–1660," forthcoming in *VMHB*. See also chapter 10, note 29.

[8] See Appendix.

[9] Northampton III, 242; York II, 61, 130; Hening, I, 347.

[10] Hening, I, 152, 166, 190, 246, 344, 419; Norfolk I, 358; II, 10, 122, 206; IV, 167.

in the neighborhood of present-day Williamsburg.[11] The palisade would cut off from the mainland a large segment of the peninsula between the James and the York rivers. During the boom everyone was too busy growing tobacco to attempt the job, but in 1634 they got it done. Thereafter, as soon as the wolves in the area had been exterminated, there was a safe cattle range as large, they bragged, as the English county of Kent.[12] Elsewhere, too, by fighting back the Indians and by placing bounties on wolves, the settlers succeeded in building up their herds. While the climate of Virginia continued to be perilous for human beings, it was great for cattle and swine; and once the breeding numbers passed a certain point, they multiplied a good deal more rapidly than people did and provided meat and milk to sustain Virginia's growth. Virginia swine were said to be particularly flavorful, comparable to Westphalian.[13]

Besides neat cattle and swine, the settlers kept a few goats and fewer sheep. Horses were at first a rarity. In the beginning the settlers tried to keep their livestock continually under attendance. Owners of large herds employed cowkeepers to look after them; many families kept dogs to help with the job; and both cattle and swine were sometimes penned up at night.[14] Milch cows may have continued to be thus guarded. But in 1643 Virginians passed a fencing law that in effect gave livestock the run of the land. A man had to place a sufficient fence around his crops, at least four and a half feet high, with the lowest rail close enough to the ground to keep hogs from getting under it. Unless he had such a fence in good repair, he had no chance of recovering damages if someone else's hogs or cattle got into his field and destroyed his crop. The burden of proof

[11] *WMQ*, 2nd ser., VI (1926), 118; VIII (1928), 164; C.O. 1/4, ff.21–22.

[12] *VMHB*, II (1894–95), 51–52; VIII (1900–1901), 157; C.O. 1/4, ff.21–22, 28; C.O. 1/8, ff.74–75; "Aspinwall Papers," Massachusetts Historical Society, *Collections*, 4th ser., IX (1871), 110.

[13] "A Letter from Mr. John Clayton," in Force, *Tracts*, III, No. 12, p. 36; Edmund Berkeley and Dorothy S. Berkeley, eds., "Another Account of Virginia by the Reverend John Clayton," *VMHB*, LXXVI (1968), 415–40, at 419.

[14] The use both of cowkeepers and of dogs is apparent from numerous cases in the county court records; for example, Norfolk I, 52, 204, 256, 281; II, 117a; Northampton I, 61; II, 51, 386; IV, 20. See also "Letter from Mr. John Clayton," p. 38. On the rise of cattle raising in Virginia, see Wesley N. Laing, "Cattle in Seventeenth-Century Virginia," *VMHB*, LXVII (1959), 143–64.

was on the planter to show that his fence was sufficient. The law was a boon to the burgeoning animals and probably no less so to the settlers' corn crops.[15]

It would be wrong to assume from the fencing act that Virginians were divided into planters and cattlemen. During these decades every planter was also a cattleman, and cattle constituted a large proportion of the worldly goods of both affluent and ordinary men. The inventories of the smallest estates recorded for probate usually list a cow or two. In Norfolk County, for example, in 1656, one Peter Marks left only a bed, a gun, a chest, three pewter dishes, a pot, a kettle, and two cows—a list that might be considered the basic equipment for keeping house in Virginia.[16] In York County we find in 1646 an estate worth 1,380 pounds of tobacco, of which a cow, a calf, and a young bull account for 850 pounds; or in 1647 an estate worth 700 pounds, of which a cow and yearling heifer account for 550 pounds.[17] In large estates the proportions were frequently similar. When Cornelius Lloyd, a commissioner of Norfolk County, died in 1654, his possessions, other than debts owed him, were appraised at 40,361 pounds of tobacco, of which 87 head of cattle accounted for 25,540 pounds.[18] Cesar Puggett, of the same county, left an estate in 1645 valued at 24,215 pounds, of which 42 cattle accounted for 17,500.[19] When Edmund Scarburgh leased a plantation on the Eastern Shore to William Brenton of Boston, he included 109 head of cattle and "a parcel of hogs." [20] In 1647 Norfolk County had 360 tithables, that is, men over fifteen, and 546 cows three years or more old.[21] And in Northampton County the clerk of the court recorded cattle marks for 236 persons between 1665 and 1669, a time during which the number of households in the county did not exceed 177.[22]

Virginians had recognized that their growing herds might be a way to wealth as well as to health and survival, and so they proved to be. The spectacular increase of cattle when they were sufficiently cared for, in a land where the range was limited only by wolves and

[15] Hening, I, 244, 332, 458. There had been earlier laws requiring men to fence their planting land (*ibid.*, 176, 199), but the 1643 law seems to have been the first to assign responsibility for damage to crops. On the manner of building fences in Virginia, see Berkeley, "Another Account . . . by John Clayton," 426.

[16] Norfolk IV, 10.
[17] York II, 156, 294.
[18] Norfolk III, 168, 184a.
[19] Norfolk I, 242–43.

[20] Northampton IV, 153.
[21] Norfolk II, 56.
[22] Northampton IV, 228ff.

Indians, presented the possibility of high returns on a small investment. Even though the actual increase was seldom equal to the potential, the certainty of a very large increase was taken for granted. In 1638 a jury found that the heirs and assigns of Abraham Peirsey owed the heirs and assigns of Samuel Argall fifty head of cattle for two entrusted to Peirsey in 1621.[23] This was unrealistic and unfair, but such a rate of increase was not impossible. If we may believe the author of *A Perfect Description of Virginia*, Benjamin Symmes's free school owned forty head of cattle in 1649. They came from eight with which Symmes had endowed the school when he started it fourteen years earlier.[24] In 1651 Simon Foscutt of Northampton obtained from William Whittington a ten-year-old cow for which he agreed to deliver two cows between three and seven years old, with calves by their sides, five years later. At prevailing prices the ten-year-old cow would have been worth around 500 pounds of tobacco, and a young cow with a calf by her side around 600 pounds. Whittington made similar bargains with two other people, and in one case he was able to demand two for one in a little over three years.[25]

Virginians found a market for surplus cattle in exporting to other colonies, especially Barbados,[26] and in supplying the tobacco

[23] *VMHB*, XI (1903–4), 285–87.

[24] Force, *Tracts*, II, No. 8, p. 15; Neill, *Virginia Carolorum*, 112–13.

[25] Northampton IV, 149a, 150.

[26] John Hammond, *Leah and Rachel*, Force, *Tracts*, III, No. 14, p. 19; *A Description of the Province of New Albion*, Force, *Tracts*, II, No. 7, p. 5; Richard Ligon, *A True and Exact History of the Island of Barbados* (London, 1657), 37, 58, 113; Vincent T. Harlow, *A History of Barbados, 1625–1685* (Oxford, 1926), 283–84. It is impossible to establish the volume of this trade. For a later period C.O. 1/44, ff.246–66 shows 13 ships clearing from Barbados for Virginia in 1678. C.O. 33/13 contains Barbados shipping returns 1679–1704. The ships entering from and clearing for Virginia constitute only a small percentage of the total. Nevertheless, it would seem to have been a highly profitable trade. Ligon says (p. 113) that an ox worth £5 in Virginia could be sold in Barbados for £25. Maurice Thompson, an English merchant, bought 100 Virginia oxen for transport to Barbados in 1647. Carl and Roberta Bridenbaugh, *No Peace beyond the Line: The English in the Caribbean, 1624–1690* (New York, 1972), 84. The Virginia county court records contain numerous references to Barbados, arising from commerce between the colonies. Governor Andros in 1696, answering queries from the Board of Trade, said that Virginia exported to "New York Barbados and the islands and New England." C.O. 5/1309, No. 16. And the Virginia council, answering similar queries in 1708, said that Barbados was

ships that waited long periods in Virginia rivers to gather cargo. Because immigration kept both the domestic and export markets growing, the rapid increase in cattle brought no slump in prices. And since cattle for the most part sustained themselves by foraging in the woods and marshes,[27] the periodic scarcity and high cost of corn did not affect their value either. During the 1640s and 1650s prices of cattle showed no marked fluctuation.[28]

Although virtually everybody in Virginia raised cattle, corn, and tobacco, a few men specialized in the industrial trades that enabled the colony to carry on business. Shipwrights built small vessels and repaired ships that came from abroad to collect tobacco; coopers made the hogsheads (barrels) in which tobacco was packed for shipment; and carpenters built tobacco sheds and houses for the expanding population.[29] But there were never enough artisans to fill all the colony's needs. To get around the shortage, wealthy Virginians sometimes imported craftsmen as servants and hired them out to others. A variety of skilled men (including tailors, carpenters, shoemakers, and even physicians) thus crossed the ocean, but either too few came or too few stuck to their trades after serving out their indentures. The number of "unfixed" guns in inventories and complaints of the difficulty in getting them repaired testify to the shortage and the high cost of ironwork, as does the law forbidding people to burn dilapidated houses for the sake of obtaining nails.[30] One of the colony's largest needs was for shoes, which wore out rapidly in

---

then the only other colony with which Virginia carried on trade of any size. H. R. McIlwaine et al., eds., *Executive Journals of the Council of Colonial Virginia* (Richmond, 1925–66), III, 193.

[27] Nathaniel Shrigley, *A True Relation of Virginia and Maryland* (London, 1669), Force, *Tracts*, III, No. 7, p. 5.

[28] The available prices are mainly from several hundred inventories in wills in the Norfolk, Northampton, and York county records. Thus they do not usually represent actual sales. Prices naturally varied according to the age and condition of the animals, but the range of variation remained much the same during these two decades. A mature cow was worth from 300 to 600 pounds of tobacco, a cow with calf about 100 pounds more, a yearling from 100 to 200, a bull from 200 to 400, a steer from 200 to 600, with valuations only occasionally rising a little above or falling a little below these levels.

[29] Lumber, in spite of Virginia's remaining forests, was considered valuable enough for planters to bring lawsuits against anyone cutting timber on their land. Norfolk I, 264; II, 33a; Northampton IV, 91, 104; V, 71–72a; XII, 154.

[30] Hening, I, 291 (cf. *ibid.*, I, 326–27); Norfolk III, 12, 21a; *Executive Journals*, I, 183.

the rough new clearings; and with so many cattle Virginia had the raw materials for making them. But attempts to set up tanneries and cobbler shops proved unsuccessful.[31]

Raising tobacco, even at twenty shillings the hundredweight, was still too lucrative a way of spending one's time to allow serious competition from other pursuits. Tobacco occupied a man nine months of the year, what with sowing, transplanting, weeding, topping, worming, striking, and curing. The remainder of the year he cleared land, fenced, and cut boards for casks. But the tasks, if demanding, were lightened by what the settlers had learned from the Indians' easy manner of agriculture. They did not attempt to use their livestock for dunging the fields or for pulling plows. They did not even attempt to establish permanent fields, cleared of roots and stumps, where they could drive a plow. Instead, they adapted their tobacco farming to the Indians' primitive but labor-saving system: clear a field by girdling the trees, plant it to tobacco for three or four years, to wheat or corn for a few more, and then clear another stretch and let the first recover its fertility by reverting to forest.[32] It was a mode that continued to horrify those who measured the merit of a farmer by the neatness of his fields, and it did require a lot of land. But in a country where land was more plentiful than labor it made sense. With a place to live, a couple of acres in corn, a couple in tobacco, a few cattle and swine, and firewood everywhere, a man needed to buy only clothes and tools (hoes and axes and if

[31] *Perfect Description*, Force, *Tracts*, II, No. 8, 15; Northampton V, 123. Artisans are frequently identified as such in the records, as, for example, Peter Porter, carpenter; Thomas Cooper, joiner; William Dunford, boatwright. On industrial enterprises in one county see Susie M. Ames, *Studies of the Virginia Eastern Shore in the Seventeenth Century* (Richmond, 1940), 109–46. To encourage industry, the House of Burgesses at various times tried to place embargoes on wool, hides, and old iron, but the shortage of craftsmen continued. Hening, I, 174, 199, 307, 314, 488, 525.

[32] Williams, *Virginia Richly Valued*, Force, *Tracts*, III, No. 11, p. 48; "Letter from Mr. John Clayton," Force, *Tracts*, III, No. 12, p. 21; Henry Hartwell, James Blair, and Edward Chilton, *The Present State of Virginia and the College* (1697), Hunter D. Farish, ed. (Williamsburg, 1940; Charlottesville, 1964), 8–9. This continued to be the practice in Virginia through most of the colonial period. See William Tatham, *An Historical and Practical Essay on the Culture and Commerce of Tobacco* (London, 1800), 6–11. At the end of the eighteenth century, partly as a result of the influence of English agricultural reformers, Virginians began to chide themselves for their slovenly methods. There grew up a notion that these methods had "exhausted" the soil, a notion accepted by historians (Avery Craven, *Soil Exhaustion as a Factor in the Agricultural History of Virginia and Mary-*

possible a gun). By the 1640s he could produce 1,500 pounds of tobacco in a year (men were sometimes hired by the year for that much or more), probably twice what a man could grow in the 1620s.[33] Between his cattle and his tobacco he could count on coming out ahead.

---

land, 1606–1860 [Urbana, Ill., 1925]). Actually the Virginians, like many other American colonists, were practicing a "long-fallow" system. They had enough land to be able to allow a large part of it to grow back into forest, a process that took twenty or thirty years after its abandonment. Robert Beverley noted in 1705 that "Wood grows at every Man's Door so fast, that after it has been cut down, it will in Seven Years time, grow up again from Seed, to substantial Fire-Wood; and in Eighteen or Twenty Years 'twill come to be very good Board-Timber" (*History and Present State of Virginia*, 125–26). And Hartwell, Blair, and Chilton in 1697 observed that "As fast as the Ground is worn out with tobacco and Corn, it runs up again in Underwoods, and in many Places of the Country, that which has been clear'd is thicker in Woods than it was before the clearing" (*Present State of Virginia*, 8–9). Edmund Ruffin, in denouncing the Virginia practice at the opening of the nineteenth century, stated that "After twenty or thirty years, according to the convenience of the owner, the same land would be again cleared, and put under similar scourging tillage" (*An Essay on Calcareous Manures*, J. C. Sitterson, ed. [Cambridge, Mass., 1961], p. 17). Ruffin thought that it did not recover its original fertility, but one of the most ardent Virginia agronomists, Thomas Jefferson, disagreed. Although he acknowledged that tobacco and Indian corn quickly brought diminishing returns, he maintained "that the James river lowgrounds with the cultivation of small grain, will never be exhausted; because we know that under that cultivation we must now and then take them down with Indian corn, or they become, as they were originally, too rich to bring wheat." Edwin M. Betts, ed., *Thomas Jefferson's Garden Book, 1766–1824: With Relevant Extracts from His Other Writings* (Philadelphia, 1944), 192. For an analysis of tobacco production in one tidewater Maryland county, see Edward C. Papenfuse, Jr., "Planter Behavior and Economic Opportunity in a Staple Economy," *Agricultural History*, XLVI (1972), 297–311. Papenfuse shows that Maryland plantations in this county were able to sustain production during the eighteenth century with no evidence of a decline in output per acre.

[33] It has proved impossible to find any records of actual production that would reveal the average output per man of labor devoted to tobacco. L. C. Gray, *History of Agriculture in the Southern United States to 1860* (Washington, D.C., 1932) I, 218–19, has cited most of the estimates of contemporary observers. They range from 1,000 to 4,000 pounds, but the last figure is clearly an exaggeration. The amount undoubtedly varied with the quality of land used, the length of time it had been in use, the time spent in weeding and worming, the type of tobacco grown, and, most of all, with the weather. There were no improvements in technology to increase productivity during the colonial period, though it may be that the

Having found a way to stay alive and even to live more comfortably than most men did in England, Virginians during the second quarter of the seventeenth century at last began to look upon their raw new land as a home rather than a temporary stopping place. And they tried to re-create for themselves the security they associated with home in England, where life was bounded by time-honored social, legal, and political restraints and freedoms.

At the highest level in England those restraints had operated against the king, barring him from arbitrary interference with the lives of his subjects. And the subjects who were most careful to restrain him were those who themselves controlled the counties where they lived. The big men of England exercised a rather larger influence in the everyday lives of their neighbors than the king did. Virginia's big men were a good bit smaller than England's, but they aspired to the same local influence and the same autonomy for their colony as the English nobility enjoyed in their counties. In Virginia English freedom meant, paradoxically, to be as free as possible from interference by England.

Since Virginia's tobacco barons were not to the manner born, they could scarcely expect that the king would defer to the likes of them as he did to his nobility.[34] Still, they had the advantage of distance, and three thousand miles of ocean might prove an even more effective bulwark of local autonomy than their lordly counterparts in England gained from rank. They had already experienced the power that distance gave them in circumventing the orders sent by the Virginia Company. And even before the king took control of Virginia's government, they took steps to secure their position. Meeting in the last assembly under the company, the governor's council and the House of Burgesses affirmed that the governor (who would henceforth be appointed by the king) should have no power to levy taxes without the consent of the assembly. At the same time

---

hours of work were increased as time went on, especially after the transition to slave labor in the eighteenth century. Although in 1644 the assembly in a message to the king said that 1,000 pounds per man was "the uttmost that can be imagined to bee planted in good and seasonable years" (Ms. Clarendon 24, Bodleian Library), the assembly was seeking to minimize. The fact that planters would sometimes pay 1,500 or more for a year's labor argues that some at least expected to make more than that. For examples see Northampton IV, 30; V, 37a, 116a. A law passed in 1658 required the father of an illegitimate child to pay to the mother's master or mistress 1,500 pounds of tobacco or one year's service. Hening, I, 438.

[34] Bernard Bailyn, "Politics and Social Structure in Virginia," in Smith, *Seventeenth-Century America*, 90–118, esp. 93–96.

they sent a letter to the Privy Council, requesting the continuation of the assembly under the new government and advising the king of the need also to rely on local talent for a proper management of the colony.[35]

The assembly's worries about the shift to royal government centered on the governor whom the king might send, especially if he were someone not familiar with Virginia or not prepared to stay there. Governors sent from England, their letter claimed, "for the first yeare are rawe in experience and for the most part in Ill disposition of health through the change of the Clymate, the seconde yeare they beginn to understand the affaires of the Country, and the thirde provide for their retorne." Moreover, any instructions sent from England, though they might seem good at that distance, were likely to prove otherwise when they came to be carried out. In fact, no "main project" should be undertaken without prior approval of the governor's council, men who knew the country and knew what would work and what would not.[36]

Between the lines the assemblymen were saying that Virginians would find ways of defeating any English policy toward them that they did not approve. And they soon showed that they could defeat projects sponsored by the king as easily as those sponsored by the company. Although Charles I pointedly refrained from continuing the assembly when he took over the government of Virginia, royal governors found that they could not get along without it or without the council. Actually, the council had been officially continued, and to it the king, like the company, appointed the most successful and powerful men in the colony. As the number of such men grew, however, they could not all be given places on the council, and yet it was necessary to take them into account. The assembly offered the easiest way to do it. Though without instructions to do so, governors called the assembly together on several occasions in the 1620s and 1630s to deal with problems of defense and other local matters. They handled these effectively, but they also exhibited the usual independence of representative assemblies. When the governor asked them to comply with the king's wish for a contract to market their tobacco, they turned him down, as we have seen. In 1632 they took the occasion of their meeting to affirm their own exclusive

[35] *RVC*, IV, 581; *Journals of the House of Burgesses, 1619–1658/59,* 26–27.

[36] *Ibid.*

authority to tax the colony.[37] It was plain that they intended to exercise that authority whether the king recognized it or not. To be an Englishman was to be ruled only by laws that the country's best men had approved in Parliament; the assembly was Virginia's parliament, and its members were Virginia's best men.

Even though the best might be none too good, they enjoyed a wider popular constituency than any member of the House of Commons in England could boast. There were no legal restrictions on voting in Virginia until 1670. It went without saying that neither women nor children could vote, and it seems unlikely that servants were allowed to. But a man who had finished his term of service, whether he had set up his own household or not, could cast his vote for a representative in the House of Burgesses. It did not follow that he cast it for men like himself. The best men were better than he, and the very best did not need his vote, because they were on the council. Whether appointed by the king or elected by the people, they would not be bashful about telling a royal governor what he could or could not do in Virginia.

The governor who had to contend with Virginia's best men during the 1630s was John Harvey. No newcomer to Virginia, he had been a member of the royal commission sent to investigate the colony in 1623 and knew the people he would encounter when he arrived in 1630. During the next four or five years he made every effort to win them away from tobacco. At the same time he made peace with the Indians, assisted the Catholic colonists who in 1633 planted the colony of Maryland across the Potomac, and called into question some of the shady deals that council members had engaged in during the 1620s. None of these measures won him friends among the men who had been running Virginia. Many of the magnates of the 1620s were dead by this time, but Samuel Mathews, William Peirce, and Dr. John Pott were very much alive, and new potentates were rising in the place of the Yeardleys and Peirseys, aided frequently by judicious marriages to the widows of their predecessors. They showed their power by seizing Governor Harvey in 1635 and shipping him back to England. When he won vindication and returned in triumph to send his persecutors to England for trial, they there defended themselves so persuasively that in 1639 Harvey was dismissed from office in disgrace.[38]

[37] Hening, I, 171.
[38] Harvey's administration and his quarrel with his council have been

Virginia's next two governors were more closely attuned to the facts of political life in Virginia. Francis Wyatt—the old company governor—arrived with royal instructions that finally recognized the assembly and confirmed its claim to legislative authority.[30] Wyatt was already identified with Virginia's ruling class. He had long been one of them; and his successor in 1641, Sir William Berkeley, quickly became one and proved as ardent a defender of Virginia's autonomy as anyone could ask of a man who retained his loyalty to the king.

Berkeley's loyalty to the king was unquestioned. His brother John, the first Baron Berkeley, was a favorite at court; and Sir William himself was also an accomplished courtier, a man of ready wit and sophisticated taste. He nevertheless showed his commitment to Virginia by building at Green Spring, near Jamestown, the most substantial house that Virginians had yet seen in their country.

Berkeley won the hearts of Virginians at once. And during his years as governor he repeatedly gave them cause to be grateful for his appointment. Twice he crossed the ocean to seek help for the colony in England. On his first trip in 1644 he found that the king needed help more than Virginia did; and he stayed for a year to fight against the Roundhead forces that had carried the gentry's contest with the king from Parliament to the battlefield. But he returned to Virginia to champion the cause of the colony, no matter who challenged it.

During the Civil Wars, king and Parliament were so occupied with one another in England that neither gave much attention to what was happening in the New World. All talk of a tobacco contract was forgotten now, and the Virginians elevated England's salutary neglect into a matter of principle by asserting their right to a free trade and by affirming it as "the libertye of the Collony and a right of deare esteeme to free borne persons . . . that noe lawe should bee established within the kingdome of England concerninge us without the consent of a grand Assembly here." When a rumor

the subject of several varying interpretations: Thomas J. Wertenbaker, *Virginia under the Stuarts* (Princeton, 1914), 60–84; Wilcomb E. Washburn, *Virginia under Charles I and Cromwell, 1625–1660*, Jamestown 350th Anniversary Historical Booklet, No. 7 (Williamsburg, 1957), 10–29; Richard L. Morton, *Colonial Virginia* (Chapel Hill, N.C., 1960), I, 122–46; Bailyn, "Politics and Social Structure," 94–98; J. Mills Thornton, "The Thrusting Out of Governor Harvey," *VMHB*, LXXVI (1968), 11–26.

[30] *VMHB*, XI (1903-4), 50–54.

was spread in 1647 that Parliament had violated this right by forbidding foreigners to trade with English colonies, the assembly dismissed it as "a forgerye of avaritious persons [i.e., the London merchants] whose sickle hath bin ever long in our harvest allreadye." [40] The assembly invited Dutch merchants to bring their "wares and merchandizes" to Virginia and "to trade or traffique for the commoditys of the collony in any shipp or shipps of their owne." [41] The Dutch responded so warmly that the Virginians once again enjoyed something like prosperity. Though their tobacco never again brought the bonanza prices of the 1620s, the abundance of Dutch traders resulted in a pretty steady price of twenty shillings the hundred pounds during most of the 1640s and 1650s.

Throughout the fight between royal and Parliamentary forces Berkeley remained a staunch partisan of the king, but he was an equally staunch partisan of Virginia and an enthusiastic supporter of the colony's development of the Dutch trade.[42] When Parliament beheaded Charles I in 1649 and established the Commonwealth to replace the monarch, Berkeley and his coterie proclaimed the succession of the king's son as Charles II and warned any potential rebels against taking the occasion of the king's execution to challenge the authority of the king's government in Virginia. Berkeley had only to point to his record and to remind Virginians that Parliamentary control could mean the return of "the same poverty wherein the Dutch found and relieved us." [43] And indeed it could have; for in spite of the Virginia assembly's brave words, Parliament was more than willing to listen to the London merchants, and in 1651, at the merchants' behest, it did forbid the Dutch trade. Not all of Berkeley's supporters placed as high a value as he on loyalty to the king. But they all shared his preference for keeping Virginia's trade free; and so in 1652, when Parliament finally sent commissioners with an armed force to secure the colony's allegiance to the Commonwealth, there was no great enthusiasm for complying. When Berkeley capitulated, he dictated terms that gave the Virginians virtual autonomy.

[40] *Journals of the House of Burgesses, 1619–1658/59*, 74; *VMHB*, XXIII (1914–15), 244–47. The pungency of language in this declaration suggests that Berkeley himself may have been the author of it.

[41] Hening, I, 258; cf. *ibid.*, 540.

[42] William Berkeley, *A Discourse and View of Virginia* (London, 1663), 6–7. Berkeley himself apparently engaged in the trade. See York II, 93.

[43] *Journals of the House of Burgesses, 1619–1658/59*, 76.

The new governor installed by the commissioners, Richard Bennett, had been in the colony since the 1620s, when he came to take over the estate of his brother Edward, one of the original tobacco barons of the boom years. He was imbued with the same views as other Virginians, and he made no effort to enforce the act that Parliament had passed making Dutch trade in Virginia illegal. His own power was in any case somewhat less than Berkeley had enjoyed. The Parliamentary commission, in replacing Berkeley, had underwritten the authority of the Virginia assembly, enabling the members even to choose the colony's future governors and councillors. The governors they chose were men of their own kind, like Bennett, and Samuel Mathews, Jr., whose father had married Abraham Peirsey's widow and died the richest man in Virginia (as Peirsey had been before him). In 1660, just before Charles II recovered his throne in England, the assembly decided that Berkeley, who had remained in Virginia, should again have the job; and they summoned him back to the post, which he retained for the next sixteen years (during which he married the widow of Peirsey's grandson).[44]

The men who governed Virginia in the 1640s, 1650s, and 1660s, whether under king or Commonwealth, showed themselves to be only a little less ruthless than those who dominated the colony in the boom period. They continued to sit in judgment on disputes in which they themselves were involved; and their servants frequently had to bring suit in order to obtain freedom when the term of indenture was up.[45] They demanded handsome support and deference from their inferiors and usually got it. The expenses incurred by the representatives who sat in the House of Burgesses were paid by the people of the counties they represented, and in many cases the amounts can be found in the county court records. A few weeks' attendance generally brought more than an ordinary man was likely to make in a year. Among other expenses that the burgesses of Norfolk County charged to their constituents were 150 pounds of tobacco for a fiddler in 1653 and 500 pounds for a trumpeter in 1660. Charges for such items as "an anchor of drink" or "2 cases of strong waters" suggest that the Virginians' capacity for sack and strong

[44] Hening, I, 362–73; Washburn, *Virginia under Charles I and Cromwell*, 39–62; Morton, *Colonial Virginia*, I, 174–87; Craven, *Southern Colonies*, 262–69.
[45] For examples: Northampton IV, 215a; X, 39, 52, 55; Norfolk I, 8, 9, 85, 88, 305; II, 52a, 147a; III, 213a, 221; IV, 20, 40, 46, 55, 226; Lancaster IV, 257.

waters had not decreased and that a legislator considered it his prerogative to be paid for as much as he could drink while doing the public's business.[46]

Though their standard of living remained high, the authority of the men who governed became somewhat diluted, partly because there were a great many more of them as time went on and they were by no means united in their political views and interests. Furthermore, with the expansion of population through several counties, local institutions modeled on English ones began to assume a larger importance in day-to-day life and imposed a familiar network of remembered relationships, of which deference to wealth and birth and success was only a part.

These developments were accelerated after 1644, when the Indians, now vastly outnumbered, launched a last desperate attempt to recover their patrimony. In a surprise attack they killed an estimated five hundred people, but Governor Berkeley himself led the colonists against them and reduced the remaining Pamunkeys and the constituent tribes of their dominion to a tributary status. The way was thus opened for English expansion, and in the next ten years five new counties were formed, each with a county court to maintain order and mediate disputes between neighbors.[47]

In establishing counties and county courts, the Virginians were taking one step toward re-creating the security of English society. By dividing their counties into parishes, each with a vestry and a number of churchwardens, they took another. Not every parish was able to obtain or support a minister of its own. Sometimes two or three parishes shared one in rotation. On the whole, Virginians were much less concerned with the world to come than were the settlers of New England. Although the rise of Puritanism in England was reflected in both political and ecclesiastical disputes in Virginia, the most ardently puritanical settlers were driven out by Governor Berkeley or else left voluntarily, many of them for Maryland.[48] But

---

[46] Norfolk I, 74; III, 62a; IV, 269.

[47] Washburn, *Virginia under Charles I and Cromwell*, 29–39; W. F. Craven, *White, Red, and Black: The Seventeenth-Century Virginian* (Charlottesville, 1971), 55–58. The counties, besides Northumberland (1645), were Lancaster, Gloucester, Westmoreland, New Kent, and Rappahannock.

[48] Virginia was founded at a time when Puritan tendencies were strong within the Church of England. Puritanism and subsequently Quakerism seem to have been strongest in the region south of the James River. But the Quakers secured a following in several counties, sometimes among fairly

the frontier environment tended in Virginia, as it did so often in American history, to invigorate transplanted institutions and especially those concerned with moral behavior. The settlers had stretched themselves out along Virginia's network of rivers over areas much larger than the usual English parish. Without proximity to promote a sense of community that would make them feel at home, they tried to bind themselves together by imposing on each other a strict standard of behavior. Without being Puritans in any theological or ecclesiastical sense, they looked a little puritanical in the way they dealt with offenses against conventional morality.

Anyone could report moral offenses to the churchwardens, who were charged with preserving the good behavior of church members. If an accusation seemed justified, the churchwardens presented the offenders to the county court; and the court tried, judged, and sentenced them. Thus the county court in Virginia took the place not only of the English county's quarter session court but also of the English ecclesiastical court and sometimes even of the vestry, which was charged with the care and running of the church. Since the vestrymen and the commissioners who sat on the county court were often identical, and since the same clerk sometimes transcribed the business of both in the same book, it is often difficult to distinguish in the early records between a meeting of the vestry and a meeting of the court. It was the court, however, that prescribed the punishment of delinquents brought before them by the churchwardens. The courts, for example, prescribed penances for couples who appeared with children too soon after marriage, requiring them in the traditional manner to appear at church the next Sunday dressed in white robes and carrying white wands. As in England, they prescribed whipping for the unmarried woman who produced a child, while her lover usually got off with doing penance and paying for the child's support. That the Virginians were not quite Puritans is apparent from the fact that they seldom punished adultery more se-

prominent families. Evidence of Puritanism or Quakerism will be found in Surry II, 86; Norfolk II, 74–75, 120–22, 129, 131; IV, 302, 360, 374, 380, 386, 392, 396; Henrico I, 116, 140–41, 193–94; II (transcript), 41–42; Hening, II, 198. See also Babette M. Levy, "Early Puritanism in the Southern and Island Colonies," American Antiquarian Society, *Proceedings*, LXX (1960), 69–348; Jon Butler, ed., "Two Letters from Virginia Puritans," Massachusetts Historical Society, *Proceedings*, LXXXIV (1972), 99–109; *WMQ*, 1st ser. XI (1902–3), 29–33.

verely than ordinary fornication.[49] But they joined the New Englanders in trying to prevent as well as punish both. If a man and woman were suspected of "incontinency," they were forbidden to go near each other.[50]

The courts sometimes punished a man for habitual drunkenness. One addict, for example, was required to stand at the church door with a pot tied about his neck.[51] Since the justices often held their meetings at a tavern, where liquor was readily available, they occasionally had to rebuke drunken behavior during their sessions (even on the part of those sitting on the bench).[52] But they took an indulgent view of the social drinking that acquainted a man with his neighbors, even though it might lead him to brawl with them. A meeting of the court was an occasion not only for settling disputes but for lifting a glass at the tavern before or after court time. How heavily the taverns were patronized is suggested by the fact that in 1648 eighty men in the parish of Elizabeth River in Norfolk County owed money to William Shipp, who kept the tavern there.[53] At the time the whole county contained only 334 men over fifteen.[54]

Those who gathered at the tavern were also expected to gather every Sunday, with the rest of the parish, at church. Wherever a minister was on hand to preside, the courts insisted that men observe this ancient fellowship, which assumed a new importance in binding the far-flung planters together. Working or traveling or "goeing a fishing" on Sunday instead of going to church brought fines or perhaps a requirement to build a bridge across a creek that would ease the route to church for others. And when the sheriff discovered that church was a good place to serve writs, he was forbidden to do so—too many people stayed home for fear of receiving a summons.[55]

Drinking and worshiping with one's fellow men were but two

---

[49] Norfolk I, 65, 86, 177, 279, 305, 306, 312; II, 106a, 113a. For an example of adultery treated as fornication, see Norfolk I, 183.

[50] Northampton IV, 89a; Norfolk I, 146, 191, 230, 296; II, 10; IV, 7, 78; York II, 414.

[51] Northampton III, 159a.   [52] Hening, II, 384; Lancaster IV, 389.

[53] Norfolk II, 65–66.

[54] Ibid., 93. Elizabeth River Parish had 165 tithables in 1645 (Norfolk I, 291). Thus nearly half the men in the parish were indebted to the tavern keeper.

[55] York II, 386; Hening, I, 457.

threads in the web of community that the settlers were building. The commissioners recognized the fragility of the web and did everything they could to bolster the mutual respect that made it possible for people to live peaceably together. They came down especially hard on any kind of slander. Argall Yeardley, son of Sir George, had come of age in 1642 and had been forthwith made commander of Northampton County. When Thomas Parks scoffed that Yeardley's father "was but a Taylor that Lept off a shopp board in Burchin Lane" and that his mother "was but a middwife not to the honour-Cittizens but to bye blowes," Parks got thirty lashes.[56] Yeardley was a big man, to be sure, but slander, whether of the high or low, called for punishment. It was almost as dangerous to accuse another person of adultery as it was to commit it. John Dennis had to sit in the stocks and ask forgiveness of Goodwife Williams because he called her "a whore and a base whore" after she had called him "knave and base knave." [57] These were ordinary people, and so were Francis Millicent and Mary Jolly, a servant. Millicent spread some stories about Jolly, who was apparently sick abed, saying that "if she were not with child, she was lately with child." The court decided that Millicent had "unjustly and wrongfully scandalized and defamed Mary Jolly, servant to Mr. John Neale." In the usual phrasing of Virginia courts, it was "therefore thought Fitt and soe ordered by this Court that the said Francis Millicent shall be whipt and have thirty lashes and to aske the said Mary Jolly forgivenes publiquely in the Congregation the first Sabbath that she is able to come to Church and the said Millicent to pay the charges of the suite." [58]

The courts had to spend a good deal of their time in protecting the reputation of Virginia's women, mainly from each other. When the Northampton commissioners heard "that about 3 weeks since Alice Robins said that Mary Hudson was as badd as any salte Bitch," Alice Robins and her husband Sampson both got twenty lashes.[59] Mary Rayman had to do penance and beg forgiveness of Anne Johnson for saying that Anne was "naught" with her "black shaggy dog." [60] Eady Hanting had to apologize merely for saying:

> that Matthew Haywards wife did live as brave a life as any Weoman in Virginia for she Could lie abead every morninge till

[56] Northampton II, 313, 351.   [59] Northampton I, 117.
[57] Northampton I, 157–58.   [60] Northampton III, 227, 229.
[58] Northampton I, 86–87.

hir husband went a milkinge and came Back againe and washt the dishes and skimd the milk and then Mr. Edward Floide would come in and say my Deare will you walke and soe she went abroad and left the Children Crienge that hir husband was faine to Come home and leafe his worke to quiett the Children." [61]

Eady Hanting, who spoke these words, was one of the more impulsive members of the parish of Elizabeth River in Lower Norfolk. Shortly after this episode she married Thomas Tooker, but not soon enough. The churchwardens presented her and her husband for fornication before marriage; and when she came to stand before the congregation in her white sheet and was admonished by the minister "for her fowle Crime Committed" she "like a most obstant and graceless person cutt and mangled the sheet wherein she did penance." She got twenty lashes for that.[62]

The courts also protected the inhabitants from defamation that might injure their economic standing in the community. When George Hawkins accused James the Scot, servant to Saville Gaskins, of stealing bacon and could not prove it, the court awarded James 200 pounds of tobacco for the damage to his reputation.[63] An imputation of dishonesty might lead to loss of business if the accusation were not publicly disproved in court. Accordingly, when Amy Cottell called the merchant John Lownes a rogue and charged him with presenting a false bill, he brought suit. Although Governor Berkeley himself had called the man a villain some years earlier, Amy was obliged to apologize, saying, "I am heartily sorry and do desire this to be published I have done him great wrong." She also had to pay him 400 pounds of tobacco for his expenses in bringing the suit.[64] Similarly, Richard Lemon, a merchant, had to pay John Stringer, a carpenter, 300 pounds for calling him "a cheating fellow." [65]

The creation of a sense of community in Virginia was complicated by the fact that the English colonists, even while getting a footing in the New World, had to absorb a substantial minority of foreigners. The records show Portuguese, Spanish, French, Turks, Dutch, and Negroes.[66] Many of them can be identified, for they

[61] Norfolk I, 42.　　[63] Norfolk IV, 7.
[62] *Ibid.*, 64, 86, 93.　　[64] Norfolk II, 201; IV, 220.
[65] Northampton IV, 144. John Stringer, carpenter, was apparently no relation to the physician of the same name mentioned below.
[66] Norfolk I, 105; II, 50. 135, 142; IV, 225, 244, 356; Northampton III, 116–19; IV, 147.

were frequently designated as Andrew the Spaniard or Cursory the Turk. Or the name itself may be indicative. One Frenchman in Norfolk was invariably known as "James the La Balle." He was officially made a denizen in 1658 and became a churchwarden.[67] We can watch the gradual transformation of foreign names that appear frequently in the records. But for some reason Dutch names were Anglicized almost at once; the Dutch seem to have absorbed the Virginia version of English ways rapidly and unobtrusively. Often we learn only by chance that someone named William Westerhouse or Jenkin Price is Dutch.[68]

A more conspicuous set of non-English immigrants were the Negroes. They were nevertheless few in number, probably no more than five hundred by 1650. Whether they were brought by traders directly from Africa or by way of the West Indies is not clear. Many had names like Anthony or Ferdinando that suggest a Spanish or Portuguese connection. Whatever their origin, they already occupied an anomalous position. Some were undoubtedly slaves in our sense of the term, that is, they and their offspring were treated as the property of other men; and it seems probable that all Negroes, or nearly all, arrived in the colony as slaves.[69] But some were free or became free; some were servants or became servants.[70] And all, servant, slave, or free, enjoyed rights that were later denied all Negroes in Virginia. There is no evidence during the period before 1660 that they were subjected to a more severe discipline than other

[67] Norfolk IV, 180, 235.

[68] Northampton IX (no paging), session of April, 1658.

[69] The status of Virginia's first Negroes has been widely debated. Oscar and Mary Handlin surveyed the previous discussions of the subject and gave their own view, that the first Virginia Negroes were not held in slavery, in "The Origins of the Southern Labor System," *WMQ*, 3rd ser., VII (1950), 199–222. The fullest recent appraisal, by Winthrop Jordan in *White over Black* (Chapel Hill, N.C. 1968), 71–82, and also in his "Modern Tensions and the Origins of American Slavery," *Journal of Southern History*, XXVIII (1962), 18–30, concludes that some were enslaved and some were not. The evidence is too fragmentary to prove that any Negroes were imported as servants on the same terms as white servants, but the evidence *is* sufficient to show that Negroes were held as slaves in the 1640s and 1650s. See for example Northampton III, 139, where in 1648 a deed is recorded for a "Negro woman and all her increase (which for future tyme shall bee borne of her body)." For other clear examples of slaves in the 1640s and 1650s see Northampton II, 324; III, 120, 180a; IV, 124, 151, 165a; V, 17a, 86–87, 94a; York I, 96; II, 63, 390.

[70] Northampton III, 150, 152, 205; IV, 226.

servants. Some slaves were allowed to earn money of their own and to buy their freedom with it.[71] They bought and sold and raised cattle of their own.[72] In one case in 1646 the sale of a slave from one master to another was made to depend upon the slave's consent.[73] Another slave was able to purchase the freedom of his daughters and apprenticed them to a white master until they should reach majority.[74] Two Negroes who showed an unwillingness to work were given an indenture guaranteeing their freedom in return for four years' work and 1,700 pounds of tobacco.[75] And this is not the only sign in the records that rewards were thought more effective than coercion as a means of extracting labor. In 1645 Edwin Connaway, clerk of the Northampton court, in a remarkable deposition declared:

> That being at the house of Capt. Taylor, about the Tenth day of July last past the said Capt. Taylor in the morning went into the quartering house and this deponent coming forth of the dwelling house did see Capt. Taylor and Anthony the negro goeing into the Corne Feild and when they returned from the said Corne Feild, the said negro told this deponent saying now Mr. Taylor and I have devided our Corne And I am very glad of it now I know myne owne, hee finds fault with mee that I doe not worke but now I know myne owne ground I will worke when I please and play when I please, And the said Capt. Taylor asked the said Negro saying are you content with what you have And the Negro answered saying I am very well content with what I have or words to that effect.[76]

While racial feelings undoubtedly affected the position of Negroes, there is more than a little evidence that Virginians during these years were ready to think of Negroes as members or potential members of the community on the same terms as other men and to demand of them the same standards of behavior. Black men and white serving the same master worked, ate, and slept together, and together shared in escapades, escapes, and punishments. In 1649 William Watts, a white man, and Mary, a Negro servant, were required to do penance for fornication, like any other couple, by standing in the church at Elizabeth River with the customary white sheet and white wand; and in 1654 the churchwardens of the upper parish in

[71] Northampton IV, 118a; IX, session of Jan. 30, 1659/60; Surry I, 349.
[72] Northampton III, 83; IV, 114; V, 38a.
[73] Northampton IV, 81a.
[74] Northampton III, 82a; IV, 82.
[75] Northampton V, 25a, 27, 54, 60a.   [76] Northampton II, 457.

Northampton presented both a white couple and a Negro couple for fornication.[77]

There are several cases where masters set up conditions in their wills whereby Negro slaves would become free or could purchase their freedom. And the terms indicate an expectation that they would become regular members of the free community. Argall Yeardley provided that a Negro boy, then aged three, should be free at the age of twenty-four and be given two cows. The boy's godfather was made a witness to the agreement.[78] Richard Vaughan provided that each of his three Negro girls should "bee brought upp in the feare of god and to bee taught to reade and make her owne cloaths." When they came of age, they were each to get two cows with calf, and two suits of clothes, two blankets, a rug, a bed, four barrels of corn, and a breeding sow; together they were to have a plantation of 444 acres with a new house 25 feet by 20 feet.[79]

The success of these early efforts at integration is nowhere more dramatically shown than in the behavior of Anthony Longo, a free Negro who had learned not only the merits of industry and thrift but also the truculent attitude to authority which so many Englishmen carried wherever they went and which the courts had so often to put down. One John Neene was sent by Major Walker, a commissioner of the court, to serve a warrant or subpoena on Longo in connection with a case in which Neene needed Longo's testimony. Neene reported his experience in these words:

> Sayth that comeinge to Tony Llongo his house with a warrent of Major Walkers your Deponent asked him whether hee would goe alonge to Mr. Walkers with mee. his answere was what shall I goe to Mr. Walkers for: goe about your business you idle Rascall: Upon those slightinge tearmes, I told him I had a warrant for him, sayeinge, will you goe with that, hee made mee answer, shitt of your warrant have I (said hee) nothinge to doe but goe to Mr. Walker, goe about your business you idle Rascall as did likewise his wife, with such noyse that I could hardly heare my owne words, reading the warrant to them, which when I had done readeinge, the said Tony stroke att mee, and gave mee some blowes, soe perseavinge it was to little purpose to staye with him,

[77] Norfolk II, 113a; V, 55. See also Northampton X, 30; *Minutes of Council*, 477; Hening, I, 551.

[78] Northampton V, 117a–119a.

[79] Northampton V, 102. See also *ibid.*, 57a, 100a; York I, 233; Henrico I, 139; II (transcript), 64.

I went to Mr. Littleton's house and requested Daniel Baker to goe to Tony Longos with mee only to testifie that I had a warrant from Mr. Walker for his appearance before him; Daniel Baker att my request went with mee which when wee came, I desired him to read it to him which he did his answers were that hee would not goe, hee must gather his corne, Nowe it beinge about the sun settinge (or somethinge after) I told him wee might goe to night and neither hinder himselfe much, nor mee, But his answer was thats a goode one nowe I have bine att worke shall goe to Mr. Walkers I your said deponent requested him to goe alonge with mee And as I could not make my debt appear I would give him for his payment 20 lb of tobacco. Well said hee I cannot goe, why when shall I attend you said your deponent tomorrowe or next daye, or next weeake Ile goe with you att any time his answer was in generall, well, well, Ile goe when my corne is in whereupon I bad him goodnight, and left him, and on the morneinge returned the warrant. All which to the best of my remembrance were his very words (or to same effect).[80]

The commissioners understandably punished Longo for contempt of court.[81] But it was the kind of contempt that Englishmen often showed to authority, and it was combined with an assiduity in pursuit of calling that English moralists were doing their best to inculcate more widely at home. As England had absorbed people of every nationality over the centuries and turned them into Englishmen, Virginia's Englishmen were absorbing their own share of foreigners, including Negroes, and molding a New World community on the English model, a pasture-farming empire stretched out and magnified, altered by the nature of the terrain and the universal preoccupation with tobacco but still recognizably English. Yet this empire upon closer examination will be found more different from England than at first appears.

[80] Northampton V, 60a.   [81] *Ibid.*, 54a.

8

LIVING
WITH DEATH

THE most obvious difference between Virginia and England was the abundance of land and the absence of people. The native population which might have made the two countries radically different was small to begin with and became rapidly smaller under the onslaught of European diseases and weapons. Once the English pushed the remnants out of the way, they had several million acres of fertile tidewater lands available for a mere handful of settlers. The relative abundance of land and the shortage of people would shape Virginian—and American—history for centuries to come. But during the colony's first half century the shortage of people was different in kind from any experienced in Americans' later absorption of the continent. It was not just that the colony was new. It was not just a matter of time, needed to build up the stream of immigrants. It was a matter of death. The rich lands of the tidewater were empty not simply for lack of immigrants but because the men who did come to settle on them died so fast. We have seen that after 1625 the colony grew rapidly. But the growth was achieved in the face of a continuing death rate of appalling proportions.

It is well known that before 1624 Virginia was a death trap for most of those who went there. One reason why the king dissolved the Virginia Company was that it seemed to have sent so many men to their deaths without taking adequate measures to feed and shelter them. It is well known, too, that summer in Virginia was a dangerous time for new arrivals. This was "seasoning" time, and those who survived it were said to be "seasoned" and thus immune to the dangers of future summers.[1] What is not generally known is that either

---

[1] David Peter de Vries, in New-York Historical Society, *Collections*, 2nd ser., III (1857), 75; Neill, *Virginia Carolorum*, 109.

the diseases involved in seasoning (probably typhoid fever) [2] or other diseases continued to kill Virginians in large numbers long after 1625. The years from 1625 to 1640, when population more than quintupled, from 1,300 to about 8,100, included the period of the Great Migration from England. During these years it is probable that immigrants to Virginia averaged at least 1,000 a year. The governor wrote in February, 1628, of 1,000 "lately receaved," [3] and in February, 1634, of 1,200 as "this yeares newcomers." [4] Persons arriving "this year" were reported in July, 1634, as 1,500,[5] in May, 1635, as 2,000,[6] and in March, 1636, as 1,606.[7] We have actual records for the year 1635 of 2,010 persons embarking for Virginia from London,[8] and London was not the only port of embarkation. Perhaps these years were exceptional, but other scattered records indicate a continuing heavy exodus from England.[9] If immigrants did average 1,000 a year during the years from 1625 to 1640, then 15,000 immigrants increased the population by a little less than 7,000. Since most immigrants came as servants and were bound for periods of four to seven years in order to repay their passage, it is unlikely that there was a heavy return migration of men ready to pay an equally heavy price to go back where they came from. No matter how one reads the figures, they show that Virginians had to cope year after year with a death rate comparable only to that of severe epidemic years in England.

There is literary evidence to support such a conclusion. Samuel Maverick, returning from Virginia to New England in August, 1636, said that 1,800 had died there the year before.[10] A Dutch ship captain who called at the colony in the summer of 1636 noted that thirty-six sail of ship were there but that they had arrived before the seasoning months were over and that fifteen of the thirty-six captains had consequently died.[11] In 1638, the House of Burgesses

[2] Gordon W. Jones, "The First Epidemic in English America," *VMHB*, LXXI (1963), 3–10.

[3] C.O. 1/4, f.109.

[4] C.O. 1/8, ff.9–10; *VMHB*, VIII (1900–1901), 155.

[5] Massachusetts Historical Society, *Collections*, 4th ser., IX (1871), 110.

[6] *VMHB*, I (1893–94), 417.   [7] *Ibid.*, IX (1901–2), 37.

[8] John C. Hotten, *Our Early Emigrant Ancestors: The Original Lists of Persons of Quality* . . . (New York, 1880), 35–145.

[9] C.O. 1/10, ff.94–95, 126; P.C. 2/50, f.643; P.C. 2/51, ff.16–18; P.C. 2/52, ff.714–15; P.C. 2/53, ff.182, 187, 199.

[10] John Winthrop, *The History of New England*, James Savage, ed. (Boston, 1853), I, 228.

[11] New-York Historical Society, *Collections*, 2nd ser., III (1857), 37, 75, 77.

doubted the feasibility of the king's scheme for limiting tobacco production because of the impossibility of determining the size of such a perishing population as theirs. "In respect," they said, "of the uncerten nomber of people yearely comeinge and the mortallity of people here farre greater some yeares then others . . . wee are not at anie tyme certen of the nomber of our Inhabitants." [12] At the same time the burgesses objected to a request from the king for an account of the debts owed by each planter. The information could not be had, they said, because a third of the debts outstanding in the country were contracted by persons since deceased and could be ascertained only as suits were brought by creditors.[13] That the colony would have expired but for the annual transfusion of immigrants is suggested by the complaint of the inhabitants in 1638 that a proposed monopoly contract for the purchase of Virginia tobacco would prevent any ships from coming "excepting some few belonging to the Contractors." The result would be that "the Collonye will in short tyme melt to nothing for want of supplyes of people." [14]

Although Virginia was supposed to be particularly deadly for new immigrants, seasoned inhabitants too may have experienced a death rate higher than was common in England. The absence of parish registers makes it virtually impossible to obtain the birth and death dates of any substantial group of seventeenth-century Virginians after the census taken in 1624/5. But one crude index of longevity can be gleaned from the records of the Norfolk County court, which include a substantial number of depositions. At the beginning of a deposition, the witness ordinarily gave his name and age. The ages are doubtless rough, for people frequently did not know their exact age and added "or thereabouts" to the number given. The witnesses were of all social classes, including servants. Of the 207 persons who gave depositions between 1637. when the records begin, and 1664, when the number of depositions drops off, the approximate date of death for 99 shows up incidentally in the records by 1700. For these 99 persons identified (all but three of whom were male) the average age at death was 48.[15]

<hr/>

[12] C.O. 1/33, ff.239–40; printed in *Journals of the House of Burgesses, 1619–1658/59*, 59–61. Another copy of this document is printed, wrongly assigned to the year 1668, in H. R. McIlwaine, ed., *Journals of the House of Burgesses of Virginia, 1659/60–1693* (Richmond, 1914), 53–54.

[13] *Ibid.*   [14] C.O. 1/9, f.228.

[15] The median age was between 47 and 48. The oldest was 80 and the youngest 24. The average age at which the persons made their depositions

It is difficult to measure such a figure against the life tables produced with more precise and abundant figures for England or Europe at the time, but it would seem that the life expectancy of seasoned adults in Norfolk County was somewhat lower than life expectancy in contemporary England and very much lower than in New England, where the men who settled Andover, Massachusetts, at about the same period, lived to an average 71.8 years.[16] We get a

---

and thus came under observation was 34 and the median 33. The youngest was 20 and the oldest 60. It is doubtful that a search of the records beyond 1700 for persons who may have died after that date would be fruitful, for the names of those whose death had not been mentioned by then had long since ceased to figure in the records. The date of death has been taken as the date when the person's will was proved, or the date of the inventory of his estate, or the date when he is first referred to in the records as "deceased" (frequently one learns of a death only from the mention of someone's having married the widow). The figures thus tend to exaggerate a little the length of life. It should be noted too that longevity in Norfolk may have been lower than in other parts of Virginia. The county apparently had the reputation of being "an unhealthy place." See Francis Nicholson to Board of Trade, August 1, 1700. C.O. 5/1312, f.1; Henry Howe, *Historical Collections of Virginia* (Charleston, S.C., 1845), 395. Kevin P. Kelly, "Economic and Social Development of Seventeenth-Century Surry County, Virginia" (unpublished doctoral dissertation, University of Washington, 1972), 224–38, attempts to construct life tables for men born in that county between 1650 and 1680, based on 63 persons.

[16] On longevity in England see Peter Laslett, *The World We Have Lost* (London, 1965), 93–94; on Andover, Mass., Philip J. Greven, Jr., *Four Generations: Population, Land, and Family in Colonial Andover, Massachusetts* (Ithaca, N.Y., 1970), 26–27. A slightly different measure of longevity in Norfolk can be obtained from the county commissioners. Of the forty men who sat as commissioners between 1637 and 1660, the age at death can be ascertained for twenty-four. The average age at death was 49 and the median between 47 and 48. The oldest was 74 and the youngest 31. The average age at which they became commissioners and thus come under observation was 36 and the median between 37 and 38. The youngest was 22 when he became a commissioner and the oldest 56. The figures accord with the observation of an anonymous Virginia clergyman in 1689. Speaking of the Indians, he said, "They seldome live longer than 40 or 50 years. Neither do the Inglish who are born in Virginia live beyond that age ordinarily" (Pargellis, "Account of the Indians in Virginia," 230). Three other studies of longevity in Virginia show somewhat different results. Wyndham B. Blanton found average longevity in Virginia, "based on a study of 205 seventeenth century families," to be 51 years and 5 months. "Epidemics, Real and Imaginary, and Other Factors Influencing Seventeenth-Century Virginia's Population," *Bulletin of the History of Medicine*, XXXI (1957), 454–62,

glimpse of what Virginians considered to be old age in the orders of
the Norfolk court relieving aged persons of taxation. Bartholomew
Hoskins was relieved of taxes when he was 47, because he was aged
and infirm and had been in the colony since the time of Sir Thomas
Dale.[17] Rowland Morgan got the same privilege at 54 because he
was a "poor ancient man" and Samuel Turbey at 53 because he was
"ancient, poor, and decrepit." [18] On the other hand, Moses Linton
lived to 80 and got along without exemption until 73 as far as the
records show.[19]

It seems likely that the colony's women and the children they
bore (or at least those that survived infancy) enjoyed more favorable prospects than men. Simply by surviving infancy children were,
in a sense, seasoned, and stood a better chance against the colony's
endemic diseases than those entering from outside. Women had already exhibited their durability in the early days of the colony. In
1624 it was the opinion of Sir Francis Wyatt, after living several
years in the country, that "the weaker sexe . . . escape better than
men, either that their worke lies chiefly within doores, or because
they are of a colder temper." [20] Wyatt may not have been a proper
authority on the temper or temperature of women, but he was right
about their capacity for survival. A list of the living and the dead in
Virginia in February, 1624, shows that 35 out of 279 women (12.5
percent) had died in the preceding ten months, as against 294 out of
1,288 men (22.8 percent). In the following year another list shows
that 14 out of 282 women died (5 percent) as against 100 out of
1,042 men (9.6 percent).[21]

---

at p. 461. Kelly, "Economic and Social Development of Surry County," 28–
29, using genealogies of 62 families, found a mean age at death of 57.65 for
men born 1620–50, 56.25 for men born 1651–80, and 61.52 for men born
1681–1710. Martin H. Quitt, "The Virginia House of Burgesses, 1660–1706:
The Social, Educational, and Economic Bases of Political Power" (unpublished doctoral dissertation, Washington University, St. Louis, Mo., 1970),
estimated the median age at death for 30 immigrant burgesses at 60.5 and
for 74 natives at 55. But Lorena S. Walsh and Russell R. Menard, in a more
widely based study of longevity in Charles County, Maryland, found life
expectancy for men born in the county to be between 24.5 and 27.5 years at
age 20. Immigrants, even if they survived seasoning, had an even lower life
expectancy. "Death in the Chesapeake: Two Life Tables for Men in Early
Colonial Maryland," *Maryland Historical Magazine,* LXIX (1974), 211–27.
    [17] Norfolk II, 50.   [18] Norfolk IX, 274.   [19] Norfolk VII, 311.
    [20] *WMQ,* 2nd ser., VI (1927), 117.
    [21] See Appendix, esp. note 3. The deaths in the 1625 list are incomplete.
I have not counted persons whose sex is not clearly indicated by a forename.

The lists, while showing the superior resistance of women to disease, also reveal how small their total numbers were in the population. In 1625 there were 350 men for every 100 women. Subsequent immigration kept the ratio uneven. Of the 2,010 immigrants from London in 1635, less than 14 percent were women. And all the evidence indicates that during the rest of the century women continued to be a minority in Virginia (see Appendix).

We are observing, then, a society that during its first forty or fifty years grew under conditions differing dramatically from those in the world that the settlers had known before. Women, and therefore children, constituted a much smaller proportion of the population in Virginia than anywhere in Europe. Unmarried men constituted a much larger proportion. And the whole population, but especially its men, was dying off rapidly and could sustain itself and grow only by continuing heavy immigration. These unfamiliar and unwelcome circumstances, no less than the colonists' wish to create familiar institutions, dictated the shape of their developing society.

One much lamented development came in the position gained by physicians, or by persons at any rate who claimed to be able to cure disease. Sick men are not likely to be hard bargainers, and dead men cannot bargain. Virginia accordingly became a land of opportunity for doctors and quack doctors; and in the seventeenth century the ministrations of the one were not likely to be more effective than those of the other. The fees charged by people who practiced medicine were by any other standards outrageous. Men who were unable to pay sometimes bound themselves as servants for a year or more in return for a cure. But since the services performed were often unavailing, the physician or "chirurgeon" commonly collected his charges from the estate of his newly deceased patient. Sums of 1,000 pounds of tobacco were not uncommon, and they went as high as 2,500.[22]

The House of Burgesses noticed that the effect of these "imoderate and excessive rates" was to prevent men from summoning help for sick servants, because "it was the more gainfull and saving way to stand to the hazard of their servants then to entertain the certain charge of a physitian or chirurgeon whose demands for the most parte exceed the purchase of the patient." To prevent gouging by physicians, the burgesses provided that anyone thinking a charge excessive could bring the case to court, where the commissioners would

[22] Norfolk III, 136, 172, 212a; IV, 162; Northampton IV, 155, 203; V, 138, 142; York II, 152.

allow what they considered reasonable.[23] But the law seems to have been ineffective. The only complaints that were successful in court were those where the patient had obtained a genuine contract in which payment was to depend on being cured.

In every county a number of physicians set up practice. In Charles City County between 1656 and 1660, when the population was probably about a thousand, at least nine persons are mentioned in the records as practicing medicine. In Northampton County between 1640 and 1660, at least twenty physicians or chirurgeons are mentioned, though no more than four or five were active at the same time. The county in 1660 probably had fewer than a thousand inhabitants. In Norfolk County between 1637 and 1660 sixteen are mentioned, for a population of around 800.[24] Not all those who tried to practice made a go of it; and, in view of their greater exposure to disease, the mortality among physicians may have been above average. But a few of the colony's big men began in this way: John Pott, who was governor for a time; Obedience Robins, one of the most important men in Northampton County; and Colonel John Stringer, another Northampton commissioner, who affected the title of "philomedicus" rather than plain "chirurgeon."

But the unusually large role played by physicians in the colony was the least important consequence of Virginia's continuing high death rate. More significant was the effect on the role of women. In a society where men died early, the relatively small number of women could expect to wear widow's weeds and to wear them often, though not for long. Women were too rare in Virginia to be left for long without husbands. The case of Jane Sparrow in 1660 was doubtless extreme. She was sick, and her husband called in a doctor. The cure was successful, but the husband died, leaving the doctor to collect 1,200 pounds of tobacco from his estate. The recovered wife remarried five days later.[25]

Most Virginia women waited a couple of months; but they were, in the records at least, a singularly unlovely lot. Given their small numbers, they account for a high proportion of the cases of

[23] Hening, I, 316.

[24] On population estimates see Appendix. In counting "chirurgeons" I have omitted persons who appear to be surgeons aboard ships lying in the Virginia rivers, except when they later became residents. But ships' surgeons did become involved in court cases ashore, and it may be that I have inadvertently included some.

[25] Charles City County, Orders 1658–61, in Beverly Fleet, ed., *Virginia Colonial Abstracts*, XI (Richmond, 1941), 89, 92.

slander heard by the courts, and they were also in court too often for abusing their servants. In three cases where servants died after abusive treatment, women were defendants.[26] In none of these cases was the woman found guilty, but one, Anne Charlton (widow of Stephen Charlton, a Northampton commissioner), was required to give bond for good behavior in the future. The commissioners had had trouble with her before, when she was the widow of Anthony West. At that time, she had gone after her overseer with a club.[27] Another commissioner, Henry Woodhouse, of Norfolk, had to be given protection from the unkind usage of his wife while he was sick. His fellow commissioners ordered that the neighbors should "have free libertie to resorte to the house of Mr. Woodhouse to see that hee have what shalbe both sufficient and necessarie for him dureinge his sickness, and according to his quallitye." At the same session the court placed in the sheriff's custody for protection a maidservant of Mrs. Woodhouse who had been "Most unchristian-like used by her mistress." But the court's efforts were not enough. By the next session both Woodhouse and the maid were dead. Within the year Mrs. Woodhouse had remarried.[28]

If an awareness of their scarcity value induced an imperiousness or even downright tyranny in Virginia's women, it also gave them greater economic advantages than they enjoyed in England. By Virginia's law, as by England's, a widow was entitled to a life interest in one-third of her husband's estate,[29] and in Virginia the annual usufruct of an estate was likely to amount to a larger proportion of its value than in England. Furthermore, men of property generally favored their wives with more than the law required. It was common to give specific bequests to the children and everything else to the wife,[30] but there was great variety in wills. John Valentine gave his widow one-third of the estate as her own and the use of the rest of it while she remained a widow.[31] Rowland Burnham gave his wife half the servants, half the cattle, all the furniture, but none of the

---

[26] Norfolk II, 117a. 120; III, 20a; Northampton II, 22, 26; IV, 223a–227; cf. Northumberland III, 454; R. A. Brock, ed., *The Official Letters of Alexander Spotswood*, Virginia Historical Society, *Collections*, n.s., I and II (Richmond, 1882–85), II, 202–3.

[27] Northampton IV, 97, 223a–227.

[28] Norfolk III, 157a, 165a, 170a, 181, 221.   [29] Hening, I, 405.

[30] This is an impression formed from reading the numerous wills recorded in the county courts. In the examples cited below, however, I have taken wills available in print.

[31] *VMHB*, VI (1898–99), 118–20.

land.[32] Abraham Peirsey gave his widow one-third plus one-twelfth.[33] Adam Thorowgood gave his widow a mare and a foal, one of the best cows in the pen, half a dozen goats, four sows, and part of his plantation for life, "all which I give her as a memorial of my love—not any ways intending to cut her off from a equal share in my estate with my children."[34]

Besides getting a large share of the estate, the widow was often appointed administrator. This meant that claimants against the estate had to make their claims to her, and she, by delaying payment, might continue to enjoy the whole for some time. Captain John Sibsey left most of his land, his servants, his plate, and two-thirds of everything else to his widow, one-third to his daughter. But the daughter's husband had to sue her mother in order to get what was given her.[35] If a widow had a jointure (which excluded a part of the estate as belonging to her before any inventory was taken), she was in a particularly advantageous position. Whether she had a jointure or not, she was not responsible for her husband's debts beyond the value of his estate.[36]

The wealthy widow has always had an edge on competitors in the marriage market. In Virginia the death rate produced such a rapid turnover of husbands and wives that widowhood became a principal means for the concentration of wealth. It has been suggested that the men who made their way to the top in the 1620s and 1630s in Virginia were unable to perpetuate their family lines; the famous first families of Virginia came to the colony later.[37] In a patrilineal sense this was the case. But while the high mortality lasted, with women apparently resisting it more successfully than men, Virginia was on the way to becoming an economic matriarchy, or rather a widowarchy. The man who needed capital could get it most easily by marrying a widow. And she was likely to get it back again, with whatever return he had added to it, when he died. The next husband would have an even larger base to build on.

We can sometimes watch the process taking place among the more successful planters, whose extensive holdings brought them frequently into the court records. One of the men, for example, who made it to the top in Virginia in the late 1620s and early 1630s was

[32] *WMQ*, 2nd ser., II (1922), 269.   [34] *Ibid.*, II (1894–95), 416.
[33] *VMHB*, I (1893–94), 188.   [35] Norfolk III, 12a, 42a, 43.
[36] For examples, Norfolk III, 201; IV, 120.
[37] Bailyn, "Politics and Social Structure."

Adam Thorowgood. Though he came as a servant, he was of good family and in 1627 married Sarah Offley, daughter of a London merchant and granddaughter of a Lord Mayor. Thorowgood died in 1640 at the age of 38. Within a year Sarah married Captain John Gookin, whose father had established one of the largest particular plantations under the Virginia Company. John Gookin died in 1643 at the age of 30. Sarah stayed single for four years, playing the grande dame of Norfolk at her house on Lynnhaven Bay. In 1647 she married Francis Yeardley, aged 23, son of Sir George Yeardley, the former governor. She saw to it that most of their property would be hers and not included in the estate if he should die before her, which he did, at the age of 31. Something of her scale of living can be judged from the fact that five years after their marriage Francis traded seven head of cattle to buy jewelry for her (which did not include a diamond necklace that she had at her death).[38]

The game, of course, could be played the other way around. If a man could stay alive long enough, he might become a repeating widower. And as might well be expected in such a perishing society, repeating widows often married repeating widowers. William Burdett, who arrived as a servant in 1615, was able to marry the widow of Roger Sanders, one of the first commissioners on the Eastern Shore. She had already been a widow at least once before she married Sanders, and evidently Burdett's pursuit of her was a matter to bet on. The Northampton court recorded a deposition "that Mr. George Scovell did laye a wager with mr. mountney £10 starling to £5 starling Calling of us tow to witness the same: That mr. william Burditt should never match in wedlocke with the widow Sanders while they lived in Virginia. Soe the sayd Scovell not Contented but would lay £40 starlinge more to £10 starlinge that the sayd mr. william Burdett should never have the widdowe Sanders." Scovell lost. Burdett got her, outlived her, and before dying at the age of forty-six, he married another widow. When Burdett died, he left 66 head of cattle, 32 goats, a parcel of hogs, 10 servants, and a stack of debts.[39]

The man with his eye on the main chance went for the widow rather than the daughters when a wealthy Virginian died. Governor Harvey and Thomas Hill both married daughters of Abraham Peir-

[38] *VMHB*, II (1894–95), 416; Norfolk III, 24a, 193, 201; IV, 117; Gookin, *Daniel Gookin*, 56–57.
[39] Northampton I, xxxii, 10; II, 419–25.

sey, the richest man in Virginia. But Samuel Mathews, whom George Sandys had earlier identified as a man addicted to profit, got the widow (she had been the widow of Nathaniel West when Peirsey married her) and with her assistance hung on to the whole estate, even though Governor Harvey in a lengthy lawsuit tried to get it away.[40]

As women in Virginia generally became widows sooner or later, children generally became "orphans," as fatherless children were called in Virginia even when their mothers were still alive. And although orphans usually came off second best in contests with their mother or stepfather for an estate, Virginians were conscious of the orphans' disadvantages and took measures to protect them. In making a will, men often named a guardian other than the mother to protect the children's interests, and in addition appointed feoffees in trust to see that the guardian did his job properly. Where a child was left without either parent, the county court appointed a guardian. At the lowest rank in the social scale an orphan without either father or mother was better off than in England. Because he was a potential source of valuable labor, the community seldom had to subsidize his bringing up unless he was a mere infant. Unlike the penniless orphan in England, the parish apprentice, he could expect to be taught a trade, and frequently he received tools and clothes when he attained majority. Sometimes his guardian was required also to set aside a cow calf for him and take care of her increase until he reached majority.[41]

Fathers, anticipating that they would not live to see their children launched in the world, frequently deeded cattle to them at birth and appointed feoffees in trust to see that the child received the female increase when he married or came of age. The male increase was usually assigned to pay for the child's upbringing. Grandparents and godparents often made the same sort of gift. A large portion of the surviving court records consists of these deeds of gift, in which a cow is carefully identified by her appearance, earmarks, and name (Golden Locks, Gentle, Whitefoot, Nightingale, Frisky, Buttermilk). So prevalent was the practice that orphans ranked among Virginia's principal cattle owners. Parents who did not provide a "stock" for their children by deeds of gift took care of the matter

[40] *VMHB*, XI (1903–4), 171, 174–82.
[41] For examples, Northampton III, 125; IV, 177; Fleet, *Virginia Colonial Abstracts*, X, 46.

in their wills. Susan English spelled out the usual arrangement with unusual explicitness: After bequeathing various cattle to her three children, she wrote:

> whereas there wilbe charge in bringing upp the abovesaid Children both for diet Cloathing and scooling I desire it may be entered upon the records in the court booke that whosoever bringeth upp the children unto the age of discresion with all things necessary and fitting shall have the male cattle for soe long tyme as the Children be with them.[42]

The acquisition of all the male cattle produced during the orphan's minority was such a lucrative compensation for bringing him up that men on every social level competed for the privilege of guardianship. How serious a matter this could be is revealed in a contest between Governor Harvey and Ambrose Harmer over the guardianship of Benoni Buck, the idiot orphan of the Reverend Richard Buck. Harvey proposed to rotate the guardianship among members of the council in order to help support the government, but Harmer (who claimed the guardianship through his wife, the widow of one of the overseers of Buck's will) carried the case to England's Court of Wards and to the Privy Council. The Privy Council sided with Harmer, much to Harvey's chagrin.[43]

There was so strong a temptation for guardians and stepfathers to appropriate more than the male increase or whatever was allowed in the writs and deeds of gift that the House of Burgesses in 1643 passed a law requiring a yearly accounting of all orphans' estates by their guardians. Henceforth each county court held an annual session known as an "Orphants Court," in which guardians reported the previous and present number of every orphan's cattle.[44] Even mothers who were guardians of their own children had to render accounts. Ordinarily the courts allowed no expenditure for an orphan that would diminish the cattle whose increase had been assigned for his upbringing. Mary Woodhouse Batts had to ask special permission of the court to sell two steers in order to buy clothes for her children by Henry Woodhouse. The court granted permission on the condition that the steers be replaced by two younger steers.[45]

[42] York II, 339.

[43] *VMHB*, IX (1901-2), 178-79; XII (1904-5), 390-93.

[44] Hening, I, 260. For other legislation protecting orphans, see *ibid.*, 260-61, 269-70, 416-17, 443-44, 451. For examples of orphans courts, see Norfolk I, 204-5, 257-58, 270-71; II, 137a-139a; York II, 180-84, 399-408.

[45] Norfolk IV, 217.

Sarah Offley Thorowgood Gookin was harder to handle. The commissioners of Norfolk County, who were obviously afraid of her, asked her politely but unsuccessfully on ten different occasions to render account of the cattle of her children by Adam Thorowgood. Finally they sent the high sheriff, Thomas Ivey, to levy a fine of 500 pounds of tobacco on her. She replied to the sheriff's hesitant communication with a letter in which she flatly refused to pay a fine or to appear at court, and hinted broadly that the court was going beyond its jurisdiction. It was unheard of, she said, that a mother should be asked to account for the property of her own children. She closed with a characteristic feminine touch: "my respects to your selfe and wyfe most kindly remembred to whome I have sent a small baskett of apples per the bearer." The next sheriff, the following year, like Ivey, lacked the nerve to press the matter further. The court threatened to fine him if he did not proceed. But before anyone else dared to face up to her, Francis Yeardley married her, and upon *his* promise that *he* would render the account, the court with undisguised relief repealed its 500-pound fine.[46]

But not everyone was Sarah Offley Thorowgood Gookin Yeardley. The courts frequently did curb mothers and stepfathers and guardians, even of exalted rank. Richard Vaughan, who was feoffee in trust for Stephen Charlton's stepdaughter Bridget, complained to the court, of which Charlton was a commissioner, when Charlton sold a mare and horse belonging to the girl. His fellow commissioners ordered Charlton to replace the mare and horse by a Negro man and the produce of the crops he should make annually. When Charlton died, Vaughan saw to it that Bridget's cattle and other possessions were not included in the inventory of Charlton's estate and also prevented her stepmother from making use of a mare that belonged to her.[47] When Matthew Phillips, a commissioner of the Norfolk court, got with child a maidservant who belonged to some orphans of whom he was guardian, his fellow commissioners made him pay the orphans' estate 600 pounds of tobacco for loss of the maid's time during pregnancy and lying-in.[48]

In making provision for children in wills, Virginians usually followed the English pasture-farming pattern of partible inheritance. Each child was likely to get something; but if one had already been given a substantial amount of property by deed of gift, his share in

[46] Norfolk II, 13a, 36a, 41, 48–48a, 52, 52a, 53a.
[47] Northampton IV, 218a; V, 125a, 135.   [48] Norfolk I, 305.

the estate might be smaller. Thus Stephen Charlton left only small bequests to his daughter Elizabeth, but he had already deeded her 1,700 acres of land, a slave, a mare, 3 cows, 6 ewes, and several thousand pounds of tobacco.[49] John Valentine excluded his eldest daughter Ann "in regard she hath a considerable stock already confirmed her, therefore I only give and bequeath to her at marriage one cow." [50] Commonly the eldest son got more than other children, especially of land, but not much more. Occasionally the youngest child got a larger share.[51] Often all shared "by the rule of proportion, that is to say, share and share alike." [52] Wills, like deeds of gift, thus contributed not simply to the accumulation of property by women but also to the dispersion of property among women and children, or widows and orphans.

If we examine the property that was being tossed about so rapidly from the dying to the living, we will discover that mobility was only one aspect of its instability. Property itself was evanescent, shifting in value, perishable. Specie was virtually nonexistent, for the export of coin from England to the colonies was forbidden, and whatever came into the colony from other sources quickly found its way out again. And land, the symbol of stable value in England, was the least valuable investment a Virginian could make during the first half of the century, unless he was remarkably farsighted and willing to wait a generation or two for the payoff. It was so abundant and so easy to acquire that the price rose very slowly. Public lands could be obtained by producing evidence of having paid for the transportation of others to the colony, at the rate of fifty acres per person or "headright"; and if a man did not need all the headrights he was entitled to, he could sell them. Such headrights were bought and sold at 40 to 50 pounds of tobacco in the 1650s.[53] To convert a headright into actual ownership of a specific tract of land, the secretary of the colony exacted a fee for making out a patent, 30 pounds of tobacco in the 1630s, increased to 50 pounds in 1643 and 80 pounds in 1658.[54] Even at the highest figure, a hundred acres

[49] Northampton V, 17a, 56a–57a.   [50] *VMHB*, VI (1898–99), 119.

[51] Northampton IV, 223.

[52] *VMHB*, VI (1898–99), 119. This continued to be the common practice in the eighteenth century. See Robert E. and B. Katherine Brown, *Virginia, 1705–1786: Democracy or Aristocracy* (East Lansing, Mich., 1964), 81–83.

[53] Norfolk III, 205a; Westmoreland I, 51.

[54] Hening, I, 201, 265, 463.

of public land could be had for 160 to 180 pounds of tobacco, less than 2 pounds per acre.

Precise valuations of private land are hard to obtain, because lands were seldom appraised in the inventories of estates, and most deeds do not mention the price. Deeds which do mention the price indicate that unimproved river land could be had throughout the 1640s and 1650s for from 4 to 10 pounds of tobacco per acre. At this rate, a hundred acres was worth no more than a couple of cows, worth less than a year's wages for a servant hired by the year. Where a man's plantation was appraised in his estate, it usually accounted for only a small proportion of it. Robert Glascock, for example, left an estate in Norfolk County in 1646 worth 35,850 pounds of tobacco. The plantation and its buildings amounted to only 3,500 pounds.[55] An orphan left with nothing but land would be poor indeed, and a wise guardian would trade the land for whatever cattle it would buy, as Alexander Mountney did in 1642 with 150 acres belonging to the orphans of Edward Hill and Thomas Spilman, because vacant land "was noe wayes beneficiall to the said Orphants." [56]

While unimproved land was a poor inheritance and a poor investment because its value increased so slowly, improved land was not much better, because it could decline in value. Tobacco could be grown on a piece of land for only three or four years before the crop began to diminish. The planter therefore counted on abandoning a field after that length of time. Efforts to restrict tobacco growing only hastened the process. Tobacco grown on virgin land was of better quality than that from used land, and each plant produced more.[57] Whether restricted to a certain number of pounds or to a certain number of plants, a man would go for virgin land to make the maximum profit. And as long as land remained abundant, even in the absence of restrictions, there was a temptation to keep moving in search of better crops.

Because of the abundance of low-cost land wealthy Virginians (unlike wealthy men in England) were at first relatively indifferent to the opportunities for acquiring land. Sometimes they waited years

[55] Norfolk II, 45–46.

[56] Northampton II, 213; cf. *ibid.*, 219. The value of land in Maryland at this time seems to have been about the same. See William A. Reavis, "The Maryland Gentry and Social Mobility, 1637–1676," *WMQ*, 3rd ser., XIV (1957), 418–28, at 423*n*.

[57] "Letter from Clayton," Force, *Tracts*, III, No. 12, pp. 20–21.

before claiming the acres due them by headright for servants they had transported.[58] Often they sold their headrights rather than patent the land for themselves. When later generations of Virginians settled down, after the tidewater land next to the rivers had been taken up, they felt that a tobacco plantation needed fifty acres per working hand.[59] Even though a man could care for only three or four acres at a time in tobacco, some was needed for corn and a great deal for pasture and for a long recuperative, fallow period. In the first half of the seventeenth century, however, few Virginians saw the advantage of acquiring large reserves for future use. Good land lay everywhere around them. Something of the cavalier attitude of landed men toward their holdings can be seen in Stephen Charlton's recollection in 1648 of how Francis Pott came to settle on the Eastern Shore:

> Sayth that beinge att Mr. [Argall] Yardley his howse about three yeares since (or thereabouts) Capt. Francis Pott alsoe beinge then there and newly come over the Baye, with some servants (whereby to make a cropp) And beinge unprovided of a place to plant, this Deponent spoake and said hee could helpe him to ground: And Mr. Peter Walker hee said alsoe then, that hee could helpe him to grounde to plant on; but Mr. Yardley said noe William Berry his plantation laye voyde and was fenced and hee should have yt for nothinge.[60]

Houses, of course, increased the value of land where they were located but not usually by more than a couple of thousand pounds of tobacco. While land remained abundant, men hesitated to invest much in a house that they might one day wish to abandon. Virginia houses continued to be for the most part small and insubstantial. Even the more well-to-do planters contented themselves with a few rooms, a "quartering house" for their servants, tobacco houses for curing the crop, and perhaps a milkhouse. Though the houses were doubtless better than they had been in the 1620s, most were made of wood and were typically fifteen feet by twenty, twenty by twenty, or twenty-five by twenty. For building a house twenty feet square a carpenter charged 600 pounds of tobacco in 1655, worth

---

[58] See E. S. Morgan, "Headrights and Head Counts: A Review Article," *VMHB*, LXXX (1972), 361–71.

[59] Harry J. Carman, ed., *American Husbandry* (New York, 1939), 165.

[60] Northampton III, 158a.

only a little more than a cow.[61] The most valuable parts of the building were the nails and sawn boards, the doors, and the glass; and a deserted building was likely to disappear in a hurry from people scavenging these.[62] But decay rather than pillage was the principal enemy of Virginia houses. Land and houses rapidly declined together. When Philip Chapman in his will ordered his plantation sold to buy cattle for his son John after his death, it was, he said, because the land and house alike would be worn out by the time the boy came of age.[63]

Even tobacco, the colony's principal commodity, was highly perishable. Stored for a year or more, it was likely to rot, especially if in packing the leaves had been wet down to make them more pliable, or if improperly cured leaves had been included. In these early years Virginians had not acquired the skill in packing necessary to make tobacco keep, and so most planters were eager to get it off their hands as quickly as possible.

If the ships that carried it to market failed to arrive in sufficient numbers, the hogsheads left behind might be a total loss by the next season. Sometimes litigation would hold up shipments, with disastrous results. One Dutch merchant lost heavily when his agent collected 17,000 pounds of tobacco from Edmund Scarburgh before he had conveyance ready for it. A subsequent lawsuit further delayed shipment, so that two years later in the summer of 1654 it was still packed in hogsheads in Scarburgh's tobacco sheds. By that time it was so rotten that Scarburgh's overseer reported he "was forsed to flinge it awaye for wante of roome to cure our crops nor could bee noe longer kept by reason of the extreame stincke it yeilded in the summer tyme." [64]

[61] Norfolk III, 180. Another contract, in 1645, called for 240 pounds and one ewe kid (worth perhaps £3 in all) to build a house 15 by 20 feet with a "Welch chimney." Northampton II, 395. In the following year another man contracted to build a house 25 by 20 feet, the cost of the lumber not included, for five pairs of shoes and the soling of a sixth pair. Northampton III, 7a. Shoes at this time cost 50 pounds of tobacco a pair. Northampton III, 24a, 151a, 171a. For other building contracts see Surry I, 55, 96; Henrico I, 88; Norfolk II, 186a.

[62] Norfolk III, 215; Henrico I, 100, 490; Northumberland III, 248.

[63] Northampton V, 87a–88.

[64] Northampton V, 62a–65a. In February, 1656/7, John Jeffries, a London merchant who had been trading in tobacco for the preceding twelve years, testified before the High Court of Admiralty that planters in Virginia who had not disposed of their crop by March made it a practice

Virginia's most stable, most secure commodity was cattle. Hence the practice of deeding cattle to children. But even cattle were by no means a sure thing. Throughout the seventeenth century, Virginians were still collecting bounties on wolves (which may even have multiplied as a result of the introduction of cattle) and still fending off Indian poachers. A herd might be cut down by a bad winter or by epidemic disease, or the animals might run wild beyond recovery in the woods. You could not store up cattle and forget them, like acres of land, and expect to find them when you went looking. In demanding an annual accounting of orphans' cattle, the courts were guarding not merely against embezzlement but against the neglect that could destroy an inheritance overnight.

Servants were Virginia's most valued form of property but also the most risky. It was noted in 1648 that servants were "more advantageous . . . than any other commodityes" for importation from England.[65] The initial cost for a man for four or five years was no more in tobacco than he might make in a year.[66] The risk came from the mortality to which servants were no less subject than masters. During a man's first year in the country it was considered safer not to work him in hot weather, when tobacco needed most care. The risk of losing him anyhow was so great that when the House of Burgesses passed a law against engrossing imported commodities to sell for a profit, they provided that "Nevertheless it shall be lawfull . . . for any person haveing bought a servant and undergone the charge and hazard of seasoning of any such servant, to make his best advantage by putting off or bartering such servant to any other inhabitant within the collony." [67] The risk was reflected in prices. A seasoned hand, even if he had only two or three years to serve, might be considered more valuable than a new hand for his full term.[68]

"to send their tobacco when March is past by any shippe they can or if noe shipp bound for England bee then there to barter it away to any that will take it for the like quantitie of tobacco to bee paid the next yeare following or send the same for New England, rather than keepe it in Virginia after March is past, by reason it is a Commoditie which with the heate of the Country in Virginia will bee spoiled if it bee kept after the moneth of March next following after the yeare it groweth." H.C.A. 13/71 (P.R.O.).

[65] Northampton IV, 15a.

[66] Assuming an output of 1,500 to 2,000 pounds. See chap. 7, note 40.

[67] Hening, I, 245.

[68] For example, a new man with four years to serve was exchanged in 1642 for a seasoned man with two years to serve. Norfolk I, 159. In 1643 a

The price for a servant just arriving from England with five years or more to serve ranged from 600 pounds or more in the 1630s up to 1,000 pounds or more in the 1640s and 1650s; a seasoned hand with three years or more to serve was worth from 1,500 to 2,000 pounds during the 1640s and early 1650s.[69]

A servant, though seasoned and in reasonably good health, was valuable only for the work that could be extracted from him in the given time of his service. But servants unless closely supervised were no more diligent in later decades than they had been in the early days of the colony. With this fact in mind, Governor Harvey in 1639 failed to act against one Thomas Loving, who by marrying a widow had gained control of an estate entrusted to her deceased husband by a London merchant. There was no doubt that Loving was detaining the estate illegally, but the governor refrained from taking it away because there would then be no one to look after it, "the servants being thereby left without oversight by whose neglect the Estate in question might suffer much prejudice."[70] Harvey later explained the servant problem to his superiors in England: ". . . daily experience informeth how much a Virginia estate (which consisteth for [i.e., of] servants for tearme Yeares and Cattell) is wasted in the absence of a Master, through the neglect of Servants whose tyme expire with certaintye of charge to supplye them and noe advantage to the Master."[71] A Virginia estate, in other words, might be here today and gone tomorrow simply from failure to make use of it.

Virginia's high rate of mortality and the fleeting value of property, whether servants, land, tobacco, or—to a lesser degree—cattle,

---

man with six years to serve was exchanged for a man with two years to serve plus 300 pounds of tobacco. *Ibid.*, 202. In 1655 an inventory evaluated three new men and boys for a total of 4,500, while two seasoned men for three and four years respectively totaled 4,000. Norfolk III, 19. In Northampton a 1648 inventory listed a man with two and a half years to serve at 2,000 and one with five years to serve at 1,800. Northampton III, 180a. In a York inventory in 1653 a man with three years to serve was valued at 1,000 and "a new hand" with seven and a half years to serve at 900. York I, 143.

[69] A shipload of servants in 1636 brought from 450 to 600 pounds of tobacco apiece. Martha W. Hiden, ed., "Accompts of the Tristram and Jane," *VMHB*, LXII (1954), 424-47. The values for subsequent years are drawn mainly from inventories in Norfolk, Northampton, and York. See also chap. 15, note 4.

[70] *VMHB*, XII (1904-5), 389.   [71] *Ibid.*, 393.

precluded any secure accumulation of wealth within the colony and invited theft and embezzlement of all kinds. It was not merely a question of widows and their new husbands hanging on to estates that did not belong to them, or of men claiming, taking, and using up an estate before the true heir could show up. A clever crook could take advantage of almost any transfer of property in a community where every business transaction was a high-risk adventure delicately balanced against the perishability of both the property and the participants involved.

In spite of the handicaps thus imposed by mortality and by the evanescence of property, Virginians did manage in the decades after 1630 to bring a measure of stability to their economic transactions. In the absence of coin they made tobacco their principal medium of exchange, and because it was so perishable a medium, they often made their exchanges in advance, in promissory notes stated in pounds of tobacco "payable at the next crop." Big men, who could take the risk, became merchant planters. They bought shiploads of English goods and supplied their neighbors with clothes and tools in return for such notes. Thus Hugh Yeo, a merchant planter on the Eastern Shore, in April, 1647, supplied seventeen persons there with goods valued at a total of 9,469 pounds of tobacco payable the following October.[72] Even fines levied as punishments by the courts were made payable at the next crop.[73]

Although the system was simple, its operation was complicated by the death rate. A not uncommon case occurred in the Norfolk court when the clerk recorded a suit for 966 pounds of tobacco against John Laurence because he had married the widow of John Stratton who was the security for a debt due to Thomas Bridge, because Bridge had married the widow of George Bateman who had married the widow of John Holmes to whom the debt was originally owed.[74] With the parties dying off so rapidly, it was easy to lose the documents and difficult to keep track of who owed what to whom. Frequently the courts had to arbitrate disputes on the basis of oral testimony from witnesses to a transaction.

In order to lend a greater stability to the system, the House of Burgesses at one point ordered markets to be set up, with the intention of establishing what amounted to an exchange, with the clerk

---

[72] Northampton III, 73–75; cf. Northampton IV, 74a; V, 42.
[73] For example, Northampton IV, 178a.   [74] Norfolk IV, 282.

of the market witnessing every transaction. The measure failed and was repealed,[75] but the courts themselves took on the character of an exchange. All conveyances had to be recorded there; and book debts (those recorded only in a merchant's account book) were made not actionable.[76] In order to speed collections, debtors could simply "confess judgment," that is, admit that they owed the amount demanded and have the fact recorded without going through the expense of a trial. Speed was essential because of the importance of oral testimony and the mortality of witnesses. For example, creditors who had already collected from a man sometimes tried to collect again from his heirs and often succeeded if death had also removed witnesses to the payment. The courts responded by adjusting the statute of limitations to the character of their society, ordering that no bill or bond should be good after three years from its date.[77]

In requiring the speedy settlement of debts, the courts aimed primarily at preventing fraud. But they were also recognizing the importance of time in the colony's economy. Perhaps because Virginians had less time to reckon with than other people, they came to value it more highly. It was not only that a man had a short while to live. His servants, his most lucrative income-producing property, were worthless unless used before their time ran out. And he had to have them on hand when he and his crop needed them. A Virginian who made a contract to buy servants would go to court if they were not delivered on the agreed date. When John Neale promised to furnish John Harloe with a new man for four years' service but was unable to obtain one by the specified time, he had to turn over his own servant, Richard Bayley, until he could get a new one. Time was money, or at any rate it was tobacco and tobacco was money. The courts recognized the equation by making debts payable in days of work. A debt in work might even be collectible from a dead man, as when the Northampton court in 1641 ordered the estate of Daniel Cugley, deceased, to pay eight days' work to Henry King.[78]

As the courts took on the function of an exchange, they acknowledged the equation of time and money in other ways too. When a man brought suit against another and failed to appear to prosecute it, he subjected the defendant to a waste of time for which

---

[75] Hening, I, 362, 397.   [76] *Ibid.*, 301–2, 417, 472–73, 485–86; II, 111.

[77] *Ibid.,* I, 390. The limit was later extended to five years. *Ibid.*, 483–84; II, 104–5.

[78] Northampton I, 98, 112; II, 76.

he ought to pay. It accordingly became the practice in such cases to nonsuit the plaintiff and award the defendant a sum for the amount of work time lost. In an early instance the Norfolk court spelled out the reasoning: Tristram Mason, having caused Robert Taylor "to leave his afaires and to appeare at this court It is therefore ordered that the said masonn shall pay the said Robert Taylor for one dayes worke and his Charges for his diett the said day and likewise the charges of the suite." [79] In later instances the court specified an amount of tobacco, usually at the rate of twenty pounds a day, with ten pounds reckoned as the value of a day's work and ten pounds for diet. Witnesses subpoenaed in a suit were entitled by the same reasoning to payment for their time, and the courts ordered the losing party or the party in whose behalf they were summoned to reward them at a similar rate.

Thus Virginians built a local system of credit and exchange that recognized their peculiar conditions of life and created a kind of stability out of instability. Virginia could not quite be England. As long as the heavy mortality lasted it must be vastly different. Yet the differences were not all in England's favor. The very abundance of land and scarcity of people that made land a poor investment gave Virginia an irresistible attraction for ordinary men. Land was the anchor of every Englishman's hope for security, and English political philosophers attributed their country's freedom to the vigilance of its landowners, whose representatives in Parliament could curb the tyranny of ambitious monarchs. But in England the landowners were few, while in Virginia anyone who survived his seasoning and service could take up a plot, grow his crop, make his voice heard in voting for representatives, and perhaps even aspire to represent his neighbors in the House of Burgesses. Those who survived learned to live with the other risks, even to overcome most of them. And when mortality finally began to decline, it looked for a time as though Virginia might become the center of a New World empire where Englishmen and English liberty would thrive together.

[79] Norfolk I, 39.

9

THE TROUBLE
WITH TOBACCO

Wᴴᴇɴ and why Virginians began
to live longer is almost as much a mystery as why they had died so
rapidly. Concrete if indirect evidence of the rise in longevity comes
from the rise in population after 1644. It had taken thirty-seven
years to achieve the roughly 8,000 people present in that year. In
the next nine years the number grew to more than 14,000; and in the
nine years after that it reached a probable 25,600.[1] While it is not
impossible that an increase in immigration contributed to the accelerated increase in population during these years, there is no clear
evidence of it; nothing, for instance, like the letters of the 1630s remarking on the large numbers of arrivals in Virginia.[2] The population, to be sure, continued to be composed primarily of immigrants.
Although the New England colonies were able to grow without
many new arrivals after 1640, Virginia and Maryland, like the sugar
islands of the West Indies, would have expired without a steady
flow of new workers. But the sharp increase in Virginia's population
after 1644 probably came not from a corresponding rise in the num-

[1] See Appendix.
[2] W. F. Craven has attempted to estimate the volume of immigration
during the seventeenth century from the number of headrights claimed
annually in land patents. On this basis he finds the heaviest immigration in
the quarter century after 1650. *White, Red and Black*. But because of the
long and irregular lag between the arrival of an immigrant and the claiming
of a headright for him, the annual volume of land patented bears no direct
relation to the annual volume of immigration. See my "Headrights and Head
Counts."

ber of annual arrivals but from the fact that the newcomers had begun to live longer. They did not live as long, perhaps, as they would have if they had stayed in England, and certainly not as long as they would have if they had gone to New England, but they did live longer than their predecessors. More of them were surviving their "seasoning," living out their terms of service, and taking a place in the community.

The decline in mortality was not sudden. Seventeenth-century Virginia never became a health resort. In the 1680s royal governors fresh from England still fled to New York to escape the summer fevers, and seasoning still left many newcomers looking like skeletons. A visiting physician in 1684 noted that "their fingers stand stifly bent, the hands of some hang as if they were loose at the wrists from the arms . . . and at length those that seemeingly recover are oft troubled with a sort of a gout." [3] On top of the regular summertime fevers there came winter epidemics. An especially severe one of some unrecognized disease in 1686–87 and 1687–88 carried away large numbers (though probably not one-third of the tithables, as Governor Howard estimated).[4] In 1693 measles and in 1696 smallpox took a toll.[5] But these epidemics serve to underline the decline in deaths from the seasoning sicknesses of summer. In two parishes where records of deaths survive, the dates show that summer was no longer the deadliest time in Virginia. In Charles Parish, York County, 54 percent of the deaths recorded in the years 1665–1700 occurred in the five months from November through March. And in Christ Church Parish, Middlesex County, 57 percent of the deaths, 1678–1706, occurred in these months.[6] If

[3] John Clayton to ———, April 24, 1684. Sloane Mss. 1008, ff.334–35, British Museum.

[4] To William Blathwayt, March 21, 1686/7. Blathwayt Papers, XIV, Colonial Williamsburg. On May 10, 1688, Governor Howard proclaimed a day of fasting for what he then called "the greatest mortality that hath been knowne." Effingham Papers, microfilm in the Library of Congress. Most of the lists of tithables in the counties for which records survive do show a dip in these years, but not as large as the governor's words suggest.

[5] C.O. 5/1307, f.48; C.O. 5/1308, ff.58, 60.

[6] The number of deaths in Charles Parish was 589, in Christ Church Parish 228. Charles Parish Register (photostat), Virginia State Library; Sally N. Robins, ed., *The Parish Register of Christ Church, Middlesex County, Virginia, from 1653 to 1812* (Richmond, 1897), 31–54. Cf. Kelly, "Economic and Social Development of Surry County," 33.

Virginia's earlier high mortality was the product of diseases prevalent in the summer, those diseases had apparently declined in intensity, at least by comparison with winter diseases.

Another straw in the wind, suggesting an over-all decline in disease in the second half of the century, is the decreasing number of persons identified as physicians or chirurgeons in the county court records. The Norfolk records mention fourteen in the years from 1661 to 1700, as against sixteen for a population perhaps half the size or less during the shorter period from 1637 (when the records begin) to 1660. Moreover, lawsuits involving physicians were far fewer than in the earlier period.

More direct evidence of improved health comes from people who observed it. In 1648 a writer signing himself "Beauchamp Plantagenet" said that formerly five out of six immigrants had died in seasoning but now it was only one in nine.[7] By 1656, John Hammond, who had spent twenty-one years in the country, was able to affirm Virginia to be "wholesome, healthy and fruitfull" because the colonists had improved their food and drink "and therefore enjoy better healths."[8] And Governor Berkeley, reporting to the Privy Council's Committee on Foreign Plantations in 1671, offered the opinion that all new plantations were unhealthful for "an age or two" but that Virginia had now passed this stage: "there is not often unseasoned hands (as wee terme them) that dye now whereas heretofore not one of five escaped the first yeare."[9] Thirty-five years later William Byrd, the robust founder of a famous Virginia family, complained to a British correspondent about Virginia's continuing evil reputation for disease. He admitted that "the many Rivers, and the vast quantity of water all over the country incline people now and then to agues, especially at the time of year when people eat fruit without any other measure than the bigness of their bellys." But in general he thought that Virginians were no less healthy than other people.[10]

One reason for the decline in mortality may have been the very fruit to which Byrd attributed the country's agues, for a disease often mentioned as afflicting Virginians, especially new arrivals, was

[7] *A Description of the Province of New Albion*, Force, *Tracts*, II, No. 7, p. 5.

[8] *Leah and Rachel*, Force, *Tracts*, III, No. 14, p. 10.

[9] C.O. 1/26, f.198; Hening, II, 515.

[10] Byrd to Sir Hans Sloane, April 20, 1706, Sloane Mss. 4040, ff.151–52, British Museum.

scurvy.[11] Though it is impossible to tell whether the diagnosis was accurate, it may be that the development of orchards and the availability of fresh fruit furnished the settlers with a supply of badly needed vitamins.

Fruit may have helped in another way too, by contributing to a change in drinking habits. Early Virginians were notoriously fond of anything with alcohol in it, but in the absence of beer or cider they were normally obliged to drink water. The water table in tidewater Virginia was doubtless high and wells therefore shallow and easily contaminated. As long as Virginians drank from them, they would be exposed to a great variety of bacilli, including those responsible for typhoid fever. We are told that Virginians in the early years moved about a great deal in search of land that would make a bigger crop of tobacco, a practice that would have discouraged the laborious construction of deep wells in locations more favorable to health than to tobacco culture. Moving about also kept men from planting orchards. A remonstrance by several prominent Virginians, dated 1638, argues for a tobacco contract with English merchants on the grounds that "hereby wee shalbe enabled to build Comodious Habitations and Townes Whereas now the gredines after great quantities of Tobacco causeth them after 5 or 6 yeares continually to remove and therefore neither build good Houses, fence their grounds or plant any Orchards etc." [12]

The last point is perhaps important. By midcentury we find increasing mention of orchards in the deeds and leases recorded in county courts; and John Hammond asserted that while during the boom years the settlers had neglected to plant orchards, by 1656 "Orchards innumerable were planted and preserved." [13] The settlers had finally settled down and were therefore getting something better than water to drink. The purpose of an orchard was not so much to get fruit to eat as to get cider to drink. Cider and other fermented beverages would have been much less lethal than contaminated water.

Still another factor contributing to survival may have been an improvement in the conditions of transportation to the colony. The Virginia assembly in 1662 ordered masters of ships to provide ade-

---

[11] For example, Hamor, *True Discourse*, 19; Northampton IX, 193–96. It is impossible to tell whether the word was used customarily to designate the disease to which we ordinarily confine the word today or in its other usage, more common then, to indicate skin disease.

[12] C.O. 1/9, ff.248–49. [13] Force, *Tracts*, III, No. 14, p. 9.

quate clothing and four months' provisions for every passenger carried from England.[14] Though there was no method of enforcing the order, it or other measures may have improved shipboard conditions that had brought immigrants to Virginia half dead from undernourishment and exposure. And the newcomers may have had a better chance of survival because of a change in the time of arrival of ships. In the 1630s, despite pleas from the colonists, ships were still reaching Virginia in the summer months.[15] By the 1660s they were arriving in the fall or early winter (as they did for the rest of the colonial period), thereby avoiding the danger from seasoning (and from the worm that ate ships' hulls in the lower reaches of Virginia's rivers during the summer).[16] The immigrants had time to recover from the voyage and were consequently better able to withstand the killing summer.

The decline in mortality did not much alter the patterns of life that Virginians had built during the deadly years. The credit system continued to operate through promissory notes. Orphans' courts continued to look after the fatherless. Widows continued to be sought after. And everyone who could afford to continued to import servants. The lengthening life span, however, did create rising expectations. With death no longer staring them so closely in the face, more and more of the incoming servants could count on making it through their term of servitude to set up a place of their own in a society that was now in a position to offer them increasing security. John Hammond, in his account of Virginia and Maryland published in 1656, perhaps painted too idyllic a picture, but there was reason for his remark "that never any servants of late times have gone thither, but in their Letters to their Friends commend and approve of the place, and rather invite than disswade their acquaintance from comming thither." [17] And why not? With the mortality diminished, Virginia looked like the best poor man's country in the

[14] Hening, II, 129.

[15] David Peter de Vries, "Voyages from Holland to America A.D. 1632 to 1644," New-York Historical Society, *Collections*, 2nd ser., III (1857), 77.

[16] This is evident from letters in the 1660s. (For example, Thomas Ludwell to Richard Nicolls, April 28, 1667. Blathwayt Papers, Huntington Library; Berkeley to Council for Foreign Plantations, 1666. C.O. 1/20, f.11.) But the pattern of arrivals in the fall and winter and departures by May or June probably was fixed earlier, in the 1640s or 1650s.

[17] Force, *Tracts*, III, No. 14, p. 12.

world. A whole continent lay behind it; it had plenty of room for everyone.

But everyone, unfortunately, wanted to make tobacco. As more and more of the newcomers stayed alive, Virginia's annual tobacco harvest rose; and (as had happened before and would happen again) there was a limit to how much the rest of the world would buy at the prices formerly given. Crops of half a million pounds had ended the boom prices of the 1620s. By 1663 the official count of tobacco reaching the port of London alone was over seven million pounds, in 1669 nine million, in 1672 ten and a half million; and the planter had to sell for half or less of what he had generally got in the 1640s and 1650s.[18]

It was not difficult to see that Virginia was too dependent on tobacco. Thoughtful men had said so from the beginning; and Virginians, in whom a nascent local patriotism was beginning to stir, felt ashamed of their colony's continuing failure to live up to expectations by producing something more useful. It was surely not the fault of the land. The colony could boast of what amounted to the largest harbor in the world, with its great rivers that allowed ocean-going vessels to sail deep into the interior. It had rich soil, abundant timber, and an infinite expanse of unexplored territory. Such a land should become a rich dominion, the source of all kinds of wholesome commodities, the seat of great cities.[19] But instead of gathering together in cities and towns like the civilized men of England, the inhabitants still spread out over the countryside. Instead of attempting to discover and develop the true riches that the country could surely be made to yield, they still produced nothing but tobacco.

Virginia houses continued to stand—and fall—as symbols of the colony's failure. Civilization to Englishmen still meant living in durable houses, and some of Virginia's big men did build of brick. But everyone else still lived in the rotting wooden affairs that lay about the landscape like so many landlocked ships. A heavy storm would knock them down or fire devour them in an instant. But no matter—sift the ashes for nails and put up more—wood was cheap.

[18] Stanley Gray and V. J. Wyckoff, "The International Tobacco Trade in the Seventeenth Century," *Southern Economic Journal*, VII (1940), 20–21; *WMQ*, 1st ser., VIII (1899–1900), 263; William Berkeley, *A Discourse and View of Virginia* (London, 1663), 5; see chap. 10, notes 10 and 29.

[19] This is the burden of many tracts published in the 1640s, 1650s, and 1660s. See Force, *Tracts*, II, Nos. 7, 8; III, Nos. 11, 13, 14, 15.

To some Virginians this seemed a sorry way to live. They wanted the place to look more like England, more civil, more like a promised land that was fulfilling its promise. The reason it did not, they thought, was because of tobacco.

Everybody blamed tobacco, and no one mentioned that Virginians had been far more miserable in the years before they discovered it than they had ever been since. Although during the boom years they had defeated every move to limit the tobacco crop and promote the production of other commodities, we have seen that after the price collapsed they themselves tried to limit the crop. The impetus for their efforts had come from a drop in tobacco prices, but the purpose of limitation then and later was not merely to raise prices but also to encourage new products. Limitation would give men time for other lucrative activities; and the anticipated higher price of tobacco would furnish the capital needed for starting more wholesome enterprises. The argument was so appealing that Virginians fell for it again and again. Each scheme was abandoned before its promoters thought it had had a fair trial, so the next scheme always had a reservoir of hope to build on. In the later 1650s as population and production figures headed up and tobacco prices headed down, the stage was set for the most ambitious effort of the century to save Virginia from tobacco and the evils that accompanied it. And a man to direct the rescue was already on the scene.

Sir William Berkeley was energetic and talented, and he brought to his task a thorough familiarity with the country. He had watched Virginia grow, under his direction, into a relatively stable community. After he was deposed from office by Parliament, he stayed at his plantation in the colony and enjoyed the prosperity that Dutch shipping continued to bring, despite parliamentary prohibitions. But he was one of those not satisfied with the colony's continued dependence on tobacco. He wanted Virginia to become the brightest jewel in the restored king's crown; and when the assembly summoned him back to office, at a time when the colonists' health had improved, he was filled with visions of also improving the colony's economy.[20]

---

[20] Berkeley developed his views most explicitly in *Discourse and View of Virginia.* The best secondary accounts of his efforts to reform the colony's economy are: Sister Joan de Lourdes Leonard, "Operation Checkmate: The Birth and Death of a Virginia Blueprint for Progress, 1660–1676," *WMQ,* 3rd ser., XXIV (1967), 44–74; and John C. Rainbolt, "The Virginia Vision: A Political History of the Efforts to Diversify the Economy of the Old

To the north the New Englanders had achieved a much more balanced economy than Virginia, but Berkeley had no wish to learn from Puritans. He retained his scorn and hatred for the Roundheads who had killed his king; and he despised the New Englanders, who continued to embody their seditious tenets after 1660.[21] When answering some queries about Virginia in 1671, he gave his opinion that the colony's Anglican ministers were well paid but that he would be happy to see them paid even better "if they would pray oftener and preach less." Preaching was a Puritan specialty, and he did not like it even from the mouths of men whose orthodoxy was assured. And he wanted no more of those other Puritan specialties: schools and books. In Virginia, he said, "I thank God, there are no free schools nor printing, and I hope we shall not have these hundred years; for learning has brought disobedience, and heresy, and sects into the world, and printing has divulged them, and libels against the best government. God keep us from both!"[22] He would tolerate no doctrines that nourished sedition in his colony.

And yet Berkeley's plans for Virginia sound a little like New England with the Puritanism left out. The settlers must gather in towns, where they could better protect themselves from savage enemies without and from the savage nature that lurked within them all. Only towns and cities could nourish the arts and skills that distinguished civil men from barbarians. Surrounded by paying customers, artisans would no longer be tempted to relinquish their skilled callings to earn a living by tobacco. They would build ships so that the colony could develop its own commerce. They would smelt and forge iron from the mines that would be discovered. They would spin and weave cloth from the wool and linen that the farmers outside the towns would produce. For the farmers too would give up their addiction to tobacco and cease to be dependent on the vagaries of the tobacco market. They would expand corn and wheat production for export to the sugar plantations of the West Indies. Economically, if not ideologically, Berkeley was ready to try the Yankees' game, and with a fair chance of winning. After all, Vir-

---

Dominion, 1650–1706" (unpublished doctoral dissertation, University of Wisconsin, 1966), 85–203.

[21] Berkeley to Richard Nicolls, May 20, 1666; May 4, 1667; April 26, 1668. Add. Mss. 28,218, ff.14–17, British Museum; Blathwayt Papers, Huntington Library. Berkeley to Henry Coventry, April 1, 1676. Coventry Papers, Longleat House (microfilm in Library of Congress), LXXVI, 68.

[22] Hening, II, 517.

ginia enjoyed a central position in North America, close to the West Indies, and close (it was then supposed) to the rich Spanish settlements on the Pacific. Virginia should be the center of England's New World empire.[23]

Berkeley hoped to renovate the economy through government action, with the help of the king and of a few public-spirited gentlemen like himself. He was convinced that in the long run his scheme would serve not only the best interests of the colony and the mother country but of every individual bent on profit. Indeed, no one denied it. He was so confident of the colony and of himself, so sure that England must see the problem as he did, that he took himself there in 1661 to place the case before the king and secure the capital to get things going.

In England he found it no problem to persuade the royal advisers that Virginia should be producing something more than tobacco. Instructions to Virginia's royal governors had repeatedly called upon them to set the people building towns and growing other crops. Moreover, Berkeley's drive to diversify production in Virginia coincided with a renewed English interest in expanding the mother country's own economy. In spite of the exodus to the New World, England still harbored a larger population than she could employ. But England's self-appointed economists were now moving to the view that surplus people could be an asset instead of a liability, a means to increase the products the country could manufacture for sale abroad.[24]

With such parallel sentiments developing in England, Berkeley expected to find encouragement for his own plans for Virginia. But he quickly found that encouragement was limited to kind words. Neither the king nor his advisers nor the English merchants who marketed Virginia tobacco were willing to invest capital in diversifying Virginia's exports. The funds would have to come from the Vir-

[23] The plans are detailed in Berkeley's *Discourse and View of Virginia*, which says nothing, however, about building towns, a project in which Berkeley took an active role.

[24] Peter Chamberlen, *The Poore Mans Advocate* (London, 1649); Roger Coke, *A Discourse of Trade* (London, 1670); Thomas Firmin, *Some Proposals for Imploying of the Poor* (London, 1672); Andrew Yarranton, *England's Improvement by Sea and Land* (London, 1677); *The Trade of England Revived* (London, 1681); Walter Harris, *Remarks on the Affairs and Trade of England and Ireland* (London, 1691); John Bellers, *Proposals for Raising a Colledge of Industry* (London, 1695).

ginians themselves, which meant that in the end they would have to come from the crop that the new enterprises were supposed to replace. But how could that happen with Virginia already depressed by the low price of tobacco and with her lucrative Dutch trade outlawed by a new navigation act? At the prompting of the king and the merchants, Parliament in 1660 had required that henceforth all tobacco from the colonies be shipped to England, where the king could collect a duty on it and the merchants a profit.

England's interest in having towns in Virginia was not quite the same as that felt by Virginians. England expected the towns to become export centers for shipping tobacco more swiftly and surely. English merchants would benefit by a reduced turnaround time in loading tobacco ships from a central location; and the customs revenue would benefit by the reduction of clandestine sales to foreign ships from the scattered private wharves of the planters. King, Parliament, and merchants were all more interested in the certain profits of taxing and selling Virginia tobacco than in uncertain profits from the uncertain staples that they continually enjoined the Virginians to produce.[25]

Berkeley was saddened by the king's want of confidence in Virginia and angered by Parliament's prohibition of tobacco shipments to foreign markets. His own confidence in the colony was undiminished, however, and he returned to see what he could do on the spot, hopeful that if he could show results he would be able to persuade the king and his advisers to do more. He carried with him royal instructions that repeated the usual injunctions to Virginia governors, but made more specific, probably at his own request. A town was to be built on each river. The governor and each of his council should build houses in them. The people should plant mulberries and grow silk. They should produce flax, hemp, pitch, and potash.[26]

In Virginia Berkeley found among some of the wealthy planters who sat on his council the same indifference to the colony's future and the same addiction to tobacco that he had encountered in England. The burgesses, however, were convinced of the benefits of his plan and agreed in particular that the colony must have a genuine town or city, for "without one we could not long be civill rich or happy, that it was the first stepp to our security from our Indian

[25] See again Leonard, "Operation Checkmate."
[26] *VMHB*, III, (1895–96), 15–20; C.O. 1/16, f.182.

Enemies and the onely meanes to bring in those Commodities all wise men had so long expected from us." [27] The assembly accordingly voted that, in order to make Jamestown a real city, every county should be responsible for putting up a real house there, "built with brick," and a slate or tile roof. The buildings would be laid out in whatever pattern Berkeley might think convenient. Even before Berkeley's return the assembly also took steps to implement his diversification program by establishing bounties for various products made in Virginia: fifty pounds of tobacco per ton for every boat or ship built; three pounds of tobacco for every yard of linen cloth; five pounds of tobacco for every yard of woolen cloth; fifty pounds of tobacco for every pound of silk made. They revived a former law requiring every landholder to plant mulberry trees. They required every county to erect a tanhouse at public expense and forbade the exportation of hides, wool, and iron in order to encourage manufactures. A few years later they required every county to set up a loom at public expense. [28]

The costs of the program were not small. The record of expenditures by the assembly is available only for its first year of operation, 1663. In that year, though the program was just getting started, the assembly paid bounties amounting to 10,700 pounds of tobacco on 32¼ pounds of silk, 177 yards of woolen cloth, and four vessels totaling 164 tons. This was modest enough, but the bill for surveying the new town at Jamestown, for starting a statehouse and eleven other houses, plus the bill for bricks and lime, amounted to 251,400 pounds. The total cost of the new program was over 262,000 pounds, nearly half the public expenses for the year and equal to more than 22 pounds for every tithable person in the colony. [29]

Berkeley himself, never bashful about claiming public funds, collected 80,000 pounds for building eight houses and 30,000 for the statehouse "to be built." [30] The amount was about the same (£500) as he was investing annually of his own funds in wages for workmen, whom he had engaged to make silk, flax, hemp, and potash.

[27] Berkeley to [Thomas Povey?], March 30, 1663. Egerton Mss. 2395, ff.362–64, British Museum.

[28] Hening, II, 120–23, 172–76, 238–39.

[29] Clarendon Mss. 82, f.275, Bodleian Library, Oxford. According to Francis Moryson, the taxes levied for the program caused hundreds of Virginians to move to Maryland. Letter to the Earl of Clarendon, 1665. Ms. Clarendon 83, Bodleian Library.

[30] Clarendon Mss. 82, f.275.

Within two years, he assured Thomas Povey, (secretary of the Privy Council's Committee for Trade and Plantations), he expected to send a ship loaded entirely with flax, hemp, and potash produced by his own men. Meanwhile he begged the English government to send over agents whom the king trusted, to view the colony so that they could assure His Majesty of its promise. Berkeley also pleaded for flax and hemp seed and skilled men to grow them and to work their fibers. He needed men skilled in silk culture too.[31]

There is no evidence that skilled men were sent to Berkeley or that he got off his shipload of flax, hemp, and potash in two years' time. Nor did he get the financial backing he needed for diversification from Virginians who might have helped push the scheme to success. With the restoration of the monarchy and of a degree of stability in England, these men had become afflicted with the old tendency to look upon Virginia as a place of short sojourning, where a man could seek a present crop and a hasty return. Though an ordinary man could scarcely make enough to stay out of debt on the low tobacco prices of the 1660s and 1670s, a man with the capital or credit to deal on a large scale could find opportunities to make substantial profits by buying and selling at the right time and by working his men a little harder. And with England back on an even keel, it might be more attractive to invest the profits there rather than risking them again in Virginia. The biggest men in Virginia were all too prone, Governor Berkeley observed in 1663, to keep "looking back on England with hopes that the selling of what they have here will make them live plentifully there and many have not been deceived in that opinion, which has been a stopp to the growth of this Country, for on it they expend no more then what is usefull to them in order to their return for England." [32]

In spite of his inability to tap private capital, Berkeley did not lose faith in his project. In 1666, when Governor Nicolls of New York mentioned that the people there were starting to grow flax and make linen, Berkeley assured him that if they persevered, every woman in New York would be able to earn more in a year than three men planting tobacco in Virginia.[33] In 1668 he collected 300 pounds of Virginia silk to send the king, as a token of what the colony could achieve, even without the skilled men he had asked for. Frustrated in his efforts to get such men from England, he was pre-

---

[31] Egerton Mss. 2395, ff.362–64.   [32] *Ibid.*
[33] July 30, 1666. Blathwayt Papers, Huntington Library.

pared to go to France himself and bring some back, if the king would give him permission.[34] Berkeley during the 1660s had not confined his energy to promoting textiles. He had boosted corn production and had gone into trade with the West Indies, like the hated New Englanders. In 1667 he was able to write to Governor Nicolls, "I am now turning an absolute corne merchant and am sending great quantities to the Barbados." [35]

In addition to promoting diversification, he had made a major effort to limit Virginia's tobacco crop. In the absence of outside capital, it was essential to Berkeley's scheme—and to every other attempt to reform Virginia's economy—that the production of tobacco be limited. Two ways of achieving the goal were considered. The more drastic one, which would probably have effected an immediate rise in tobacco prices as well as turning the planters to other tasks, was a total cessation of tobacco planting for a year. Another way would have been to prohibit planting after a certain date every year. In either case it would have been necessary for Virginia, Maryland, and possibly North Carolina (as yet a mere outpost of Virginia but with a separate government) to agree on whatever was done. For Virginia alone to reduce production would have benefited only her neighbors.[36]

The Virginia assembly had shown its commitment to the diversification program in the provisions for bounties and for the building of towns. When it came to a cessation or reduction of planting, the members were equally prepared to further the scheme and so were the members of the Maryland assembly. Most of the members of both assemblies were merchant planters with large investments in tobacco. Probably many of them had substantial amounts on hand, unsold. They would be happy to hold it for the expected price rise and could probably wait out the interval without much spoilage, because by the 1660s Virginians had so improved their curing and packing practices that hogsheads could be stored longer without rotting. But as they considered the matter, they had to reckon with the effect on the small planter and on the growing numbers of freedmen (as servants who had served their terms and

[34] C.O. 1/23, ff.41-43.

[35] Jan. 22, 1666/7. Blathwayt Papers, Huntington Library.

[36] Virginians had always been resentful of the king's grant of Maryland to Lord Baltimore. Even in their earlier major effort to control production in 1640 and 1641, they had felt the need for Baltimore's cooperation, which he had been reluctant to give. See P.C. 2/52, ff.680a-680d (P.R.O.).

become freemen were frequently called). For men living close to the edge of poverty, with no stocks of tobacco or anything else on hand, a year without planting might be too strong medicine. For that reason many favored the second alternative of prohibiting planting after a certain date. For three years, while Berkeley exercised his not inconsiderable talents for diplomacy, the colonies argued about which alternative to take; but in 1666, when a huge amount of tobacco was left unsold, all three colonies agreed to halt planting from February 1, 1667, to February 1, 1668.[37]

For three American colonies to agree about anything in the seventeenth century was a rare triumph. Unfortunately the assemblies had not counted on the fact that other men had a larger stake in the proceeds of their constituents' labor than they did. Because the people of Virginia and Maryland contributed so heavily to the income of the British government, of Lord Baltimore, and of British tobacco merchants, they were not free to perform this kind of economic experiment, even though its object was precisely the diversification that had been enjoined upon them ever since the founding of their colonies. The assemblies might have been forewarned by the action of the Privy Council three years earlier in rejecting a petition asking that the king himself interdict tobacco planting in Virginia and Maryland for a year.[38] A cessation would interrupt, or at least sharply reduce, the flow of customs duties from tobacco into the royal treasury; and if the diversification scheme succeeded, though perhaps the empire would benefit in the long run, the short-run loss to the treasury would not be insignificant. Tobacco duties from Virginia and Maryland accounted for perhaps 25 percent of England's customs revenue and 5 percent of the government's total income in the 1660s.[39] The duty levied by Lord Baltimore on to-

[37] C.O. 1/20, f.338 and passim.

[38] C.O. 1/18, f.323; cf. C.O. 1/16, ff.145, 160, 161; Philip A. Bruce, *Economic History of Virginia in the Seventeenth Century* (New York, 1895), I, 389.

[39] England's total revenue, 1660–67, was £10,291,436, or an average of £1,470,201 for the seven years. William A. Shaw, ed., *Calendar of Treasury Books, 1660–1667* (London, 1904), xxxiv. The revenue from customs averaged £310,079. *Ibid.*, xxviii–xxix. In 1663, the only one of these years for which figures are available for tobacco imports, 7,371,100 pounds were imported at London alone. Assuming a reexport of one-third, the import duty would have amounted to about £46,000. Figures for the outports are not available, but in 1672, when London imported 10,539,000 pounds, the outports imported 7,020,000, or 67 percent of the amount imported at London. (Gray and

bacco exported from Maryland probably constituted a larger share of his income. In 1667 Baltimore relieved the Privy Council of the need for turning down the intercolonial agreement that Berkeley had worked so hard to achieve. Baltimore vetoed Maryland's participation, thereby, as Berkeley said, robbing Virginia and Maryland alike "of all future hopes of the advancement of our commodity." [40]

Baltimore offered a number of reasons (not including the loss to himself) for rejecting the cessation. He was not persuaded that the state of the trade was so bad as to require so drastic a measure. Industrious planters in Virginia and Maryland, as he heard it, "live in much greater plenty and gain estates much sooner than those of their quality in England." But he recognized that not everyone was prosperous, for he went on to argue that a cessation would ruin the poor and enrich the rich. He was not surprised, he said, "that the Councill and major part of the Assemblies of both Colonies (which consist of the ablest Planters) should agree to such Cessations, or that the Merchants here should desire the same, it being in truth the way to make them rich in one year." Like the merchant planters in Virginia, the merchants in England had the tobacco already on hand to benefit from the cessation; but the small man, as Baltimore pointed out, would be prevented from his only means of livelihood. [41]

Baltimore may have been shedding crocodile tears. He had discovered a personal reason why he and the king should be particularly concerned for the welfare of the men who did the actual labor in Virginia's and Maryland's tobacco fields. He had heard from Maryland that a cessation might result in rebellion by the growing mass of poor planters, and a rebellion might reduce the volume of tobacco production—and hence the revenue—even more drastically than a prohibition of planting. The size of the revenue from Virginia and Maryland depended on keeping as many colonists as possible working in the fields.

As this became increasingly clear to the king and his advisers, the possibility of limitation and diversification, of transforming Virginia into something other than a collection of tobacco plantations,

Wyckoff, "International Tobacco Trade," 20–21.) If the proportions were the same in 1663, the total would have been about £77,000, or roughly 5 percent of total revenue and nearly 25 percent of total customs revenue. Sir John Knight in 1673 estimated royal revenue from Virginia at £150,000. C.O. 1/30, ff.197–98. This was apparently an exaggeration, but the 1672 imports must have brought in close to £110,000.

[40] C.O. 1/21, ff.109–12.   [41] C.O. 1/21, ff.269–70.

grew correspondingly smaller. Perhaps with the assistance of the ethical imperatives of Puritanism something resembling Berkeley's dream for Virginia could have been achieved. Certainly the New Englanders, though without the handicap of a soil and climate well suited to tobacco, did achieve something like it. But given the Virginians' attitudes toward servants, work, and time, it would have been difficult at best to sustain a program like Berkeley's, a program that required short-term losses (from reduction of the tobacco crop and from artificial support of new enterprises) for the sake of a possible long-term gain. The temptations to corruption that the program presented in a society where corruption in government office was already familiar were apparent in the large sums received by individuals, including Berkeley himself, for building houses which, according to one complaint, "fell down again before they were finished." [42] But corruption in the carrying out of the scheme was only symptomatic of the forces working against it. It was caught in the competition of the king, Lord Baltimore, and the tobacco merchants on the one hand and successful large planters on the other, to squeeze as much profit as possible, as quickly as possible, out of Virginia's servants and small planters. The patterns of raw exploitation established in the boom time of the 1620s had subsided but not disappeared in the decades of settling down that followed. As mortality dropped and population rose, new possibilities for exploitation appeared; and Virginia became a land of opportunity, not for the men who survived their seasoning and continued to work in the fields, but for kings and lords and other men who knew how to put the power of government to work for them.

[42] *Journals of the House of Burgesses, 1659/60–1693*, 102.

10

A GOLDEN FLEECING

O F those who profited from the labor of Virginia's tobacco growers after 1660, the king stood foremost. Royal interest in the wealth that came from tobacco long antedated Berkeley's efforts to renovate Virginia's economy. Already in 1619 James I, even as he denounced the evils of tobacco, had tried to gain for the crown some of the profits of supplying Englishmen with it.[1] Charles I had also tried, also unsuccessfully, to talk Virginians into giving him or his favorites the exclusive right to market their product.[2] But the royal government had another way to collect the lion's share of the profits from tobacco: by requiring the colonists to ship their crop to the mother country, where an import duty could be collected on it.

The first edict requiring shipment to England was issued in 1621,[3] but could not be effectively enforced; and while the English were preoccupied with their Civil Wars, the Dutch had taken the opportunity to enter the trade. During the years when the Virginians were establishing their society, it was mainly the Dutch who carried off their tobacco. When Cromwell first began to gather in the strings of empire in the 1650s, London merchants stood behind him in the attempt to wrest from the Dutch their control of trade everywhere. And when Charles II took the throne in 1660, the same merchants had joined him in moves to make as much as possible out

[1] Beer, *Origins of the British Colonial System*, 117-42; Gray, *History of Agriculture*, I, 238-40.

[2] Beer, *Origins*, 142-75; Gray, *History of Agriculture*, I, 240-41.

[3] *RVC*, I, 537.

of the rising tobacco crop. In that year the king's ministers secured the passage of the navigation act mentioned in the preceding chapter that cut off Virginia's trade with the Dutch. The act required tobacco produced in any English colony to be shipped only to England or to another English colony. It had to be shipped in an English or English colonial ship, manned by a crew that was at least three-quarters English or English colonial.[4] When it entered England, it would pay a duty of twopence a pound, a tax roughly equal to the price the producer then got for it and more than he would get during the next two decades.

Although 1½ pence of the twopenny duty was returned if a merchant reshipped his tobacco to a foreign market, the revenue from tobacco was spectacular. In 1675, when roughly a third of the tobacco was reexported, the annual proceeds from tobacco duties were estimated at £100,000.[5] In 1685 the customs levy on what stayed in England was raised to fivepence.[6] Reexportation rose steadily and reached 63 percent of imports in the last years of the century.[7] Even so, the king must have received roughly £1,894,000 from the Virginia and Maryland tobacco crop during the six years from 1697 to 1702.[8] By 1708 one observer estimated the annual revenue at £400,000.[9]

The drop in the price of tobacco after mortality declined and production increased was no catastrophe for the king. The customs duty was levied not on value but on weight. If the planter got only a halfpenny a pound—tobacco dropped that low in 1666 [10]—the king still got twopence a pound. The larger the crop, whatever its price, the greater the royal revenue. No other colonial product carried such a burden of imperial taxation: in the 1670s it could be calculated that every man who worked in the tobacco fields earned

---

[4] 12 Charles II, c. 18.   [5] Hening, II, 526.   [6] 1 James II, c. 4.

[7] Sloane Mss. 2717, British Museum. In the period 1712–17 home consumption was calculated at 8,175,226 pounds annually and reexports at 17,142,755. King's Mss. 205, British Museum. Jacob M. Price, *The Tobacco Adventure to Russia*, American Philosophical Society, *Transactions*, n.s., LI, part 1 (1961), 1–120, at p. 5.

[8] The total imports for these years were 197,203,000 pounds, of which 118,062,000 were reexported. Gray and Wyckoff, "International Tobacco Trade," 25. Egerton Mss. 921, British Museum.

[9] Egerton Mss. 921, British Museum.

[10] C.O. 1/21, ff.109–12; *VMHB*, IV (1896–97), 237; Gray, *History of Agriculture*, 264. See note 29.

£7.10.00 annually for the royal treasury, which was more than he earned for himself or for a master.[11] No other colonial product yielded so much revenue.[12] The value and weight of sugar brought to England from the West Indies was greater than that of Virginia and Maryland tobacco, but the duties collected on it were smaller. More than once in the course of the century Virginia's governors reminded the king that Virginia produced a larger share of the royal revenue than any other colony.[13]

Although the king, or the government he represented, became the principal tobacco profiteer as soon as the Navigation Acts were passed, tobacco seems to have invited exploitation by men of every rank in the seventeenth century; and the development of Virginia society after 1660 must be viewed with an eye to the toll that everyone who came near tobacco tried to collect from it.

Every year, after the danger from the summer fevers was past and the great harvest was beginning to come in from the fields to be cured, the tobacco ships would converge on Virginia, beat their way through the passage between Cape Charles and Cape Henry, and spread out into the watery landscape, up the great rivers and into the bays, Lynnhaven, Mockjack, Chesapeake, to familiar wharves. The first loaded and back to England would enjoy an advantage in the European market. But many, for safety's sake, sailed together. In a small way it was like the gathering of the Spanish treasure fleet at Nombre de Dios or San Juan de Ulúa. Tobacco was scarcely gold or silver, but the quantities carried out through Virginia's capes every year were enough to attract some of the same kind of attention that Englishmen had given to the treasure of New Spain a century earlier. As the volume of shipping rose, pirates of all nations became a serious problem. Sometimes they lurked off the capes to catch the tobacco ships homeward bound. Often they came inside and ranged along the shores, pilfering and plundering. Occasionally they were caught and executed,[14] but they kept coming. In 1700 an English man-of-war, with Virginia's Governor Nicholson aboard, captured one in Lynnhaven Bay after a battle that lasted from five in the morning till three in the afternoon, the two ships

[11] Assuming a modest crop of 1,200 pounds per man and reexportation of one-third. *VMHB*, IV (1896–97), 237.

[12] See chap. 9, note 39.

[13] Berkeley, *Discourse and View of Virginia*, 5; C.O. 1/30, f.113; C.O. 1/48, f.53.

[14] C.O. 1/57, f.300.

within pistol shot of each other and blasting away with everything they had.[15]

The naval patrols were not always so assiduous. Some of the men entrusted with fending off pirates and interlopers were distinguishable from the pirates only by the flag they flew. Roger Jones, an old navy captain, assigned in 1683 to command an armed sloop and twelve men, managed to make do with eight men while collecting pay for the full twelve and thus began his Virginia career with a tidy bonus. The small number of men he retained would scarcely have been effective against pirate ships, which sometimes mustered crews of over a hundred, but they served as a bargaining force. Jones, it was claimed, laid the foundation of a great estate by "adviseing Tradeing with and Sheltering Severall Pyrates and unlawfull Traders . . . but more perticulerly by tradeing with and assisting one Davis and other Pyrates to whome as is credibly repoarted he struck the Kings Collours But they Soone understood he was of their owne Tribe or a well wisher to them, and therefore dismissed Captain Jones againe with a Considerable quantity of French wines and other valuable goods." [16]

Jones was succeeded by Captain Thomas Allen and Captain John Crofts of the royal navy, with two naval ketches, *Deptford* and *Quaker*. Allen and Crofts seem to have been anything but Quakers. Allen had a mistress aboard and Crofts a wife, or at least a woman he called his wife (Governor Howard was not persuaded that she was). Crofts was often in his cups, but when sober he knew how to take advantage of the opportunities that lay before him. He and Allen apparently made a practice of shaking down the masters of tobacco ships already cleared by the local customs officers. Though they went about it crudely, they took in according to a Rappahannock planter, about £500 yearly apiece and might easily have raised the sum to £1,000 apiece if the one had not been a sot and the other a fool.[17] There were enough technicalities in the customs regulations to offer a pretext for holding a ship for a time. A

[15] C.O. 5/1311, f.29.
[16] C.O. 5/1306, No. 111; Lewis H. Jones, "Some Recently Discovered Data Relating to Capt. Roger Jones," *WMQ*, 1st ser., xxvii (1918–19), 1–18; W. R. Palmer, ed., *Calendar of Virginia State Papers* (Richmond, 1875), I, 38–40.
[17] Richard B. Davis, ed., *William Fitzhugh and His Chesapeake World, 1676–1701* (Chapel Hill, N.C., 1963), 193, 215. The activities of Crofts and Allen are detailed in C.O. 1/62, ff.179–200.

master with a cargo aboard was always eager to get it to market as soon as possible, and made the more eager by the fact that it was difficult to scrape together provisions for the voyage. Once your ship was ready to go, it was worth paying a substantial bribe to be out and away, especially if you were intercepted by Captain Crofts.

Crofts was a violent man and good at intimidating those he stopped. When in drink, he and his alleged wife regularly threw everything in sight at each other—she even tossed coals from the fire about the cabin, terrifying the men in the powder room. The crew sometimes had to take to the shrouds to get clear of the captain, as he thrashed about with drawn sword, threatening to split them all. When Crofts stopped William Gennes, headed for Plymouth in the *Daniel and Elizabeth* with full clearance papers, Gennes asked why. In reply Crofts "belched out a thousand Oaths, that [he] was come there to gaine an Estate, and he would gett one before he left the Country." [18]

Taking the hint, Gennes gathered up what plate and gold and silver rings he could find aboard and presented them as a contribution toward the captain's goal. It was not enough for Crofts. His response, according to Gennes, was to swear "Damne him againe, he would nott be Contented with such toys." [19] He demanded fifty guineas. But this was too much for Gennes, and Crofts finally settled for £25 sterling plus the plate and some clothes. Unfortunately for Crofts, the owner of the vessel, William Martin of Plymouth, was not a man to take this sort of thing lying down. Hence the case ultimately came before the Privy Council, to whom the secretary of the colony attested that "Tho many merchants have suffered by Captain Crofts in this Nature, none have taken soe good resolutions to make knowne their sufferings as this Mr. Martin hath done." [20]

A more talented crook than Captain Crofts was Captain James Moody of H.M.S. *Southampton*. Though he had a nasty habit of horsewhipping Virginians who displeased him, Captain Moody avoided the crude form of shakedown favored by Crofts. Instead, when stationed in Virginia waters in the 1690s, he turned his sailors into lumberjacks and went into the lumber business. He had the men fell cedar and black walnut timber, much prized in England but expensive to transport there. After his men had sawed it into planks and billets, Moody delivered these, marked with his name, to the

[18] C.O. 1/62, f.195a.   [20] C.O. 1/62, ff.204-5.
[19] C.O. 1/62, f.194.

tobacco ships riding in the James and York rivers. Those captains who refused to carry the lumber or demanded that Moody pay freight charges found their sailors impressed for service aboard the *Southampton* and their ships thereby stranded. Moody managed to get into the tobacco business also, but not by having his sailors grow tobacco for him. Though unable to pay for provisions for his crew, he seems to have had no trouble buying tobacco on credit for himself, and this too he got shipped freight free by the same tactics.[21]

Officers of the royal navy were not the only government officials to fatten on the tobacco trade. Virginians serving in the colony government got into the act too. In order to reduce direct taxes, the House of Burgesses in 1658 tried a duty of two shillings per hogshead exported from Virginia. They repealed the act the next year but reimposed it in 1662 and in 1680 made it perpetual.[22] The governor usually named members of his council to collect the duty: two for the James River, two for the Potomac, and one each for the Rappahannock, the York, and the Eastern Shore. After 1673, when Parliament levied a penny a pound duty on tobacco shipped to another English colony instead of to England, the collectors were usually entrusted with gathering this too and with enforcing the other Navigation Acts. As compensation they were entitled to fees for entering and clearing ships and to a 10 percent commission on the duties they collected.[23]

But a collector's salary (a commission was always known as a salary in seventeenth-century Virginia) was not as important as the opportunities the office presented. Nicholas Spencer, collector for the lower precinct of the Potomac, admitted as much in asking his brother to secure him a royal confirmation of the office in perpetuity (in case the next governor should give or sell it to another): "the proffit of sallery is not soe much as the many advantages it gives mee otherwayes." [24] Precisely what Spencer meant by "otherwayes" he

[21] C.O. 5/1313, ff.133-34.

[22] Hening, I, 491-92, 498, 523; II, 130-32, 176-77, 466, 469.

[23] Hening, II, 443-44; Hartwell, Blair, and Chilton, *Present State of Virginia*, 58-59; Ms. Locke C. 30, f.61, Bodleian Library, Oxford; *Journals of the House of Burgesses, 1659/60–1693*, 500, 502; *Minutes of Council*, 424. The office of naval officer was separated from that of collector in 1699, on instructions from England, in spite of protests from the councillors. *VMHB*, IV (1896–97), 52; Hening, III, 195–97; C.O. 5/1310 (Library of Congress transcript), pp. 165–70.

[24] Sloane Mss. 3511, ff.133-34, British Museum.

did not say. Perhaps the collectors could get free freight for their own tobacco in return for overlooking certain duties; possibly they commanded a more direct form of bribery as eighteenth-century customs officials did. At any rate, when the zealous Edward Randolph came to inspect Virginia's collectors in 1692, he found them a venal lot, who regarded their offices simply as perquisites "intended to enrich the members of the council." [25] As councillors they were able to block all efforts at reform, for they constituted the colony's supreme court. In 1698 Benjamin Harrison (who was about to gain a seat on the council himself) observed how they stood by each other.

> and if any one of themselves does happen to Speake a little freely of the Miscarriages of his Brethren, tho' perhaps there may be truth enough in it, Yet upon Second thoughts they, takeing it to be their Common Interest to agree among themselves, do generally let such things sleep without moving any further. Thus about two years since Coll. Parke [collector for the lower James] of his own knowledge accused Coll. Hill [collector for the upper James] (in the presence of Severall People) of Frauds and abuses in Collecting the penny a pound on Tobacco imposed by the 25 Car. 2. c. 7; but 'tis probable the Consideration how fatall a prosecution of that nature might in Consequence prove to himself amongst the Rest, caused him to desist from makeing any legall information.

Harrison was ready to cite other names and figures to demonstrate his conclusion that "There is not perhaps in all the Kings Dominions any place where the methods of Managing both the trade and Revenues are so exactly calculated to defraud the Publick, and abuse the subject." [26]

As might be expected from the hints of bribery, the collectors seldom felt obliged to seize a ship for violating the Navigation Acts. When they did, the circumstances were likely to be unusual, as in the case of the ship *Phoenix*. The *Phoenix* belonged to William Fisher, a merchant in Terceira (Azores), whose factor in La Rochelle shipped him £12,000 sterling worth of goods aboard her in 1675. The master, Leonard Haynes, ran away with the ship, tried unsuccessfully to peddle the goods in Newfoundland, and then headed for Virginia, where he perhaps knew of kindred spirits. He

[25] To William Blathwayt, April 21, 1692. Blathwayt Papers, Colonial Williamsburg.
[26] C.O. 5/1309, No. 55.

brought her into Cherry Stone Creek on the Eastern Shore and conspired with John Bellamy, a substantial planter there, to unload the ship as though consigned to Bellamy. But the *Phoenix* was a foreign ship, forbidden to trade in an English colony, and Colonel John Stringer, the collector for the Eastern Shore, made it known that he would not overlook so blatant a violation. Bellamy and Haynes therefore contrived to beach the ship, as though she were wrecked, and on the pretext of this distress were able legally to remove the cargo. That Colonel Stringer connived at this move seems apparent from the fact that the cargo quickly disappeared into the hands of "Colonel Stringer, Coll. Kendall, Coll. Waters, Major Spencer, Capt. Foxcroft, Coll. Thomas Ballard and several others." These were all commissioners of Northampton County with the exception of Ballard, who was from James City County, a member of the governor's council and collector for James River.[27]

When Governor Berkeley heard of this fraud, he ordered the ship and goods seized, to be retained for the owner, whom he promptly informed of his action. Fisher gratefully sent off an agent to bring them back to Terceira, but before the agent arrived, Colonel Stringer had a better idea. As collector for the Eastern Shore, he now seized the ship and goods as forfeited for violation of the Navigation Acts. His fellow councillors and collectors constituted the court to try the case, and with no one to contest it they obliged by condemning the ship and cargo. The governor was now entitled to one-third of the proceeds, Colonel Stringer to another third, and the king to the remainder. When Fisher's agent arrived and demanded the goods, he found them in the hands of Virginia's great men. They had punished Bellamy for attempting to smuggle, but they met all of Fisher's claims for the goods by citing their own condemnation of the vessel. Fisher could not collect a penny, and fifteen years later he was still trying in vain to secure a special royal order for Governor Berkeley's share, which another Virginia magnate, Philip Ludwell, had obtained in a characteristic Virginia manner. Ludwell had married Berkeley's widow.[28]

Virginia's officials did not often get windfalls like the *Phoenix*, but from the way they gathered about the spoils it is obvious that the talents so evident in the boom times of the 1620s had not disappeared. The 1660s and 1670s were far from being a boom time. The expansion of population and the corresponding expansion of

[27] C.O. 1/47, f.78.   [28] C.O. 1/51, ff.37-41; C.O. 5/1305, No. 61.

tobacco production combined with the restrictions of the Naviga-tion Acts to keep tobacco prices in a twenty-year trough.[29] The market recovered in the 1680s and 1690s but only sporadically. Only those who dealt with tobacco in large volumes could count on mak-ing profits from growing or selling it.

In this situation the control and use of government became more than ever the key to successful exploitation of Virginia's growing population. It was the force of government that enabled the royal treasury to collect a legal toll and officers like Captain Crofts an illegal toll on the tobacco trade. And it was the force of govern-ment that enabled the most successful Virginians to supplement the income from their own tobacco with dues and fees and perquisites that placed a heavy burden on the lesser men who hoed the weeds and stripped the stalks.

As the profits of tobacco growing fell in the 1660s and 1670s, the profits of government office in Virginia rose. The most lucrative office, of course, was the governor's. When Berkeley was returned to the chair—with the restoration of the monarchy in 1660—the House of Burgesses voted him a gift of a bushel of corn from every tithable in the colony, an amount that would have been worth more

[29] Russell R. Menard, "Farm Prices of Maryland Tobacco, 1659–1710," *Maryland Historical Magazine*, LXVIII (1973), 80–85, has constructed a useful table of tobacco prices in Maryland during this period. The figures, based on valuations in inventories, generally averaged from 6 to 8 shillings per 100 and seldom rose above 10 shillings per 100 (1.2*d* per pound). Virginia prices were probably somewhat higher, but no such table is available for Virginia, and it seems unlikely that a reliable one could be constructed. The usual conversion rate in Virginia in official transactions during the four decades from 1660 to 1700 was 10 shillings per 100. See Norfolk V, 63a (1667); VI, 33 (1669); Hening, II, 55 (1662), 222 (1665), 288 (1671), 419 (1677); III, 153 (1696); Davis, *Fitzhugh*, 138 (1683), 176 (1686), 209 (1687), 237 (1688); C.O. 5/1306, No. 32 (1691). But it is likely that the actual price often fell below this rate to a penny a pound or less: Norfolk VIII, 15a (1687), 108 (1689), 171 (1692); Henrico II, 31 (1678), 240 (1689), 323 (1691); Davis, *Fitzhugh*, 226 (1687), 252 (1689). See also references in note 10 and Kelly, "Economic and Social Development of Surry County," 256.

In 1698 the price went up to 20 shillings per 100 for Orinoco and 25 shillings for sweet-scented, but it was back to 10 shillings by 1700. See C.O. 5/1309, No. 74; Letter Book of Robert Anderson, Junior, Alderman Library; Gray, *History of Agriculture*, I, 264–67. In 1705 Robert Beverley reported that "of late years" tobacco had generally sold at nearly 20 shillings per 100. *History and Present State of Virginia*, 261. The problem of tracing the actual course of Virginia tobacco prices is complicated by the fact that sales were commonly made in barter for English goods. Such goods were

than £1,000.[30] In later years too they often voted special gifts of money in addition to his annual salary of £1,000 and in addition to various perquisites that grew over the years. They gave him 200,000 pounds of tobacco (roughly £1,000) to pay for his fruitless trip to England in 1661.[31] Beginning apparently in 1663, he was given the proceeds of a special ten-shilling duty on every hogshead of tobacco shipped to other English colonies. Later this was set at a fixed £200 per year, so that his annual salary was £1,200.[32] In 1661 Berkeley forbade anyone to kill unmarked cattle in the wild "hee laying claime to them as dew to him as beinge Governor." [33] He also claimed an annual tribute in beaver from the subject Indian tribes,[34] plus 200 pounds of tobacco for every marriage license issued in Virginia, plus 350 pounds annually from every tavern that retailed drinks, plus 5 shillings from every person leaving the colony.[35] After 1680 governors of Virginia also got 40 shillings from every non-English person naturalized; and, without apparent authorization,

---

sometimes stated to be valued "at the first penny" of their cost in England. That is, the planter was to pay nothing for the freight charges. But often an "advance" was made on the first cost of the goods. Obviously a price of tobacco calculated in goods "at the first penny" cannot be compared with a price calculated in goods at an "advance." Yet where we have records of sales, there is usually no way to tell which sort of transaction has taken place. For indication of the effect of these different kinds of reckoning on prices see Davis, *Fitzhugh*, 224-27, and Francis Jerdone to William Buchanan, May 26, 1750, *WMQ*, 1st ser., IX (1902-3), 156-57.

[30] Hening, II, 10. There were about 11,000 tithables in the colony, and corn was worth about 20 pounds of tobacco per bushel (100 pounds a barrel). Thus the gift would have amounted to 220,000 pounds of tobacco at a time when tobacco was worth about 10 shillings per 100.

[31] *Journals of the House of Burgesses, 1659/60–1693*, 60, 141; Hening, II, 17. Berkeley, in a letter to Thomas Ludwell in 1676, expressed relief, in the midst of growing discontent over taxes, that the assembly had given him no gifts in the preceding three years (C.O. 1/36, ff.67–68); but according to Giles Bland the assembly's gifts to the governor were nevertheless a source of discontent (C.O. 1/36, ff.111, 113).

[32] Hening, II, 133, 315; *Journals of the House of Burgesses, 1659/60–1693*, 501. The governor was already collecting a similar fee (60 pounds of tobacco per hogshead) in the 1650s. See Northampton V, 82a. A hogshead at this time might hold from 350 to 670 pounds of tobacco. See Appendix, note 48.

[33] Norfolk IV, 309.

[34] Effingham in 1686 said that this was now much reduced and worth only £50 a year. Minutes of the Council, April 24, 1686, Effingham Papers.

[35] Hening, II, 20, 55, 113; C.O. 1/38, f.81.

they collected 20 shillings from incoming ships under a hundred tons and 30 shillings from ships over that weight.[36]

Most of these perquisites became permanently attached to the office, and the men who succeeded Berkeley kept reaching for more. Lord Culpeper, who was appointed governor in 1678, got the regular salary jacked up to £2,000, plus £150 for house rent.[37] At that rate he was able to spend all but nine months of his seven-year governorship in England simply by hiring a lesser man to preside over the colony as lieutenant governor at the rate of £1,000 a year. Culpeper was one more of that long line of men who came to Virginia with only a brief sojourning and a quick profit in mind. And so was Lord Howard of Effingham, whom the king appointed to replace Culpeper in 1684.

Lord Howard may not really have been a grasping man, but he was hard up and regarded the office as a heaven-sent boon to repair his ailing fortunes. During his first year in Virginia, while his wife remained in England, he bombarded her with love letters (in which he also adjured her to "keepe your children from taking Gods name in vayne," and to keep young Charles "from being amongst the servants").[38] To allay the pain of their parting, he presented her with calculations of the future profits of his office. His first expectation was that the various perquisites would bring the total annual income to £2,500, and that he might be able to put aside £1,500 a year in spite of the lavish hospitality expected of him. But within two months of his arrival in 1684, he had already collected £300 in perquisites and predicted that he would be able to live on these alone and have the whole salary clear profit. One way in which he managed to increase the perquisites was by charging a fee of 200 pounds of tobacco for affixing the colony seal to every document issuing from the secretary's office, the chief of these being patents for land. In this way alone, a local planter estimated, he got 80,000 to 100,000 pounds of tobacco annually.[39] Virginians objected to the innovation, and the king eventually stopped it. Nevertheless, Governor Howard was able to shore up his estate more rapidly than he had expected. Within six months of his arrival he had sent back bills

[36] Hening, II, 464–65; C.O. 1/64, ff.46–48, 66; Beverley, *History and Present State of Virginia*, 89.

[37] Hartwell, Blair, and Chilton, *Present State of Virginia*, 32.

[38] Effingham Correspondence (the volume so labeled consists of Effingham's letters to his wife), Effingham Papers.

[39] Davis, *Fitzhugh*, 215.

of exchange totaling £1,220 and was planning to send £1,000 more by the next ship. He could honestly rejoice in writing to his "dearest dearest dearest Life and Joy" that God had put him "in such an honorable and proffitable imployment." [40]

Next to the governor in rank and emoluments stood the secretary, whose profits came mainly from fees. He collected something for nearly every official document issued or recorded in the colony: 80 pounds of tobacco for every land patent, 40 pounds for every marriage license, and two shillings sixpence (doubtless collected in tobacco at the going rate) from every person leaving the colony. He appointed all clerks of county courts and received a percentage of the fees they charged in every action at law. He issued writs for elections to the assembly and thereby collected a fee of 350 pounds from each county, or a total of about 7,000 pounds for every meeting.[41] At the end of the century the secretary's total was running over 135,000 pounds of tobacco annually, worth at that time from £600 to £1,200 sterling or more.[42]

The members of the council were directly rewarded only by £350 sterling proportioned among them for expenses in attending meetings; but they were first in line for valuable positions as secretary, escheator,[43] or collector, which they could hold simultaneously with their seats on the council.[44] Every officer involved in the collection of revenues in Virginia claimed a share of them. The auditor got 5 percent (later 7½ percent) of the 2 shillings per hogshead duty simply for examining the collectors' accounts;[45] and the high sheriff in each county added 10 percent for himself to the taxes he collected, as well as charging assorted fees for serving warrants and making arrests. All public officers exacted fees for performing

[40] Effingham Correspondence.   [41] Hening, II, 144–45.

[42] VMHB, VIII (1900–1901), 184. In 1699 tobacco was up to 20 or 25 shillings the 100 pounds (see note 29). This price was not maintained, but even at 10 shillings the 100 the secretary would have made £675.

[43] Escheators, of whom there were four, got £5 sterling from the purchaser of every tract of land that had reverted to the king because the owner had died without heirs. Hartwell, Blair, and Chilton, Present State of Virginia, 20.

[44] Ibid., 33–36; Michael Kammen, ed., "Virginia at the Close of the Seventeenth Century: An Appraisal by James Blair and John Locke," VMHB, LXXIV (1966), 141–69, at 167–68; Ms. Locke e 9, ff.144–47, Bodleian Library, Oxford.

[45] Journals of the House of Burgesses, 1659/60–1693, 500, 502; Coventry Papers, LXXVI, 319; Virginia Historical Register, III (1850), 187.

their duties and continually increased their charges, authorized and unauthorized, for both real and nominal services.

The largest expense borne by Virginia's taxpayers arose from meetings of the assembly, which usually lasted less than a month. Besides the secretary's fees for summoning the meeting, each session entailed payments ranging from 6,000 to 20,000 pounds of tobacco apiece for the speaker, the clerk of the House of Burgesses, the clerk of the council, and the clerk of the assembly.[46] In the 1670s the House sometimes passed special acts naturalizing foreigners and awarded the speaker 800 pounds and clerk 400 from each of them. Thus ten new Virginians paid the speaker 8,000 and the clerk 4,000 in September, 1672.[47] Even the three doorkeepers got 1,500 pounds each per session, and the drummer who alerted members to the daily sittings got 3,000, a good deal more than a man could make in a year in the fields.[48] The individual counties paid their representatives in the House of Burgesses on a per diem basis, 150 pounds a day until 1677, when the amount was reduced to 120 pounds. In addition each burgess was entitled to miscellaneous expenses and also to a servant and horse or else to a boat with servants to row it, depending on whether he came to the assembly by road or water. Even after the reduction of the per diem rate the cost, to the county for a session lasting less than a month could run to 4,000 or 5,000 per burgess, besides the 300-pound fee each county paid the clerk of the assembly for a copy of the laws passed.[49] By comparison the inhabitants of New England starved their representatives on two or three shillings a day (equivalent to twenty or thirty pounds of tobacco) from which they had to pay all expenses, including travel. Other New England government officers were paid proportionately; for example, the elected governor got £120 a year in Massachusetts, £80 in Connecticut, and £10 in Rhode Island.[50]

[46] Surviving records of the authorized disbursements of particular assemblies are in Mss. Clarendon 82 (for 1662); *Journals of the House of Burgesses, 1659/60–1693*, 499–502 (for 1675, 1676); Coventry Papers, LXXVI, 294, 319 (for 1673, 1674).

[47] Hening, II, 289–90, 302.   [48] References in note 46.

[49] Hening, II, 23, 106, 309, 398–99. The costs to a county are usually detailed in the county court records in November or December of each year.

[50] N. B. Shurtleff, ed., *Records of the Governor and Company of the Massachusetts Bay* (Boston, 1853–54), I, 228; IV, part I, 154; J. H. Trumbull, ed., *The Public Records of the Colony of Connecticut* (Hartford, 1850–90), III, 129, 165, 191, 219, 245; J. R. Bartlett, ed., *Records of the Colony of Rhode Island and Providence Plantations* (Providence, R.I., 1856–65), II, 443,

The princely sums exacted from Virginians for support of their government, as well as those they paid for ministers' salaries and the building and upkeep of churches, came almost entirely from poll taxes, levied by the county courts on every "tithable" person (defined in general as men over fifteen and any women engaged in tobacco production).[51] Since masters were obliged to pay the tax for their bound servants, and since servants were a principal form of wealth, the poll tax was a less inequitable form of taxation than would have been the case in a society where wealth lay more in land or goods than in people. Nevertheless, the burden lay heavy on a new freedman who had only his own labor to support him. He might have to pay in direct taxes anywhere from a hundred to two hundred or more pounds of tobacco a year, which could amount to 10 percent of his total income. And after the numbers of freemen began to increase, few of them could expect to share, by holding public office, in the benefits of the taxes they paid. A study of the House of Burgesses in the period 1660–1706 has shown that no servant who arrived after 1640 made it into the ranks of the burgesses.[52] And certainly no former servant after 1640 became a member of the council. Virginia in the second half of the seventeenth century may still have been by comparison with England a land of opportunity, but the range of opportunity had narrowed. The largest opportunities were preempted by those who had already achieved success, either in Virginia or in England.

It was the already successful who could lay claim to government office and to the perquisites that went with it. And the office was generally commensurate with the success. Only the very successful could expect the highest offices. Governor Nicholson, in recommending trustworthy Virginians to the king for high position, revealed the premise when he declined to recommend appointment to the council for Thomas Milner, speaker of the House of Burgesses in 1691. Though Nicholson praised Milner for having "behaved himself very well" as speaker, he simply did not have "Estate enough to bee a Counsellor." Nicholson therefore recommended that the

---

473; III, 309; Edward J. Brandon, ed., *The Records of the Town of Cambridge . . . 1630–1703* (Cambridge, Mass., 1901), 102. When Massachusetts acquired a royal governor under her new charter of 1691, his salary was £500 and rose to £1,000. L. W. Labaree, *Royal Government in America* (New Haven, 1930), 352–53.

[51] On the changing definition of "tithable" see Appendix.

[52] Quitt, "Virginia House of Burgesses," 274.

king give him some lesser "place of Profitt." [53] The same assumption was evident when the people of Warwick County complained in 1677 that too many places of profit were held by the same men: they were told that if properly qualified men were confined to one office, there would not be enough men of the right sort to fill the places.[54] Multiple officeholding was the rule not only among Virginia councillors but also at the county level. The coveted position of high sheriff was held on an annual basis, and the commissioners in a county generally rotated it among themselves, though the formal appointment came from the governor.[55]

Virginia's successful men were usually as quick to defer to those who ranked above them as they were to demand deference from those they had surpassed, for it was to their advantage that men be big enough to fit the offices they held. When Lord Culpeper in 1680 condescended to spend some time in the colony he governed, they were delighted to welcome a real peer as governor, for they knew that he could press their interests far more effectively than a lesser man. Culpeper lived up to expectations. He had the aristocrat's contempt for bureaucrats and could nonchalantly brush aside instructions they sent him if people on the spot persuaded him they were unwise. For example, he had orders to discharge Robert Beverley as clerk of the assembly because of complaints received in England about Beverley's rapacity. But when the assembly unanimously supported Beverley for the position, rapacious though he indeed was, Culpeper had none of the compunctions that an ordinary governor might have felt in paying more heed to the local pecking order than to instructions concocted by superiors whom he did not really consider superior: he accordingly reappointed Beverley forthwith and scarcely bothered to apologize for doing so.[56]

Before leaving for Virginia, Culpeper had discovered that one Robert Ayleway had managed to wangle from the Privy Council an appointment as auditor general of Virginia. Rightly suspecting that this intrusion of a non-resident into a "place of profit" formerly reserved for residents would offend aspiring Virginians, Culpeper told

[53] C.O. 5/1306, No. 41. Milner was accordingly given the post of escheator for the south side of the James. *Executive Journals*, I, 239.

[54] C.O. 1/39, f.222.

[55] This practice was prescribed by statute in 1662 (Hening, II, 78) and is evident in all the surviving county court records. See also C.O. 1/20, ff.220–21.

[56] C.O. 1/47, ff.258–60.

Ayleway flatly that he was dismissed. When Ayleway pleaded that he held a commission under the Great Seal, which Culpeper had no authority to revoke, His Lordship was unimpressed. It took more than the Great Seal to frighten him, and he assured the hapless Ayleway that if he succeeded in hanging on to the office, he, Culpeper, would see to it that "it should not bee worth to him one penny." [57] The burgesses were so grateful for this gesture that they passed an act, urgently desired by the king, that they had unanimously been refusing to accept.[58]

In supporting Beverley and suppressing Ayleway, Culpeper did what to him seemed best both for the peaceful government of the colony and for his own fortune. Culpeper, like other official beneficiaries of Virginia tobacco, had reason to seek the well-being of the colony. The larger the revenue a man drew from the planters' labors, the more interest he had in seeing that revenue continue undiminished. The king, the governor, the councillors, the burgesses, the sheriffs—the fortunes of all seemed to be linked to the colony's prosperity. Yet the prosperity that Virginia had enjoyed in the 1620s from high tobacco prices was no boon to the rights and liberties of those who worked for other men. In the prosaic decades that followed, Virginians had developed institutions that gave a greater security and freedom and even a kind of prosperity to ordinary men, especially to those who managed to survive the term of years when a master could claim their services. But after midcentury the prosperity of Virginia's big men, in the face of low tobacco prices and rising crops and population, could not be widely shared, nor could the governmental authority that made it possible. As death loosened its grip on the colony, kings and captains and governors tightened theirs and began once more to reduce the rights of those on whose labors they depended.

[57] C.O. 1/45, f.169. Though Culpeper was momentarily victorious, Ayleway did hang on to his commission and years later was able to sell his interest in it to William Byrd. Philip A. Bruce, *Institutional History of Virginia in the Seventeenth Century* (New York, 1910), II, 599; *VMHB*, XXV (1917), 263; XXVI (1918), 133, 390.

[58] C.O. 1/47, ff.258-60; Hening, II, 466-69; *Journals of the House of Burgesses, 1659/60-1693*, 130, 134-35, 144-45.

Book III

THE VOLATILE SOCIETY

11

THE LOSERS

THE society Virginians established during the first fifty years of the colony's existence had been geared to function in the face of heavy mortality. One of its features was the annual arrival of new workers to replenish the dying labor force. The decline of mortality and the increase in population did not stop the flow of immigrants. Until the last two decades of the century the annual arrivals were probably not much under 1,000 a year and in some years much more. New workers were still necessary, because Virginia's increase in population did not solve the labor problem of the planters. When servants became free, they preferred to work for themselves even though that might mean going into partnership for a term with one or more other freedmen. And they had been able to set up for themselves because of the cheap public land that was another feature of Virginia society.

Before the middle of the century, while the heavy death rate continued, the men who survived their terms of servitude and managed to set up households of their own were too few in number to offer serious competition to their former masters or to invite systematic exploitation. As they began to live longer, however, as more became free each year, their very numbers posed a problem for the men who had brought them. If the ex-servants continued as freemen to make tobacco, though they would automatically contribute to the fees and duties levied on the trade, they would be competing with their former masters. By adding to the volume of the crop, they would help to depress the price. If they did not make tobacco but lapsed into an idle, perhaps dissolute life such as many had led in England, they would corrupt the labor force and contribute nothing to the revenue derived from the colony. As things were going then, the increasing number of freedmen, whether diligent or delinquent, would increasingly cut into their former masters' profits.

In efforts to handle this problem, the men who ran Virginia began to alter their society in ways that curtailed and threatened the independence of the small freeman and worsened the lot of the servant. During the last thirty or forty years of the seventeenth century, while tobacco was enriching the king and so many others, most of the men who worked in the fields were losers, and they did not much like it.

One approach to the problem of increasing freedmen was to impose as long a servitude as possible before allowing men to become free. During the extra years of service they would create profits rather than competition for their masters, who would also be able to keep them out of mischief. Servants who came to the colony without an indenture in which the terms were specified were vulnerable to such a move. In 1642 the assembly had prescribed that they could be kept for four years if over twenty at the time of arrival, for five years if between twelve and twenty, and for seven years if under twelve. Between 1658 and 1666 the assembly, as always a collection of masters, revised the terms to give themselves and other masters a longer hold on their imported labor. Henceforth persons nineteen or over when they arrived would serve five years, and persons under nineteen would serve until they were twenty-four.[1] The new law meant that most servants who came without an indenture had to serve three additional years, because most of them were in their teens. In fact, so far as surviving records show, most were not over sixteen. The laws required that a master who imported a servant without an indenture bring him to court within six months to have his age determined and his consequent term of service recorded. In the Lancaster records from 1662 to 1680 only 32 of 296 servants were judged to be nineteen years of age or more. The median age was sixteen, and 133 were younger than that and therefore had nine years or more to serve.[2] In Norfolk County in the same period only one of 72 servants was judged to be as old as nineteen, and the median fell between fifteen and sixteen.[3]

Another way to prolong the term of service was to attach greater

[1] Hening, I, 257, 443; II, 113, 240.
[2] Lancaster III and IV, passim.   [3] Norfolk IV, VI, and VII, passim.

penalities to the servants' favorite vice, running away. Early laws had already provided that servants who ran away should have their terms of service extended by double the length of time in which they absented themselves.[4] In 1669 and 1670 new laws provided rewards to anyone apprehending a runaway, with the provision that the servant not only reimburse his master by double service for the time missed, but that he also reimburse the public by serving further time at the rate of four months for every 200 pounds of tobacco expended on the reward for apprehending him.[5] The rate thus set for reimbursement was about half the current wage for hired labor. In practice the courts sometimes set more equitable rates. but they favored masters by allowing the high recovery charges usually claimed by a man who pursued and caught his own servant. In addition to requiring the servant to reimburse those charges by longer service, the courts added time to the servant's term for presumed losses incurred by the master as a result of the servant's absence from his job. Though in past decades the provision for double service had ordinarily been considered adequate recompense for crop losses incurred by the servant's absence, the courts in some counties in the 1670s began adding time, above and beyond double service, for the loss of crop. Thus in Lancaster, Christopher Adams, absent for six months, was required to serve three years extra: one year for the six months' absence, one year for the loss of the crop that he would otherwise have made, and one year for 1,300 pounds of tobacco expended in recovering him.[6] James Gray, absent 22 days, got fifteen months' extra service: three months for 22 days and loss of crop, and twelve months for the cost of recovery.[7] Three servants absent for 34 days were required to serve 68 days for the 34, eight months for the loss of crop, and four months, ten days for the cost of recovery.[8]

Servants who engaged in forbidden pleasures also had their terms extended. A maidservant who had a child served two years extra for it. And the surreptitious feast in the forest with which servants sometimes indulged themselves became yet another means of extending their terms. The penalty for killing a hog was 1,000 pounds of tobacco or a year's service to the owner and 1,000 pounds or a year's service to the informer.[9] If the owner and the informer

[4] Hening, I, 254, 401, 440.
[5] Hening, II, 273–74, 277–79.   [7] *Ibid.*, 163.
[6] Lancaster IV, 161.   [8] *Ibid.*, 263.
[9] Hening, II, 129 (1662). In 1679 the assembly provided further that second offenders should have their ears nailed to the pillory and then

were the same man, as was often the case, he got both. Thus Richard Higby was required to serve his master six years extra for killing three hogs.[10]

In spite of such legal contrivances for prolonging servitude, men did become free. When they did, they looked for land of their own. With land of their own they could begin to reap the profits that their labors had hitherto earned for others. But in their need for land lay another means of controlling them and extracting a part of their earnings. In the early years few Virginians had thought it worth the trouble to acquire large tracts of land, and men who became free in the first half of the century probably had no trouble finding good land still unclaimed on the James or York rivers or their tributaries. But as life expectancy rose, the expectancy of land-ownership rose with it, and anyone could see that the demand would send land values up. It would be worthwhile to acquire land not merely for future use or to hand on to children and grand-children, but also to sell or to rent to the rising body of new free-men. In this way the established planters might continue to share in the fruits of their former servants' labors.

In the Old World, by controlling access to the soil, landlords had been able for centuries to exact a portion of other men's earnings in the form of rents.[11] In Virginia the method could not be as effec-tive as in Europe, because land was too plentiful. But because it was so plentiful and so cheap, it could be acquired in much larger amounts than European landlords aspired to, in amounts large enough to place most of Virginia's river lands in private hands long before actual settlers reached them.

It was not very costly to acquire large holdings. The head-rights on the basis of which public land could be claimed were bought and sold in Virginia separately from the servants for whose transportation they were issued. Headrights were valid whether the person in whose name they were claimed was alive or dead. The

---

cut off, and that third offenders be treated as felons under English law, i.e., be subject to the death penalty. Hening, II, 440–41.

[10] Lancaster IV, 142.

[11] It has been argued that in times and places where land was abundant and rents consequently low, as in early America and in late sixteenth- and early seventeenth-century Russia, the result was to make entrepreneurial classes develop some form of serfdom or slavery. Evsey D. Domar, "The Causes of Slavery or Serfdom: A Hypothesis," *Journal of Economic History*, XX (1970), 18–32. The hypothesis would seem to be borne out by the de-velopments under way in seventeenth-century Virginia.

years of heavy mortality, when land was scarcely worth patenting, had left Virginians with a large reservoir of unused headrights. In the 1650s they could be bought for 40 or 50 pounds of tobacco apiece, each headright entitling the owner to fifty acres of land.[12]

As mortality fell and population rose, Virginians who had a little capital to spare began to assemble headrights and were soon scrambling to patent the colony's best remaining lands. By the time the land boom began, the best acres were already gone along the lower reaches of the James and York and much of the Rappahannock. Speculators began at once to reach for the plums in more remote areas, including the Potomac region. In 1650 Virginians were just beginning to patent land on their side of the Potomac, where Northumberland County had been formed in 1648. By 1651 they were already staking out claims as far up as Potomac Creek, eighty miles upriver. By 1654 Westmoreland County had been formed, and they were acquiring land along the tributary Occoquan and the Potomac "freshes" in the future counties of Stafford and Prince William.[13] Much of the speculative fever centered in Charles City County, where Howell Price, clerk of the court, seems to have served as a broker to speculators. Between 1655 and 1659 he bought up headrights worth 38,500 acres, most of which he sold to other men, who used them to patent land on the Potomac.[14] Before the decade was out, a few individuals held title to most of the land on the Virginia side downstream from the present site of Alexandria. A mere scanning of the patents reveals over 100,000 acres held by only thirty persons.[15]

During the 1650s speculators were also patenting huge tracts

[12] Norfolk III, 205a; Westmoreland I, 51.

[13] *VMHB*, XXIII (1915), 249–50; Hening, I, 352–53, 381; Nell M. Nugent, *Cavaliers and Pioneers: Abstracts of Virginia Land Patents and Grants* (Richmond, 1934), 185–316.

[14] Fleet, *Virginia Colonial Abstracts*, X, 29, 33, 39, 46, 53, 64, 78, 84, 88, 91, 101; XI, 27, 33, 74. The names of the persons for whom headrights were claimed were usually certified by a county court and copied in its records. The rights could then be sold, as Price sold his, and the person ultimately exercising the rights would then record the names again in the patent he obtained. It is thus possible to trace, through the excellent index in Nugent's *Cavaliers and Pioneers*, the ultimate use made of Price's certificates. He seems to have exercised rights to only 1,000 acres himself.

[15] Nugent, *Cavaliers and Pioneers*, 185–390. Some of the larger patentees were John Wood, 10,000 acres; Samuel Mathews, 5,200; Gervase Dodson, 11,400; Thomas Wilkinson, 6,500; Henry Corbin, 3,900; Giles Brent, 6,000; and Nathaniel Pope, 5,100.

on the upper York and Rappahannock rivers,[16] and the boom did not stop there. In 1664 the number of headrights used reached the peak of the century, when 3,243 rights were expended on 162,150 acres. In Accomack County alone Colonel Edmund Scarburgh presented certificates for 191 headrights and got 9,550 acres; John Savage got 9,000, and eleven other persons 15,200 acres. And in 1666 eight patents accounted for 34,600 acres (in Rappahannock, Isle of Wight, and Accomack).[17] Altogether in the years 1650 to 1675 Virginians patented 2,350,000 acres, more than half the total for the whole period 1635–99.[18]

After securing a patent, the owner was supposed to "seat" the land, that is, build a house and plant corn or tobacco. He was also supposed to pay annual quitrents to the king at the rate of two shillings for every hundred acres. But until late in the century the quitrents were only sporadically collected, and according to Edward Randolph, an English revenue agent, the way the planters seated the land was to "cut down a few trees and make therewith a little Hut, covering it with the bark and turn two or three hogs into the woods by it: Or else they are to clear one Acre of that land, and to plant and tend it one year: But they fell twenty or thirty trees, and put a little Indian Corn in the ground among them as they lye, and sometimes make a beginning to fence it, but take no care of their Crop, nor make any further use of their land." [19]

Such a procedure sufficed to establish a man's claim to a tract, however large. As a result, the land still appeared to visitors to be "one continued wood." John Clayton in 1684 observed that "every one covets so much and there is such vast extent of land that they spread so far they cannot manage well a hundredth part of what they have." [20]

Managed or not, the acres were owned. And the servants who became free after 1660 found it increasingly difficult to locate workable land that was not already claimed. In order to set up their own households in this vast and unpeopled country, they frequently had to rent or else move to the frontiers, where they came into conflict with the Indians.[21] Many preferred safety in the settled area even though it meant renting land from the big men who owned it. In

---

[16] *Ibid.*, 194–96, 200, 244–45, 324.   [17] *Ibid.*, 424–524, 548–61.

[18] Craven, *White, Red, and Black*, 15–16.

[19] C.O. 5/1309, No. 5. Aug. 31, 1696.   [20] Sloane Mss. 1008, ff.334–35.

[21] C.O. 1/39, f.196; Massachusetts Historical Society, *Collections*, 4th ser., IX (1871), 164.

turning down a proposal to levy taxes on land instead of polls, the House of Burgesses in 1663 argued that this would properly entail limiting the right to vote to landholders. And such a limitation would be resented by "the other freemen who are the more in number." [22] Thus the burgesses implied that the majority of freemen were without land. This was probably an exaggeration, perhaps motivated by the realization of burgesses with very large landholdings that they would have to pay more in taxes on their acres than on their servants' polls. In 1676, however, Thomas Ludwell and Robert Smith, two members of the council, maintained that at least one-fourth of the population consisted of "merchants and single freemen and such others as have noe land." [23] And in the same year Francis Moryson, another former council member, explained the term "freedmen," as used in Virginia, to mean "persons without house and land," implying that this was the normal condition of servants who had attained freedom.[24] In any case, land had been so engrossed by this time that newcomers, even with substantial capital and a supply of servants, often rented. In 1678, when the Privy Council instructed the governor to confine voting in the colony to landholders, Thomas Ludwell (the secretary of the colony) objected that this would create inequities, because of "many tennants here (especially in James River which hath been longest planted) haveing more tythable servants then their landlords." [25]

There are no records from which we can estimate the exact proportion of tenants and owners at any time in the seventeenth century. But there is evidence that in Surry there were 266 resident owners of land in 1704, and 422 households in 1703.[26] Thus approxi-

[22] George Bancroft, *History of the United States*, 15th ed. (Boston, 1856), II, 207, quoting from "Richmond Records, no. 2, 1660 to 1664, p. 175." (These records were destroyed in the burning of Richmond in 1865.) John Daly Burk, who also had access to the destroyed records, says of the proposed change: "The attempt probably originated in a desire of contracting the right of suffrage, in order as it was pretended that the poorer classes might not have it in their power to elect to the assembly men disaffected to the government." *The History of Virginia, from Its First Settlement to the Present Day* (Petersburg, 1804-16), II, 137.

[23] Coventry Papers, LXXVII, 128.

[24] *Ibid.*, 204.

[25] *Ibid.*, LXXVIII, 202.

[26] The first extant quitrent roll, showing the owners of land, dates from 1704 and is reproduced in Thomas J. Wertenbaker, *The Planters of Colonial Virginia* (Princeton, 1922), 183-247. The only county in which the number

mately 156 (37 percent) of the householders appear to have been tenants. The earliest date for which it is possible to make comparison of landowners and householders in exactly the same year is in 1720, in Christ Church Parish, Lancaster County. There, out of 146 householders, 86 were owners, and the other 60 (41 percent) apparently tenants (including several who held large numbers of tithables).[27]

How large a share of a tenant's produce did the landlord get? That varied greatly according to the location and quality of the land. In Surry a 300-acre tract described as poor was worth 350 pounds of tobacco a year in 1673; a 100-acre tract rented in 1656 for a barrel of Indian corn (worth about 100 pounds of tobacco).[28] In each of these cases the tenant was also to plant an orchard and build or maintain a tenantable house, to be left on the plantation at the termination of the lease (a common requirement). In Henrico County in 1686 a plantation was rented at 100 pounds per year for every person working on it.[29] In Lancaster, where land was richer than in Henrico or Surry, a plantation of 100 acres was leased in 1664 for ten years at 60 shillings (about 600 pounds of tobacco) a year for the first two years and 50 shillings (500 pounds) thereafter.[30] One man's crop in Lancaster was almost certainly larger and more valuable than the yield from the cheap lands of Surry. But 2,000 pounds would probably have been a good crop even in Lancaster.[31] Hence the rent of a plantation ran from perhaps 5 to 8 percent to 25 percent or more of the annual produce of a single man. Since a plantation, unless it was exceptionally small, would support

---

of households is known at about that time is Surry, where the tithable lists exist for the year 1703. Surry V, 287–91. Kelly, "Economic and Social Development of Surry County," 124, says that the 1703 tithable list shows a total of 462 freemen in that year. Such a number is not incompatible with the total of 422 households listed, but it is not clear how Kelly has identified freemen living in other men's households. From recorded deeds and land patents Kelly estimates that in the last thirty years of the seventeenth century over 40 percent of Surry's freemen were non-landowners (p. 125).

[27] Thirty-eight (31 percent) of the 124 landowners on the rent roll were apparently non-resident. The list of tithables is in Lancaster IX, 335–36; the rent roll is in the Virginia State Library.

[28] Surry I, 151–52; II, 24.   [29] Henrico II, 127.

[30] Lancaster II, 285. These are only samples of numerous leases recorded in the court records of various counties. More are cited in Bruce, *Economic History*, II, 413–18.

[31] See chap. 7, note 33.

more than one man, the rent was not high, but it usually represented a good profit for the owner above the quitrent he owed to the king. Moreover, many owners saved themselves this expense by making their tenants responsible for the quitrent.

Perhaps more important than the actual rent obtained by Virginia's landlords was the effect of the artificial scarcity of land in keeping freedmen available for hire. If a man could not get land without paying rent for it, he might be obliged to go back to work for another man simply to stay alive. The pressure to do so would of course be stronger if he entered on his freedom without tools, clothes, or provisions. According to the "custom of the country" (legally enforceable), a master was required to furnish a servant at the end of his term with freedom dues of three barrels of corn and a suit of clothes (probably worth 500 to 600 pounds of tobacco). But as freedom time drew near, it was tempting to both parties to strike a bargain in which the servant gave up his freedom dues in return for an early release. If his term expired in the slack season from December to May, his labor during the last few months would be worth a good deal less than his dues, perhaps less than his board. But, impatient for immediate freedom or intimidated by an overbearing master, servants often did give up their freedom dues and thus found themselves very quickly back at work for their bread in another man's household.[32]

Those who did make it into the ranks of the householders, whether by renting or buying land or staking out a new claim in the interior, faced yet another drain on their earnings. Though it required no more than a piece of land, a hoe, an axe, a few barrels of corn, and a strong back to set up a tobacco plantation, marketing a small crop could be difficult. If a man's land was on a river or creek, one of the ships that rode in the great rivers from November to June would send hands to roll the hogsheads to the shore and hoist them aboard a boat or small sloop.[33] But the prices offered for

[32] The three barrels of corn were worth about 300 pounds of tobacco. On the value of the clothes given as freedom dues see chap. 17, note 16. In 1677 the assembly limited the right of masters to make bargains with their servants, "especially some small tyme before the expiration of their tyme of service." Hening, II, 388.

[33] It is difficult to determine how hogsheads were loaded in the seventeenth century, but Hugh Jones in 1724 said that it had been the custom "in some places" for sailors to roll the hogsheads, sometimes for some miles. Jones, *The Present State of Virginia*, Richard L. Morton, ed. (Chapel Hill,

tobacco varied greatly from year to year, and so did the availability
of ships to carry it. A big man with labor to grow tobacco on a
large scale could command more attention and better prices from the
ships, because his large crop made it possible for a ship to load
rapidly and get back to England for a more favorable market than
later ships. It was often easier for a small man to sell his crop to his
larger neighbor than to gamble on the chance of getting it aboard a
ship himself. If his land did not abut a river, he might have no choice
but to sell to someone who could get it aboard for him.

The larger planters in this way came to be merchants—many
described themselves as such. Some made regular trips to London in
order to market a shipload at a time. And, as always, the man who
marketed the crop generally made more from it than the man who
grew it. Virginians often spoke bitterly about the low prices that
the London merchants paid them, but the local Virginia merchant
planters could play the same role toward their small neighbors that
the London merchants played toward them.[34] And as it became
common for Virginia's big planters to be heavily indebted to London merchants, so the small planter became indebted to his larger
neighbor. His crop in one year might not buy the clothes and other
supplies he needed for the next. The merchant planter would advance the goods against the next year's crop. And as the London
merchants charged Virginia debtors premium prices for goods purchased on credit, it is altogether probable that local debts produced
the same advantage to the creditor. To be sure, most creditors were
also debtors. In seventeenth-century Virginia, as elsewhere and
always, debt was not merely an unfortunate condition to which the
poor were subject. Fortunes can often be made by going into debt
on a large scale, and the whole Virginia economy was based on
credit, often supported by little more than the promise of next year's

---

N.C., 1956), 89. Thomas Adams in a letter to the London merchants Perkins,
Buchanan, and Brown, April, 1770, says it had always been the custom for
the buyer to pay the cost of getting tobacco aboard ship, though not to
take the risk of loss in the process. *VMHB*, XXIII (1915), 54–55. One case
that reached the Northampton County court in 1652 shows a ship captain
hiring a man with a shallop to get tobacco aboard. Northampton IV, 88.

[34] Aubrey C. Land has emphasized the entrepreneurial activities of the
Chesapeake merchant planters in the eighteenth century. "Economic Behavior in a Planting Society: The Eighteenth-Century Chesapeake," *Journal
of Southern History*, XXXIII (1967), 469–85. The behavior he describes was
characteristic of seventeenth-century planters also, though on a smaller scale.

crop. Nevertheless, for a man without servants, whose next year's crop would be the result only of his own labor, debt might be a road back to servitude. When a man could not pay up at harvest time, and there was no good prospect he ever would be able to on his own, when he had no cattle, no land, and not even a feather bed [35] to his name, or when these had already all been attached for debt, he might be required to work out his indebtedness by a term of service to his creditor or to someone else who would discharge the debt. In the early 1660s, when tobacco prices were low, one Virginian estimated that three-fourths of the planters were so poor they would have to become servants to the others, "who being merchants as well as planters will bee better able to subsist." [36]

It was doubtless an exaggeration to place three-fourths of the population in so desperate a condition. But it seems plain that by the 1660s Virginia was acquiring a new social structure. Outside the structure entirely were the remaining tributary Indians, segregated in what amounted to reservations, beyond the limits of settlement but rightly uneasy about their future. Inside the structure at the bottom were a number of slaves, perhaps more than a thousand but still a minor component of society. A little above them were a much more numerous body of servants, working out the terms assigned them or agreed upon by indenture to repay the cost of their transportation. At the other end, at the top of the scale stood the elite group of men who had inherited, amassed, or arrived in the colony with estates large enough to assure them a continuing supply of servants and to win them lucrative government offices. A little below them were the other established householders, usually with one or more servants. In between the established householders and the servants working out their terms stood the part of the population that had begun to grow most rapidly: the freedmen who had finished their terms of service. They were entitled to set up households of their own, but they were finding it harder to do than the men who became free in the preceding decades.

From the annual lists of tithables that survive for four counties

[35] Feather beds were a highly valued item in Virginia, being listed in inventories for 400–600 pounds of tobacco, about the same value as a cow. One of Governor Berkeley's enemies, complaining of Virginia tax levies, accused Berkeley of saying that if people "had not tobacco they had cowes and fetherbeds sufficient to discharge their leavies." Coventry Papers, LXXVII, 144.

[36] Ms. Rawlinson A 38, Bodleian Library, Oxford.

it is possible to form some estimate of the ability of freedmen to enter the ranks of householders. The most conspicuous change observable in the lists during the third quarter of the century is the increasing number of households containing only one tithable, that is, one male over fifteen years old.

Percent of Households with Only One Tithable [37]

	1653	1663	1668	1675
Lancaster	13	18	13	32
Accomack		23	40	51
Northampton		30	41	53
Surry			38	57

Although some of the new one-man households were doubtless headed by the sons of older families who had married and set up for themselves or by new immigrants who had come on their own, the majority probably consisted of men, with or without wives, who had formerly been servants. The increase in one-man households would seem to indicate that the freedmen were doing well, but if we dig a little deeper, a slightly different picture is uncovered. In Lancaster, of 247 servants who either are known to have become free or were legally entitled to freedom between 1662 and 1678, only 24 show up as householders by 1679 (after that date the lists are incomplete because of damage to the records).[38] Lancaster in the seventeenth century was a rich man's county, in the area be-

---

[37] The first year in which a figure appears is the first year in which a record is available for that county. The total number of households in each county was as follows: Lancaster had 92 in 1653, 175 in 1663, 191 in 1668, and 196 in 1675; Accomack had 128 in 1663, 188 in 1668, and 297 in 1675; Northampton had 151 in 1663, 177 in 1668, and 205 in 1675; Surry had 182 in 1668 and 245 in 1675. Lancaster in 1653 included the future counties of Rappahannock (1657) and Middlesex (1669). The figures are from Lancaster I, 90; III, 234–38; IV, 85–87, 335–38; Accomack I, 35; II, 80; V, 326; Northampton VIII, 175–76; X, 54–55; XIII, 73–75; Surry I, 315–17; II, 92–94.

[38] 205 servants who had their ages judged before 1678 were to become free by that year. An additional 42 of unstated age received their freedom by court order after suing for it. Lancaster III and IV, passim.

tween the York and the Potomac, where population and tobacco production were expanding most rapidly. But the figures suggest that it was not a land of opportunity for its newly freed servants.

Northampton County, on the Eastern Shore, was a poorer region, but even there, although a servant might make it into the ranks of householders, the odds were against it. From 1664 to 1677, of 808 non-householders who appear on any of the Northampton tithable lists, only 230 later appear as householders; and 88 men who appear as householders later appear as non-householders. Those who lost status, with a few known exceptions, were presumably freemen who had set up on their own and then had to give up and go back to work for someone else. Only 80 of the 329 white non-householders present in the years 1664–67 were still in the county in 1677; 49 of them had become householders, but 31 had still not made it.[39]

The tithable lists of Northampton and Lancaster argue that Virginia in the 1660s and 1670s furnished fewer opportunities to the poor than either we or seventeenth-century Englishmen may have supposed. A man who came to Virginia with nothing but the shirt on his back expected several years of servitude, but after that he expected something more of life in the New World. When he got to Virginia, however, he found that he might never make it out of the ranks of servants. If he did, it was not likely to be in one of the counties where rich land would insure him success. Land was still abundant but no longer free, except in areas where the danger from Indians or the lack of transportation for tobacco made it uninviting. Those who managed to set up on their own were likely to find themselves still paying tribute to their former masters in the form of rent, not to mention the tribute they paid in yearly poll taxes, export taxes, and fees, as well as the tribute exacted by the king in customs duties at London. Under the circumstances it is not surprising that Virginia's freemen in these years were reputedly an unruly and discontented lot of men.

The distribution of discontent in Virginia, like the distribution of spoils, was uneven. Geographically the gravest concentrations of unhappiness and unruliness lay probably in the counties that attracted the largest numbers of new freemen. These were not necessarily the most rapidly growing areas. The rich counties on the lower York, Rappahannock, and Potomac were growing very

[39] See Appendix, pp. 423–31, where the Northampton lists are analyzed in detail. The figures that follow are derived from that analysis.

rapidly during most of the second half of the seventeenth century, but they probably grew by the importation of increasing numbers of servants who, when freed, moved elsewhere, perhaps after hiring out for a time to gain capital to set up for themselves in some corner of Virginia less engrossed by the wealthy.

Although it is impossible to tell where the freemen of any county came from, two areas seem for a variety of reasons to have drawn a larger than average number of small planters. The first was New Kent, extending from the upper reaches of the Chickahominy, which empties into the James, to those of the Pianketank, which empties into Chesapeake Bay (see map, page vi) and embracing the various branches of the Mattapony and Pamunkey. The second was the "Southside," the counties of Surry, Isle of Wight, Nansemond, and Norfolk, along the south bank of the James River. The table of one-man households shows the Southside county of Surry with the largest percentage by 1675 and Lancaster, in the Northern Neck, with the smallest. For one year, 1679, the records allow us to determine the size of households in two additional counties, Northumberland (another Northern Neck county) and Henrico (at the head of the James, embracing both sides).

Tithables per Household in 1679

County	Average number of tithables per household	Percent of one-man households	Percent of households with 2 to 5 tithables	Percent of households with over 5 tithables
Surry	1.98	58.0	36.7	5.3
Henrico	2.72	37.5	55.0	7.5
Northumberland	2.27	33.9	55.4	10.7
Lancaster	3.18	36.4	52.3	11.4
Accomack	2.49	45.6	47.1	7.3
Northampton (1677)	2.29	53.7	39.0	7.3
TOTAL	2.60	44.2	47.5	8.3

Again Surry appears to be the poorest, not only in having the largest percentage of one-man households and the smallest percentage with more than five tithables, but also in the number of tithables per household, a related but not identical index of wealth.[40]

No figures are available for the other Southside counties or for New Kent during the seventeenth century, but for the year 1704 it is possible to determine the number of tithables per landowner in all the counties south of the Rappahannock.[41] Though this is a less reliable index of wealth than the number of tithables per household, it is the best we have. In 1704 both New Kent and the Southside counties averaged 3 tithables per landowner, while the other counties averaged 4.5. Since we know Surry was in a comparable position thirty years earlier, it seems likely that the other Southside counties were too. As for New Kent, we may perhaps find a clue in the fact that well-to-do residents of nearby counties in the 1670s designated the New Kenters as "rabble." [42]

Another clue that New Kent and the Southside counties held a smaller than normal proportion of prosperous planters is the fact that few men from these areas were appointed to the governor's council. In spite of New Kent's proximity to Jamestown (a prime consideration in appointments to the council), only one resident of

[40] The Surry, Lancaster, and Accomack lists are part of the annual listing of tithables in those counties and are in Surry II, 225–27; Lancaster IV, 514–17; and Accomack VIII, 99–101. I have also included the Northampton figures for 1677 (from Northampton XII, 189–91) since the year is so close, and no later figures for Northampton survive. The Henrico and Northumberland figures derive from a law requiring each county to raise a soldier for every 44 tithables. In calculations made to implement the law in these two counties the court set down the number of tithables in each household. The records are in Henrico I, 102–3, and Northumberland III, 37–38. The number of households in each county was as follows: Surry 226, Henrico 160, Northumberland 289, Lancaster 176, Accomack 274, Northampton 205.

[41] The tithable figures are in Evarts B. Greene and Virginia D. Harrington, *American Population before the Census of 1790*, 149–50. The list of landowners in Wertenbaker, *Planters of Colonial Virginia*, 183–247, does not include the counties of the Northern Neck, between the Rappahannock and the Potomac.

[42] William Sherwood to Sir Joseph Williamson, June 1, 28, 1676; Philip Ludwell to same, June 28, 1676, *VMHB* I (1893–94), 167–85. Note p. 174 for identification with New Kent. See also Massachusetts Historical Society, *Collections*, 4th ser., IX (1871), 165, 166, 170.

New Kent sat on the council before 1676. More distant counties supplied several members: before 1676 there were three from Rappahannock, three from Westmoreland, five from Lancaster, two from Middlesex, and two from Northampton, all considerably more remote from Jamestown than New Kent. The Southside counties were apparently not as lacking as New Kent in men of sufficient stature to sit on the council, but they too were less well represented than their proximity to Jamestown would have warranted. In the period before 1676 Surry furnished two members and Isle of Wight only one, Nansemond five and Norfolk three. By contrast the counties of York, James City, and Charles City, lying just across the river, furnished sixteen, sixteen, and eight, respectively.[43]

If the Southside and New Kent had many small householders living on the edge of subsistence, the distress occasioned by low tobacco prices and profit-hungry officials and merchants would have been particularly keen in these two areas. And it would have been made worse by the fact that they both faced more acutely than most other areas a problem that was never far from the consciousness of all seventeenth-century Virginians: the Indians. An act of the assembly in 1669, which specifies the numbers of warriors or "bowmen" in the various neighboring tribes, also indicates the county to which each tribe was adjacent. Of 725 warriors in 19 tribes, 280 in 6 tribes were adjacent to Nansemond, Surry, and Charles City (the southern part), and 200 in 5 tribes were adjacent to New Kent. Of the remainder Henrico accounted for only 40 and the counties on the Rappahannock and Potomac for 190.[44]

These were all supposedly peaceful Indians, defeated in war and pushed back from the coast. That discontented freedmen and displaced Indians should have been concentrated in the same areas was scarcely accidental. Both were losers in the contest for the richer lands of the tidewater. And both held an uncertain place in the way of life that was developing in Virginia.

If Berkeley's schemes for Virginia had been successful, both might have had a different future. In keeping with his vision, Berkeley had urged a shift from poll taxes to land taxes, a move that would have reduced the large accumulations held for speculation and that would at the same time have reduced the pressure on the Indi-

[43] Figures drawn from William G. and Mary N. Stanard, *The Colonial Virginia Register* (Albany, N.Y., 1902).
[44] Hening, II, 274–75.

ans. Berkeley's whole drive to free Virginia from dependence on tobacco, like Sir Edwin Sandys' forty years earlier, was accompanied
by a consistent effort to find a modus vivendi with Virginia's Indians.

Not that the governor was a lover of Indians. He had earned
his popularity in the colony by subduing them after their last concerted assault on the settlers in the 1640s. In the treaty made in 1646
he had established the ascendancy of the English once and for all,
by prescribing boundaries within which the Indians were not to enter without permission (all the tidewater from the York River to
the Blackwater, south of the James). As a symbol of their submission the Indians thereafter paid him a yearly tribute of twenty beaver
skins and selected their rulers only with his approval.[45]

Responding to the demands of the expanding English population, Berkeley almost immediately allowed the opening up of the
tidewater north of the York, but he clung to the policy of keeping
Virginia's Indians as tributaries rather than enemies, specifically requiring them to assist the colony against any "strange" Indians.[46]
Other governors followed the same policy during the interregnum
of the 1650s, and for a time Virginians even made efforts to convert
the Indians to a more English mode of existence. Protection of their
title to land, it was felt, would make them think twice about for-
feiting it in rebellions. Since they were good hunters, they were offered bounties on wolves (though less than those paid to Englishmen) in the form of a cow for every eight wolves' heads they
brought in. Possession of a cow was expected to serve as "a step to

[45] Hening, I, 323–26. The treaty of 1646 seems to have required this
tribute only from Necotowance, who was evidently the successor of
Opechancanough as head of the empire that Powhatan had formed. But by
the 1660s that empire had crumbled, and at some point the English began
collecting the tribute from each neighboring tribe. A treaty in 1677 spelled
out the obligation of "every Indian King and Queen" to pay it. *VMHB*,
XIV (1906–7), 294.

[46] Hening, I, 353–54; II, 34, 35, 39, 138–43, 193–94, 218–20; Craven,
White, Red, and Black, 58, W. S. Robinson, "Tributary Indians in Colonial
Virginia," *VMHB*, LXVII (1959), 49–64. See also the letter of Berkeley to
the commissioners of the Northampton County court in 1650, warning
against taking lands from "the Indyans commonly called by the name of
the Laughinge Kinge Indyans" who "have beene ever most faithfull to the
English And particularly that neither they nor their Kinge in the last bloody
massacry could bee enjoined to engage with our Enemyes against us And
soe by consequence kept the remoter Indyans att Least Neutrall. . . ."
Northampton III, 207a. Cf. Berkeley to Lancaster commissioners, Dec. 7,
1660. Berkeley Papers, Alderman Library.

civilizing them and to making them Christians." They were also invited to send their children into English homes to be brought up as
Christians, and were assured that the children would be treated as
other servants and not be enslaved.[47]

But the Indians mostly refused to send their children for lessons
in servility, and the cows proved no more successful as missionaries
than the few ministers who tried their hand at it. The Indians were
more assiduous in growing corn than the English; and cattle, whether
their own or the English, only created fencing problems for them.
They already practiced an economy that was more self-sufficient and
more diversified than that of the English and a way of life that was
more urban, if not more urbane. They were the only Virginians
who did in fact live in towns, using the surrounding land for their
cornfields as well as for hunting and gathering. They needed a good
deal of space for these activities but not nearly as much as the thousands of acres claimed by Virginia's new land barons.

As the English population swelled, and the two economies came
increasingly in contact, they did not mesh. Berkeley's land tax had
been rejected by a House of Burgesses loaded with aspiring speculators. The new freedmen were multiplying in numbers every year,
and, unable to afford land elsewhere, moved to the frontiers, where
they viewed the Indians not as fellow victims but as rivals for the
marginal lands to which both had been driven. They brought their
cows and hogs with them; they brought their guns; and they brought
a smoldering resentment, which they had been unable to take out on
their betters. The Indians, they had been taught (if they needed
teaching), were not their betters.

The government itself had taught them in the very measures by
which it attempted to protect Indian rights. To the Indians who participated in the peace of 1646, the remnants of the old Powhatan
confederacy, Virginia conceded that they should not be killed simply for trespassing on the lands that had been taken from them, but
only for committing "what would be felony in an Englishman."
The felony was to be proved by "two oathes at least." [48] But the act
did not say where or to whom the oaths must be sworn or who was
entitled to do the killing once the oaths were taken. Perhaps it
was intended that the facts be proved in court, but the act did not
say so. When an Indian damaged an Englishman's property, the law
required the victim to seek satisfaction from the Indian's king and

---

[47] Hening, I, 393–96.   [48] *Ibid.*, 415.

not attempt to recover his losses in the customary frontiersman's do-it-yourself manner. But in applying this procedure the government displayed a contempt for the rights of individuals that would have been unthinkable in the treatment of any European. When John Powell complained to the assembly about damages done him by Indians in Northumberland, the commissioners of the county were empowered to determine the value of the damage and, after due notice to the "cheife man or men among those Indians," to seize enough of them to satisfy the award by selling them "into a forraigne countrey." [49]

Perhaps these were foreign or "northern" Indians, who had not participated in the peace of 1646 or had not subsequently been reduced to tributary status, but the measure so casually recorded for enslaving them speaks volumes about prevailing attitudes. Berkeley himself proposed all-out war on the northern Indians. In June, 1666, he told Major General Robert Smith of Rappahannock, "I thinke it is necessary to Destroy all these Northern Indians." To do so would serve as "a great Terror and Example and Instruction to all other Indians." Moreover, an expedition against them would pay for itself, for Berkeley proposed to spare the women and children and sell them. There were enough, he thought, to defray the whole cost. [50]

Thus even Berkeley seems to have thought it appropriate that hostile Indians be enslaved. The standard justification of slavery in the seventeenth century was that captives taken in war had forfeited their lives and might be enslaved. Yet Englishmen did not think of enslaving prisoners in European wars. And it is inconceivable that a raid, say by the Dutch, would have resulted in authorization to seize a suitable number of Dutch men, women, or children for sale into slavery. There was something different about the Indians. Whatever the particular nation or tribe or group they belonged to, they were not civil, not Christian, perhaps not quite human in the way that white Christian Europeans were. It was no good trying to give them a stake in society—they stood outside society. Even when enslaved, it was best to sell them into a foreign country. If the freedman on the frontier failed to discriminate between good Indians and bad, or between Virginia Indians and foreign Indians, if he looked upon all Indians as creatures beneath the rights of Englishmen, if he took potshots at any he saw near his plantation, he would find many of his betters in the House of Burgesses to support him.

[49] Hening, II, 15–16.   [50] *WMQ*, 2nd ser., XVI (1936), 591.

In the end, Virginia's way of life would be reshaped by the freedmen and their betters, joined in systematic oppression of men who seemed not quite human. But before that alliance was devised, Englishmen continued to oppress Englishmen, and the men at the top allowed the discontent of the men at the bottom, in New Kent and the Southside, to reach the point of rebellion. Once rebellion began, there was enough discontent in the rest of Virginia to bring the whole colony to a boil.

12

DISCONTENT

VIRGINIANS could be so heavily exploited, legally and illegally, partly because they were selected for that purpose: they were brought to the colony in order to be exploited. From the beginning Englishmen had thought of their New World possessions as a place in which to make use of people who were useless at home. Although the hoped-for transformation was supposed to be morally uplifting to those who experienced it, the purpose was not merely charitable. The wretches who were rescued from idleness and unemployment must be sufficiently able-bodied to make the rescue worth the rescuer's trouble. They should be young, but not too young to work in the fields. And they should be male rather than female, because, for reasons not altogether clear, English women were not ordinarily employed in growing tobacco or other work in the ground. The planters imported three or four times as many men as women. The fact that the population was therefore predominantly male and predominantly young helped to make heavy exploitation possible. If the men who grew the tobacco had had more women and children to support, they could not have contributed so large a share of their produce to the men who profited from their labors.[1]

But the very imbalance of sex and age that made Virginia's servants highly exploitable made them potentially dangerous when freed. Bachelors are notoriously more reckless and rebellious than men surrounded by women and children, and these bachelors were

[1] Cf. Joseph J. Spengler, "Demographic Factors and Early Modern Economic Development," *Daedalus* (Spring, 1968), 433–46, esp. 438.

a particularly wild lot. The way they got to the colony helped to guarantee that they would be so. The planters' demand for labor generally outran the supply of volunteer emigrants from England, for the exploitation of the boom years combined with the continuing mortality of the first half century to give Virginia an evil image. The depressed tobacco prices after 1660 and the consequent misery of the small planters helped to sustain the bad reputation of the colony. Although a large proportion of yeomen and skilled workmen could be found among the immigrants who came with written contracts (indentures), it was often only the desperate who could be induced to enroll for ordinary service.[2]

For a time in the 1660s ship captains brought in convicted felons, whose sentences had been commuted to service in Virginia. Though the planters snapped them up, the skill of these old hands at resisting authority eventually alarmed their masters, and the government put a stop to the practice.[3] But ship captains were good at finding desperate men, whether in jail or out, and they also knew where to find men too drunk to know what they were doing. When the king tried to crack down on the transportation of unsuspecting and unwilling persons, the tobacco merchants of London interceded on behalf of the captains and their customers. The people carried to Virginia, the merchants assured the king, were "the scruffe and scumme of the People . . . if they were not transported to the Plantations, its to be feared many of them would to Tyburne."[4] So the operation continued by catching convicts before conviction, making Virginia, as one irritated Virginian observed, "a sinke to drayen England of her filth and scum."[5]

[2] Northampton III, 140a; Abbot E. Smith, *Colonists in Bondage: White Servitude and Convict Labor in America, 1607-1776* (Chapel Hill, N.C., 1947), 67–86. Cf. Mildred Campbell, "Social Origins of Some Early Americans," in Smith, *Seventeenth-Century America*, 63–89: Craven, *White, Red, and Black*, 6–9; and Lois Green Carr and Russell R. Menard, "Immigration and Opportunity: Servants and Freedmen in Early Colonial Maryland," in The Seventeenth-Century Chesapeake: Essays Delivered at the 32nd Conference in Early American History, November 1 and 2, 1974, College Park, Maryland.

[3] Hening, II, 509–11; C.O. 1/25, ff.59–60, 62; C.O. 1/27, f.16. *Minutes of Council*, 209–10.

[4] C.O. 1/50, ff.51–53. Cf. Bullock, *Virginia Impartially Examined*, 49. Lionel Gatford, *Public Good without Private Interest* (London, 1657), 4–5.

[5] Nicholas Spencer to Lord Culpeper, Aug. 6, 1676. Coventry Papers, LXXVII, 170. Cf. C.O. 1/49, f.107.

Virginia masters did their best to tranform the reluctant immigrants into useful citizens. Hard work was supposed to be their redemption, and while they remained in service they had plenty of it.
But the experience did not always effect a reformation. Perhaps they
would have caught the work habit and the aspiration to continue it
if land and a wife had seemed within reach. But with conditions as
they were after 1660 men were unlikely to be struck with such an
aspiration after they got to Virginia. Even men who came with a
positive goal and determination to reach it could lose heart. Why
should a man continue to work hard after he became free if his
work would only continue to enrich the rich? Better to hit the road.
In Virginia if a man was young and free and wanted only to be let
alone, there were ways of getting along without work.

Given the way cattle and hogs roamed free and multiplied in
Virginia's unfenced forests, it was not difficult for a man with a gun
to keep alive indefinitely without owning or renting land. The
burgesses did their best to cut off this recourse by enacting the severe law noted in the preceding chapter, against killing other men's
hogs in the woods.[6] The penalty of 2,000 pounds was about twenty
times what a hog was worth; and the fact that half of it went to the
informer made the easy life a risky one. The county courts assiduously enforced the law, and Norfolk went beyond the burgesses
with a by-law of its own. Because "severall Idle persons have and
doe for the most part imploy themselves in hunting and killing of
wild cattle," the county court placed a 2,000-pound fine on anyone
who killed any *un*marked beast, that is, a beast with no ascertainable
owner.[7] Moreover, when a man was convicted, the court usually forbade him thereafter to carry a gun in the woods.[8] But as more and
more servants turned into freedmen, the numbers of idle young men
multiplied.

Behind the mounting number of households with only one tithable we may discern a substantial number of footloose single freedmen, who drifted from county to county. They appear on the records in Northampton County: between 1664 and 1677 a total of
1,043 tithable persons were at some point present in the county; but
248, or nearly a quarter, were there for only a year, while 134 more
were there more than once but not in consecutive years.[9] In Acco-

[6] Hening, I, 350–51; II, 129, 440–41.
[7] Norfolk V, 14; see also *ibid.*, 96.
[8] Norfolk V, 74; VI, 47a, 49, 92, 92a.   [9] See Appendix.

mack in the 1690s the taxpayers complained of what was almost certainly true earlier, that "loose and vagrant persons that have not any setled Residence do too comonly enter themselves singly and not in any House Keepers List of Tithables . . . and when the time comes that the Sheriff goes about to collect the publique Dues they abscond and remove from place to place on purpose to defraud the County of their Levies being sensible they having no visible Estates by which the Sheriff can make distress for the same by reason whereof the Taxes grow the more burdensome and grievous to the Setled persons. . . ." [10]

So here they are again, the terrible young men. In old England they slept in the sun when they should have been cutting Robert Loder's wheat. They bowled in the streets of Jamestown when they should have been planting corn. England poured them into Virginia by the thousands, and good riddance. Virginia welcomed them and fattened on their labors, as long as they could be kept alive and working for their betters, five, six, seven, maybe ten or twelve years. After that, if they had not resigned themselves to earning more every year for their betters than they earned for themselves, they often offended the community by more than idleness and tax dodging. They enticed servants to steal hogs with them and feast in the forest. They helped servants to run away "in troops." They settled themselves far up the rivers, where Indians could mount guerrilla attacks on them and drag the whole colony into war.[11] And they gathered at the polls at election time and so upset their former masters that in 1670 the assembly decided it was unsafe to allow them to vote. In a candid explanation of its order, the assembly declared that newly made freemen "haveing little interest in the country doe oftner make tumults at the election to the disturbance of his majesties peace, then by their discretions in their votes provide for the conservasion thereof." Hence only landowners and housekeepers should be allowed a voice in choosing burgesses.[12] As long as homeless freemen had been few, they could safely be allowed to share in all the privileges of their society, including the choice of its governing assembly. It was their growing numbers that made them a threat to the country and required curtailment of the rights extended to them earlier.

[10] Colonial Papers, folder 11, No. 4, Virginia State Library; Palmer, *Calendar of Virginia State Papers*, I, 52.

[11] Hening, II, 35; C.O. 1/39, f.96; C.O. 5/1309, No. 5; Coventry Papers, LXXVIII, 202.

[12] Hening, II, 280.

But depriving the homeless of the vote did not make them settle down. In England it was possible to catch the vagabonds and have them whipped from constable to constable until they were back in the parish where they belonged—and where nobody wanted them. In Virginia, where everybody wanted them, it was not only harder to catch them, but the very measures taken to exploit their labor drove them to the road. If you engrossed the land, to collect a little rent from them, or if you got them in debt, they might take off for the frontiers or to Maryland or Carolina. Because the proprietors of Carolina had difficulty keeping a governor in residence in the northern part, the men who squatted there on Albemarle Sound were often able to escape not only their creditors but also the taxes and customs duties that Virginians paid. "Carolina," observed Governor Culpeper, "(I meane the North part of it) alwayes was and is the sinke of America, the Refuge of our Renagadoes." [13]

While the wealthy planters and officials regarded the terrible young men as so much labor lost, they could not ignore the thought that the men might also be dangerous. Footloose young Englishmen had always been dangerous when armed, as the Spanish in the Caribbean could attest. And Virginia was full of guns. Though there were not enough blacksmiths to keep guns in proper repair, though powder and shot had to be brought from England, life in Virginia required guns. You needed guns to protect your cattle from wolves; and the counties, even long established ones, paid bounties throughout the century for the wolves killed within their boundaries every year. You needed guns to protect your cornfields, not only from birds but from the animals that broke into them. Although it was against the law, many a farmer took angry shots at the horses that could jump a fence. Horses had multiplied so rapidly after 1660 as to become a nuisance.[14]

Above all, you needed guns to stay alive when marauding Indians came upon your plantation. Although Governor Berkeley had tamed the tribes of Powhatan's empire by 1646, there was no telling when stray parties of "foreign" Indians might descend on a plantation.

[13] C.O. 1/47, f.261.

[14] Hening, II, 267, 271, 279; Coventry Papers, LXXVII, 332; Ms. Rawlinson A185, Bodleian Library, Oxford. The change was reflected in valuations. In the 1640s and 1650s horses appeared only rarely in inventories, but when they did, the values ranged from 1,500 to 3,500 pounds for a mare. By the 1680s a mare seldom was valued at more than 1,500 and usually at less than that.

Stretched out so widely over the landscape, the planters could never gather against a surprise, hit-and-run attack. A man had to be ready to shoot it out by himself. Even to warn each other, the planters needed guns to signal with. Indeed, the law required every able-bodied man to be armed, and Virginians were so fond of accompanying drinking bouts with musket fire, easily mistaken for signals of distress, that another law forbade shooting at "drinkings," except for marriages and funerals (where gunfire was apparently considered a necessary part of the ritual).[15] William Blathwayt, the auditor general of the colonies, who was better informed about them than any other Englishman of his time, observed in 1691, "that there is no Custom more generally to be observed among the Young Virginians than that they all Learn to keep and use a gun with a Marvelous dexterity as soon as ever they have strength enough to lift it to their heads."[16]

Because every man was supposed to keep a gun, because every man wanted to keep one and feared to be without one, the armed men of Virginia inevitably included the "loose and vagrant" fellows who dodged the tax collectors, the small planters who were in debt to their neighbors and on the verge of renewed servitude, the men who lived in danger on the frontiers. These were the men, in addition to the annual supply of servants, whom the king, the collectors, and the merchant planters were trying, with some measure of success, to exploit. It was a risky business. Men with guns are not as easily exploited as men without them.

The danger was greatest in time of war. In peacetime there were few occasions when men who were separated by rivers and creeks and miles of woodland could assemble in dangerous numbers. Some gathered on Sundays at church, more gathered at the meetings of the county courts. But a wartime march against Indians or invading Dutch meant bringing together as many men as possible. They would all be armed, and who could tell if they might not turn their weapons against their merchant-planter leaders and begin pulling down houses, to collect as plunder what they had lost in rent and taxes.

The wars that grew out of the mother country's quarrels with the Dutch and French created special hardships in the colony and increased tension among the struggling poor. European wars always brought dramatic reductions in the tobacco ships. The few that ar-

[15] Hening, I, 401–2, 525.   [16] T. 64/88 (Blathwayt's journal), 360.

rived could load to the brim at a farthing a pound, while tobacco rotted onshore for want of transport. Deprived of the usual supply of imports, the planters, large and small, worried about the clothes that were falling from their backs and the shoes that were falling from their feet. Without a supply from England, they complained, they would shortly be naked.[17] The lucky merchants whose ships got through could enjoy low tobacco prices in Virginia and high ones in London. Nicholas Spencer, later secretary of the colony, wrote to his brother in London in 1672, trying to pull strings at court to get a ship sent to him at Rappahannock. If she slipped through the Dutch and got safe back to England, Spencer said, "I will not then take one thousand pounds [i.e., sterling] for my share of the profits."[18] But most Virginians, who now had to pay extra taxes for raising troops and building forts, were deprived not only of their customary income but even of the tools and clothes they needed to keep working.

It took a brave man to put himself at the head of a troop of ragged but armed tobacco planters who might regard him, and not without reason, as a source of their misery. Governor Berkeley did it. In 1667, when a Dutch warship sailed up the James and captured twenty ships, including the royal frigate that was supposed to be defending the rest, Berkeley gathered a force and at least prevented the Dutch from landing.[19] In 1673 he led the planters out again to prevent a Dutch invasion. No one knew the danger behind his back better than he, but he had to take what men he could get. He took only freemen, because Virginians feared to furnish their servants with arms. According to Berkeley, there were as many servants as freemen, and merely to leave them behind unattended gave every planter "fearfull apprehentions of the dainger they Leave their Estates and Families in, whilest they are drawne from their houses to defend the Borders." But Berkeley saw more to fear from the planters in his army. Of the able-bodied men he could draw out to defend the colony, he estimated that "at least one third are Single freemen (whose Labour will hardly maintaine them) or men much in debt, both which wee may reasonably expect upon any Small advantage the Enemy may gaine upon us, wold revolt to them in hopes

[17] C.O. 1/30, ff.114–15; C.O. 5/1305, Nos. 22, 50; C.O. 5/1306, No. 64; C.O. 5/1308, No. 6; *Executive Journals*, I, 213–14.
[18] Sloane Mss. 3511, ff.133–34, British Museum.
[19] C.O. 1/21, ff.109–12; *VMHB*, IV (1896–97), 230–36.

of bettering their Condicion by Shareing the Plunder of the Country with them." [20]

Berkeley had not wanted war with the Dutch. He remembered how their ships had rescued the planters from poverty when the English Civil Wars broke up the English market in the 1640s. In Berkeley's opinion, which was shared by many other Virginians, it was the English interdiction of Dutch trade that had tumbled Virginia tobacco prices. The two Dutch wars of 1664–67 and 1672–74 were particularly grievous because they were brought on by English efforts to stop the Dutch from trading with the colonies. During these years, when Dutch ships came to Virginia rivers they came not to trade but to burn. And they seemed to be accompanied by the wrath of God. When they came in 1667, it had been in the midst of an almost biblical series of misfortunes. In 1667, the year when Baltimore thwarted the cessation of tobacco planting, the weather almost achieved it—along with the destruction of every other crop. In April a hailstorm not only destroyed most of the newly planted tobacco and corn but even killed young hogs and cattle. The planters were getting on their feet when the Dutch raid hit them in June. This was followed by a forty-day rain that again ruined most of the tobacco. And on August 27 came "the great gust," the fiercest hurricane Virginians had ever seen. It knocked down nearly every wooden house, and the falling trees broke fences, so that cattle and hogs roamed freely through cornfields and trampled whatever tobacco was left by the storm. High tides were driven up the rivers and overflowed the lowlands. The roads were so clogged with tree trunks that it took years to clear them.[21]

Virginia produced only thirty shiploads of tobacco that year. Yet there was so much unsold tobacco left over from the previous year that the next spring, when the war had ended and the tobacco fleet was back on the job, it took eighty ships to carry off what was on hand. The secretary observed that the planters could harvest as much in two years as the whole tobacco fleet could carry in three. But again it was the man with enough capital to wait out a lean year who profited. The storms in 1667 that served in place of a cessation did not hurt him as they did the small man, who lost his only means for purchasing tools and clothing for the next year. It was a ragged lot of men who grew the king's tobacco that year. And only

[20] C.O. 1/30, ff.114–15.
[21] C.O. 1/21, ff.288–93; Norfolk VI, 27a, 38a, 52a, 53.

six years later they had to face another bout with war and nature. When the Dutch came to Virginia again in 1673 and burned or sank eleven ships in the James River, it was after a winter in which, according to the council, disease had killed fifty thousand cattle and the inhabitants had exhausted their corn supplies in order to preserve the surviving animals.[22]

Wartime hurt the planters not only by reducing the number of ships that came for their tobacco, but by generating directives from England for the construction of costly forts to protect the shipping that did come. Virginians knew that a fort was worthless in their country against an enemy ship, especially when the king called for it to be placed at Point Comfort, in order to command the entrance to the colony's rivers. Anyone looking at a map of Virginia could see that Point Comfort, at the end of the peninsula between the York and the James, was an ideal place for a fort; anyone looking at Point Comfort's swampy ground could see that it was no place for a fort. But distant British superiors kept repeating the mistake, right down to Sir Henry Clinton, who ordered Lord Cornwallis to fortify Point Comfort in 1781. Cornwallis took one look at the place, ignored the order, and settled, not altogether successfully, at Yorktown. A peer like Cornwallis (or Culpeper, who gave equally short shrift to silly orders) could afford to use his own judgment in defiance of less knowing superiors, but most Virginia governors, even the redoubtable Berkeley, did not dare assume such independence. Berkeley knew that "a nimble frigate that can take and leave will be master of any merchant man that comes within our capes" and that the only effective protection was a naval patrol "to guard the entrance into our bay which the best forts in the world are not able to doe." [23] But when war came, the king would insist on a fort; and another 80,000 pounds would go on the tax bill, welcomed perhaps by the contractors who undertook to build the useless structure.[24]

In the 1660s and 1670s everything seemed to be working against Virginia: the Navigation Acts and the drop in prices; the king's fail-

[22] C.O. 1/23, ff.31–32; C.O. 1/30, ff.41, 114–15.

[23] To Richard Nicolls, July 30, 1666. Blathwayt Papers, BC 77, Huntington Library.

[24] Thomas Ludwell to ——, July 18, 1666, and Berkeley to ——, July 20, 1666, Ms. Clarendon 84. T. Ludwell to ——, Feb. 12, 1666/7, Ms. Clarendon 85, Bodleian Library, Oxford; *VMHB*, IV (1896–97), 234–35; governor and council to king, June, 1667, C.O. 1/21, ff.109–12; *VMHB*, IV (1896–97), 240–45.

ure to support Berkeley's scheme for diversification; Lord Baltimore's veto of the cessation agreement; war, weather, and disease.
All contributed to the misery of the exasperated planters and to the
nervousness of those Virginians who sat at the top of the heap. To
compound the difficulties, the king showed a reckless indifference
to the welfare of the province that was contributing so heavily to
his revenue. Not content with Virginia's contribution to the crown
in tobacco taxes, he used the colony's lands to reward his favorites
at court.

His generosity at Virginia's expense had begun at a time when
he had little but Virginia with which to reward anyone. In 1649,
after the execution of his father when he was just beginning his exile
from England, he had given to seven of his loyal supporters the
whole peninsula between the Rappahannock and Potomac, the so-
called Northern Neck.[25] Word of the grant may never have reached
Virginia, for the colonists were already patenting lands in the area
in 1650, and when Virginia surrendered to Parliament in 1652, the
land boom in the Northern Neck was well under way. By 1660,
when Charles regained the throne, the choicest lands had all been
patented.

For those who held patents in the Northern Neck the Restoration was cause for alarm, especially after Governor Berkeley received instructions from the king, early in 1663, to give his assistance
to a number of English investors who had leased the 1649 grant
from the proprietors. The colony dispatched one of its ablest men,
Colonel Francis Moryson, to England to try to secure a revocation
of the grant. Unsuccessful in that, he finally obtained in 1669 a
restatement of the grant that recognized all patents issued in the area
by the Virginia government through 1661.[26] This left the best lands
along the Potomac secure in the hands of the speculators who had
grabbed them in the 1650s, but made vastly uneasy everyone who
had taken out patents in the years after 1661. The Northern Neck
had grown in population more rapidly than any other part of Virginia in the years since 1652. The inhabitants had risen from about
1,300, or about 9 percent of Virginia's population in 1653, to per-

[25] The fullest account of the proprietary grant of the Northern Neck
is in Douglas S. Freeman, *George Washington* (New York, 1949–57), I,
447–519. Many of the documents involved are in Hening, II, 518–43, 569–83.
More are in the Coventry Papers, LXXVI and LXXVII.

[26] Freeman, *Washington*, I, 456–57.

haps 6,000, or about 19 percent, in 1674.[27] Though this was still a frontier region, exposed to Indian attack on the upper reaches of its rivers, it was filling up rapidly, and those who owned land had already experienced a sharp rise in values and could anticipate a continuing appreciation—provided their titles were secure.

Governor Berkeley may have had mixed feelings about the region since one of the proprietors was his brother and another was his brother-in-law. Nevertheless, he and other Virginians recognized the proprietorship as a threat to the future of the colony; and the assembly prepared to raise money to buy out the proprietors, which they hoped to do for £2,400 sterling. Berkeley himself was ready to lend half the sum (at 8 percent interest).[28] It was, of course, the taxpayers who would ultimately have to pay the bill, yet another heavy toll on their tobacco.

But before negotiations were fairly under way, the king stunned the colony with another blow. Major General Robert Smith, who had been entrusted with buying the Northern Neck, discovered in February, 1674, that the king had just given all the rest of Virginia's public lands, for a period of thirty-one years, to his two dear friends, Lord Thomas Culpeper (one of the proprietors of the Northern Neck) and Henry, Earl of Arlington. And to show his further love for Culpeper he granted him, two years later, the governorship of Virginia, to begin when the aging Berkeley (then 69) should die.[29]

To the king it may have seemed that he was only giving up his quitrents from the land. Since these had seldom brought him much anyhow, he had little to lose by turning them over to his friends. The inhabitants could go on making tobacco for him. But the Virginians could not take the matter so casually. They expected that the proprietors would require new surveys that might upset existing claims and that they would exact more in land prices and be more assiduous in the collection of quitrents. In September, 1674, the assembly, loaded with native land speculators, sent the secretary of the colony, Thomas Ludwell, to join Smith and Moryson in England, to seek a revocation of both grants and to plead for a royal charter

[27] These are rough estimates based on the information in the Appendix, tables 1 and 6. The estimation is complicated by the fact that Lancaster spanned the Rappahannock River in 1653 and Rappahannock County spanned it in 1674.

[28] *Journals of the House of Burgesses, 1659/60–1693*, 61.

[29] Freeman, *Washington*, I, 461–64; Hening, II, 569–78.

for the colony, a charter that would protect Virginians from future
fits of irresponsible generosity on the part of their monarch. To defray expenses of the mission, the assembly voted a tax of 100 pounds
of tobacco per tithable. In addition, they imposed a fine of 50
pounds on the loser in every lawsuit in the county courts (70
pounds in the General Court).[30]

At this point the burgesses must have known that the burden
on tobacco growers, which is to say on virtually every man in the
colony, was reaching the breaking point. But who could say how
close it might be? As early as 1661 York County had weathered a
servant rebellion, brought on when one bold fellow suggested that
it had formerly been the custom of the country for servants to have
meat three times a week.[31] This insolence had no sooner been suppressed than a conspiracy was discovered among the servants in
Gloucester. In 1663 a group of nine of them met secretly and
planned to seize their masters' arms and lead a march of servants on
the governor to demand their freedom. Another servant disclosed
the plot, and the assembly was so relieved at what seemed to be a
narrow escape that they not only rewarded the informer with freedom and 5,000 pounds of tobacco but proclaimed "that the thir-
teenth of September, the day this villanous plott should have been
putt into execution, be annually kept holy to keep the same in a
perpetual comemoration."[32] Two years later in Lancaster, when
the county court sentenced a man to the stocks for uncivil behavior
in court, the judges were so threatened by the angry populace that
they beat a retreat. They "thought it not safe to sitt any longer," the
clerk reported, "being in a manner forced to adjourne."[33]

Governor Berkeley, who expected from his people the same
loyalty that he himself gave to his king, was good at keeping the lid
down. In 1674, in spite of his nervousness about the growing ranks
of impoverished freedmen, and in spite of the succession of disasters
and disappointments that followed one after another, he stifled two
"mutinies" begun "by some secret villaines that wispered amongst
the People that there was nothing entended by the fifty pound leavy
[the first installment of the 100-pound levy for buying out the
proprietors of the Northern Neck] but the enriching of some few

[30] Hening, II, 311–14.   [31] *WMQ*, 1st ser., XI (1902–3), 34–37.
[32] Hening, II, 191, 204; *VMHB*, XV (1907–8), 38–43. One deposition
says that they were going to demand only a one-year reduction in their
terms of service.
[33] Lancaster III, 364, 369.

people." When the next installment was levied the following year, he had no trouble.[34]

But to keep the lid on, Berkeley had to inhibit the development of free institutions that had begun in the years of trade with the Dutch and twenty-shilling-a-hundred tobacco. It was not enough to deprive landless freedmen of the vote and to keep the council in line by judicious dispensation of offices. There was the House of Burgesses to deal with too, and Berkeley dealt with it by keeping the same men sitting as long as possible. For fifteen years, beginning in 1661, he did not call a general election of representatives. Men who had been elected in 1661 were more apt to be the right kind than those who might be chosen by people who were feeling the pressure of debt and taxes. They would support the governor and the governor would support them.

Berkeley counted on the council and the burgesses to help him keep the rest of the population under control. He also counted on the men he appointed as commissioners in the county courts. It was they who represented authority in the day-to-day life of most Virginians. And it was important that they generate a certain awe among their neighbors. Indeed, the men at the top in Virginia, whether councillors, burgesses, or county commissioners, could keep control only if they commanded a deference exceeding what their birth or wealth would have entitled them to in England. They had few other resources for keeping the peace. The church was a particularly weak reed to lean upon. Many of Virginia's pulpits were empty, despite ministerial salaries that were generous by New England standards.[35] And the few ministers who settled in the colony were not of a type to fill the populace with respect for order. There was no trained constabulary. The county commissioners, who annually chose the constables in each county, usually rotated the job among men of small means, who could not afford the fines for refusing to take it. There was no army except the militia, composed

---

[34] C.O. 1/36, ff.67–68; *WMQ*, 1st ser., III (1894–95), 122–25.

[35] The standard salary in the seventeenth century was at first £100, later £80, though Lord Culpeper maintained that few parishes actually paid this much. C.O. 1/20, f.220; C.O. 1/52, f.249. On the scarcity of ministers see Darrett B. Rutman, *American Puritanism* (Philadelphia, 1970), 49–51; Beverley, *History and Present State of Virginia*, 253. On the moral character of Virginia ministers see Norfolk II, 129; IV, 151; William S. Perry, ed., *Historical Collections Relating to the American Colonial Church*, vol. I, *Virginia* (Hartford, 1870), 30, 38, 253, 363.

of men who would be as unlikely as the constables to make effective instruments for suppressing the insubordination of their own kind.

In the absence of other modes of social control, the first gentlemen of Virginia had to keep before the rest of the population an exalted view of their position. If John Jones of Lancaster said he was as good a man as Mr. Henry Corbyn, one of the commissioners, he must be fined for his insolence.[36] Nor could John Sandford of Norfolk get away with saying that he was "as good a subject as any man in court." [37] If Richard Price pushed into the pew reserved for Edward Dale, the high sheriff, he must be sent to Jamestown for trial before the governor and council.[38] The records do not show what happened to Bartholomew Owens of Surry County, who in a private conversation called Captain George Jordan a "Raskell and Roge and shorte Arsed Raskell" and added that "he Longed to kick that short arse." [39] Such outbursts could happen anywhere, of course, but in Virginia they were probably prompted by the same pathetic frustration that is revealed in a speech reported of William Spring. Spring was a small planter of Surry (the tax list shows that he was the only tithable in his household) who in a fury against his creditor, Colonel Thomas Swann, declared, "I will meete him at Court, and shall not be afraid to speake to him for he is but a man . . . and soe I will tell the Court before his face, I shall not be afraid to speake it . . . and the forexprest William Spring furder said (his Anger still flaimeing) . . . that he the said Spring knew what the Colonel aimed at, it is my Cattle (said he) to be bound over." [40]

Again, the records are silent as to what Spring actually did say when haled before the court, but it is likely that he ate humble pie. It was not for the likes of William Spring to suggest that Colonel Thomas Swann was but a man. Colonel Swann was a commissioner, a judge of the county court; men like William Spring must be taught that they were not as good as he and had best hold their tongues.

In spite of the proclivity of Englishmen, especially when in drink, to sass their superiors, the commissioners could count on a deep-seated habit of deference and were determined to see it kept up. Although Virginia could boast no genuine peer, the men who

---

[36] Lancaster III, 87.   [37] Norfolk VII, 61.
[38] Lancaster IV, 206; *Minutes of Council*, 299.
[39] Surry I, 166.   [40] Surry II, 103.

presided over the county courts were usually able to overawe any challenge to their authority simply by expressing their outrage against anyone who slighted them, in or out of court. If Virginians lacked the complex of institutions by which ordinary men were kept in their place in England, most of them had been through the school of servitude and had been taught there the lessons of subjection with more rigor than was customary in England.

There was nevertheless a limit beyond which it would not be possible to maintain order simply by swaggering. It would appear that the two mutinies in 1674 approached that limit. But the mutineers were apparently all small men,[41] and could be overawed by the majesty of the governor and by "the advice of some discreet persons that had then an Influence upon them." [42] But what if persons of influence used their influence the other way? The level of discontent was so high throughout the colony that solidarity among the men of influence was essential. It was a situation that invited the talents of any overmighty subject who thought that he was not getting his proper share of the winnings. It might even generate a compassionate leader who genuinely believed that the impoverished were not getting *their* proper share. If a mutiny should be led not by a William Spring but by a Colonel Swann, who then would be able to suppress it?

[41] Most were listed for only one tithable in 1674 and in earlier lists. Those listed for two or three were probably partners. *WMQ*, 1st ser., III (1894-95), 123; Surry I, 372-74; II, 62; *Minutes of Council*, 367.

[42] Giles Bland to Sir Joseph Williamson, April 28, 1676, C.O. 1/36, ff.111-12.

13

REBELLION

I N 1676 civil war came to Virginia. The chain of events that led to it began in 1675 with an Indian conflict on the Potomac. There the big men had always taken the lead in harassing the Indians. Early in 1662 Colonel Gerald Fowke, a representative of Westmoreland in the House of Burgesses, had been convicted, along with Giles Brent, George Mason, and John Lord, of seizing and imprisoning without cause a king of the Potomac Indians. Fowke and Brent were declared "incapeable of bearing any office civil or millitary in this countrey," and Mason and Lord were suspended from such offices. But somehow their names continued to appear as justices, burgesses, and sheriffs.[1] In 1675, when the county of Westmoreland had grown to 538 tithables and adjacent Stafford County to 436, a new round of Indian troubles began.

This time Susquehannahs, Doegs, and Piscattaways were involved.[2] None of them had participated in Berkeley's 1646 Indian

---

[1] Hening, II, 150–51. Lord and Mason were justices of Westmoreland at the time of the first records that give the composition of the court in 1662/3, a year after the assembly's decree. Fowke was the county's representative in the assembly in September, 1663. (Westmoreland III, 6, 11, 13, 16, 18, 24, 25, 30, 38, 39; *Journals of the House of Burgesses, 1659/60–1693*, 21.) Lord was still justice of Westmoreland in 1676. In 1669 Mason was sheriff of Stafford County, formed from Westmoreland in 1664. Warren M. Billings, "Virginia's Deplored Condition 1660–1676: The Coming of Bacon's Rebellion" (unpublished doctoral dissertation, Northern Illinois University, 1968), 245.

[2] Doeg may have been a generic term for Maryland Indians, including the Piscattaway and several other tribes. Lurie, "Indian Cultural Adjustment," 42.

treaty. They were, however, on good terms with the government of Maryland, which had given the Piscattaways a fort as a refuge against hostile tribes. They stayed for the most part on the Maryland side of the Potomac; but the Susquehannahs, who lived at the head of Chesapeake Bay, traded north to Manhattan and south behind the Virginia settlements to the Carolinas. In July, 1675, a group of Doegs, who were apparently trading in Stafford County, Virginia, took some hogs belonging to Thomas Mathew, alleging that he had failed to pay for goods he had bought of them. Mathew or his men pursued them, recovered the hogs, and killed or beat several Indians. The Doegs retaliated with a raid in which they killed one of Mathew's servants.[3]

Now the Masons and Brents could go into action. Colonel Mason (for he now bore that title) and Captain Brent (son of the first Giles Brent) took the Westmoreland militia across the river. Brent, after asking the Doegs for a parley, killed a king and ten of his men. Mason, by accident or indifference, killed fourteen Susquehannahs before discovering that he had the wrong Indians.[4] The Susquehannahs had just been driven from their headquarters at the head of the bay by invading Seneca Indians and had taken refuge with their friends the Piscattaways. From the Piscattaways' fort on Matapoint Creek, east of the Potomac, they conducted retaliatory raids on the Virginians.[5] In response, Berkeley commissioned Colonel John Washington and Major Isaac Allerton of Westmoreland to investigate and punish the raiders.[6] On September 26, with "neer a thousand" Virginia and Maryland militia, Allerton and Washington laid siege to the fort. Five chiefs who came out to treat for peace were seized and murdered. Although the English greatly outnumbered the Indians, they did not attempt to storm the fort, but con-

---

[3] The sequence of events that make up what is called "Bacon's Rebellion" must be pieced together from a variety of accounts, many of which have been gathered in Charles M. Andrews, ed., *Narratives of the Insurrections* (New York, 1915), 15–141, and in Force, *Tracts*, I, Nos. 8–11. The two most thorough secondary accounts are T. J. Wertenbaker, *Torchbearer of the Revolution* (Princeton, 1940), which is highly favorable to Bacon, and Wilcomb Washburn, *The Governor and the Rebel* (Chapel Hill, N.C., 1957), which is equally favorable to Berkeley. For the Doeg episode, Andrews, *Narratives*, 16, 105–6.

[4] *Ibid.*, 17, 106.

[5] Fairfax Harrison, *Landmarks of Old Prince William* (Richmond, 1924), I, 75.

[6] *WMQ*, 1st ser., IV (1895–96), 86.

ducted a leaky siege of it for several weeks, at the end of which the Indians killed ten of the sentinels and escaped.[7]

Within a short time the Susquehannahs were across the Potomac filtering through the forests of the upper Rappahannock, avenging themselves wherever they found opportunity.[8] Up to this point the pattern of conflict was familiar. The Indians were far too few in number to constitute a serious threat to the English. The Susquehannahs in the fort had numbered only 100 warriors, and in 1669 the total number of warriors in all nineteen of Virginia's tributary groups had been only 725.[9] The English population of Virginia in 1674 included more than 13,000 men fit to bear arms, and they were much better supplied than the Indians could have been with both arms and ammunition. Most Indians, in the long run, depended heavily on their cornfields to stay alive. They could not have sustained a prolonged conflict against an enemy superior in numbers and arms. But the Indians had a few short-run advantages. They were better woodsmen, perhaps better marksmen, better able to live off the land, and at least as ready as the English to offer instruction in terror. Given the straggling mode of English settlement, it was easy for a few warriors to descend on a plantation, slaughter everyone there, and then disappear into the woods. No one could tell where they might strike next. To those who were threatened, it seemed that Indians were everywhere, "so many that none can guess at their number." And as usual the settlers suspected all Indians had joined in a "confederation" to destroy them.[10] As the terror mounted, the people who felt it wanted action.

Berkeley at first appeared willing to give them action. In January, 1676, he commissioned Sir Henry Chichely to raise a force and march against the Susquehannahs, who were reported to be edging southward along the heads of the rivers. But just as the men were ready to set out, Berkeley recalled them.[11] It was a costly change of mind. Not that the expedition might have ended the Indian menace. Whether Sir Henry Chichely (whom Lord Culpeper later

---

[7] Washburn, *Governor and Rebel*, 21–24; Andrews, *Narratives*, 19, 47–48, 106; *WMQ*, 1st ser., II (1893–94), 38–43; IV (1895–96), 86; Force, *Tracts*, I, No. 9, p. 3.

[8] Berkeley to Thomas Ludwell, April 1, 1676. C.O. 1/36, ff.67–68; Andrews, *Narratives*, 19–20.

[9] *Archives of Maryland*, V, (Baltimore, 1887), 134; Hening, II, 275.

[10] *WMQ*, 1st ser., IX (1900–1901), 8; Coventry Papers, LXXVII, 66–67, 73.

[11] Andrews, *Narratives*, 107.

characterized as "that Lumpe, that Masse of Dulnesse, that worse than nothing") [12] would have been able to locate a hundred roving Susquehannahs in Virginia's forests is an open question. But Berkeley had apparently decided that a defensive policy was preferable to an assault. In doing so, he forfeited his influence with the restless men whose mutinies over taxes he had been able to suppress a couple of years before.

Those mutinies had taken place in Surry on the Southside and in New Kent, areas in close contact with the local tributary Indians.[13] Though the tributaries were bound by law [14] to assist the colony against invading tribes, the settlers were reluctant to trust them in any conflict. No one doubted that the invaders were headed south, and no one could be sure that the tributaries would not make common cause with them.

When Berkeley heard that the Susquehannahs had been seen at the falls of the James, he called a special session of the assembly. It met on March 7 and adopted measures that added political grievances to the settlers' anxieties over the Indians. The legislators decided to build a fort at the head of each great river and to man the forts with a standing army of 500 soldiers drawn from the lower counties; the tributary Indians were to be enrolled against the enemy and rewarded with trading cloth, but private trade with the Indians was forbidden.[15] To people in New Kent and the Southside, the act that was supposed to end the Indian menace looked like a prescription for profiteering. The frontier forts would contribute more to the wealth of the men who built them than to the security of the people they were supposed to protect. The new ones would doubtless be located on the unoccupied upriver lands of the "great men" who sat in the assembly and would thus help to raise the value of their speculative holdings.[16] The soldiers, recruited in the lower counties,

[12] Culpeper to William Blathwayt, March 20, 1682/3. Blathwayt Papers, XVII, Colonial Williamsburg.

[13] *Minutes of Council*, 515; *WMQ*, 1st ser., III (1894–95), 123–25; Surry II, ff.40–43.

[14] The treaty of 1646 said nothing on this point, but it did make the tributary Indians subjects of the English. The assembly had interpreted this to mean that their assistance could be required against any foreign Indians "as being part of the articles of peace concluded with us." Hening, I, 403.

[15] Hening, II, 326–38.

[16] Coventry Papers, LXXVII, 445; C.O. 1/21, ff.157–58 (this paper is misdated as 1667, it is obviously from 1676); C.O. 1/39, ff.205, 223–28, 234, 238, 245, 246, 250; *Journals of the House of Burgesses, 1659/60–1693*, 101, 103.

would be paid 1,500 pounds of tobacco apiece, more than a frontier farmer on poor land was likely to make in a year. There would have to be another huge levy to pay for the troops and the forts, and both would be useless against roving Indians who melted into the woods after every attack. It almost seemed that the assembly had wished to guarantee the ineffectiveness of the scheme, because they had included a provision that if the enemy was discovered, he was not to be attacked until the governor was notified and gave his approval, by which time, as every frontiersman knew, the Indians would have vanished. The provision may have arisen from Berkeley's anger at the reckless commanders who had murdered the Susquehannah chiefs at the fort when they came out to a supposed peace parley ("If they had killed my Grandfather and Grandmother, my father and Mother and all my friends, yet if they had come to treat of Peace, they ought to have gone in Peace"),[17] but it would scarcely reassure frontiersmen of the government's ability to handle the Indian danger.[18]

Among those not reassured was Nathaniel Bacon, a young newcomer to the colony, on whom the governor had showered extraordinary favors. Bacon's wife was friendly with Lady Berkeley—their correspondence suggests that they had known each other in England—and Bacon had arrived with enough capital (£1,800) to make a good start in Virginia.[19] He was a kinsman and namesake of one of Virginia's elder statesmen; and though he was only twenty-nine years old, Berkeley nominated him at once to the council. At Berkeley's advice, Bacon settled himself upriver from Jamestown on the north side, apparently with some intention of engaging in the fur trade with the Indians.[20] He also set up a plantation still higher at the falls.

Bacon seems to have felt a certain disdain for wealthy Virginians who had reached their position from "vile" beginnings or "whose tottering fortunes have bin repared and supported at the Publique chardg." [21] He was no leveler by temperament and perhaps harbored something of the scorn of the wellborn Englishman for the provincial parvenus among whom he found himself. Several of the men who later joined him were also new arrivals of the same

---

[17] Andrews, *Narratives*, 23.   [18] *Ibid.*, 112.
[19] Coventry Papers, LXXVII, 8, 41; Washburn, *Governor and Rebel*, 18.
[20] Coventry Papers, LXXVII, 6, 100.
[21] *VMHB*, I (1893-94), 56-57.

kind, such as Giles Bland, who arrived in the colony with a royal appointment as customs collector. Bland's disdain for the local gentry resulted in the council's barring him from office after he called Secretary Ludwell a "mechanick fellow" (as well as a "puppy" and a "son of a whore").[22] But if Bacon was no leveler and only a very recent Virginian, he had already acquired one attitude of his upriver neighbors: their contempt for the Indians (with whom he still proposed to trade). In September, 1675, he had taken it upon himself to seize a number of Appomattox Indians for allegedly stealing corn (not his or his neighbors'). Berkeley had rebuked him at the time, mildly but firmly, reminding him that he was not the governor of Virginia, and that attacking friendly Indians was just the way to produce what everyone wanted to avoid, namely, "a Generall Combination of all the Indians against us."[23] But Bacon had his own ideas about that.

One day in the following April, Bacon and some of his neighbors, James Crews, Henry Isham, and William Byrd, got together for a sociable glass or two. Byrd had lost three servants killed by the Indians. Bacon had lost his overseer at the falls. They were all unimpressed by the measures the March assembly had taken and were "making the Sadnesse of the times their discourse, and the Fear they all lived in, because of the Susquahanocks, who had settled [i.e., encamped] a little above the Falls of James River."[24] They were also uneasy about the tributary Indians who lived close by. It was said that these Indians were not planting corn, which suggested that they intended leaving their towns for the warpath. Bacon in particular believed the country must defend itself "against all Indians in generall for that they were all Enemies." "This," he told Berkeley later, "I have alwayes said and doe maintaine."[25]

While Bacon and his friends were telling each other their troubles on the north side of the James, the less prosperous planters on the south side were doing the same. They were even more upset than Bacon about the assembly's measures and also about the assembly itself. The 150 pounds a day plus expenses that the burgesses allowed themselves was as much a grievance as the useless forts that would enrich the great men. And Giles Bland was apparently encouraging them to appeal to the king against the extor-

[22] C.O. 1/31, ff.179, 228; *Minutes of Council*, 390, 399.
[23] Coventry Papers, LXXVII, 3.   [24] Andrews, *Narratives*, 110.
[25] Coventry Papers, LXXVII, 89, 101.

tionary local magnates. Bland was ready to carry the message himself.[26]

The immediate problem, however, was the Indians. The Southsiders were eager to march against them with their own arms and without pay, and had appealed to the governor to commission someone to lead them.[27] When he declined to do so, they lost patience and began to gather on their own in an encampment at Jordan's Point, just below the mouth of the Appomattox. Hearing of the move, Bacon and his friends left their talk and crossed the river to see what was up. Bacon's feelings about Indians were evidently known. He was a friend of the governor, a member of the council; and his appearance in the crowd, doling out a supply of rum like a good politician, gave a semblance of governmental approval to the gathering. "A Bacon! a Bacon! a Bacon!" went the cry. The young man was evidently not displeased, and he agreed to lead them against the Indians, perhaps assuming that Berkeley would not deny a commission to *him*.[28]

And, indeed, if Berkeley had been willing to follow the line of least resistance, he would have been well advised to grant the commission gracefully. In April of 1676, however, the Southsiders' proposed march on the Indians apparently looked more dangerous to the safety of the colony than the depredations of the Susquehannahs. For months Indian tribes up and down the continent had been restive. King Philip's War, a concerted attack on the New England settlers, had broken out at about the same time as the skirmishes on the Potomac, a fact that looked sinister in itself. It was rumored that the Susquehannahs were negotiating for assistance from tribes three hundred miles to the north. All in all, Berkeley was convinced that the Indians were "generally conspired against us in all the western parts of America." [29] With a larger Indian war brewing, Berkeley thought it desirable to keep a firm but friendly grip on Virginia's tributary Indians, not only because they might be useful as spies against hostile tribes but also to prevent them from joining the enemy. Berkeley, knowing the frontiersman's contempt for all Indians and his greed for their lands, would not risk sending out an expeditionary force that might not differentiate between friend and foe any more carefully than the Westmoreland militia who had started

[26] C.O. 1/36, ff.109–13; C.O. 1/37, ff.84–86; cf. Coventry Papers, LXXVII, 156.
[27] C.O. 1/36, f.139.   [28] Andrews, *Narratives*, 109–11.
[29] C.O. 1/36, ff.67–68; Coventry Papers, LXXVII, 66–67.

the whole conflict with the Susquehannahs. Nor could Berkeley risk creating an armed force of his most disgruntled inhabitants, men who were even more likely to turn against him than those he had led against the Dutch. The assembly may have been swayed by this danger when voting to garrison the new forts with men from the downriver counties.

Although Bacon seriously differed with Berkeley about the way to deal with Indians, he fully appreciated the danger of rebellious freemen. Living in Henrico County, he was in a better position than Berkeley to sense their mood, and he was not likely to underestimate it. As a prosperous government official in an area surrounded by men angry with the government, he could anticipate a rough time if discontent turned to rebellion. By leading the discontented in their proposed expedition against the Indians, which he relished as much as they did, he would gain their good will and at the same time avert their anger from the governor and assembly. According to Bacon, his leadership at Jordan's Point had precisely that effect. "Since my being with the volunteers," he wrote to Berkeley, "the Exclaiming concerning forts and Leavys has beene suppressed and the discourse and earnestness of the people is against the Indians. . . . "[30] Bacon was offering Berkeley a way to suppress a mutiny. The Indians would be the scapegoats. Discontent with upper-class leadership would be vented in racial hatred, in a pattern that statesmen and politicians of a later age would have found familiar.

Berkeley did not take the offer. Virginia needed the friendship of the local Indians, and he did not trust the freemen. Furthermore, he did not know whether to trust Bacon. Though it is difficult to establish the sequence of events (many of the documents are undated), Berkeley was apparently convinced that everything had been quiet until Bacon "infused into the People the greate charge and uselessnesse of the forts."[31] It seems unlikely, however, that the people needed to have these grievances pointed out to them. Apprised of the accusations against him, Bacon sent dispatches of his own to the governor, protesting his loyalty and assuring him that he did not want command over any forces except by Berkeley's order. And he urged Berkeley not to listen to reports conveyed by

[30] Coventry Papers, LXXVII, 99. On the dating of this statement, see Washburn, *Governor and Rebel*, 189–90.
[31] Coventry Papers, LXXVII, 103.

"unworthy and base fellowes of noe faith or trust."[32] Bacon was probably referring to base fellows who had scrambled up the ladder of success. For himself, he was busy among the base fellows who had not made it. In order to enlarge the force he hoped to lead against the Indians, he crossed from the Southside and headed for New Kent.

There, as on the Southside before Bacon appeared on the scene, people had apparently already begun "to mutiny, and complaine of the proceedings of the Assembly."[33] There too he found and reported to Berkeley that "The whole country is much alarmed with the feare of Generall Combinacion [of the Indians] and I thinke not without reason."[34] And there too his eminence as a council member contributed to the readiness of the people to follow him.[35] According to a later account, "they of New Kent envieing the pamunkeys [the principal tributary tribe] and coveting the good Land on which they were seated, perceiveing the Governors just inclinations to preserve them as Spyes, to finde out the Susquehanoes and other Indian enimies, Mr. Bacon taketh advantage of the discontents he had raised, beateth up drums, lists his tumults in a military posture, and appeareth at the head of them, and then sends to the Governor for a Commission."[36] Again Bacon was offering the governor a way to divert a mutiny. But Berkeley and his supporters seem to have been transfixed by the dangerous character of Bacon's following: they were a "Rabble Crue," said the council, "only the Rascallity and meanest of the people . . . there being hardly two amongst them that we have heard of who have Estates or are persons of Reputation and indeed very few who can either write or read."[37] Virginia's rulers failed to see that it might be more dangerous to withhold government sanction from such men than to grant it.

When Berkeley refused Bacon a commission, Bacon chose to proceed without one, but he issued a conciliatory "Humble Appeale of the Voluntiers to all well minded and Charitable People." The appeal recited the uselessness of the forts, the need for a "moving force," and the willingness of the volunteers to "become both actours and paymasters of this necessary defensive warr" without charge to the colony. It asked "the Enactours themselves of this late

[32] *Ibid.*, 99, 100.

[33] "Aspinwall Papers," Massachusetts Historical Society, *Collections*, 4th ser., IX (1871), 165.

[34] Coventry Papers, LXXVII, 73.   [35] "Aspinwall Papers," 166.

[36] *Ibid.*   [37] Coventry Papers, LXXVII, 95–96.

Act for forts," to judge in their consciences "whether our proffer be not wholly clear from any dregs of Rebellion, and mutiny, and be not rather to be esteemed an honourable purchase of our Countries quiett and benefitt with our owne hazard and charge." It closed with a denunciation of all Indians and their combination against His Majesty's good subjects, who were the only rightful inhabitants and possessors of Virginia.[38] Bacon also wrote a personal letter to the governor as he was about to set out on May 2: "I am just now goeing out to seeke a more agreeable destiny than you are pleased to designe mee," and he begged Berkeley not to believe evil reports of him.[39]

Whatever Bacon's intentions may have been in assuming leadership of the self-starting crusade against the Indians, he was guilty of a greater insubordination than Berkeley could tolerate. On May 10, in a public proclamation, Berkeley denounced him and removed him from the council.[40] On the same day Berkeley offered the colony another way to defuse a mutiny: he called for a new election of burgesses and a new meeting of the assembly; and he invited the voters to present any complaints they might have against him.[41] He was giving Virginians the opportunity to elect men who knew their views and the opportunity to have their views made law.

Meanwhile Bacon continued to conduct the crusade against Indians—all Indians. He began by marching his men southward to a fort held by the Occaneechees on the Roanoke River near the present Carolina border. The friendly Occaneechees captured a number of Susquehannahs for him. After the prisoners had been killed, Bacon's men turned their guns on the Occaneechees and dispatched most of them too, thus demonstrating their evenhanded determination to exterminate Indians without regard to tribe or tribute. Upon returning, Bacon reiterated his loyalty to the governor. All he wanted, he said, was to make war "against all Indians in generall," neglecting to add that friendly Indians were somewhat easier to catch than hostile ones, and made a satisfactory substitute as far as he and his men were concerned.[42]

The massacre of the Occaneechees was probably no more than Berkeley had been expecting of the expedition. He evinced neither

---

[38] *Ibid.*, 445.
[39] *Ibid.*, 76.
[40] C.O. 1/37, f.2.   [41] C.O. 1/36, f.137.
[42] Washburn, *Governor and Rebel*, 40–46; Coventry Papers, LXXVII, 89.

surprise nor anger, for during Bacon's absence he himself had somehow become convinced that it was no longer feasible to distinguish
between friendly and unfriendly Indians. The view that all Indians
were enemies had been a self-fulfilling prophecy, an attitude that
necessarily turned friend into foe. And Berkeley was now prepared
to admit that the transformation had taken place. "I believe all the
Indians our neighbours are engaged with the Susquehannoes," he
wrote to Colonel Thomas Goodrich on May 15, "and therefore I
desire you to spare none that has the name of an Indian for they are
now all our Enemies." [43]

Although he still blamed Bacon for aggravating the Indian troubles, Berkeley seemed willing for the moment to accept the propo-
sition that Bacon's true intention was what Bacon had steadily maintained it to be, Indian fighting rather than rabble-rousing. When
Bacon returned from his triumph over the Occaneechees, Berkeley
invited him to submit, hinted at a pardon, and offered to let him go
to England and state his case before the king if he preferred.[44] But
Bacon preferred to make his case before the people of Virginia. On
May 28, still writing in highly respectful terms, he declined to apologize for what he had done "in so Glorious a cause as the Countrys
defence," and renewed his request for a commission.[45] Berkeley interpreted this posture, perhaps correctly, as confirmation of his original view of Bacon's purpose. That view would now fulfill itself
just as Bacon's view of the Indians fulfilled itself. Berkeley and his
council, upon receipt of Bacon's letter, denounced him and all his
"Ayders Assisters and Abettors" as rebels, and called upon all loyal
subjects to "Joyne in prosecution of him and them according to the
Nature of their Offences." [46]

The nature of those offenses was treason, and the proper punishment death. In order to make that plain, Berkeley issued a "Declaration and Remonstrance" in which he explained that the mighti-
est subject in the land, even a peer of the realm, would deserve
death if he successfully protected the country against an enemy
without authorization from the king.[47] This was an unfortunate line
of reasoning to a people who put preservation ahead of loyalty to a
governor who was not, after all, quite a king. And among men who
as a matter of course believed that all Indians were alike, Berkeley

[43] Coventry Papers, LXXVII, 85.   [45] Ibid., 93.
[44] Ibid., 90, 91.   [46] Ibid., 94.
[47] Ibid., 157–58.

could not at this stage of the game start winning points by stating that he too was now against all Indians, especially when he added that earlier "I would have preservd those Indians that I knew were hourely at our mercy to have been our spies and intelligence to find out the more bloody Ennimies." He also misread the situation in stating that "Mr. Bacon has none aboute him but the lowest of the people." [48] Those he had in plenty, but there were men of the better sort too who shared Bacon's racist hatred of Indians.

With Berkeley's Declaration not only Bacon but all his followers and supporters became, by definition, rebels. They undoubtedly retained their zeal for killing Indians, but they were now invited to save a share of their hostility for the governor and council, the biggest men in Virginia. In a colony where the level of discontent was already so high and the means of suppressing a rebellion were so scant, it required a degree of foolhardiness in the governing circles to adopt such a position. With the local Indians fleeing out of range, and the Susquehannahs too elusive to lay hands on, the dangerous young men of New Kent and the Southside might well consider attacking their rulers, especially if led by men who could themselves lay claim to high position. As Giles Bland had recognized some weeks earlier, a bona fide rebellion could easily develop out of the existing situation, precisely because the freemen were led "by persons of quality there, which was wanting to them in 1674 when they were suppressed by a Proclamation, and the advice of some discreet persons, that had then an Influence upon them; which is now much otherwise, for they are at this time Conducted by Mr. Nathaniel Bacon, lately Sworne one of the Councell, and many other Gentlemen of good Condition." [49]

In the last days of May the elections to the new assembly that Berkeley had called for took place. The results of the elections in many counties are unknown. We do not know, for example, who was elected from New Kent. But the voters of Henrico chose Bacon (no longer a councillor) and his friend James Crews. According to Isaac Allerton of Westmoreland, the Southside counties all chose delegates suited "to their factious and Rebellious humours," and Berkeley himself thought that all but eight out of perhaps forty burgesses were sympathetic to Bacon.[50] Later a royal investigating commission reported that most were "Free men that had but lately

---

[48] *Ibid.;* "Aspinwall Papers," 178–81.   [49] C.O. 1/36, f.111.
[50] Coventry Papers, LXXVII, 102, 160–61, 352.

crept out of the condition of Servants." [51] Of the twenty-three known members, however, none fits that description.[52] Most had been members before, and were men of standing in their counties. If the rabble controlled the election, they seem to have demonstrated the same deference to their superiors that they had shown in earlier elections. If the members were sympathetic to Bacon, it was because men of standing were ready to back him.

When Bacon appeared at Jamestown to take his seat in the assembly on June 6, he took the precaution of coming in a sloop on which he was accompanied by fifty armed men. But when it came to the use of armed men, the old governor still knew a few tricks himself. Berkeley not only outwitted the rebel and captured him, but presented him to the House of Burgesses on his knees. At the governor's dictation, Bacon had written a confession of his sins, and once he presented it, Berkeley did an about-face. Having publicly reestablished his authority, he gambled on a move that might conciliate Bacon's followers and again solidify the ruling class of Virginia. He not only pardoned Bacon but restored him to his seat on the council and, astonishingly, promised him the commission he had been seeking.[53] No longer qualified to be a burgess (because he was a councillor), Bacon asked leave to return home to visit his wife. Berkeley granted him permission, but with the humiliating proviso that he stay out of New Kent. And on June 10 Bacon departed, still without the commission that had been promised him.[54]

[51] Andrews, *Narratives*, 113.

[52] Billings, "Virginia's Deplored Condition," 109–12, 264. Billings identifies 21 out of the possible 41 members and observes that all but four were justices of the peace. In addition to these 21 it is possible to identify several others. The representatives from Lancaster were Thomas Haynes and Colonel John Carter (Lancaster IV, 394). Carter was the wealthiest man in Lancaster, listed for 37 tithables in 1675 and 44 in 1677. Haynes was far from poor, listed for 8 in 1675 and 11 in 1677. Richard Lawrence, who was probably one of the representatives from James City, was a graduate of Oxford (Andrews, *Narratives*, 96). Thomas Mathew, whose dispute with the Indians had started the troubles, was a member, and he tells us that the two commanders at the siege of the Indian fort, Isaac Allerton and John Washington, were members (*ibid.*, 23). Both were men of high standing. Mathew also identifies Colonel Edward Hill, perhaps the biggest man in Charles City County, as present (*ibid.*, 26). Allerton and Hill were later members of the council but do not seem to have been so at this time and so must have been burgesses.

[53] Andrews, *Narratives*, 21–23, 54, 114–15.

[54] Force, *Tracts*, I, No. 9, p. 5; Coventry Papers, LXXVII, 160–61.

In his absence the assembly proceeded with a set of enactments designed to pacify all parties except the Indians. The right to vote was restored to freemen who owned no land and did not keep house for themselves. Representatives were to be chosen in each county to sit with the justices when the county levies were being laid. Vestries of parish churches were to be elected instead of being chosen by co-optation. Councillors were no longer to be exempt from levies. Clerks, secretaries, surveyors, collectors, and sheriffs were forbidden to take fees except for work actually performed. And to spread the perquisites of office more widely among deserving gentlemen, no one was to hold the office of sheriff for more than a year. None of these or of the assembly's other enactments breathes the spirit of rebellion. They provide mainly for the remedy of abuses that had enabled a few men in every county to milk the public for more than their fair share. Though the new laws did nothing to reverse the trend toward a more severe exploitation of servants, they gave the small freeman a degree of protection against corrupt officials, and restored to him a share in the choice of his rulers in both state and church.[55]

Perhaps more significant than these mild measures were those taken by the assembly to deal with the Indians. Berkeley, recovering his earlier view of the proper strategy, lectured the assembly against rash and unjust assaults on friendly Indians; and the assembly in the preamble to its principal enactment acknowledged that some Indians might not be engaged in the supposed combination against the English. The queen of the Pamunkeys was even invited to an interview, where with great dignity she gave her unanswerable reasons for not trusting English justice and declined to send more than a dozen warriors to aid the English against the Susquehannahs. The assembly then gave its definition of enemy Indians: any who left their towns without English permission. The lands of such Indians were to be forfeited, and this presumably meant private cornfields as well as tribal hunting and gathering lands, for the assembly did not distinguish between the two. In order to carry on the war against them, the assembly abandoned the plan for forts and voted to raise 1,000 troops instead of 500, to be drawn from the several counties in proportion to population, and to be paid for by the counties. Included in the provision was a clause better designed than any other to deflect the growing hostility of the freemen from their governors to

[55] Hening, II, 341-65.

the Indians: besides being paid 1,500 pounds of tobacco for foot soldiers and 2,250 for horsemen, the troops were to "have the benefitt of all plunder either Indians or otherwise." By "otherwise" was probably meant furs, guns, corn, and other Indian possessions. By "Indians" was meant Indians; and this was spelled out: "that all Indians taken in warr be held and accounted slaves dureing life." [56]

Bacon had been in Jamestown long enough to know, before he left, the composition of the new assembly and its intention of redressing the freemen's grievances. He may have realized that once the freemen were satisfied, Berkeley would have nothing more to fear from him and might even revive the charges against him. His best insurance, in that event, would be to gain and keep as large a popular following as possible. Then, if Berkeley did turn on him, Bacon could play the rebel role that Berkeley had been thrusting upon him. Meanwhile the role of Indian crusader still suited him. After all, it was as the suppressor of Indians that Berkeley himself had originally won his popularity in Virginia. Whether for these reasons or others, Bacon kept his focus on the Indians. He was apparently determined to be the leader of the war against them and believed that the freemen would support him in that aim. He disobeyed Berkeley's instructions to stay out of New Kent, and wherever he went he gathered more volunteers.

By June 22 Bacon was back in Jamestown with 500 of the upriver men behind him. Again he demanded a commission, and again Berkeley saw the demand as a rebel's challenge to his authority. As Bacon stood before the statehouse, with his ragged band of armed men around him, the governor strode out and proposed to settle the matter in good knightly fashion by single combat. Baring his breast, he cried, "Here! Shoot me, foregod, fair Mark, shoot." But Bacon continued to insist that he had no rebellious intentions. "No May it please your honor," he said, "We will not hurt a hair of your Head, nor of any other Mans, We are Come for a Commission to save our Lives from the Indians, which you have so often promised, and now We Will have it before we go."

This time there was iron in the demand. At gunpoint Bacon got his commission and also a vote by the assembly empowering him to raise whatever volunteers he could, and, if he saw fit, to suspend the levying of the 1,000 troops previously voted. He was thus officially authorized not only to raise men but to lead them in enslaving

[56] Andrews, *Narratives*, 25–27; Hening, II, 346.

Indians and collecting plunder, and he could legitimately transform the men he had brought with him from rebels to government troops.[57]

These men, according to Philip Ludwell, the acting secretary of the colony, were "a Rabble of the basest sort of People, whose Condicion was such, as by a change could not admitt of worse." There were not twenty among them, he said, "but what were Idle and will not worke, or such whose Debaucherie or Ill Husbandry has brought in Debt beyond hopes or thought of payment."[58] But if Bacon's followers were rabble, they were evidently tax-paying rabble, that is, freemen rather than servants, for their cry outside the statehouse was "noe Levies, noe Levies."[59] And Ludwell himself explained the willingness of the burgesses to accede to Bacon's demands by their fear that if they did not the servants of the country would be drawn into the act and "carry all beyond remedy to Destruction."[60] Bacon's men demonstrated that they had something to lose (servants would not have) when news arrived on June 25 that eight persons had been killed by Indians in New Kent. Off they went the next day to protect their houses or families.[61]

As troops led by a commissioned officer, Bacon's men could think themselves entitled to military supplies. Two of Berkeley's supporters, Laurence Smith and Thomas Hawkins, had been raising horses, arms, and ammunition in nearby Gloucester County for a march of their own against the Indians. Bacon and his men accordingly helped themselves to what had been raised and hurried on to New Kent. In this move Berkeley and his friends thought they saw at last an opportunity to crush the rebel.

Gloucester was at this time probably the richest county in Virginia. The prosperous householders there would surely resent the commandeering of their horses and arms by Bacon's New Kent rabble. Apparently with Sir Henry Chichely's encouragement, Robert Beverley and Philip Ludwell[62] concocted a petition in the name of

[57] Andrews, *Narratives*, 29, 116–17; Hening, II, 349; cf. *Journals of the House of Burgesses, 1659/60–1693*, 65.

[58] C.O. 1/37, ff.35–38; *VMHB*, I (1893–94), 178–86.

[59] "Aspinwall Papers," 171.

[60] Coventry Papers, LXXVII, 137; C.O. 1/37, f.38; *VMHB*, I (1893–94), 184.

[61] *Ibid.*; "Aspinwall Papers," 172.

[62] "Aspinwall Papers," 173; Coventry Papers, LXXVIII, 321; C.O. 1/41, ff.279,304; Burk, *History of Virginia*, II, 268.

the inhabitants of Gloucester, asking for protection against Bacon. The governor responded with a declaration that Bacon's commission, obtained by force, was void. He marched to the county and summoned the people to join him. One account says that Berkeley succeeded in getting 1,200 men. But all accounts agree that when the Gloucestermen learned that Berkeley wanted to use them against Bacon, they quickly departed. They were willing to fight Indians under Berkeley's leadership, but they were not willing to fight Bacon and their fellow Virginians.[63] Bacon, at this point on the verge of a march against the Pamunkeys (who had disappeared into the interior), turned back to deal with the governor; and Berkeley with a handful of supporters fled by ship to the Eastern Shore, pausing only to issue a new proclamation declaring Bacon a rebel.[64]

By this time Bacon himself was ready to believe the proclamation. If Berkeley could not see the merits of his crusade against the Indians, if Berkeley and his friends wished to make it a contest for superiority among white Virginians, Bacon was finally ready to oblige them. Arriving at Middle Plantation (the present site of Williamsburg) on July 30, he issued a "Declaration of the People" that combined a denunciation of Berkeley's crowd of placeholders with a statement of his own intention "not only to ruine and extirpate all Indians in generall but all Manner of Trade and Commerce with them." It was no leveling manifesto. Though it condemned the levying of taxes "upon specious pretences of Publick works for the advancement of private Favourites and other sinister ends," it attacked those same favorites on the grounds that they were socially unworthy of their riches. "Let us observe," it said, "the sudden Rise of their Estates compared with the Quality in which they first entered this Country . . . and lett us see wither their extractions and Education have not bin vile."[65] Bacon was not suggesting that true gentlemen should forgo the profits that belonged to social distinction. What was intolerable was that upstarts like the Ludwells and the Beverleys should have been able to collect so large a share of the winnings. It was time to redistribute some of their ill-gotten wealth, time to plunder the estates of a few upstart grandees as well as time to plunder the Indians.

In a society where success had always depended on exploitation

---

[63] "Aspinwall Papers," 173, 181–84; Andrews, *Narratives*, 34, 56–57, 119–21; Coventry Papers, LXXVII, 161.

[64] Andrews, *Narratives*, 57; Force, *Tracts*, I, No. 9, p. 5.

[65] C.O. 1/37, f.173; *VMHB*, I (1893–94), 55–61.

that fell little short of plunder, it was an appealing formula to men of every class. Bacon had earlier complained that "Things have been carried by the men at the helme as if it were but to play a booty game, or divide a spoyle." [66] Now he would give everyone a chance to play the booty game and redivide the spoils. As was only proper, gentlemen would come first. He invited them to attend him at Middle Plantation on August 3 and there presented them with an oath denouncing Berkeley for starting a civil war and agreeing to support Bacon even if royal forces should be sent to suppress him. The principal gentlemen and officers of the militia in the several counties had already agreed to serve under Bacon at the time when he extracted his commission from the governor. They had feared, as one related later, that if they refused, he might appoint some of his New Kent rabble in their places. [67] There was now even more to be lost by not joining him. If there was to be civil war, it seemed clear that Berkeley would be the loser. And so the gentlemen, led in fact by Colonel Thomas Swann of Surry (still no mere man), put their names to the oath. [68] Even those who had opposed Bacon stepped forward to enroll. George Jordan of Surry, for example, had privately complained of the rebels' "false and base complaints against the government," but nevertheless signed. Jordan had also observed that "every magestrat that hath loyally declared his descent [dissent] against these late monstrous proceedings is threatened with plundering and pulling down their houses." [69] Better to plunder than be plundered.

And for the next three months Virginians of all ranks vied with one another in plundering. In England Thomas Ludwell concluded that Bacon intended to collect as much booty as possible and then make off with it by sea. [70] But Bacon, true to his declared priorities, made the Indians his first object. While other gentlemen went about the task of protecting their own estates and dismantling those of the few who had placed their bets on Berkeley, Bacon marched through the back country looking for Indians. Before setting off, he had dispatched two of his lieutenants, Giles Bland and William Carver, to the Eastern Shore to capture the governor. But Philip Ludwell turned the tables and captured Bland and Carver. [71] Encouraged by

[66] Coventry Papers, LXXVII, 442.   [67] Andrews, *Narratives*, 30–34.
[68] C.O. 1/37, f.130; Coventry Papers, LXXVII, 162.
[69] Coventry Papers, LXXVII, 156.   [70] *Ibid.*, 254.
[71] "Aspinwall Papers," 174–75; Andrews, *Narratives*, 36–37, 64–65, 123–28; Burk, *History of Virginia*, II, 270–72.

this success and by Bacon's absence in the wilderness, Berkeley tried for a comeback. To do so, he appealed for support in such a way as to risk a graver civil war than Bacon had yet threatened.

Hitherto, while worrying about the rabble of New Kent and the Southside, Virginia gentlemen had taken pains to offer no opportunities for rebellion to the country's most oppressed groups, the servants and slaves. In the previous Dutch and Indian wars, fear of a servile insurrection had troubled the planters more than fear of invasion. And Thomas Ludwell, in England, assured the Privy Council that Bacon was unlikely to try to gain support by offering freedom to servants who joined him. If he did, Ludwell explained, "I verely beleive it will in a short time ruine him, since by it he will make all masters his Enimies." [72] But Berkeley was willing to take the risk, or so at least the word went. As he prepared to return to Jamestown, he not only promised the people of the Eastern Shore the plunder of the estates of those who had signed Bacon's oath, but it was said he offered freedom to the servants of the signers in return for support.[73] The two proposals were not wholly consistent, since servants were the principal form of wealth worth plundering, but Berkeley was desperate. Too desperate. Evidently even servants felt that he was unlikely to win. He did reach Jamestown by ship on September 7, but neither freemen nor servants rallied to his cause.

Bacon, in the meantime, had located the peaceful Pamunkeys in the Great Dragon Swamp between the Mattapony and the Pianketank rivers in New Kent. He captured forty-five, along with most of the tribe's worldly goods, consisting of furs, wampum, and English trading cloth. He had only to march on Jamestown, parading his captive Indians as he went, to win supporters. And he now emulated Berkeley by offering freedom to the servants and slaves of loyalists. His forces quickly outnumbered Berkeley's; and after a brief siege Berkeley and his remaining friends left on the ships that had brought them. Bacon burned Jamestown to the ground on September 19.[74]

From there, accompanied by William Byrd, he returned to Gloucester County to gather loot from loyalists. Witnesses later gave a graphic description of Byrd handing out goods from the stores

[72] Coventry Papers, LXXVII, 332.

[73] Andrews, *Narratives*, 36, 65–66; Washburn, *Governor and Rebel*, 79–80, 208.

[74] Andrews, *Narratives*, 66–71, 129–36; Washburn, *Governor and Rebel*, 80–83, 209. Andrew Marvell to Henry Thompson, Nov. 14, 1676. HM21813, Huntington Library.

of Augustine Warner, at Warner Hall: ". . . whensoever he mett with any fine goods, as silks fine Hollands, or other fine Linnings, silke stockings, Ribbond, or the like he sent them into Bacons roome, where he was often called in and was very conversant." Byrd finally passed out from drinking too much of Colonel Warner's cider and Malaga wine, but "the soldiers then with him, lifted him up, and removed him soe asleep from place to place, and from chest to chest [Byrd apparently had the keys firmly fastened to himself] and tooke such goods as best liked them." [75]

Such was the sordid culmination of Bacon's Rebellion. During September and October the scene at Colonel Warner's was repeated at the houses of other loyalists.[76] But when Bacon died of the "bloody flux" (probably a form of dysentery) on October 26, the rebellious mood of the Virginians ran out. Shortly thereafter armed vessels from England arrived. One of them, operating in James River, produced conversions to loyalty in the Southside counties as she moved up and down the riverbank there. Another in York River obtained the surrender of the New Kent men who had marched with Bacon. Most of them switched their allegiance back to Berkeley and were allowed to go home. By January Berkeley was back at his Green Spring plantation, ready to hang the unrepentant and to recoup his and his friends' property losses by more legal methods of plunder.

Given its extent, the rebellion had caused little bloodshed among white Virginians. Beginning as a crusade against the Indians, who proved elusive targets, it ended as a series of plundering forays against those who had stuck with Berkeley. At the end there were eighty slaves and twenty English servants who refused to surrender, but these were easily captured and returned to their owners.[77] It was a rebellion with abundant causes but without a cause: it produced no real program of reform, no revolutionary manifesto, not even any revolutionary slogans. Bacon had probably never intended it to turn into a rebellion. Considering the grievances of Virginia's impoverished freemen, it is surprising that he was able to direct their anger for so long against the Indians. Berkeley either did not perceive or chose not to exploit the opportunity presented by the hatred of white Virginians against Indians. But for those with eyes to see, there was an obvious lesson in the rebellion. Resentment of an alien race might

---

[75] C.O. 1/42, f.178.   [76] *VMHB*, III (1895–96), 250; Surry II, 134.
[77] C.O. 1/37, ff.181–86; Coventry Papers, LXXVII, 301–2; Washburn, *Governor and Rebel*, 85–89.

be more powerful than resentment of an upper class. For men bent on the maximum exploitation of labor the implication should have been clear. But Virginians did not immediately grasp it. It would sink in as time went on; but with the rebellion over, those who had been profiting from tobacco thought at first only of recovering what they had lost—and maybe a bit more.

14

STATUS QUO

ALL governments rest on the consent, however obtained, of the governed. In 1676 the king of England was not pleased by the failure of his government in Virginia to retain the consent of his subjects there. Governor Berkeley had continually reminded him of the importance of Virginia's big men in keeping the multitude of servants and freedmen in their proper place. And the king certainly was no leveler. He counted on his magnates, whether in England or Virginia, to see that his subjects expressed their consent to his government by paying their taxes, working at their jobs, and obeying their superiors at every level. When the Virginians took to fighting rather than growing tobacco, it meant that the men he entrusted with power had failed; and he was not ready to take at face value their diagnosis that the trouble was only the wickedness of an ambitious young man.

As already noted, the king had a large stake in the good behavior of Virginia's laborers. As long as they kept at their jobs, each of them earned him anywhere from £5 to £10 sterling a year, regardless of what they earned for themselves or their employers. When they stopped growing tobacco and attacked their superiors, the king suspected that they were being pushed too hard, that the local ruling class was trying to levy too large a toll of their own on Virginia labor. The king accordingly sent a commission to investigate and remedy the grievances of his subjects, regain their consent, and get them growing tobacco again.[1]

---

[1] Washburn, *Governor and Rebel*, 92–113, presents a different view of the activities of the commission than that offered here.

The three commissioners were well equipped to restore order in Virginia. One of them, Colonel Francis Moryson, was familiar with the colony from having served as lieutenant governor and then as the colony's agent in England. Colonel Herbert Jeffreys, who was the brother of John Jeffreys, a well-known London merchant in the Virginia trade,[2] came with a regiment of more than 1,000 troops in his charge; and Sir John Berry, a naval officer, had been given command of the small fleet of ships that brought them. The commissioners carried with them a royal proclamation offering pardon to every rebel who submitted, instructions to Berkeley for ending the rebellion, and a commission to Jeffreys to take his place, with the title of lieutenant governor, while Berkeley reported back to England.[3] But when they arrived in Virginia on February 2, 1677, the commissioners discovered that Berkeley had recovered the upper hand and was restoring law and order in his own way.

His way was to reverse the plundering forays of the preceding months and seize for himself and his friends all the property they could lay their hands on. He had set up headquarters at his plantation, Green Spring; and his agent, William Hartwell, was bringing in men and cattle and hogsheads of tobacco as fast as he could find them.[4] There was no need, in Berkeley's view, to wait for a trial to convict a man of treason before seizing his goods. Much simpler just to take what was available and wait for conviction later—a foregone conclusion, anyhow—or else compound with a man for pardon, in return for everything he had or could earn in the next year or two. Given the extent of the rebellion, opportunity for retaliatory plunder was almost unlimited, for, as Berkeley himself acknowledged, there were not five hundred persons in the country who had stayed out of the rebellion.[5] Although willing to pardon those who turned fast enough with the wind, like Colonel Thomas Swann of Surry or

[2] The relationship is evident in John Jeffreys' letter to Leolin Jenkins, Jan. 4, 1680/1, C.O. 1/46, f.167.
[3] C.O. 1/38, f.8; Coventry Papers, LXXVII, 262; Hening, II, 424–26; *VMHB*, XIV (1906–7), 356–59.
[4] C.O. 1/39, f.24; C.O. 1/40, ff.1–41; C.O. 1/43, f.35.
[5] C.O. 1/39, ff.66–67; Coventry Papers, LXXVII, 389. The commissioners' view was shared by the governor of Maryland, who reported to Lord Baltimore in January and again in May, 1677, that Virginia would remain on the brink of renewed rebellion unless new people were sent to govern: "they have beene strangely dealt with by theire former magistracy, and have as yett little hopes of an amendment and are generally dissatisfied." C.O. 1/39, ff.20–21; C.O. 1/40, f.186.

Gregory Walklett of New Kent, Berkeley had already begun hanging the recalcitrant.[6]

The commissioners were dismayed. Though the rebellion appeared to be over, the situation was exactly as the king had feared. The governor and his crowd were squeezing the people to the point where the king's whole revenue from Virginia might be lost. Berkeley had succeeded in making them lay down their arms, but it did not follow that they would pick up their hoes. They were at present, the commissioners reported,

> of soe sullen and obstinate an humour, that if not treated as befitts their present condition, with easie and timely methods of Redresse, tis to be more than fear'd (as the common Rumour indicates) that they will either abandon their Plantations, putt off their servants and dispose of their stocks and away to other parts, or else the most part of them will only make Corne, instead of Tobacco, and soe sullenly sitt downe—carelesse of what becomes of their owne Estates or the Kings Customes.[7]

What was worse, when the commissioners informed Berkeley of the king's intention that he return to England, he showed no indications of complying. When they showed him Jeffreys' commission to replace him, he refused to acknowledge it.[8] When they presented him with the king's proclamation of pardon for all rebels, he at first refused to issue it; and when he finally did so, he accompanied it with a proclamation of his own denying pardon to eighteen persons.[9] Aghast, the commissioners reported to England that Berkeley intended "to hang upon this Rebellion more then ever suffered death for the horrid murther of that late glorious martyr of blessed memory [Charles I]." Hang them he did, and continued to compound with those he spared, selling the pardon that the king had freely given, filling the jails as fast as they were emptied.[10]

Berkeley retained the upper hand, over the country and over the commissioners. When he called for a new assembly, apparently anyone suitable to serve as burgess or willing to vote was eager to be on the right side of the vindictive old governor. The counties elected

[6] *Minutes of Council*, 454–55; Coventry Papers, LXXVIII, 170–73.

[7] C.O. 1/39, ff.66–67; Coventry Papers, LXXVII, 389.

[8] Coventry Papers, LXXVII, 398–403. [9] C.O. 1/39, ff.55, 65.

[10] *Ibid.*, ff.66–67, 180–82; Coventry Papers, LXXVII, 389; LXXVIII, 19; Burk, *History of Virginia*, II, 254–55. For the reaction of the king and his council see the undated drafts of letters in Ms. All Souls 254, Bodleian Library, Oxford.

the kind of men to please him, and he had them meet at Green Spring, where they could enjoy his hospitality. There they passed "An act of indemnitie and free pardon," allegedly confirming the king's pardon (which was in any case beyond their power) but exempting from pardon (which was still further beyond their power) those whom Berkeley had already hanged and all others (some of them specifically named) who "did beare any command in the service of the rebells." They also obligingly passed "An act for the releife of such loyall persons as have suffered losse by the late rebells," which enabled those identified by the governor and his friends as "loyal" to recover property from those identified as rebels. By the time the so-called loyal party finished their work, the commissioners concluded, the country would be worth nothing to the king.[11]

In May, 1677, when Berkeley finally condescended to return to England, he left Jeffreys with a council and House of Burgesses determined to continue the lucrative lawsuits made possible by the assembly's act and determined to frustrate any redress of grievances that might interfere with their traditional methods of exploiting the country. Robert Beverley, the clerk of the assembly, and Philip Ludwell, the acting secretary, were as obstructive as Berkeley himself had been. The commissioners were convinced by their investigations in Gloucester County that these two had cooked up "that fatall petition of Gloster" and thus persuaded Berkeley into the venture that turned Bacon's expedition against the Indians into civil war. Ludwell, to be sure, had later done Berkeley a real service in capturing the ship that Bacon sent to the Eastern Shore. But Beverleys main activity, it seemed, had been to conduct plundering raids that were difficult to distinguish from those carried out by the rebels. Betweentimes, he had put the troops assigned him to work for his own benefit felling trees and splitting rails. According to the commissioners, "The services hee did against the Rebells in Virginia (upon which hee soe highly values himself) was noe more than sculking out to surprize small Guards of Rebells by night, and Plundering People without distinction of parties. . . ." Indeed, he was heard to say that as far as he was concerned, the rebellion ended too soon, because "hee had not plundered enough."[12] But regardless of

[11] Hening, II, 366–73, 381–86; Coventry Papers, LXXVIII, 19; cf. C.O. 1/42, ff.46–48.

[12] C.O. 1/41, ff.260, 279, 297–304; Burk, *History of Virginia*, II, 268; *VMHB*, II (1894–95), 168, 405–13; Coventry Papers, LXXVIII, 321.

the commissioners'-opinion of Robert Beverley and Philip Ludwell, these were the men they had to deal with. Beverley was entrenched in his place in the assembly. Ludwell held the strongest office short of governor in the colony. And when Berkeley died soon after his return to England, Ludwell was able to buttress his position by marrying Lady Berkeley. He dismissed Jeffreys as "a pitiful Little Fellow with a Perriwig" and a "worse Rebel than Bacon." [13]

Faced with this pair and with their counterparts in every county, Jeffreys, Moryson, and Berry, though armed with the king's pardon, could do little to stop the legalized plundering by which the loyal party were accumulating property at the expense of everyone they could label a rebel. In August, 1677, when their investigation of the rebellion was completed, Berry and Moryson returned to England, leaving Jeffreys to cope with the wolves alone. The king a few months earlier, on being apprised of Berkeley's lèse majesté in modifying his pardon, had sent a sharp letter (dated May 15, 1677), revoking Berkeley's proclamation. It reached the council by September, but they concealed it until October 26 and went on compounding and suing.[14] William Sherwood, a supporter of Berkeley during the rebellion, had the temerity to appear as attorney for some of the alleged rebels. As a result, he was disbarred from practice and charged with raising a mutiny. By Sherwood's account, his only fault was that those who "called themselves the loyall party" resented his "endeavours to prevent their designes of greedily extorting compositions from the people." "Those things doe already run soe highe," he wrote early in 1678, "that there is seizure made of some mens goods and Lands who never had one penny of the estate of those that have obteyned Judgements against them." [15] In 1680 the plundering was still going on, and the king was still sending instructions to end it.

Berry and Moryson had returned to England with a good idea of why the Virginians rebelled. The commissioners had not been unprepared for what they found in the colony, for the messages sent to England by Giles Bland had been taken seriously. Bland had warned that the annual royal revenue of £100,000 was endangered by the exactions of the local magnates, and among other examples he had singled out the high pay the burgesses voted themselves. The commissioners had accordingly been instructed specifically to get

---

[13] *Executive Journals*, I (1680–99), 472; Coventry Papers, LXXVIII, 134.
[14] C.O. 1/42, f.60; Hening, II, 428–30.　　[15] C.O. 1/42, ff.60–61.

burgess salaries reduced.[16] At the close of the Green Spring assembly in March, 1677, after continual urging, the burgesses had finally complied, and the commissioners were able to report that the pay was now reduced from 150 to 120 pounds of tobacco a day, "which is the very lowest allowance the Burgesses can support their charges under" (New England legislators somehow got by on a quarter of that). Ironically, in the same letter the commissioners reported the hanging of Giles Bland, one of those whom Berkeley had excepted from the king's pardon.[17]

The assembly had taken other steps to alleviate discontent. After repealing all the acts passed at the turbulent assembly of the preceding June, they proceeded to reenact provisions from several of them—with modifications. They did not reenact the one restoring the vote to landless freemen, but they did formulate one of their own to prevent masters from coercing servants into giving up their freedom dues in exchange for early freedom. The commissioners knew, however, that much more was needed. Immediately on their arrival, they had ordered the sheriff of every county to summon a meeting for the statement of grievances.[18] In response they had received a barrage of documents telling them what was wrong.[19]

Some counties turned in lengthy lists with detailed descriptions of the extortions they suffered at the hands of particular local officials; others offered more generalized statements. The pervasive complaint in all, as might be expected, was the high cost of government. The people wanted to reduce not only the daily pay of their burgesses but also the number of their meetings, so that there would be fewer days to pay for.[20] They wanted an end to fruitless government expenditures. Much of their tax money, they suspected, was going to line the pockets of a pack of officials. To remedy the situation, they wanted a public accounting of public funds—they wanted

[16] Coventry Papers, LXXVII, 285–86, 336.

[17] Hening, II, 398–99; C.O. 1/39, f.182; *Journals of the House of Burgesses, 1659/60–1693*, 92–94.

[18] *Ibid.*, 94; Coventry Papers, LXXVII, 376.

[19] Most of the documents are in C.O. 1/39, ff.196–252. Several have been printed in *VMHB*, II (1894–95), 166–73, 289–92, 381–92; III (1895–96), 35–42, 132–59, 239–249; IV (1896–97), 1–15; and *Journals of the House of Burgesses, 1659/60–1693*, 99–113.

[20] C.O. 1/39, ff.203, 212, 236, 240, 244; *Journals of the House of Burgesses, 1659/60–1693*, 92, 107, 108, 111; *VMHB*, II (1894–95), 168.

to be told specifically what their taxes were paying for.[21] They wanted some elected representatives to join with the appointed justices of the peace in calculating the amount of the annual county levy, and they wanted the calculation to be performed in public.[22] There were also complaints against multiple officeholding, suggestions that land rather than tithables should bear the brunt of taxation, and objections to the penny-per-pound "plantations duty" levied by England since 1673 on tobacco shipped from one colony to another.[23]

The grievances added up to a bill of particulars of the ways in which the few were fleecing the many. As the commissioners considered each item, they found little that they could do without offending the beneficiaries—not least of whom was their royal master—and without undermining the authority of government. The commissioners' response to the grievances was, in fact, as revealing of what was wrong in Virginia as the grievances themselves. To begin with, the commissioners had to dismiss out of hand the objections to the plantations duty. The duty had been introduced by Parliament in order to counteract the practices of sharp New England traders who, after passage of the Navigation Acts, legally carried Virginia tobacco to Boston or New York and then, claiming they had thereby satisfied the Acts, reshipped it to the Netherlands for a better price than they could get in England. The New Englanders had thus been able to offer small planters a better rate in their exchanges of merchandise for tobacco than English merchants or Virginia merchant planters did. Although most tobacco probably went to England, the small men's trade with New Englanders had been a safety valve that moderated the distress caused by the falling tobacco market and the Indian troubles. But abolition of the plantations duty was out of the question: the king's solicitude for the welfare of his subjects in Virginia did not extend to a reduction of England's share in the fruits of their labors. He wanted only to reduce the excessive local exactions. And so the commissioners were obliged to tell the

[21] C.O. 1/39, ff.203, 221, 234, 243, 248; *Journals of the House of Burgesses, 1659/60–1693*, 103, 105, 107, 110, 112; *VMHB*, II (1894–95), 171, 388.

[22] C.O. 1/39, ff.214, 238; *VMHB*, II (1894–95), 172, 289–90, 389.

[23] C.O. 1/39, ff.196, 220, 246–50; *Journals of the House of Burgesses, 1659/60–1693*, 108, 109; *VMHB*, II (1894–95), 170, 388; III (1895–96), 38, 142–47, 239–52, 342–49; IV (1896–97), 1–5.

Virginians that it was "wholly mutinous to desire a thing contrary to his Majesties Royall pleasure and benefitt and also against an Act of Parliament." [24]

They gave equally short shrift to the requests that would have given the government a more popular cast. The king, however concerned to prevent the oppression of his subjects, would surely not be eager to do it by giving them a larger hand in their own government. To have elected representatives sitting with the county justices to apportion taxes might open the way to all kinds of popular demands. "This," the commissioners said, "wee account an Innovation and in Derogation of those persons appointed by the Public [actually by the governor] to assess the County Leavy." If the measure was adopted, they said, "the consequence we beleeve will be noe Levies wil be laid but the time spun out in wrangling." [25] The same considerations applied to a request from one county that freemen without land be again allowed to vote for representatives in the assembly, since they paid the same taxes as the housekeepers did. The request was dismissed as "repugnant to the Lawes of England and to the Lawes and Peace of the Colony." [26]

The request for a land tax in place of the levy on polls did seem a good idea to the commissioners. This, too, Giles Bland had urged, as had Berkeley before him, and the king's advisers were in favor of it. But the commissioners knew that most of the huge tracts acquired in the preceding twenty-five years were in the hands of the men who controlled the burgesses, council, and county courts.[27] They were not likely to consent to a land tax. It was, the commissioners reported, "a thing to be wished" but not to be accomplished unless "injoyned from hence [England] by royall authority which if soe wee knowe not how it will be relished by the landed men. . . ." [28] The most they could recommend was a royal decree imposing a tax

[24] *VMHB*, II (1894–95), 170; C.O. 1/39, f.202.

[25] C.O. 1/39, ff.215, 239.

[26] *Ibid.*, f.199; *Journals of the House of Burgesses, 1659/60–1693*, 106. Freemen without land had been deprived of the vote in 1670. It was restored to them by the June, 1676, assembly. The acts of this assembly were all rescinded by the Green Spring assembly of February, 1676/7. Most were repassed, but not this one, which the king had specifically interdicted. Hening, II, 280, 356–57, 380–81, 425.

[27] See above, p. 219. Members of the council continued to be favored in land patents in subsequent years. See Manning C. Voorhis, "Crown versus Council in the Virginia Land Policy," *WMQ*, 3rd ser. III (1946), 499–514.

[28] C.O. 1/39, f.222.

equal to the tax on one tithable for every 100 acres that a man held over 1,000. If "the greate Ingrossers of Lands" had to pay up for their unused lands, they might give them up and thus remove "one of the most apparent causes of the misery and mischiefs that attend this colony by occasioning the Planters to stragle to such remote distances when they cannot find land neerer to seat themselves but by being Tenants which in a Continent they think hard." [20] But the king did not see fit to attempt this reform by royal decree, and the misery and mischief continued.

From the commissioners' reports on Virginia grievances, from their dealings with the assembly, and from Governor Jeffreys' plaintive letters after their departure, it was clear that the king had in Virginia a set of overmighty subjects, many of whom would risk plunging the colony into rebellion again if it would assist in the catch-as-catch-can struggle for riches. But there seemed to be little that the king could do about it without upsetting the precarious peace, and Virginia's magnates were quick to press their own solution to the problem on him, namely, that he should keep troops and ships in the colony—at his own expense.[30] The continuing discontent in Virginia, Thomas Ludwell assured the English authorities in June, 1678, came from "the meaner sort who pressed by their necessityes and desiring againe to have the spoyle of other mens estates are in my humble opinion not to be trusted without a force of 200 foot and 50 horse." [31] Two companies of the foot regiment that accompanied the commission were accordingly kept in the colony after Berry and Moryson returned to England. But no one decided who was to pay them, the king expecting the Virginians to do it and the Virginians expecting the king to do it. As a result, the soldiers remained on the point of mutiny and added yet another element to Virginia's burden of discontent.[32]

After Jeffreys died in December, 1678, the colony sustained its shaky peace under Lieutenant Governor Sir Henry Chichely, while Lord Culpeper, who had succeeded Berkeley as titular governor, remained in England. At this point the settlers at the heads of the rivers were complaining again about Indian attacks, and Chichely summoned the burgesses to deal with the situation. When the members assembled, two adventurers lured them into a scheme that showed how little they had learned from Bacon's Rebellion. William Byrd,

---

[29] *Ibid.*, f.196.
[30] Coventry Papers, LXXVIII, 157, 162, 168.
[31] *Ibid.*, 202.
[32] *Ibid.*, 264, 396, 398, 406; C.O. 1/45, ff.189-90.

who had somehow emerged from the rebellion with both plunder and reputation intact, was sitting in the House as representative for Henrico. He suggested what seemed to be a cheap way to secure the river heads for the future. He and Laurence Smith, another go-getter from Gloucester County, would each undertake to seat what amounted to a town, the one along the upper reaches of the James (where Byrd had patented large holdings) and the other on the upper Rappahannock (where Smith had done so). The inhabitants would include 250 armed men in each town, who would be recruited by guaranteeing them, along with Byrd and Smith, freedom from arrest and from lawsuits for twelve years, and freedom from taxes for fifteen years. These men would stand ready to protect the frontier farmers at a moment's notice.[33]

The House of Burgesses liked the idea. Members of the council had reservations, but a majority of both bodies agreed to it. Perhaps in another colony it might have worked. But it required only a little reflection to see what it could mean in Virginia. William Byrd, who had already displayed his talents for leading restless men, was proposing to "cantonize" the frontier. At the heads of the rivers, in a domain of his own, he would welcome the discontented, penniless freemen, the debtors, the hog-stealers, the terrible young men. With guns in their hands, ammunition, and freedom from arrest, the defensive force promised, as one skeptical council member put it, "more sting than Hony."[34] Secretary Nicholas Spencer spelled out the dangers in a report to England:

> It carries with it a specious gloss of seeming futuer safety but if I rightly apprehend the matter and truely understand of what that body will be composed of, it carryes with it a prospect of as dangerous consequences as is possible to be contrived, for if all the ill humors of a naturall body be collected and settled in any one part it will be of power and efficacie to endanger the whole, which being diffused into all the parts of the body, its malignitie is not of force to offend, thus it will be in the settlement intended, whither all loose, idle, stubborne, and ungoverned people will retier as an asylum: and how dangerous that may be in our wilderness your Honors quick sight will soon descerne.[35]

The Privy Council did discern and promptly disallowed the act. And the king ordered Lord Culpeper to get over to his province

---

[33] Coventry Papers, LXXVIII, 378–87, 444; Hening, II, 448–54.

[34] Philip Ludwell to Coventry, June 16, 1679. Coventry Papers, LXXVIII, 386. See also *ibid.*, 406.

[35] *Ibid.*, 398, 400.

himself and straighten it out. For several years now the Privy Council had been impressed with the growing importance of the colonies to England and was trying to exercise a closer supervision over them through a standing committee, the Lords of Trade and Plantations. The commissioners who investigated the rebellion had given the Lords a full set of the freemen's grievances and a more candid interpretation of the colony's troubles than they could have received from Berkeley and the Virginians who controlled the government. As a result, the Lords formulated instructions for Culpeper, designed to bring Virginia's unruly ruling class into line. He was to repeal by proclamation a whole series of acts offensive to the king. He was also given three acts, drafted by the Privy Council and already affixed with the royal seal, which he was supposed to have passed by the Virginia assembly.[36]

The move was ominous for the future control of Virginia by Virginians. The Lords apparently intended to remove from the House of Burgesses the whole initiative in legislation, for they also instructed Culpeper that he and his council were to draft all future laws and send them to the king for revision before submitting them to the burgesses. Indeed, he was not to call assemblies except at the express command of the king. Moreover, the assembly, which had hitherto been the highest court of appeals in the colony, was to lose that position. Hereafter no appeals were to be allowed from the General Court (consisting of the governor and council) except to the king himself in his Privy Council.[37]

The Lords also provided instructions for a variety of legislation to allay discontent in Virginia. To ease the lot of the actual tobacco makers, and to make immigration attractive to servants, Culpeper was to draft a bill "for the restraining any inhumane severity which by ill masters or overseers may be used toward Christian servants." For security against Indian attack, he was to see that all planters and their Christian servants were furnished with arms. He was to see that the taxes on tithables were replaced by some more equitable form of taxation. And he was to carry out the recommendation that the Virginians were always making to themselves for the establishment of towns.[38]

Culpeper's instructions were designed to substitute the benevolent despotism of the king for the rapacious local despotism that had brought on one rebellion and threatened to bring on another. That

[36] C.O. 1/43, ff.89, 315; C.O. 1/47, ff.265–66, 271.
[37] Ibid., ff.265–66, 271.   [38] Ibid., ff.266, 270, 271.

Virginians themselves had complained to the commissioners of too frequent assemblies seemed to indicate that ordinary folk shared the king's suspicions of such bodies, that they would trust him and his governors to look after their interests more assiduously than elected representatives who spun out the time at 120 pounds a day.[39]

The king's intentions were praiseworthy, but he and his Lords of Trade underestimated the value placed on representative government by Englishmen, whether in England, New England, or Virginia. Only a few years later Parliament would send a king packing for his attempts to bypass them, and New Englanders would do the same to a royal governor commissioned to rule them without an assembly. The king did not ask Culpeper to abolish the Virginia assembly but did expect him to make it agree to a host of measures that the members were not likely to find attractive. If he had tried to do everything he was supposed to, he would probably have succeeded in nothing.

Fortunately for the king, he had in Culpeper a man with the nerve and the prestige to use a discretion that was not envisaged in his instructions, a man who realized at once that an attempt to carry out most of what he was supposed to do might throw the government into disarray. For example, Virginia masters were not about to agree to the arming of their servants, and they themselves were already armed.[40] Nor was it so easy as people in England might think to draft a law against inhumane severity to servants. "This is an Extreme Ticklish and Difficult businesse," he reported, "And the keeping an aequall Hand between Masters and Servants is one of the Greatest Concernes of the Civill Government." [41] The tax on tithables he agreed was "high, unequal, and Burthensome." And it was "most commonly managed by sly cheating fellowes that combine to Defraud the publick," namely, the august justices of Virginia's county courts. He urged the assembly to reduce the tax somehow, but he did not insist on its replacement.[42] Culpeper knew the king's priorities and knew that he could not implement them except by blinking some of His Majesty's wishes. And, as we noticed earlier, he did this repeatedly. He sensed when to yield in order to win friends and support and when to press hard the advantages thus gained.

[39] On the king's policy toward the Virginia assembly after Bacon's Rebellion, see John C. Rainbolt, "A New Look at Stuart Tyranny: The Crown's Attack on the Virginia Assembly, 1676-1689," *VMHB*, LXXV (1967), 387-406.

[40] C.O. 1/47, f.266.   [41] *Ibid.*, f.271.   [42] *Ibid.*, f.260.

By concentrating his talents on what mattered most, Culpeper got the assembly to pass an act (drafted, contrary to his instructions, by Beverley rather than the council) establishing a town with tobacco warehouses in every county. From these towns all the country's tobacco was to be shipped and the king's revenue made more secure thereby.[43] Culpeper was also able to charm or bully the House of Burgesses into accepting the three bills that he had been given by the Privy Council. One was a general act of indemnity, putting an end to the civil suits arising from the rebellion. The second was an act to facilitate the naturalization of foreigners (who might thus be induced to come to Virginia and make tobacco for the king). And the last was an act granting the king, in perpetuity, for the support of the colony government, the export duty on tobacco of two shillings per hogshead.[44]

The last would free the government, and especially the governor, from dependence on the assembly. For most of the rest of the colonial period England would strive to obtain such an act from other American colonial assemblies. When the Virginia assembly first saw it, they turned it down flatly, as every assembly of every other colony did and continued to do with proposals for permanent revenue acts. But Culpeper was perhaps the most highly placed Englishman ever to occupy a colonial governor's chair. Virginia's big men felt dwarfed beside him, grateful for his cooperation and indulgences, and alert to the danger of getting on the wrong side of a man who had given ample display of his power in the imperial machine. When they turned down the tax law, Culpeper lectured them, made a few promises and a few threats, allowed them to make some minor revisions, and eight days after the unanimous rejection he had a unanimous acceptance of that and the other two acts. It was a triumph such as no other colonial governor would ever achieve for the crown.[45]

With these actions accomplished in three months' time, Culpeper thought he had done enough for the king in Virginia and was

[43] Hening, II, 471–78; *Journals of the House of Burgesses, 1659/60–1693,* xxvii–xxviii.

[44] Hening, II, 458–69; *Journals of the House of Burgesses, 1659/60–1693,* 148; C.O. 1/47, ff.258–59.

[45] C.O. 1/47, ff.258–59; *Journals of the House of Burgesses, 1659/60–1693,* 119–49; Culpeper to Blathwayt, June 15, July 8, 1680. Blathwayt Papers, XVII, Colonial Williamsburg. On the significance of Culpeper's achievement see Rainbolt, "A New Look at Stuart Tyranny," 397–400, and David S. Lovejoy, *The Glorious Revolution in America* (New York, 1972), 53–57.

off again for England, not to return for two and a half years and then only for six months. The king did not think that was enough and after Culpeper's second flying visit to Virginia dismissed him.

By Culpeper's triumph with the tax grant the king had obtained a major advantage in his campaign to control the men who ran his most lucrative American colony. By Culpeper's act for establishing towns the king gained nothing, for the measure as drafted proved a fiasco. In Virginia during the seventeenth century a plan for towns, in prospect, always seemed to offer something to everybody.[46] When it came to actually creating towns, however, the aggregation of promised advantages always fell apart, as one group or another had second thoughts or tried to twist the scheme to their own benefit. Never was this reckless pursuit of private gain more apparent than in the 1680s. When Lord Culpeper first came to Virginia in 1680, with the standard instructions to create towns, the colony was suffering from a tobacco glut and low prices. Therefore the assembly was glad to pass the bill he wanted, especially since they were under the impression, no doubt fostered by Culpeper, that the act would be an inducement for the king to agree to a year's cessation of planting in Virginia, Maryland, and North Carolina. Such a cessation would facilitate "the reduceing us to Townes," they said in a petition to His Majesty which Culpeper carried back to England. Moreover, since the establishment of towns would be so advantageous to everyone, including the king, they beseeched him to help bring it about "though to a small diminution of your owne Treasure" by forgoing his customs duties for seven years to inhabitants of these towns.[47]

Since the king had been so generous to his favorites at Virginia's expense, it perhaps seemed not unreasonable to the burgesses to ask for a few favors for Virginia. If the king had been willing to forgo customs duties from residents of the proposed towns for seven years, the towns would surely have been built. Whether they could have lasted after the seven years were up is another question. But the king was not prepared to sacrifice seven years' revenue for the sake of cities in the wilderness. And the burgesses were not willing to make sacrifices either. When the bill was being drafted, they had made its

---

[46] The various attempts are discussed in Rainbolt, "The Virginia Vision."

[47] Hening, II, 471–78; *Journals of the House of Burgesses, 1659/60–1693*, 145–46.

success virtually impossible by insisting on a town in each of Virginia's twenty counties, instead of one or two towns on each of the great rivers. The counties were the locus of political power in Virginia, and no county was ready to see its trade center in a town located in some other county. But to start building twenty towns in a colony that had hitherto had none was unrealistic.[48]

Although the act was impracticable, Robert Beverley, who drafted it, had included a proviso stating that after the first of January, 1682 (less than six months after its passage), anyone buying or loading tobacco outside the towns designated in the act would forfeit it, one-half to the king and one-half to the informer. That winter, when the crop was ready to load, the towns and their tobacco warehouses were still not there, but Robert Beverley was. When the tobacco ships went off to gather their cargoes here and there from the riverside plantations as they had done in the past, Beverley moved in with lawsuits and began seizing tobacco for himself and the king.[49]

This was a bit too much, even for the king, who suspended the act until it could be revised to prevent such tricks, but not before Beverley had accumulated (whether by seizures or otherwise) a large quantity of tobacco, most of which he apparently shipped to London on consignment. Allegedly, at least, he and a number of London merchants were particularly eager to decrease Virginia tobacco production in order to raise the price of what they had in storage. Since the king had not ordered the requested cessation,[50] Beverley and his friends apparently decided to take the matter into their own hands. According to a later report by the governor's council, they "insinuated with the Easy sort of people how advantagious an Act for a cessation of planting for one Year" would be.[51] During the winter of 1681–82 petitions circulated in Gloucester, Middlesex, and the lower parts of New Kent, asking for a meeting of the assembly to pass such an act. Sir Henry Chichely, who was again in charge during Culpeper's absence and pretty much in Robert Beverley's pocket, agreed to call the assembly for April. But by the time it met he had received instructions from the king not to call one

[48] C.O. 1/45, ff.189–90; C.O. 1/47, f.252.

[49] *Executive Journals*, I, 19, 21, 489; C.O. 1/48, ff.63, 230; C.O. 1/51, f.316.

[50] The customs commissioners had recommended its rejection. C.O. 1/46, f.165.

[51] *Executive Journals*, I, 488; C.O. 1/51, f.316; Hening, II, 562.

until November, when Culpeper was expected to return. Chichely accordingly picked a quarrel with the members and dismissed them before they had a chance to take action. The burgesses were furious. Before they broke up, one of them announced that "If care were not taken to make a Cessation, wee must all goe a plundering." [52] They returned to their constituents in a nasty mood and reported the governor's frustration of their plans.

By this time the tobacco market was so overloaded that even the king and Lord Baltimore were sufficiently worried to be willing to do something about crop limitation. Baltimore made known that he would accept a cessation if the king wanted it, and the Lords of Trade instructed him to concur in any measures the Virginians might adopt. Culpeper himself was empowered to agree to some form of limitation when he returned to Virginia. [53] But Culpeper did not reach the colony until December. Before then the Virginians had found another way to reduce the tobacco crop and to display once again the fragility of Virginia's social order.

According to Secretary Nicholas Spencer, Beverley, "the over active Clerke of the House of Burgesses," in order "to advance those great quantities of Tobacco now on his hands," persuaded the planters of Gloucester County to achieve a cessation by cutting down the tobacco plants growing in the fields. They began one day less than a week after the assembly was dissolved, when "a Rabble made a May sport to dance from plantation to plantation to cut up Tobacco Plants." [54] From Gloucester the plant-cutting parties spread to New Kent and Middlesex. When dispersed by day, the rioters often went at it by night. [55] Chichely was able to suppress them only by bringing in militia from more distant counties that had not been infected. Even so, by the end of the month, he estimated that three-fourths of the tobacco in Gloucester, half of that in New Kent, and lesser amounts in Middlesex, Rappahannock, and York had been destroyed. Things calmed down in June and July, but in August, which was cider-making time, they started up again. Spencer blamed it on the fact of "All plantations flowing with syder, soe unripe dranke by our licentious Inhabitants, that they allow no tyme for

[52] *Executive Journals*, I, 14–17, 41; *VMHB*, VIII (1900–1901), 188–89; *Journals of the House of Burgesses, 1659/60–1693*, 157–69.

[53] C.O. 1/48, ff.62–63, 69–72, 185; C.O. 1/49, f.102.

[54] C.O. 1/48, f.230; to Blathwayt, May 29, 1682. Blathwayt Papers, XVI, Colonial Williamsburg.

[55] C.O. 1/48, ff.261, 263, 275.

its fermentation but in theire braines." He also blamed Beverley and the other "stirrers up and Acters of these mischiefs and outrages" for having "soe free a mind to Rebellion." But he recognized that a rebellion required rebels and that Virginia was peopled by men with an "itching desier" to take up arms again, men "such as his Majesties good government of his other dominions spewed forth." [56]

What he neglected to point out was that the itching desire for rebellion was kept up in Virginians by the bad government of their colony, or at any rate by the itching desire of everyone at the top, whether in England or Virginia, whether a Beverley or Berkeley, a Charles or a James, to squeeze just a little more out of the men who grew tobacco.

When Culpeper finally arrived in December, he found the jails full and the redoubtable Beverley himself under arrest. Since he could not gather enough evidence to convict Beverley of treason, he barred him from public office and then hanged a couple of humbler ringleaders and pardoned the rest. [57]

At this point, Culpeper could probably have secured from the assembly a more practicable act for towns, and he was empowered to allow a cessation to go with it. But, once again, opportunities for profit intervened. The plant cutting, together perhaps with an expansion of the world market, had given the price of tobacco a temporary boost: and by the spring of 1683 it was clear that there would be a huge crop. Though this would doubtless send the price down again and generate more discontent, the king would meanwhile have a bonanza year in customs duties. Culpeper estimated that the revenue would gain an extra £50,000 if there were no limitation of the crop. He therefore kept mum about his instructions for a cessation and returned to England full of righteousness about the extra profits he had gained for the king. Besides, he assured the king, any restraint of tobacco planting would serve only to enrich "the Engrossers of the Commodity." It was they, he was sure, who had inveigled the ordinary folk into the plant-cutting rebellion. [58]

Subsequent attempts at towns and at crop limitation encountered the same kind of difficulties. If there was not a Culpeper on hand to save the king's revenue, the commissioners of customs in England were ever ready to disapprove any measure that might reduce the flow of tobacco from Virginia. And the burgesses would insist on a town for every county. One act for towns foundered in the passage

[56] C.O. 1/49, f.107.   [57] C.O. 1/48, ff.62–63, 69–72.   [58] *Ibid.*

because the burgesses, wary of the governor's growing patronage powers, refused to increase either the number of customs collectors or the fees they received. Lord Howard of Effingham, the incumbent governor who had succeeded Culpeper, would have none of the act unless he could raise the fees.[59] Thus the only measures projected that might have cured Virginia's ailing economy and truculent mood came to nothing.

Effingham's struggle with the assembly over towns and fees was but one of many between them. Being a lesser man and a lesser peer than Culpeper, Effingham did not carry the same weight with Virginians, and they gave him a hard time. "Assemblys in this part of the world are not to be managed, especially by a naked and unarmed man," he reported ruefully to his superiors.[60] It would help if he had a guard of twenty men. It would help if the king would lend a royal frigate to transport Lady Effingham to Virginia, to show how highly the king regarded him.[61] It would help if he could get rid of Robert Beverley, who was somehow clerk of the assembly again and still its most powerful member.[62] It would help, too, if he could get a better batch of councillors. In the existing council the obnoxious Philip Ludwell, fortified by his marriage to Lady Berkeley, was still taking the lead.[63]

Effingham might have been better able to handle the ruling men of Virginia if he had better understood the ins and outs of Virginia's social divisions. Virginia's big men were by no means a united bloc. They competed with one another not only in the tobacco market but also in the scramble for offices, for lands, and for wealthy widows. The members of a county court were as sensitive to the pecking order among themselves as were the members of the council. There were frequent disputes about precedence in these bodies, and a man would sometimes refuse to sit at all if not placed higher than

[59] C.O. 1/59, ff.87–89. The journal of the House of Burgesses for this assembly is in vol. I of the Effingham Papers; it is not in the printed *Journals*. The following year the assembly did get through an act prohibiting the planting of tobacco after June 30, an expedient that had been tried often before without materially reducing the crop. Even this alarmed the customs commissioners, who persuaded the Privy Council to disallow it. Hening, III, 35; C.O. 1/62, f.295.

[60] To Blathwayt, Feb. 6, 1685/6. Blathwayt Papers, XIV, Colonial Williamsburg.

[61] To Blathwayt, April 23, May 13, June 27, 1684, Nov. 14, 1685. Blathwayt Papers, XIV, Colonial Williamsburg.

[62] C.O. 1/59, ff.87–89, 153–54.   [63] C.O. 1/61, ff.245–46, 264–65.

another on the list of councillors or judges, though the placement had no apparent function. Such rivalries were frequently allied to family connections and divisions. The well to do intermarried and built up intricate networks of families who tended to act together.

There was thus ample opportunity for a knowledgeable governor to divide and conquer, but Effingham was not good at the game. He got rid of Beverley with a royal order barring him from all public office; and he dismissed Ludwell from the council and from his post as collector. But such triumphs were illusory. After his dismissal Ludwell immediately got himself elected burgess from James City County. Effingham then persuaded the House that a suspended councillor was unqualified as a burgess. But Ludwell lived next door to the assembly house, and Effingham soon found that Ludwell at home could organize opposition as easily as if he were still a member, because of "the Caball of the gang being constantly held at his house." [64]

In spite of the Ludwells and the Beverleys, Effingham did make some progress in the program to restrain Virginia's lordly ruling class. By carrying out instructions that had initially been issued to Culpeper, he put an end to the assembly's standing as the highest court in the colony and made the General Court's decisions unappealable except to the king. [65] He also repealed some more existing laws by proclamation and advised the king that proclamations would be the best way to legislate in the future. At the same time, he advised the House of Burgesses that their authority in Virginia rested solely on the king's pleasure. That the king allowed them to make laws at all was merely an act of grace and could thus be revoked at any time. The king in question was a new king, James II, who inherited the throne in 1685. He had already shown that this was his view of colonial rights by abolishing the assemblies of Massachusetts, Connecticut, Plymouth, Rhode Island, New York and New Jersey and consolidating these colonies into the "Dominion of New England." When the Virginia assembly balked at legislation requested by the governor, Effingham told them that their consent was not really necessary. [66]

[64] *Journals of the House of Burgesses, 1659/60–1693*, viii, 288; to Blathwayt, May 23, 1688. Blathwayt Papers, XIV, Colonial Williamsburg.

[65] *Journals of the House of Burgesses, 1659/60–1693*, xxxi, 196ff.

[66] *Executive Journals*, I, 75–76; Effingham to Blathwayt, April 29, 1688. Blathwayt Papers, XIV, Colonial Williamsburg; Effingham to Lord Sunderland, May 22, 1688. Effingham Papers.

Neither Effingham nor James II had Culpeper's sense of what was politically possible. It was too late to make government, whether in England or the colonies, rest on royal prerogative. The attempt to do so could only provoke contests over rights, in which England's concern for the exploitation of the colonists would be forgotten. In Effingham's hands and in those of subsequent royal governors, the effort to restrain the rapacity of Virginia's ruling class degenerated into a contest for power between colony and mother country, between royal governor and provincial legislature.

Ruling Virginians still profited from long sessions of the assembly and from the increasing number and size of official fees. And the public levy continued high, still padded with expenditures that yielded ancillary income to the men who laid it and to their friends.[67] The success of royal efforts to reduce the cost of government after Bacon's Rebellion can be measured by the average total public and county levy for ten years before and ten years after the rebellion in one county, Norfolk, for which records are available. In spite of the fact that the assembly did not meet at all in 1678, 1681, and 1683, the average annual burden on the taxpayer had not decreased. For the years 1666–75 the levy averaged 70 pounds yearly per person; for the years 1677–86 it averaged 74 pounds.[68]

Royal governors, as we have seen, exercised their own ingenuity to get as much as they could from Virginia, while lecturing the assemblies against lengthy sessions and undue charges.[69] And the king himself, not content with getting more from Virginia than anyone else, was always finding ways to extract still more. In 1684, for example, Charles II raised the fee charged for escheats (the regrant of a parcel of land that was claimed by the king when the owner died

[67] *Journals of the House of Burgesses, 1659/60–1693,* 152, 170–83, 283. These sums did not include the daily pay and traveling expenses of the Burgesses, which were met by county levies, varying according to the size of the county or the amount of its other expenses (such as bounties on wolves).

[68] Figures derived from Norfolk VI and VII.

[69] Effingham quarreled with the assembly more over his efforts to add to his perquisites through a fee for affixing seals to land patents than he did over matters contained in his instructions. The king ultimately disallowed the fee. The journal of the House of Burgesses for October, 1685, in which the House first quarreled with him over the fee is in the Effingham Papers, vol. I. See also Effingham to Blathwayt, April 29, 1688. Blathwayt Papers, XIV, Colonial Williamsburg; *Executive Journals,* I, 521; C.O. 1/59, f.89; C.O. 5/1357, No. 267.

without heirs), in spite of having agreed in 1678 to charge no more than two pounds of tobacco per acre for this kind of grant.[70] In 1685 James II got Parliament to increase the English import duty on tobacco from twopence to fivepence per pound.[71] The royal intake went up accordingly, and so did the burden on tobacco prices that kept Virginians on the verge of rebellion.

With ruling Virginians like Beverley ready to gamble on another rebellion and with the populace ready to be led, it was touch and go to keep the planters from picking up their guns again. A Culpeper could overawe everyone around him and induce a semblance of order as long as he remained in the colony. But other governors were less assured, and even Culpeper had no illusions about the powder keg he sat on. He had not dared to entrust Virginia's magnates even with emergency powers to raise troops against Indian attacks. After the suppression of the "cantonizing" scheme of William Byrd and Laurence Smith, he had felt obliged to disregard royal instructions to name emergency commanders in the frontier areas at the heads of the rivers, "there being noe persons living thereabouts fitting to be Entrusted with soe great a power that may more endanger the peace of the country then Any Advantage accruing to it can Recompence." [72] The restless young freedmen, in those areas especially and probably everywhere, still posed a greater threat to the colony than the Indians did.

Although the plant-cutting rebellion had been successfully suppressed before Effingham took charge of the colony, he too saw that another outbreak could occur at any time. "I must tell you," he wrote to William Blathwayt, the auditor general of the colonies, "here are some, I feare want only an opportunity." "I thanke God," he added, "I have them att present under foot." [73] But news of Monmouth's Rebellion in England, followed shortly by England's own Revolution of 1688, made it hard to keep them there. Effingham's only recourse was to suppress as rapidly as possible every sign of insubordination. Late in 1685, when "the unruly tongues of some of the commonalty . . . soe palpably demonstrated the wickedness of their hearts," he seized a number of them and issued a proclamation requiring the justices of every county to imprison anyone who so

---

[70] Blathwayt to Effingham, July 28, 1684. Effingham Papers, III.

[71] Although all but a halfpenny was still returned to the reexporter, a third of the crop still remained in England at the end of the century.

[72] C.O. 1/47, f.267.

[73] May 13, 1685. Blathwayt Papers, XIV, Colonial Williamsburg.

much as spread rumors tending "to sedition or faction." [74] The council, as in the past, clamped down on persons who showed an inclination to challenge authority, by whipping, pillorying, and placing men in irons for "slighting words" to themselves or the county justices. [75]

It is questionable how long Virginia could have continued on this course, keeping men in servitude for years and then turning them free to be frustrated by the engrossers of land, by the collectors of customs, by the county courts, by their elected representatives, by the council, and, above all, by the king himself. In time the "slighting words" might have turned into a more serious challenge to authority than either Bacon or the plant cutters had managed. That Virginia changed course and avoided such an outcome was owing to no conscious decision. Plans to reorganize or redirect the colony came, as we have seen, to nothing. But while Culpeper and Effingham and their immediate successors were striving to hold the freemen still for the fleecing, the colony was already moving toward a new social order, in which freemen would not have to be held still, toward a society that would nourish the freeman's freedom and at the same time make possible the unlimited exploitation of labor.

[74] Journal of the House of Burgesses, Nov. 20, 1685, in Effingham Papers, I; *Executive Journals*, I, 75; C.O. 1/59, ff.87–89.
[75] Oct. 21, 1687. Effingham Papers, II.

Book IV

SLAVERY AND FREEDOM

15

TOWARD SLAVERY

I could be argued that Virginia had relieved one of England's social problems by importing it. Virginians of the late seventeenth century seemed to be plagued by the same kind of restless, roistering rogues who had wandered through Elizabethan England. England had kept them down by the workhouse, by the gallows, by whipping them back to the parish they came from, by sending them off on military expeditions—and by shipping them to Virginia. Richard Hakluyt had hoped that the New World would save them from the gallows. It had, and although Virginians were not all happy about it, throughout the century they kept crying for more. They wanted men. They could not get enough of them. The problem was not, as in England, to find work for them but simply to keep them working for their betters.

As we have seen, Virginians had coped with the problem in several ways: by creating an artificial scarcity of land, which drove freemen back into servitude; by extending terms of service; by inflicting severe penalties for killing the hogs that offered easy food without work. They had also through rents and taxes and fees skimmed off as much as they dared of the small man's small profits for the benefit of burgesses, councillors, and collectors. But the burdens imposed on Virginia's workers placed the colony continually on the brink of rebellion.

Elsewhere the world was trying less dangerous ways to maximize labor and the returns from labor. One way, which had a large future, grew out of the ideas that we associate with Max Weber's term, "the Protestant Ethic." Whether the origin of those ideas lay in any particular religion or not, where they prevailed they excited

in employers and employed alike a zeal for work that exceeded anything the world had formerly known. Men imbued with a yearning
for salvation found in diligent, systematic work at their jobs a sign
of their predestined election to the joys of paradise. In their eagerness thus to demonstrate their sainthood to themselves and to others,
they delivered more work than could be obtained by most external
forms of compulsion. But the extraordinary capacity for work displayed by men addicted to the Protestant Ethic was the by-product
of a special religious zeal. And religious zeal of any kind was not
conspicuous among Virginians. It was the specialty of the New
Englanders whom Governor Berkeley so despised. There remained,
however, another way of compelling men to a maximum output of
labor without as great a risk of rebellion as Virginians had been running.

    Slavery is a mode of compulsion that has often prevailed where
land is abundant,[1] and Virginians had been drifting toward it from
the time when they first found something profitable to work at.
Servitude in Virginia's tobacco fields approached closer to slavery
than anything known at the time in England. Men served longer,
were subjected to more rigorous punishments, were traded about as
commodities already in the 1620s.

    That Virginia's labor barons of the 1620s or her land and labor
barons of the 1660s and 1670s did not transform their servants into
slaves was probably not owing to any moral squeamishness or to
any failure to perceive the advantages of doing so. Although slavery
did not exist in England, Englishmen were not so unfamiliar with it
that they had to be told what it was. They knew that the Spaniards'
gold and silver were dug by slave labor, and they themselves had
even toyed with temporary "slavery" as a punishment for crime in
the sixteenth century.[2] But for Virginians to have pressed their servants or their indigent neighbors into slavery might have been, initially at least, more perilous than exploiting them in the ways that
eventuated in the plundering parties of Bacon's Rebellion. Slavery,
once established, offered incomparable advantages in keeping labor
docile, but the transformation of free men into slaves would have
been a tricky business. It would have had to proceed by stages, each
carefully calculated to stop short of provoking rebellion. And if suc-

---

    [1] Evsey D. Domar, "Causes of Slavery or Serfdom," 18–32; Briden-
baugh, *No Peace beyond the Line*, 265.
    [2] C. S. L. Davies, "Slavery and the Protector Somerset: The Vagrancy
Act of 1547," *Economic History Review*, 2nd ser., XIX (1966), 532–49.

cessful it would have reduced, if it did not end, the flow of potential slaves from England and Europe. Moreover, it would have required a conscious, deliberate, public decision. It would have had to be done, even if in stages, by action of the assembly, and the English government would have had to approve it. If it had been possible for the men at the top in Virginia to arrive at such a decision or series of decisions, the home government would almost certainly have vetoed the move, for fear of a rebellion or of an exodus from the colony that would prove costly to the crown's tobacco revenues.

But to establish slavery in Virginia it was not necessary to enslave anyone. Virginians had only to buy men who were already enslaved, after the initial risks of the transformation had been sustained by others elsewhere. They converted to slavery simply by buying slaves instead of servants. The process seems so simple, the advantages of slave labor so obvious, and their system of production and attitude toward workers so receptive that it seems surprising they did not convert sooner. African slaves were present in Virginia, as we have seen, almost from the beginning (probably the first known Negroes to arrive, in 1619, were slaves). The courts clearly recognized property in men and women and their unborn progeny at least as early as the 1640s,[3] and there was no law to prevent any planter from bringing in as many as he wished. Why, then, did Virginians not furnish themselves with slaves as soon as they began to grow tobacco? Why did they wait so long?

The answer lies in the fact that slave labor, in spite of its seeming superiority, was actually not as advantageous as indentured labor during the first half of the century. Because of the high mortality among immigrants to Virginia, there could be no great advantage in owning a man for a lifetime rather than a period of years, especially since a slave cost roughly twice as much as an indentured servant.[4] If the chances of a man's dying during his first five years in Virginia were better than fifty-fifty—and it seems apparent that they were—

[3] See chap. 7, note 69.

[4] A newly arrived English servant with five years or more to serve cost 1,000 pounds of tobacco, more or less, in the 1640s and early 1650s. The earliest surviving contract for importation of Negroes, in 1649, called for their sale on arrival at 2,000 pounds apiece, but whether they actually sold for that price is unknown (Northampton III, 204a). A seasoned Negro man or woman then cost between 2,000 and 3,000. Values for both slaves and servants in inventories rose in the late 1650s, with servants fetching as much as 3,000 and slaves 4,000. See also chap. 8, notes 68 and 69.

and if English servants could be made to work as hard as slaves, English servants for a five-year term were the better buy.

If Virginians had been willing to pay the price, it seems likely that they could have obtained Negro slaves in larger numbers than they did. During the first half of the century the Dutch were busy dismantling the Portuguese empire and, in the process, taking over the African slave trade. They promoted the development of English sugar plantations in the West Indies and supplied those plantations with enough slaves to give Barbados (founded twenty years after Virginia) a black population of 5,000 by 1645 and 20,000 by 1660.[5] Virginia could scarcely have had a tenth the number at either date. Yet the Dutch were heavily engaged in the purchase of Virginia tobacco. They would surely, in the course of that trade, have supplied Virginians with slaves if the Virginians had been ready to pay.

That Virginia's tobacco planters would not pay, while Barbados' sugar planters would, requires explanation, for mortality was evidently as heavy in Barbados as in Virginia.[6] If servants for a term were a better buy for Virginians, why not for Barbadians?

Up until the 1640s, when the principal crop in Barbados was, as in Virginia, tobacco, the labor force was mainly composed, as in Virginia, of white servants. But a shift from tobacco to cotton and then to sugar in the early 1640s made the islands less attractive than the mainland for servants who crossed the ocean voluntarily. Sugar production required such strenuous labor that men would not willingly undertake it. Sugar planters, in order to get their crops grown, harvested, and processed had to drive their workers much harder than tobacco planters did. Richard Ligon in the late 1640s was scandalized to see how the Barbados planters beat their servants in order to get the work out of them.[7] Moreover, when a servant turned free, he found land much scarcer than in Virginia or Maryland. And even if he could hire a plot, at high rents, sugar production (unlike tobacco) required a larger outlay of capital for equipment than he could likely lay hands on.[8] For these reasons, when Barbados servants became free, they frequently headed for Virginia or other

[5] Bridenbaugh, *No Peace beyond the Line*, 33, 55–60, 63–68, 82–84; Richard S. Dunn, *Sugar and Slaves: The Rise of the Planter Class in the English West Indies, 1624–1713* (Chapel Hill, N.C., 1972), 312.

[6] Dunn, *Sugar and Slaves*, 327–34.

[7] Ligon, *True and Exact History*, 43–55; Harlow, *Barbados*, 302–3; Bridenbaugh, *No Peace beyond the Line*, 102–17.

[8] Ligon, *True and Exact History*, 109–17; Bridenbaugh, *No Peace beyond the Line*, 85, 287; Dunn, *Sugar and Slaves*, 91, but cf. 197.

mainland colonies. The sugar planters may thus have bought slaves partly because they could not buy servants unless the servants were shanghaied, or "barbadosed" as the word was at the time, or unless they were sent as prisoners, like the captured Scottish and Irish soldiers whom Cromwell shipped over.[9] A dwindling supply of willing servants may have forced a switch to slaves.

It is possible that the conversion to slavery in Virginia was helped, as it was in Barbados, by a decline in the number of servants coming to the colony. The conditions that produced Bacon's Rebellion and the continuing discontent thereafter did not enhance the colony's reputation. Moreover, by the third quarter of the century there was less pressure on Englishmen to leave home. Complaints of overpopulation in England had ceased, as statesmen and political thinkers sought ways of putting the poor to work. Certainly the number of white immigrants to Virginia does seem to have declined.[10] But if this was a factor in the conversion process, another, probably of greater consequence, was the decline of heavy mortality toward midcentury, for as life expectancy rose, the slave became a better buy than the servant.

The point at which it became more advantageous for Virginians to buy slaves was probably reached by 1660. In that year the assembly offered exemption from local duties to Dutch ships bringing Negroes.[11] But in the same year Parliament passed the Navigation Acts, interdicting both the export of tobacco from the colonies to the Netherlands and any trade by Dutch ships in the colonies.[12] The result was to delay Virginia's conversion to slavery. The mother country attempted to compensate for the severing of the Dutch slave trade through a royally sponsored English trading company, the Royal Adventurers, which was reorganized and rechartered in 1672 as the Royal African Company. These companies enjoyed a monopoly of supplying all the colonies with African slaves until 1698; but the men who ran them never gained sufficient familiarity with Africa or the slave trade to conduct the business successfully. And even though their monopoly could not be effectively enforced, especially against knowledgeable private traders, both tobacco and sugar plant-

[9] Bridenbaugh, *No Peace beyond the Line,* 18, 219; Dunn, *Sugar and Slaves,* 69.

[10] Smith, *Colonists in Bondage,* 309; C.O. 5/1316, f.53.

[11] Hening, I, 540.

[12] The acts excluded all foreign shipping and required tobacco to be taken only to England or another English colony, but it was the Dutch who were principally aimed at.

ers complained that it prevented them from getting the number of workers they needed.[13] Virginia thus began to change to slave labor at a time when she had to compete with the sugar planters for a smaller supply of slaves than would have been available had the freer conditions of trade still existed under which Barbados had made the conversion.

In the competition for slaves after 1660 the sugar planters still enjoyed some advantages. Although sugar and tobacco were both "enumerated" commodities that must be shipped only to England or to another English colony, England did not collect nearly so heavy an import tax on sugar as on tobacco.[14] Consequently, a larger percentage of the price paid by the consumer went to the grower. Moreover, the price of slaves in the West Indies was less than in Virginia, because the islands were closer to Africa, so that costs of transportation and risk of loss on the "Middle Passage" were therefore less.[15] The figures for slave imports into Barbados, Jamaica, and the Leeward Islands in the last quarter of the century are all far above those for Virginia.[16] That Virginia was able to get any at all was owing to the fact that while slaves had become a profitable investment for tobacco growers, the profitability of growing sugar had declined.

It is impossible to reconstruct from surviving data the returns that could be expected on capital invested in growing tobacco in Virginia in comparison with the same amount invested in growing sugar in the West Indies at different periods in the seventeenth century.[17] It is clear, however, that by the end of the seventeenth cen-

[13] K. G. Davies, *The Royal African Company* (London, 1957), 131, 133, 145, 149, 300–315.

[14] In 1668–69 tobacco imports in England valued at £50,000 paid customs duties of £75,000, while sugar imports valued at £180,000 paid customs duties of £18,000. Dunn, *Sugar and Slaves*, 206–7.

[15] The Royal African Company's proposed prices in 1672 were £15 in Barbados and £18 in Virginia. C.O. 1/62, f.133.

[16] Dunn, *Sugar and Slaves*, 363; Bridenbaugh, *No Peace beyond the Line*, 256; Philip D. Curtin, *The Atlantic Slave Trade: A Census* (Madison, Wis., 1969), 53, 55, 62.

[17] Various contemporary calculations survive of the possible return on investment in sugar; for example, Ligon, *True and Exact History*, 109–17, and C.O. 1/58, ff.155–60. But they do not rest on actual records of production. Since they were made in support of arguments that the planters were doing well or that they were doing poorly, they are either much too optimistic or much too pessimistic.

tury and probably by the third quarter of it the tobacco growers had one strong advantage in the longevity of their laborers. A smaller proportion of their profits had to go into labor replacement and was available to meet the higher initial cost of a slave. Life expectancy in Barbados, especially for the black population, continued to be low throughout the seventeenth and most of the eighteenth century. The slaves on Barbados plantations had to be replaced at the rate of about 6 percent a year.[18] It is estimated that between 1640 and 1700 264,000 slaves were imported into the British West Indies. The total black population in 1700 was about 100,000.[19] In the next century, between 1712 and 1762 the importation of 150,000 slaves increased the Barbados black population by only 28,000.[20] By contrast, while Virginia imported roughly 45,000 slaves between 1700 and 1750 (figures from the seventeenth century are sporadic), the black population increased from perhaps 8,000 or 10,000 to over 100,000.[21] In Virginia not only had the rate of mortality from disease gone down, but the less strenuous work of cultivating tobacco, as opposed to sugar, enabled slaves to retain their health and multiply. To make a profit, sugar planters worked their slaves to death; tobacco planters did not have to.[22] A slave consequently had a longer period of usefulness in Virginia than in the West Indies. The return on the investment might be less in the short run, but more in the long run.

The gap between the ability of Virginia and West Indies planters to pay for slaves was also narrowed in the course of the century by changes in the market price of their respective crops. The selling price of muscovado sugar in the islands during the 1640s, when the planters were converting to slavery, was perhaps 60 shillings the hundredweight (it brought 80 shillings at wholesale in London). In the 1650s and 1660s it dropped to about 30 shillings, in the

[18] The sex ratio among Barbados slaves was about even. Although more men were imported than women, they died faster, and total deaths outnumbered births. Dunn, *Sugar and Slaves*, 251, 309, 314–17, 323; Bridenbaugh, *No Peace beyond the Line*, 354–55. Cf. Richard Pares, *A West India Fortune* (London, 1950), 122–25.

[19] Curtin, *Atlantic Slave Trade*, 59, 119.

[20] David Lowenthal, "The Population of Barbados," *Social and Economic Studies*, VI (1957), 445–501.

[21] Appendix, p. 423, and *Historical Statistics of the United States*, 769.

[22] It is possible also that diseases in the West Indies contributed to the higher death rate there. Mortality from disease may have continued to be as high there as it was in Virginia in the early part of the century.

1670s to about 15, and in the 1680s to as low as 10, with some recovery in the 1690s.[23] Tobacco reached 10 shillings the hundredweight in the 1660s and 1670s and stayed there with occasional ups and downs for half a century.[24]

What these prices meant in profits for the planters depended in large measure on the comparative productivity of sugar and tobacco workers; and, in the absence of actual records of production, that is less easy to determine. No significant innovations in technology occurred in the growth or processing of either crop before the nineteenth century, and by 1660 both sugar and tobacco planters were thoroughly familiar with their respective crops and with ways of maximizing production. Contemporary estimates of productivity per hand on sugar plantations vary widely, but a fair medium might be 1,500 pounds a year. Because of Virginia's fickle weather the tobacco harvest probably varied more from year to year than the sugar harvest, and a man might grow a smaller but better and higher-priced crop by reducing the number of leaves left on each plant. Any estimates of productivity are therefore even more tenuous than those for sugar. It is likely, however, that by the 1660s a man would make less than 1,000 pounds of tobacco in a lean year, but more than 2,000, perhaps much more, in a good year. In the long run a man's labor for a year would probably make about the same weight of tobacco in Virginia as of sugar in the islands. But the tobacco worker could at the same time grow enough corn to sustain himself. And in the most favorable locations, especially on the York and, to a lesser degree, the Rappahannock, he could grow a variety of tobacco (known as sweet-scented) which brought a higher price and weighed more in relation to bulk (reducing freight costs) than the ordinary Orinoco.[25]

In addition, tobacco continued to enjoy the advantage, which

[23] Harlow, *Barbados*, 170, 188, 259–60; Dunn, *Sugar and Slaves*, 196, 205, 211; C. S. S. Higham, *The Development of the Leeward Islands under the Restoration, 1660–1688* (Cambridge, 1921), 158, 191–92, 194. These prices are crude, but more precise ones for London show a similar though not so steep decline. Noel Deerr, *The History of Sugar* (London, 1950), II, 528; Davies, *Royal African Company*, 365–66. In Virginia in the 1650s a pound of sugar was valued at from 3 to 7 pounds of tobacco. Northampton IV, 203a; V, 132a, 139a; Norfolk II, 180; IV, 114.

[24] Chap. 7, note 7; chap. 10, notes 10 and 29.

[25] On sugar production see Ward Barrett, "Caribbean Sugar-Production Standards in the Seventeenth and Eighteenth Centuries," in John Parker, ed., *Merchants and Scholars: Essays in the History of Exploration*

it had always had, of requiring a smaller outlay of capital for production equipment. And land, if scarcer than it had been, was still much cheaper in Virginia than in the islands. The far greater number of slaves delivered to the sugar islanders indicates that sugar remained the more attractive risk to English capital investment. Nevertheless, tobacco was so close a competitor that before the 1680s slaves were being shipped from Barbados for sale in Virginia.[26]

In financing the extra cost of slaves, Virginians were not wholly dependent on upswings in the tobacco market. They could draw on capital accumulated during the first half century. Their earnings from tobacco (apart from any they returned to England) had been invested, as we saw earlier, in cattle and hogs and servants. When they wanted to buy slaves in Barbados, they could send cattle and hogs in exchange. Land in the West Indies was too valuable to be devoted to food products, and sugar planters were eager to buy live cattle as well as barreled beef and pork. They needed live cattle not only to turn their mills but also to dung their land as the canes exhausted it. Virginia joined with New England in supplying the need; and though no figures exist to show the volume of the trade, there is a good deal of evidence in county court records of contact between Virginia and Barbados in the seventeenth century.[27] But the extra capital to buy slaves came not only from livestock. In spite of the low profits of tobacco growing after 1660, there were the entrepreneurial profits of the merchant planters and the substantial amounts accumulated by the judicious use of government office.

More important perhaps than the capital generated locally was that attracted from England by the new competitive position of tobacco. Substantial men who might earlier have headed for Barbados now came to Virginia, supplied with funds to purchase or rent land and labor. And men with small amounts of capital, insufficient for the initial outlay of a sugar plantation, could make a good start in Virginia. Though the colony had ceased to be, if it ever was, a land of opportunity for the servant who came with nothing, it offered much to the man with £300 or £400 sterling. With half of it

---

and Trade. Collected in Memory of James Ford Bell (Minneapolis, 1965), 147–70. On tobacco see chap. 7, note 33.

[26] Elizabeth Donnan, *Documents Illustrative of the History of the Slave Trade to America* (Washington, D.C., 1930–35), IV, 89.

[27] See chap. 7, note 26.

put into buying a well-located plantation, he would have enough left over for eight or ten slaves, and "a handsom, gentile and sure subsistence," as William Fitzhugh said, who had done it. Ten slaves might make 20,000 pounds of tobacco in a good year, which at the time Fitzhugh wrote would be worth from £100 to £200 sterling. The cost of feeding them would be nothing and of clothing them little. The return on the investment would be accordingly a good deal more than could be expected from any agricultural enterprise in England.[28]

Englishmen with spare cash came to Virginia also because the prestige and power that a man with any capital could expect in Virginia was comparatively much greater than he was likely to attain in England, where men of landed wealth and gentle birth abounded. Well-to-do immigrants and their sons, who came to Virginia after midcentury, dominated the colony's politics, probably in default of male survivors of earlier successful immigrants.[29] But the fortunes gathered by those early immigrants during the deadly first half century were not necessarily lost or dispersed. Capital still accumulated in the hands of widows and joined in profitable wedlock the sums that well-heeled immigrants brought with them. The Ludwells, Byrds, Carters, Spencers, Wormeleys, Corbins, and a host of others not only shared the spoils of office among themselves, but also by well-planned marriages shared the savings gathered by their predecessors. In Lancaster County, of the twelve persons who were listed for more than twenty tithables between 1653 and 1679, one was a widow and nine of the remaining eleven married widows.[30]

These were the men who brought slavery to Virginia, simply by buying slaves instead of servants. Since a slave cost more than a

---

[28] Davis, *Fitzhugh*, 279–80.

[29] Bailyn, "Politics and Social Structure"; Quitt, "Virginia House of Burgesses."

[30] The twelve (derived from Lancaster I, III, and IV) were Robert Beckingham (married widow of Raleigh Travers), John Carter I (married widow of William Brocas), John Carter II (did not marry a widow), Sir Henry Chichely (married widow of Ralph Wormely), Henry Corbyn (married widow of Roland Burnham), Anthony Ellyott (married widow of Justinian Aylmer), David Fox (married widow of Richard Wright), Robert Griggs (wife unknown), Lady Lunsford (widow of Sir Thomas Lunsford), Richard Parrott (married widow of Nicholas Dale), Robert Smith (married Lady Lunsford), and Thomas Wilkes (married widow of Robert Beckingham).

servant, the man with only a small sum to invest was likely to buy a servant. In 1699 the House of Burgesses noted that the servants who worked for "the poorer sort" of planters were still "for the most part Christian." [31] But the man who could afford to operate on a larger scale, looking to the long run, bought slaves as they became more profitable and as they became available.

How rapidly they became available and how rapidly, therefore, Virginia made the switch to slave labor is difficult to determine, partly because the Royal African Company monopoly made it necessary to conceal purchases from illicit traders. During the period of the monopoly (1663–98), slaves could presumably still be purchased legally from Barbados, but few records of trade between the two colonies have survived.[32] Nevertheless, from stray bits of evidence we do know that Virginians were getting slaves from other sources than the company and what prices they were willing to pay for them. The ship *Society*, of Bristol, carried about 100 slaves to Virginia in 1687. She was an interloper and was seized by William Cole, the collector for the lower James River, who later accounted for the sale of the cargo. The prices he obtained varied according to the age, sex, and condition of the slaves. For "5 Sick Negroes not able to goe or Stand" he got £20 sterling, for a man £23, a youth £20, another £21, another £22, and so on. All told, for 90 Negroes, including 13 sick (two "almost dead") and a number of small children who were probably under twelve (but not counting seven slaves who died on his hands), he got £1,501.13.6, an average of £16.6.0.[33] William Fitzhugh in 1683 apparently thought he could get better prices than these, for he offered to buy slaves worth up to 50,000 pounds of tobacco from a New Englander, at prices ranging from 3,000 pounds (for children aged seven to eleven) to 5,000 pounds (for men and women aged fifteen to twenty-four). Tobacco at this time was generally valued at 10 shillings per hundred pounds, so Fitzhugh's top price was equal to £25.[34]

There is no way of telling how many slaves were brought to Virginia by interlopers and how many came legally from Barbados. Edmund Jennings, inquiring into the subject in 1708, was told by

[31] H. R. McIlwaine, ed., *Journals of the House of Burgesses of Virginia, 1695 . . . 1702* (Richmond, 1913), 175.
[32] See chap. 7, note 26.   [34] Davis, *Fitzhugh*, 127.
[33] C.O. 5/1308, No. 9.

"some ancient Inhabitants conversant in that Trade . . . that before the year 1680 what negros were brought to Virginia were imported generally from Barbados." [35] It may be that many continued to come by that route. Although the Royal African Company had promised at its founding in 1672 to supply Virginia and Maryland as well as the islands, it sent only a few shiploads before the end of the century. During the 1670s somewhat more than 1,000 may have been landed, and in the 1680s perhaps another 1,000 or 1,500—if the seven or eight captains instructed to go to Virginia actually went there. In the 1690s, however, a list of fifty-four ships sent out between October 25, 1693, and February 15, 1698/9, shows only one consigned to Virginia. [36]

The company's figures for slaves sent to Virginia do not comport with hints in the colony records of the rate of importation. Up until 1699 slaves, like other immigrants, carried a headright worth fifty acres of land, and a count of slaves mentioned in patents for land shows fewer for the 1670s (421) and 1680s (629) than the numbers presumably carried by the company alone, but the number for the 1690s, when the company probably delivered few, if any, was 1,847. [37] It is impossible to say whether the discrepancies mean that the company records are unreliable or that many Virginians waited until the 1690s to claim land with the headrights of slaves they had imported in the 1670s and 1680s.

The extent to which slaves were replacing servants during the last decades of the century can be estimated with more assurance from the lists of tithables for Surry, the only county where the names of all the tithables survive (rather than the mere number of tithables per household). Of Surry tithables who belonged to another man's household, slaves amounted to 20 percent in 1674, 33 percent in 1686, 48 percent in 1694, and 48 percent in 1703. [38] Surry, as we have seen, was one of the poorer regions of Virginia. In the rich counties on the York the proportion must have been larger. To

[35] Donnan, *Documents*, IV, 89.

[36] C.O. 1/31, f.32; C.O. 1/34, f.109; Donnan, *Documents*, IV, 55; T. 70/61, pp. 3–4, 6, 30, 57, 83, 165–70.

[37] Craven, *White, Red, and Black*, 86. It is possible that part of the slaves brought by the company in the 1670s and 1680s wound up in Maryland.

[38] Surry II, 62–64; Surry III, 67–69; Surry V, 21–23, 287–90. Since some of the tithables listed in other men's households were boarders, these percentages can be considered low.

achieve such a large slave labor force by the end of the seventeenth century Virginians must have been buying at least as many slaves from interlopers and from Barbados as they got from the Royal African Company. And with the end of the company monopoly in 1698, private traders immediately began to bring many more.

If half the labor force was already enslaved by the end of the seventeenth century, much more than half must have been in that position by 1708, for official records show that in the preceding ten years 5,928 slaves were brought by private traders and 679 by the company.[39] And the company's papers testify to a great demand for slaves that raised the Virginia price far enough above the West Indies price to outweigh the costs of the longer voyage. The company's letters to captains in 1701 began advising them to head for Virginia rather than Jamaica, if they could get there in May, June, or July when the demand was greatest.[40] In 1704 they noted that Virginians were paying £30 to £35 a head as against £23 to £27 in Jamaica.[41]

But the planters in Virginia, as in the West Indies, were more eager to buy slaves than to pay for them. During the first five years of the new century, they overextended their credit, and the company was faced with a multitude of protested bills of exchange.[42] By 1705 the Virginia assembly was so disturbed by the rising indebtedness that it tried to slow down the traffic, dropping an import duty on servants while retaining one on slaves.[43] But by then the

[39] Donnan, *Documents*, 172–73.   [40] T. 70/58, Public Record Office.

[41] To Charles Chaplin et al., Dec. 7, 1704. *Ibid.*

[42] To Gavin Corbin (the company's agent in Virginia), April 26, May 15, 1705; Feb. 20, 1705/6; March 27, May 27, Sept. 30, Nov. 18, 1707; Feb. 24, April 9, June 4, 1709; March 23, April 18, 1710; Aug. 23, 1711. T. 70/58. With their letters the company returned the protested bills of exchange, numbering 274.

[43] Hening, III, 235. The import duty may also have been aimed at the old goal of reducing tobacco production (and raising prices) by reducing the growth of the labor force. And some planters who had bought large numbers of slaves may have favored it in order to increase the value of the slaves they had acquired. See Jones, *Present State of Virginia*, 132; Donnan, *Documents*, IV, 145, 151–52. The history of import duties on slaves in eighteenth-century Virginia is complex. See especially Thad W. Tate, Jr., *The Negro in Eighteenth-Century Williamsburg* (Charlottesville, 1965), 29–33; John M. Hemphill, "Virginia and the English Commercial System, 1689–1733" (unpublished doctoral dissertation, Princeton University, 1964), 34–35, 65–66, 88–91; and Darold D. Wax, "Negro Import Duties in Colonial Virginia," *VMHB*, LXXIX (1971), 29–44.

conversion to slave labor had already been made. According to Edmund Jennings, writing in 1708, virtually no white servants had been imported in the preceding six years.[44] This was not the end of white servitude in Virginia, but henceforth white servants were as much the exception in the tobacco fields as slaves had been earlier. Between 1708 and 1750 Virginia recorded the entry of 38,418 slaves into the colony.[45]

Virginia had developed her plantation system without slaves, and slavery introduced no novelties to methods of production. Though no seventeenth-century plantation had a work force as large as that owned by some eighteenth-century planters, the mode of operation was the same. The seventeenth-century plantation already had its separate quartering house or houses for the servants. Their labor was already supervised in groups of eight or ten by an overseer. They were already subject to "correction" by the whip. They were already often underfed and underclothed. Their masters already lived in fear of their rebelling. But no servant rebellion in Virginia ever got off the ground.

The plantation system operated by servants worked. It made many Virginians rich and England's merchants and kings richer. But it had one insuperable disadvantage. Every year it poured a host of new freemen into a society where the opportunities for advancement were limited. The freedmen were Virginia's dangerous men. They erupted in 1676 in the largest rebellion known in any American colony before the Revolution, and in 1682 they carried even the plant-cutting rebellion further than any servant rebellion had ever gone. The substitution of slaves for servants gradually eased and eventually ended the threat that the freedmen posed: as the annual number of imported servants dropped, so did the number of men turning free.

The planters who bought slaves instead of servants did not do so with any apparent consciousness of the social stability to be gained thereby. Indeed, insofar as Virginians expressed themselves on the subject of slavery, they feared that it would magnify the danger of insurrection in the colony. They often blamed and pitied themselves for taking into their families men and women who had every reason to hate them. William Byrd told the Earl of Egmont

---

[44] C.O. 5/1316, f.53.
[45] *Historical Statistics of the United States*, 769; Donnan, *Documents* IV, 175–220.

in July, 1736, that "in case there shoud arise a Man of desperate cour-
age amongst us, exasperated by a desperate fortune, he might with
more advantage than Cataline kindle a Servile War," and make
Virginia's broad rivers run with blood.[46] But the danger never ma-
terialized. From time to time the planters were alarmed by the discovery of a conspiracy among the slaves; but, as had happened earlier when servants plotted rebellion, some conspirator always leaked
the plan in time to spoil it. No white person was killed in a slave
rebellion in colonial Virginia.[47] Slaves proved, in fact, less dangerous
than free or semi-free laborers. They had none of the rising expectations that have so often prompted rebellion in human history.
They were not armed and did not have to be armed. They were
without hope and did not have to be given hope. William Byrd himself probably did not take the danger from them seriously. Only
seven months before his letter to Egmont, he assured Peter Beckford of Jamaica that "our negroes are not so numerous or so en-
terprizeing as to give us any apprehention or uneasiness." [48]

With slavery Virginians could exceed all their previous efforts
to maximize productivity. In the first half of the century, as they
sought to bring stability to their volatile society, they had identified
work as wealth, time as money, but there were limits to the amount
of both work and time that could be extracted from a servant.
There was no limit to the work or time that a master could command from his slaves, beyond his need to allow them enough for
eating and sleeping to enable them to keep working. Even on that
he might skimp. Robert Carter of Nomini Hall, accounted a humane
man, made it a policy to give his slaves less food than they needed
and required them to fill out their diet by keeping chickens and by
working Sundays in small gardens attached to their cabins. Their
cabins, too, he made them build and repair on Sundays.[49] Carter's

---

[46] *Ibid.*, 131–32.

[47] Tate, *Negro in Williamsburg*, 200–208. For examples of conspiracies
see *WMQ*, 1st ser., X (1901–2), 178; *Executive Journals*, I, 86–87, 510–11;
III, 234–36. Gerald W. Mullin, *Flight and Rebellion: Slave Resistance in
Eighteenth-Century Virginia* (New York, 1972), analyzes the forms of
resistance offered by slaves and concludes that it was the most "acculturated"
slaves who proved most rebellious. One might say, in other words, that the
more slaves came to resemble the indigent freemen whom they displaced,
the more dangerous they became.

[48] *VMHB*, XXXVI (1928), 122.

[49] Hunter D. Farish, ed., *Journal and Letters of Philip Vickers Fithian*
(Williamsburg, 1957; Charlottesville, 1968), 38, 96, 202–3.

uncle, Landon Carter of Sabine Hall, made his slaves buy part of their own clothes out of the proceeds of what they grew in their gardens.[50]

Demographically, too, the conversion to slavery enhanced Virginia's capacity for maximum productivity. Earlier the heavy concentration in the population of men of working age had been achieved by the small number of women and children among the immigrants and by the heavy mortality. But with women outliving men, the segment of women and their children grew; and as mortality declined the segment of men beyond working age grew. There was, in other words, an increase in the non-productive proportion of the population. Slavery made possible the restoration and maintenance of a highly productive population. Masters had no hesitation about putting slave women to work in the tobacco fields, although servant women were not normally so employed. And they probably made slave children start work earlier than free children did.[51] There was no need to keep them from work for purposes of education. Nor was it necessary to divert productive energy to the support of ministers for spiritual guidance to them and their parents. The slave population could thus be more productive than a free population with the same age and sex structure would have been. It could also be more reproductive than a free population that grew mainly from the importation of servants, because slave traders generally carried about two women for every three men,[52] a larger proportion of women by far than had been the case with servants. Slave women while employed in tobacco could still raise children and thus contribute to the growth of the productive proportion of the population. Moreover, the children became the property of the master. Thus slaves offered the planter a way of disposing his profits that combined the advantages of cattle and of servants, and these had always been the most attractive investments in Virginia.

The only obvious disadvantage that slavery presented to Virginia masters was a simple one: slaves had no incentive to work. The difference, however, between the incentive of a slave and that of a servant bound for a term of years was not great. The servant had

[50] Landon Carter, *Diary*, Jack P. Greene, ed., (Charlottesville, 1965), I, 484.

[51] From 1680 to 1705 imported Negro children were tithable at the age of twelve and imported "Christian servants" at the age of fourteen. In 1705 the age was changed to sixteen for both. Hening, II, 479–80; III, 258–59.

[52] Davies, *Royal African Company*, 299.

already received his reward in the form of the ocean passage which he, unlike the slave, had been so eager to make that he was willing to bind his labor for a term of years for it. Having received his payment in advance, he could not be compelled by threats of withholding it. Virginia masters had accordingly been obliged to make freer use of the lash than had been common in England. Before they obtained slaves, they had already had practice in extracting work from the unwilling. Yet there was a difference. If a servant failed to perform consistently or ran away, if he damaged his master's property either by omission or commission, the master could get the courts to extend the term of his servitude. That recourse was not open to the slaveowner. If the servant had received his reward in advance, the slave had received the ultimate punishment in advance: his term had already been extended.

Masters therefore needed some substitute for the extended term, some sanction to protect themselves against the stubbornness of those whom conventional "correction" did not reach. Their first attempt in this direction was an act, passed in 1661, that is sometimes cited as the first official recognition of slavery in Virginia. In it the assembly tried to handle the most common form of servile intractability, by making a servant who ran away with a slave responsible for the loss incurred to the master by the absence of the slave. The law read, "That in case any English servant shall run away in company with any negroes who are incapable of makeing satisfaction by addition of time, *Bee it enacted* that the English so running away in company with them shall serve for the time of the said negroes absence as they are to do for their owne by a former act [the act requiring extra service for double the length of the absence]." [53]

Though this measure tells us something about the relationship between servants and slaves in these early years, it was a deterrent more to servants than to slaves. And it did nothing for the master who could not get what he considered an adequate amount of work out of his slave by the methods that had sufficed for servants. One way might have been to offer rewards, to hold out the carrot rather than the stick. A few masters tried this in the early years, as we have seen, offering slaves freedom in return for working hard for a few years, or assigning them plots of land and allowing them time to grow tobacco or corn crops for themselves. [54] But to offer rewards of this kind was to lose the whole advantage of slavery. In the end,

[53] Hening, II, 26.   [54] See above, chap. 7, pp. 154–57.

Virginians had to face the fact that masters of slaves must inflict pain at a higher level than masters of servants. Slaves could not be made to work for fear of losing liberty, so they had to be made to fear for their lives. Not that any master wanted to lose his slave by killing him, but in order to get an equal or greater amount of work, it was necessary to beat slaves harder than servants, so hard, in fact, that there was a much larger chance of killing them than had been the case with servants. Unless a master could correct his slaves in this way without running afoul of the law if he misjudged the weight of his blows, slaveowning would be legally hazardous. So in 1669 the assembly faced the facts and passed an act that dealt with them forthrightly:

> *An act about the casuall killing of slaves.*
>
> Whereas the only law in force for the punishment of refractory servants resisting their master, mistris or overseer cannot be inflicted upon negroes [because the punishment was extension of time], nor the obstinacy of many of them by other than violent meanes supprest, *Be it enacted and declared by this grand assembly,* if any slave resist his master (or other by his masters order correcting him) and by the extremity of the correction should chance to die, that his death shall not be accompted Felony, but the master (or that other person appointed by the master to punish him) be acquit from molestation, since it cannot be presumed that prepensed malice (which alone makes murther Felony) should induce any man to destroy his own estate.[55]

With this act already on the books in 1669, Virginia was prepared to make the most of slavery when slaves began to arrive in quantity. Later legislation only extended the principles here recognized, that correction of slaves might legally be carried to the point of killing them. The most important extensions had to do with runaways. As the numbers of slaves increased and the plantation quarters were placed farther from the house of the master, runaway slaves would frequently hide out in the woods, visiting the quarters by night, where their friends or families would shelter and share food with them. To eliminate this problem, the assembly provided that the names of such outlying slaves should be proclaimed at the door of every church in the county, after divine worship, and then if the runaways did not turn themselves in, it would "be lawful for any person or persons whatsoever, to kill and destroy such slaves by such

[55] Hening, II, 270.

ways and means as he, she, or they shall think fit, without accusation or impeachment of any crime for the same." [56] The public would compensate the master for the loss of slaves thus killed. If one was captured alive, the owner might apply to the county court "to order such punishment to the said slave, either by dismembring, or any other way, not touching his life, as they in their discretion shall think fit, for the reclaiming any such incorrigible slave, and terrifying others from the like practices." [57]

This was no idle threat. Though the words of the law—"reclaiming," "dismembering," "discretion"—seem to soften the shock, the law authorizes not merely an open season on outlying slaves, but also the deliberate maiming of captured slaves, by judicial order. One gets a glimpse of the law in action in the records of the Lancaster County court for March 10, 1707/8:

> Robert Carter Esq. Complaining to this Court against two Incorrigible negroes of his named Bambarra Harry and Dinah and praying the order of this Court for punishing the said Negroes by dismembring them It is therefore ordered That for the better reclaiming the said negroes and deterring others from ill practices That the said Robert Carter Esq. have full power according to Law to dismember the said negroes or Either of them by cutting of[f] their toes." [58]

Such was the price of slavery, and Virginia masters were prepared to pay it. In order to get work out of men and women who had nothing to gain but absence of pain, you had to be willing to beat, maim, and kill. And society had to be ready to back you even to the point of footing the bill for the property you killed.

It has been possible thus far to describe Virginia's conversion to slavery without mentioning race. It has required a little restraint to do so, but only a little, because the actions that produced slavery in

[56] Hening, III, 460 (1705). This superseded a law passed in 1680 empowering "persons that shall by lawful authority be imployed to aprehend" an outlying Negro to kill him if he resisted. Hening, II, 482.

[57] Hening, III, 460–61. In 1723 the law was expanded to allow the dismemberment of any slave "notoriously guilty of going abroad in the night, or running away and lying out, and cannot be reclaimed from such disorderly courses." At the same time it was specified that no one was to be prosecuted for the death of a slave occurring as a result of dismemberment or correction. Hening, IV, 132–33.

[58] Lancaster VIII, 185. This Robert Carter was the grandfather of Robert Carter of Nomini Hall, mentioned above.

Virginia, the individual purchase of slaves instead of servants, and the public protection of masters in their coercion of unwilling labor, had no necessary connection with race. Virginians did not enslave the persons brought there by the Royal African Company or by the private traders. The only decision that Virginians had to make was to keep them as slaves. Keeping them as slaves did require some decisions about what masters could legally do to make them work. But such decisions did not necessarily relate to race.

Or did they? As one reads the record of the Lancaster court authorizing Robert Carter to chop off the toes of his slaves, one begins to wonder. Would the court, could the court, could the general assembly have authorized such a punishment for an incorrigible English servant? It seems unlikely that the English government would have allowed it. But Virginians could be confident that England would condone their slave laws, even though those laws were contrary to the laws of England.

The English government had considered the problem in 1679, when presented with the laws of Barbados, in which masters were similarly authorized to inflict punishment that would not have been allowed by English law. A legal adviser, upon reviewing the laws for the Lords of Trade, found that he could approve them, because, he said "although Negros in that Island are punishable in a different and more severe manner than other Subjects are for Offences of the like nature; yet I humbly conceive that the Laws there concerning Negros are reasonable Laws, for by reason of their numbers they become dangerous, and being a brutish sort of People and reckoned as goods and chattels in that Island, it is of necessity or at least convenient to have Laws for the Government of them different from the Laws of England, to prevent the great mischief that otherwise may happen to the Planters and Inhabitants in that Island." [59]

It was not necessary to extend the rights of Englishmen to Africans, because Africans were "a brutish sort of people." And because they were "brutish" it was necessary "or at least convenient" to kill or maim them in order to make them work.

The killing and maiming of slaves was not common in Virginia. Incidents like Robert Carter's application to dismember his two slaves are rare in the records. But it is hard to read in diaries and letters of the everyday beating of slaves without feeling that the casual, matter-of-fact acceptance of it is related to a feeling on the

[59] C.O. 1/45, f.138.

part of masters that they were dealing with "a brutish sort of people." Thomas Jones, of Williamsburg, was almost affectionate about it in writing his wife, away on a visit, about her household slaves. Daphne and Nancy were doing well, "But Juliet is the same still, tho I do assure you she has not wanted correction very often. I chear'd her with thirty lashes a Saturday last and as many more a Tuesday again and today I hear she's sick." [60]

Possibly a master could have written thus about a white maidservant. Certainly there are many instances of servants being severely beaten, even to death. But whether or not race was a necessary ingredient of slavery, it *was* an ingredient. If slavery might have come to Virginia without racism, it did not. The only slaves in Virginia belonged to alien races from the English. And the new social order that Virginians created after they changed to slave labor was determined as much by race as by slavery.

[60] Oct. 22, 1736. *VMHB*, XXVI (1918), 285.

16

TOWARD RACISM

Virginia slaves were introduced into a system of production that was already in working order. The substitution of slaves for servants probably increased the productivity and almost certainly increased the profitability of the plantation system. But slavery required new methods of disciplining the labor force, methods that were linked to racial contempt. If we are to understand that contempt and the role it played in the history of Virginia—and I think in American history—we must probe not only the differences but also the resemblances between servants and slaves in the plantation system and in the consciousness of those who ran it.

Ideally, from the point of view of the master, slavery should have made it possible to turn the slave's every waking hour to the master's profit. In an industrial society, where it is possible to engage in productive tasks at any time, it is tempting to think of masters thus directing their slaves. But absolute power did not in itself make for continuous employment in a pre-industrial society. We have already seen that sixteenth-century Englishmen were often idle, if only because there were times when nothing could be done. The tobacco plantation probably made fuller use of its workers' time than previous English agricultural enterprises had. But even on a plantation it was simply not possible to employ either servants or slaves usefully every day of the year.

Rain halted work on a Virginia plantation just as it did on any English farm. And for days after a rain the ground might be too heavy to hoe without damage to the soil or the crop. Freezing weather similarly closed down most activities. Sometimes weather that precluded field work might permit cutting wood, building fences, or scouring ditches. But often the workers were left without work. Landon Carter, who kept the most complete record we have of the day-to-day operations of a Virginia plantation, and who strove always to show a profit, repeatedly bemoaned the idleness imposed by the weather. "No working yesterday nor today," he writes, or "Not one day as yet from the 23 January to this day that the earth could be touched with hoe, spade or plow, that is 11 days together:" or "The Skye very heavy and the air very Cold . . . We can do no kind of work to any advantage." [1]

Landon Carter was probably not a typical Virginia planter. The very fact that he kept so voluminous a record of his activities suggests that he was not. And other planters, one at least hopes, were not as egotistical. Carter's diaries are a continuous demonstration that whatever happened he was right and everyone around him wrong. He may have been atypical also in the great variety of crops that he tried to grow in addition to corn and tobacco. But all Virginia planters went in for some diversity. Nearly all planted corn, kept cattle and hogs and sometimes sheep. Carter's idiosyncrasies were mainly of a sort that would have magnified the amount of work he expected from his slaves. He used his systematic record keeping, as Robert Loder had done in the preceding century in England, to step up the productivity of his laborers. He had each slave tend twice as many plants as other masters required.[2] And he stuck as far as possible to the hoe when other Virginians were turning to the plow, because, he said, "Carts and plows only serve to make Overseers and people extremely lazy and it is a certain truth that wherever they are in great abundance there is the least plantation work done there for both Overseers and Negroes imagine this or that work will be quickly done with the plows and Carts and of course are very little solicitous to do their proper parts of the business." [3] If Carter was atypical, it was not in demanding less of his slaves. If he had to let them loaf for days at a time, probably other planters did too.

Neither the slave's life nor the servant's was one endless round

[1] Diary, I, 158, 200, 253. Cf. Hartwell, Blair, and Chilton, Present State of Virginia, 9; Jones, Present State of Virginia, 76, says ". . . in wet or cold weather there is little occasion for their working in the fields, in which few will let them be abroad, lest by this means they get sick or die, which would prove a great loss to their owners, ..." John Hammond had written in 1656 that in Virginia servants did no work "all winter except dressing their own victuals and making of fires." Leah and Rachel, Force, Tracts, III, No. 14, p. 12.

[2] Carter, Diary, I, 448.   [3] Ibid., 386.

of toil, because it could not be. And when he was not working, the slave enjoyed one advantage over the servant: since the planters bought slave women as well as men, he could have some sort of family life. True, it could be broken any time at the whim of his master. But the slave, like the servant, in spite of his legal impotence was not entirely without the means of magnifying a part of his life that he could call his own. Like the servant he could find ways of avoiding work even on days when the weather was fair. In fact, his attitude toward work and his success in evading it were so much like that of the servant that Landon Carter's complaints about his lazy, unfaithful slaves sound for all the world like Robert Loder's tirades against his lazy, unfaithful servants.[4]

A favorite ruse was to feign sickness, even though this was a peculiarly hazardous one on Carter's plantation. Carter fancied himself a physician and seems to have been obsessed with an urge to cleanse the digestive tract of every person who came near him, by purges, emetics, and enemas administered in heroic proportions. At the slightest complaint he would lay down a barrage of these supposed remedies that left the victim half dead for several days, after which Carter would congratulate himself on his victory over the forces of bile. In spite of these ministrations—or possibly as a long-term result of them—Carter's slaves were continually visited by sickness, but never, he noted, on Sundays, when Virginia custom freed them from field work anyhow.[5]

Carter frequently found it necessary to entrust tasks to slaves without the supervision of an overseer or foreman. Then he would record how poorly the job had been done or how inordinately long it took. Old men slept and boys played, when the master's eye was not upon them. "Where the General is absent," he observed, "Idleness is Preferred to all business." Everywhere he went he saw evidence of "the same damned idleness." [6] Like Robert Loder he kept track of how much his people got done in a day, how many rows of corn they hilled, how many tobacco plants they topped or wormed. That way he could catch the shirkers and have them whipped. After recording how he had stepped up the output of his threshers, he noted, in words that echoed Loder, "This I minute down to shew that things are often judged impossible when obstinacy alone is the Cause of it." [7]

---

[4] For examples, I, 147, 159, 177, 295, 300, 302, 303, 347, 355.
[5] P. 174.   [6] Pp. 235, 417, 568.   [7] P. 138.

But there was a limit to the speedup he could achieve even under close supervision. He observed that "negroes tyre with the Continuance of the same work," and he resolved to vary their tasks by putting larger numbers to work on lengthy jobs so that they might be done faster and get on to something fresh.[8] In a hot spell in July he admitted, "I can't make my people work or do anything."[9] In 1757, when he began to reap his first corn crop, he had "but very few reapers, so many Complaining of last year's reaping."[10]

Such observations suggest that work could not always be got from men simply by use of the lash. Sometimes "correction" was actually counterproductive. When Carter's gardener disobeyed his instructions repeatedly and he struck the man across the shoulders with a cane ("which did not raise the least swelling"), the man refused to get up the next morning and would do nothing. Two weeks later when Carter gave him "one small rap" across the shoulder, he feigned total paralysis of his arm and could scarcely stand up. This time Carter discovered that the reason he could not stand was that he was drunk.[11] Indeed, drunkenness was a not uncommon problem on Carter's plantation. Since slaves were not furnished with liquor except at Christmas, this fact in itself suggests that they enjoyed a greater degree of independence than the laws allowed or their master would have liked.

What all these instances add up to is that the daily life of a slave differed from that of a servant less drastically than at first sight it appears to have. Slaves were the labor force of a plantation much as servants had been, and what is more important for an understanding of the role of race, masters, initially at least, perceived slaves in much the same way they had always perceived servants. Both displayed the same attitudes and habits: they were shiftless, irresponsible, unfaithful, ungrateful, dishonest; they got drunk whenever possible; they did not work hard enough or regularly enough.

These were the complaints that masters in every age have made against servants. And they were precisely the complaints that English economists and statesmen were making against the English poor during the years when slavery was becoming the prevailing form of labor in Virginia. As we have earlier observed, English attitudes toward the supposedly surplus population of the island changed markedly during the course of the seventeenth century. By the third quarter it was becoming a commonplace that the riches of

[8] P. 147.   [9] P. 274.   [10] P. 161.   [11] Pp. 369, 378.

a country lay in the multitude of its people, because labor was the source of wealth. England, with a seeming abundance of people, especially in and around London, should have been rich. But Englishmen could not help seeing how much richer the Dutch had become with fewer people. What was the reason for England's failure to profit by her masses? The answer, offered in a chorus, was the "exacting humour and evil disposition," the perversity, the stubborn, immoral idleness of England's poor.[12]

Virginia's conversion to slave labor and the use of slaves in other American colonies must be viewed in the context of contemporary English attitudes toward the poor and schemes for putting them to work. According to the men who wrestled with the problem of England's poor, half the English population consisted of wage earners, and all of them would rather drink than eat and rather starve than work. Worse than the wage earners were those who had never learned any trade but begging and stealing. In 1717 Lawrence Braddon estimated that there were a million and a half of them, no more than a fifth of whom were incapable of labor.[13] With so many needlessly idle hands England must be the laughingstock of Europe because of "the multitudes of People which in England Cheat, Roar, Rob, Hang, Beg, Cant, Pine, and Perish; which otherwise might help to encrease and maintain the Wealth and strength of these Kingdomes." [14]

Almost everything Englishmen said about their employed and unemployed poor we have already seen in the Virginians' similar complaints about their servants, slaves, and indigent freedmen. The English poor were "vicious, idle, dissolute." They were addicted to "Laziness, Drunkenness, Debauches, and almost every Kind of Vice," to "mutinous and indecent Discourses." They were "Miserable, Diseased, Ignorant, Idle, Seditious and (otherwise) vicious." [15]

[12] Thomas Manley, *Usury at Six per Cent Examined* (London, 1669), 19. For similar expressions see below and also references in chap. 9, note 28. The best secondary studies are Dorothy Marshall, *The English Poor in the Eighteenth Century* (London, 1926), and Furniss, *Position of the Laborer.*

[13] *An Abstract of the Draught of a Bill for Relieving, Reforming, and Employing the Poor* [London, 1717], ix.

[14] Coke, *Discourse of Trade,* 16.

[15] Furniss, *Position of the Laborer,* 128–30; *An Enquiry into the Causes of the Encrease and Miseries of the Poor of England* (London, 1738), 9; R. D., *Bread for the Poor* (Exeter, 1698), 4; *The Regular Government and Judicious Employment of the Poor* (London, 1721), introduction.

Virginia had originally been thought of as a receptacle for these wretches; but as the idea came to prevail that people are or ought to be a source of wealth, the problem in England, as in Virginia, was to hold them down and extract the maximum labor from them.

For Englishmen, as for Virginians, some kind of involuntary servitude seemed a possible solution to the problem. England had taken a step in this direction under Elizabeth when Parliament in 1576 provided for the building of "houses of correction" in which beggars could be put to work.[16] The motives at that time had been to place the beggars where they could not steal and also to lower the danger of insurrection. During the seventeenth century Europeans took a similar course but on a larger scale. In a movement that Michel Foucault has called "the great confinement," they everywhere founded institutions in which the sick, the criminal, and the poor were indiscriminately taken in charge. The purpose was not merely to get them out of the way but to make them contribute what they could to the national wealth. Imprisonment, instead of being a temporary matter, preliminary to trial, became the mode of extracting work from the criminal, the insane, and the poor alike. Indeed, crime and insanity seemed only extreme forms of the vice and ignorance that distinguished the poor from their betters. Work was the proper cure for all, and it could best be administered by incarceration.[17]

After 1660 the English too were caught up in these larger aspects of getting work from the poor and revived their interest in houses of correction. Workhouses (as they were now called) were still desirable for the old reasons, but the emphasis now was on making the poor add to the nation's wealth by producing manufactures for export. If private employers could not keep the population at work, the government should do it. Proposals sprang up on all sides for government-sponsored workhouses, where the poor could be

[16] 18 Elizabeth I, c. 3, Tawney and Power, *Tudor Economic Documents*, II, 331-34.

[17] Michel Foucault, *Madness and Civilization: A History of Insanity in the Age of Reason* (New York, 1965), 38-65; George Rosen, *Madness in Society* (New York, 1969, Torchbook ed.), 151-71; Nigel Walker, *Crime and Insanity in England*, vol. I, *The Historical Perspective* (Edinburgh, 1968), 43-44; George Rusche and Otto Kirchheimer, *Punishment and Social Structure* (New York, 1939), 63-71; E. J. Hundert, "History, Psychology, and the Study of Deviant Behavior," *Journal of Interdisciplinary History*, II (1972), 453-72. I am indebted to Professor Hundert for valuable suggestions.

supplied at public expense with flax, hemp, and wool for spinning and where they could be kept forcibly at the job.[18]

The proponents of workhouses generally saw them as educational institutions in which the poor, and especially the children of the poor, would learn habits of work. And like all advocates of education they expected great things. Sir Mathew Hale thought that workhouses would bring the poor "and their children after them into a Regular, Orderly and Industrious course of life, which will be as natural to them as now Idleness, and Begging, and Theeving is." [19] But the kind of education envisaged seems to have had little to do with the work ethic that we associate with the rise of modern capitalism and little to do with learning anything except work. The idea was to "inure" children to work, get them so used to it at an early age that when they grew older they would be unable to think of anything else. Sir William Temple would have set them to work at four years, John Locke at three.[20] Thomas Firmin, who established a scheme for employing the poor in their own homes as well as in workhouses, had a more liberal proposal than most. He was in favor of teaching poor children to read but no more than that. They should be set to work at seven years, for there was no point, after they reached that age, in having them "poring upon a Book." [21]

The English economists tended to agree with Governor Berkeley of Virginia that learning was a dangerous thing. It bred not only sedition but laziness if acquired by the children of the poor, "for few that have once learnt to Write and Read, but either their Parents, or themselves, are apt to think, that they are fit for some Preferment,

[18] Furniss, *Position of the Laborer*, 84–95; Marshall, *English Poor*, 127–32; Sir Matthew Hale, *A Discourse Touching Provision for the Poor* (London, 1683), 25–30; Henry Pollexfen, *A Discourse of Trade and Coyn* (London, 1697), 49; Charles Davenant, *An Essay on the East India Trade* (London, 1696), 27; Josiah Child, *A New Discourse of Trade* (London, 1693), 55–79.

[19] Hale, *Discourse*, 32–33.

[20] Furniss, *Position of the Laborer*, 114–15; C. R. MacPherson, *The Political Theory of Possessive Individualism* (Oxford, 1962), 221–24; H. R. Fox Bourne, *The Life of John Locke* (London, 1876), II, 377–90; cf. E. J. Hundert, "The Making of Homo Faber: John Locke between Ideology and History," *Journal of the History of Ideas*, XXXIII (1972), 3–22.

[21] Thomas Firmin, *Some Proposals for Imploying of the Poor* (London, 1672), 5–10. Pollexfen also proposed seven as the age for starting work. *Discourse of Trade and Coyn*, 54.

and in order to it, despise all Labouring Imployments and live Idle, rather than disparage themselves by Work." [22] By the next century Bernard Mandeville maintained that regular schooling was only another form of idleness for the poor.[23]

Whether from regular schooling or from lack of it, the children of the poor continued to distress their keepers. The failure of the efforts to inure them to work is evident in the repetition throughout the next century of the same contemptuous complaints about the fecklessness of laborers and the need to overcome "their obstinate Wills, and their encroaching sluggish intemperate Bents." [24] It occurred to a few people that it might be possible to entice the poor into greater zeal for work by making them less poor, by paying them higher wages or by lowering the price of food. But most of the self-appointed economists were convinced that laborers would work only when hungry. Higher wages or cheaper food would only mean more time lost in drunkenness.[25] "Every one but an idiot knows,"

[22] Pollexfen, *Discourse of Trade and Coyn*, 48; see also John Bellers, *Proposals for Raising a Colledge of Industry*, 16; *Enquiry into the Causes of the Encrease and Miseries of the Poor*, 61; Furniss, *Position of the Laborer*, 148–50.

[23] Marshall, *English Poor*, 24. The kind of education favored by the labor reformers of the late seventeenth and early eighteenth centuries is most vividly described by one of them, Andrew Yarranton, who had visited Saxony and there discovered the ideal form of school for the poor. He described it for the emulation of Englishmen: "First, There is a large Room, and in the middle thereof a little Box like a Pulpit. Secondly, There are Benches built round about the Room as they are in our Playhouses; upon the Benches sit about two hundred Children spinning, and in the Box in the middle of the Room sits the Grand Mistress with a long white Wand in her hand. If she observes any of them idle, she reaches them a tap; but if that will not do, she rings a Bell which by a little Cord is fixt to the Box, and out comes a Woman; she then points to the Offender, and she is taken away into another Room and chastised. And all this is done without one word speaking. And I believe this way of ordering the young Women in Germany is one great cause that the German Women have so little of the twit twat. And it is clear, that the less there is of speaking, the more there may be of working." Yarranton, *England's Improvement by Sea and Land*, 45–46.

[24] *The Manufacturer's Plea for the Bounty on Corn at Exportation* (London, 1754), 15.

[25] *Ibid.*, passim; Coke, *Discourse of Trade*, 14–15; Manley, *Usury at Six per Cent*, 23–26; Joshua Gee, *The Trade and Navigation of Great Britain Considered* (London, 1729), 38; Furniss, *Position of the Laborer*, 117–56; N. G. Pauling, "The Employment Problem in Pre-Classical English

said Arthur Young, "that the lower classes must be kept poor, or they will never be industrious." [26]

The object, then, was not the elimination of poverty but the discipline of the poor. In spite of the contempt in which they were held, there was no suggestion that their numbers should be reduced. Just as the Virginia planter who deplored the laziness of his slaves continued to buy more and encouraged the multiplication of those he had, so the English authors advocated acts to facilitate the naturalization of immigrants, especially poor immigrants, as well as acts to promote early marriage among the poor.[27]

In practice the discipline of the poor in England stopped short of actual enslavement. Parliament did not even discuss a motion by one of its members in 1670 "that as an expedient to make servants more tractable we might bring into this kingdom the use of Negro slaves." [28] And neither the workhouse nor its successor, the factory, enslaved its occupants, at least in any legal sense. But they can be seen as a step in that direction, and there were plenty of voices outside Parliament crying for the next step. Bishop Berkeley, who carried John Locke's epistemology a step further, also made an advance in his social philosophy by proposing that "sturdy beggars . . . be seized and made slaves to the public for a term of years." [29] James Burgh, another champion of reform, wanted a set of press gangs "to seize all idle and disorderly persons, who have been three times complained of before a magistrate, and to set them to work during a certain time, for the benefit of great trading, or manufacturing companies." [30] Francis Hutcheson, the moral philosopher, thought that perpetual slavery should be "the ordinary punishment of such idle vagrants as, after proper admonitions and tryals of temporary servi-

---

Economic Thought," *The Economic Record*, XXVII (1951), 52–65; E. P. Thompson, "Time, Work-Discipline, and Industrial Capitalism"; Keith Thomas, "Work and Leisure in Pre-Industrial Society," *Past and Present*, No. 29 (1964), 50–66; Sidney Pollard, "Factory Discipline in the Industrial Revolution," *Economic History Review*, 2nd ser., XVI (1963), 254–71.

[26] E. P. Thompson, *The Making of the English Working Class* (New York, 1963, Vintage Books), 358.

[27] Bellers, *Proposals*, 2; Pollexfen, *Discourse of Trade and Coyn*, 53; Braddon, *Abstract*, xiv–xv; Coke, *Discourse of Trade*, passim; Rusche and Kirchheimer, *Punishment and Social Structure*, 28.

[28] Basil D. Henning, ed., *The Parliamentary Diary of Sir Edward Dering, 1670–1673* (New Haven, 1940), 33.

[29] Tawney, *Religion and the Rise of Capitalism*, 270.

[30] *Political Disquisitions* (London, 1774–75), III, 220–21.

tude, cannot be engaged to support themselves and their families by any useful labours." [31]

The most comprehensive proposal came from Andrew Fletcher of Saltoun, a Scottish prophet of the Enlightenment. Fletcher attacked the Christian church not only for having promoted the abolition of slavery in ancient times but also for having perpetuated the idleness of the freedmen thus turned loose on society. The Church by setting up hospitals and almshouses had enabled men through the succeeding centuries to live without work. As a result, Fletcher argued, his native Scotland was burdened with 200,000 idle rogues, who roamed the country, drinking, cursing, fighting, robbing, and murdering. For a remedy he proposed that they all be made slaves to men of property. To the argument that their masters might abuse them, he answered in words which might have come a century and a half later from a George Fitzhugh: "that the most brutal man will not use his beast ill only out of a humour; and that if such Inconveniences do sometimes fall out, it proceeds, for the most part, from the perverseness of the Servant." [32]

None of these proposals for enslavement came to fruition; but they suggest that the English poor of this time seemed to many of their betters to be fit for slavery. The contempt that lay behind these proposals and behind many of the workhouse schemes is not easy to distinguish from the kind of contempt that today we call racism. The stereotypes of the poor expressed so often in England during the late seventeenth and eighteenth centuries were often identical with the descriptions of blacks expressed in colonies dependent on slave labor, even to the extent of intimating the subhumanity of both: the poor were "the vile and brutish part of mankind"; the black were "a brutish sort of people." [33] In the eyes of unpoor Englishmen the poor

[31] Hutcheson, *A System of Moral Philosophy* (London, 1755), II, 202; David B. Davis, *The Problem of Slavery in Western Culture* (Ithaca, N.Y., 1966), 374–78. I am indebted to Professor Davis for several valuable suggestions.

[32] Andrew Fletcher, *Two Discourses concerning the Affairs of Scotland: Written in the Year 1698* (Edinburgh, 1698), second discourse (paged separately), 1–33, esp. 16.

[33] Sir William Petty, *The Economic Writings of Sir William Petty*, C. H. Hall, ed. (Cambridge, 1899), I, 275. Pierre van den Berghe, in *Race and Racism: A Comparative Perspective* (New York, 1967), 31–33, has outlined two types of race relations, paternalistic and competitive, differing in the stereotypes attributed under each to the "inferior" race or caste. The stereotypes of the English poor and of eighteenth-century blacks do not fit

bore many of the marks of an alien race.

To be sure, poverty was not genetically hereditary, but work-houses and their schools were designed to make it culturally heredi-tary. The poor were not born of another color than the rest of the population, but legislation could offer a substitute for color; and to this kind of legislation Parliament was not averse. Since the rags worn by the poor might not sufficiently designate their differentness, an act of 1697 required them (as recipients of poor relief) to wear a prominent red or blue "P" on the right-hand shoulder.[34] And since they were not only troublesome, but also "nauseous to the Behold-ers," [35] they could be segregated, along with other vicious, insane, diseased, or impotent persons within the walls of the workhouses, hospitals, prisons, and asylums constructed to enclose them—the ghettos of the poor—or else they could be shipped to the planta-tions and contribute their share to the national income there.

The English poor seem to have borne it all without violent pro-test. During the period when they were the object of so many plans and projects, they offered no resistance beyond the laziness, drunk-enness, licentiousness, and insubordination expected of them. Nature was at its old business of imitating art, and it was only natural that they should conform to the image imposed on them. For the subject race to accept the role assigned it is a common enough phenomenon.

The members of this inferior breed of Englishmen who were shipped to Virginia could scarcely have been surprised to find that the men in charge of their lives in the New World viewed them with the contempt to which they were accustomed. In 1668 the Vir-ginia burgesses had even called for the erection in every county of

---

perfectly into either but more nearly into the competitive type, in which the lower caste is seen as "Aggressive, uppity, insolent, oversexed, dirty, in-ferior, despicable, and dangerous." All these attributes except "oversexed" were applied to the poor and to blacks. The characteristics attributed under the paternalistic type of race relations, according to van den Berghe, are "Childish, immature, exuberant, uninhibited, lazy, impulsive, fun-loving, good humored, inferior but lovable." Of these only laziness and inferiority were ascribed either to the English poor or to Virginia blacks in the eighteenth century.

[34] Marshall, *English Poor*, 102–3. Such a measure had been recom-mended by Thomas Firmin in 1672. *Some Proposals for Imploying of the Poor*, 14–15.

[35] John Cary, *A Discourse on Trade* (London, 1745), 121; cf. Joshua Gee, *Trade and Navigation of Great Britain*, 42–43.

workhouses on the English model. And they had empowered the
county courts "to take poore children from indigent parents to place
them to worke in those houses," a move that may have been motivated less by the spread of poverty than by the perennial shortage
of labor.[36] For indigent, debt-ridden parents, when freed of responsibility for their children, were also free to be pressed back into the
servant ranks. Thus Virginians shared not only English contempt
for the poor but also English ideas of what to do about them.

Although a degree of racial prejudice was doubtless also present
in Virginia from the beginning, there is no evidence that English servants or freedmen resented the substitution of African slaves for
more of their own kind. When their masters began to place people
of another color in the fields beside them, the unfamiliar appearance
of the newcomers may well have struck them as only skin deep.
There are hints that the two despised groups initially saw each other
as sharing the same predicament. It was common, for example, for
servants and slaves to run away together, steal hogs together, get
drunk together. It was not uncommon for them to make love together. In Bacon's Rebellion one of the last groups to surrender was
a mixed band of eighty Negroes and twenty English servants.[37]

The first slaves who reached Virginia came mainly from Barbados, where they could have learned some English, so that communication between servants and slaves was less of a problem than
it would have been later when slaves came directly from Africa. And
their shared experiences in field and quartering house must soon have
adjusted their initial strangeness to each other. Today the racism of
many poor and lower-class American whites is so notorious that we
tend to think of it as natural. But in Brazil, as Carl Degler has shown,
class and color divisions tend to be confounded. While social prestige attaches to whiteness, it also attaches to wealth: well-to-do
blacks may rank above whites, and many poor blacks are themselves
uncertain whether prejudice against them is the result of their color
or their poverty.[38]

In Virginia too, before 1660, it might have been difficult to distinguish race prejudice from class prejudice. And as long as slaves
formed only an insignificant minority of the labor force, the com-

---

[36] Hening, II, 266–67.   [37] Coventry Papers, LXXVII, 301.
[38] Carl Degler, *Neither Black nor White: Slavery and Race Relations
in Brazil and the United States* (New York, 1971).

munity of interest between blacks and lower-class whites posed no social problem. But Virginians had always felt threatened by the danger of a servile insurrection, and their fears increased as the labor force grew larger and the proportion of blacks in it rose. Although the replacement of servants by slaves reduced the annual increment of poor freemen, the numbers already on hand were still sufficient to keep the threat of another Bacon in everyone's mind. If freemen with disappointed hopes should make common cause with slaves of desperate hope, the results might be worse than anything Bacon had done.

The answer to the problem, obvious if unspoken and only gradually recognized, was racism, to separate dangerous free whites from dangerous slave blacks by a screen of racial contempt. Bacon himself had given the first lessons in the social usefulness of racism. He had had no special bias against blacks. Once committed to rebellion, he had welcomed servants and slaves alike to his forces. Bacon's racism was directed against Indians, and lower-class Virginians needed no instruction in hating Indians. Though by 1676 they were doubtless prejudiced against blacks as well and perhaps prejudiced in a somewhat greater degree than they were against Irishmen, Spaniards, Frenchmen, and other foreigners, the Englishmen who came to Virginia, of whatever class, learned their first lessons in racial hatred by putting down the Indians.

They had begun with the murder of Wingina at Roanoke in 1586. They had continued at Jamestown in the guerrilla raids of the early years, the wars of extermination in the 1620s, and the final reduction of the Virginia Indians in the 1640s. After the invasion of the Susquehannahs in the 1670s they had been ready and eager to follow Bacon in another war of extermination. That Bacon was not more successful in exterminating Indians or in keeping the anger of Virginia's freemen directed toward race war rather than class conflict was largely owing, as we have seen, to Berkeley's refusal to cooperate.

But if Bacon failed in his instinctive attempt to subdue class conflict by racism, his was the wave of the future that would sweep Virginians into their paradoxical union of slavery and freedom in the eighteenth century. And the rebellion did make Virginians connect their most powerful racial hostilities, publicly and officially, with slavery. Although Bacon was out to kill Indians, he was also out to enslave them. The June assembly in 1676 had given him and his men, in effect, a slave-hunting license by providing that any

enemy Indians they caught were to be their slaves for life;[39] and
the first assembly after the rebellion specifically ordered that soldiers
who had captured Indians should "reteyne and keepe all such Indian
slaves or other Indian goods as they either have taken *or hereafter
shall take.*" The order was reenacted in April, 1679.[40] If it requires
a greater degree of hatred or contempt to enslave a man rather than
simply to keep him a slave, the Virginians clearly had it by 1676.
They had made a deliberate public decision to enslave Indians.

Only six years earlier they had made a deliberate public decision not to enslave Indians. In 1670 the question had been raised
whether Indians sold in Virginia by other Indians (who had captured them in tribal wars) should be slaves for life or for a term of
years. At that time it was decided that servants who were not Christians and who were brought into the colony by land (Indians from
other regions) should serve for twelve years or (if children) until
thirty years of age. The same act stated that non-Christian servants
brought "by shipping" (Negroes) were to be slaves for life.[41] Thus
Africans purchased from traders were assumed to be slaves but Indians were not. In 1682 the assembly eliminated the difference, making slaves of all imported non-Christian servants.[42] Since only Indians and Africans fitted this description and since the assembly had
already decided in 1667 [43] that conversion to Christianity after arrival did not alter the status of a slave, the act of 1682 set the further development of slavery on a squarely racial foundation. Indians
and Negroes were henceforth lumped together in Virginia legislation, and white Virginians treated black, red, and intermediate
shades of brown as interchangeable. Even the offspring of a mixed
Indian and white couple were defined as mulattoes.[44] It had been
the original intention of the founders to exploit native labor. And
as Virginians began to expand their slave holdings, they seem to
have had Indians as much in view as Africans. If the natives of Virginia were insufficient in number, substitute natives from other regions could be brought in, whether from other parts of America or
from Africa. They were both, after all, basically uncivil, unchristian,
and, above all, unwhite.

[30] Hening, II, 346.
[40] *Ibid.*, 404, 440. Emphasis added. Cf. *ibid.*, IV, 10.
[41] *Ibid.*, II, 283.   [42] *Ibid.*, 490–92.   [43] *Ibid.*, 260.
[44] *Ibid.*, III, 252. But Indian blood was evidently considered less potent
than that of blacks, since not only a black parent but even a black grand-
parent or great-grandparent was enough to make a person qualify as mulatto.

Indians, whether captured within the colony or brought from without, never became available in sufficient numbers to form a significant part of Virginia's labor force. But the act of 1682 did result in the importation of many more Indian slaves than has usually been recognized. A law passed two years earlier had made slaves tithable at the age of twelve and required the owner of slave children to bring them to the county court to have their ages judged (within three months of passage of the act or three months after their arrival).[45] In Henrico County, as a result, in the year from April, 1683, to April, 1684, thirty-three Indian children, ranging in age from four to eighteen, were registered. In the same period no Negro children were registered. Henrico, located at the head of navigation on the James River, seems to have had more access to Indian slaves than most other counties. In Northumberland County in the two years after passage of the act, the court judged the ages of two Indians and three Negro children. In York County the figures were four Indian and twelve Negro; in Accomack four Indian and nine Negro.[46]

It seems clear that at the time when Virginians were beginning to buy Negro slaves in large numbers, they were also buying Indians. Indians were thus seen within the settlements more commonly than they ever had been before, and they were seen as slaves. Under these circumstances it was easy for Virginians to extend to blacks some of the bad feelings they harbored toward Indians. The new blacks were also at a disadvantage in coming for the most part directly from Africa and being therefore unable to communicate readily with English servants. The Indians too were outlanders, probably mostly from Carolina. Both were slaves and only they were slaves. It would have been natural not only for their owners but also for their fellow servants to lump them together in a lowest common denominator of racist hatred and contempt.

Obviously it was to the advantage of the men who ran Virginia to encourage such contempt in the colony's white servants and poor freemen. How clearly the advantage was perceived is impossible to say; but if Negro slavery came to Virginia without anyone having to decide upon it as a matter of public policy, the same is not true

[45] *Ibid.*, II, 479.

[46] Figures drawn from Henrico II, Northumberland III, York VI, Accomack IX. In the next century Virginians employed the friendly Tuscarora to capture slaves from enemy tribes, offering "the usual price of slaves for every woman and child delivered as captives." Oct. 24, 1711. *Executive Journals*, III, 287, 295.

of racism. By a series of acts, the assembly deliberately did what it could to foster the contempt of whites for blacks and Indians. In 1670 it forbade free Negroes and Indians, "though baptised," to own Christian servants.[47] In 1680 it prescribed thirty lashes on the bare back "if any negroe or other slave shall presume to lift up his hand in opposition against *any* christian."[48] This was a particularly effective provision in that it allowed servants to bully slaves without fear of retaliation, thus placing them psychologically on a par with masters. And in 1705, when the assembly ordered the dismemberment of unruly slaves, it specifically forbade masters to "whip a christian white servant naked, without an order from a justice of the peace."[49] Nakedness, after all, was appropriate only to a brutish sort of people, who had not achieved civility or Christianity.

But the term "Christian white servant" points to one of the complications Virginians had to overcome in emphasizing racial differences. There had always been in Virginia a rough congruity of Christianity, whiteness, and freedom and of heathenism, non-whiteness, and slavery. The early acts defining the servitude of Negroes and Indians had assumed that they would both normally be non-Christian. Yet neither Indians nor Negroes were immune to Christianity, and one ostensible aim of the founders of Virginia had been to convert the Indians. Although there had been little effort to carry out the aim, missionary zeal might someday effect it. And Africans, uprooted from their own environment, could be highly susceptible to the religion of their masters. By becoming Christian would they not become free?

Before the 1660s it seems to have been assumed that Christianity and slavery were incompatible. Negroes and Indians held in slavery who could prove that they had been baptized sometimes sued for their freedom and won it. Negroes who can be identified in the records as free generally had both a forename and a surname, implying baptism, instead of being designated simply as Mingo, Frank, Jack, and so on. The assembly in 1662 ordered the release of a Powhatan Indian who had been wrongly sold into servitude for life, "he speaking perfectly the English tongue and desiring baptism."[50]

As slavery became more profitable, the assembly moved to protect masters by building a wall between conversion and emancipation. As we have seen, it specifically provided that baptism should

[47] Hening, II, 280.
[48] *Ibid.*, 481, emphasis added.
[49] *Ibid.*, III, 448.
[50] *Ibid.*, II, 155.

not affect the bondage of either Negroes or Indians.[51] The avowed object was to encourage masters in Christianizing their slaves by eliminating the danger of losing a slave through his conversion. But the effect, whether intended or not, was to remove the most powerful motive for a slave to wish for baptism. And masters, perhaps from a lingering uneasiness about holding Christians in slavery, were content to be served by pagans. When the act was passed in 1667, slaves were probably still expected to attend church like everyone else, and the expectation may have continued for some years longer. But after slaves began to arrive in large numbers, it seems to have been abandoned.[52] Masters were reluctant to have their slaves become Christians, one minister noted, "because they say it often makes them proud, and not so good servants." Virginia slaves for the most part went unbaptized, despite hints from the mother country that they should be.[53] The prestige that went with being Christian instead of heathen could thus be reserved normally for the free and the white. But since the congruity could never be perfect, slaves were contrasted in the enactments not simply with Christian servants but with "Christian white servants."

The assembly's efforts to distinguish such servants from slaves went well beyond exempting them from being whipped naked. In an act that created perhaps the most invidious distinction between them, the assembly specifically protected the property of servants while confiscating what belonged to slaves. During the seventeenth century it had been common for masters to give a cow or a pig to a favored slave or to allow slaves to acquire such property by extra efforts of their own. But in 1705, in the same act that authorized the

[51] *Ibid.*, 260.

[52] The change may be reflected in the different steps taken by the assembly to make its acts about slaves known. In 1682 it provided for a twice yearly reading of the acts in church in the midst of services (after the second lesson). But in 1705 the acts were to be read after the service, at the door of the church. The change may imply that slaves were no longer allowed inside the church but might gather outside, or it may mean that masters tended to spend more time in the churchyard than in church, or it may mean that Commissary James Blair had objected to the interruption of divine service.

[53] *Journals of the House of Burgesses, 1695–1702,* 174; Journal of Francis Louis Michel (1702), *VMHB,* XXIV (1916), 116; Jones, *Present State of Virginia,* 70; Pargellis, "Account of the Indians in Virginia," 242; M. W. Jernegan, *Laboring and Dependent Classes in Colonial America, 1607–1783* (Chicago, 1931), 24–44.

dismemberment of unruly slaves, the assembly provided that servants were to have the sole use, benefit, and propriety of any property they owned or that came into their possession by gift or any other lawful means, but that "all horses, cattle, and hogs, now belonging, or that hereafter shall belong to any slave, or of any slaves mark . . . shall be seised and sold by the church-wardens of the parish, wherein such horses, cattle, or hogs shall be, and the profit thereof applied to the use of the poor of the said parish." [54] Thus even the small property previously allowed to slaves who had the excess energy and industry to work for it was to be handed over to poor whites—a highly effective device for dissociating the two.

It was in the area of sexual relations that the authorities were most assiduous to separate the races. Up to and perhaps through the 1660s it is difficult to document any indisputably racist feeling about miscegenation. A famous instance, often cited, is the case of Hugh Davis in 1630, ordered to be whipped "before an assembly of Negroes and others for abusing himself to the dishonor of God and shame of Christians, by defiling his body in lying with a negro." [55] But this could reflect religious rather than racial feeling: that a Christian should not lie with a heathen. Or it could be a case of sodomy rather than fornication. The specific order for "an assembly of Negroes" may signify only the court's intention to impress the mores of a Christian community upon the heathen in its midst. We have seen that in 1649 a pair of interracial fornicators were required to do penance like any other couple. And court records show the usual fines or whipping for fornication, regardless of the sinners' color, up to 1662.[56] In that year an act to determine the status of the children of a Negro woman by an English father declared that children should be slave or free according to the condition of the mother.[57] Even this cannot be seen unequivocally as dictated by racism. English ideas of property rights and the prudential consideration of keeping a child with its mother and reimbursing the mother's master for its support could have been involved. The act could even have offered an incentive to miscegenation by relieving the English father of a mulatto bastard from paying for its support as he would have to do in the case of a child borne by an English woman. Probably in order to deter men from seizing this open invitation to inexpensive sin, the act included a clause imposing double penalties on

[54] Hening, III, 459–60.
[55] *Ibid.*, I, 146.
[56] See chap. 7, note 77.
[57] Hening, II, 170.

Christians for fornication with Negroes. This again could be seen as prompted by moral concern and perhaps also by religious scruples about copulation between Christian and heathen. In any case, the act said nothing about interracial marriages.

Such marriages were by no means unknown in Virginia. In Northumberland County in 1656 Elizabeth Kay, a mulatto woman whose father had been free, sued for her freedom through an attorney, William Greensted, who was apparently white. After the suit succeeded, Greensted married her.[58] In Northampton County Francis Payne, a free Negro, was married to a white woman named Aymey, who remarried with a white man, William Gray, after Payne's death. Aymey's second marriage was evidently less successful than the first, for she was soon complaining to the court that her new husband was beating her and wasting the estate she brought him.[59]

Another case of mixed marriage appears in the Norfolk County records, where a question was raised in 1671 as to whether Francis Skiper's wife was tithable. The court decided that since she was a Negro she was indeed tithable. Skiper, who appears in the records at various times, was never identified as a Negro and was almost certainly white. He was executed for murder in 1679, but Ann was still living as a widow in Norfolk in 1691.[60] A more remarkable case was that of Hester Tate, an English servant of James Westcomb in Westmoreland County, who was legitimately married to James Tate, a slave of Patrick Spence. In 1691 the couple had four mulatto children, three of whom were in that year apprenticed to Spence and the other to Westcomb.[61] In that same year the assembly took action

[58] Warren M. Billings, "The Cases of Fernando and Elizabeth Key: A Note on the Status of Blacks in Seventeenth-Century Virginia," *WMQ*, 3rd ser., XXX (1973), 467–74.

[59] Northampton X, 220–21; XII, 59, 69. Francis Payne is identified as Negro in the records. That Aymey was white is evident from the fact that she was never included in the tithe lists. That William Gray was white is evident from the fact that in 1666, when he was a servant to John Michaels, he was listed with Michaels' other white servants, Michaels' Negroes being listed separately.

[60] The pair were married at least as early as February 2, 1667/8, when they sold 100 acres of land. Norfolk V, 28. The court's ruling that she was tithable is in Norfolk VI, 73, other references *ibid.*, 73a, 84a, 89, 92, 112a, 115a, 122a; Norfolk IX, 231; VII, 67, 74. Evidence of Skiper's execution in 1679 is in Norfolk VII, 95, and IX, 130.

[61] Westmoreland VI, 40, 41.

"for prevention of that abominable mixture and spurious issue which hereafter may encrease in this dominion, as well by negroes, mulattoes, and Indians intermarrying with English, or other white women, as by their unlawfull accompanying with one another." [62]

The act provided extensive punishments for miscegenation in or out of wedlock. A white man or woman who married a Negro, mulatto, or Indian was to be banished from the colony. That the act ran counter to the wishes of some inhabitants is suggested by a petition to the council in 1699, by "George Ivie and others, for the Repeale of the Act of Assembly, Against English people's Marrying with Negroes Indians or Mulattoes." [63] George Ivy was a resident of Norfolk, the son of a planter of the same name, from whom he had inherited a hundred acres of land in 1689. [64] The council referred his petition to the House of Burgesses, which ignored it. In the same session the burgesses also rejected a proposal from the justices of Surry County asking that the law in question be strengthened. [65] That the justices should have made the proposal argues that they thought mixed marriages were too common in Surry, which like Norfolk was a poor man's county. Though the assembly rejected the proposal, six years later it did alter the law, to provide a less drastic but more effective deterrent to racial intermarriage among ordinary people. Instead of banishment, which would deprive the colony of a potential laborer (or two), the assembly imposed six months' imprisonment and a fine of £10. At the same time it levied a fine of 10,000 pounds of tobacco on the minister who presided at the marriage. [66]

Both the original act of 1691 and the 1705 revision gave less attention to intermarriage than to the illicit relations of white women with black or mulatto men. A free white woman who had an illegitimate child by a black or mulatto father was to be fined £15. If she could not pay, she was to be sold for a five-year term. The child, though free because its mother was free, was to spend the first thirty years of its life in servitude for the benefit of the parish (again the white poor would profit). If the woman was a servant, she was to serve her master an extra two years, as the law provided for servants

[62] Hening, III, 86–87.
[63] H. R. McIlwaine, ed., *Legislative Journals of the Council of Colonial Virginia* (Richmond, 1918), I, 262.
[64] Norfolk IX, 86a; X, 94, 105, 181, 188.
[65] *Journals of the House of Burgesses, 1695–1702*, 148.
[66] Hening, III, 453–54.

having bastards, and then she was to be sold for another five years. The proceeds of this sale would be divided equally among the king, the parish, and the informer. All these provisions were repeated in the revision of 1705.

Women were still scarce in Virginia in 1691 and doubtless continued to be for another twenty or thirty years. At the turn of the century there were probably about three men for every two women.[67] The laws against miscegenation were aimed at confining the affections of these rare white women to white men. And there seems to have been good reason for concern. In Westmoreland from 1690 to 1698 fourteen white women were punished for having a total of nineteen illegitimate children, of which at least four were mulatto. In Norfolk in the same period thirteen women were punished for the same number of children, of whom at least three were mulatto. In Lancaster County from 1702 to 1712 twenty-six white women were punished for a total of thirty-two illegitimate children, of which nine were mulatto. It would appear that black men were competing all too successfully for white women, even in the face of the severe penalties.[68]

The result of such unions could be a blurring of the distinction between slave and free, black and white. The children would ultimately become free and might constitute an intermediate class, neither black nor white. By providing severe punishments for white women who gave themselves to blacks, the authorities not only discouraged the fraternization of slaves and poor whites but also assisted white freemen to find wives.

The laws said nothing about black women who had illegitimate children by white fathers, perhaps because few black women were free and the children of slave women were neither legitimate nor illegitimate, no matter who the father was. Given the power of white masters over women slaves, it is altogether likely that many black women bore mulatto children. But since the mother was a slave, the child, in spite of his intermediate color, would be a slave. Such mulattoes would therefore not constitute an intermediate class. They must be seen as black. And the assembly took pains in all its laws to identify them with blacks and to deny them any benefit from a free paternity.

[67] This was the ratio in Maryland in 1704. *Archives of Maryland*, XXV, 256.

[68] Westmoreland VI, Norfolk IX and X, Lancaster VIII.

The class of free Negroes and mulattoes already in existence could not be eliminated without more draconian measures than the assembly was willing to undertake. But the class could be prevented, or at least hindered, from growing. In 1691 the assembly forbade masters to free slaves unless they paid for the transportation of them out of the colony.[69] Later the assembly flatly forbade emancipation except by approval of the governor and council for some signal public service (such as revealing a slave conspiracy) and authorized the seizure and sale as a slave again of any Negro, mulatto, or Indian whose owner attempted to free him.[70]

Negroes, mulattoes, and Indians already free did manage to stay in the colony and to cling to their freedom. But it was made plain to them and to the white population that their color rendered freedom inappropriate for them. In spite of being free, they were denied the right to vote or hold office or to testify in court proceedings.[71] And their women, unlike white women, were subject to taxation, whether they worked in the fields or not. These handicaps, together with the penalties for miscegenation, successfully dissociated them from whites, however poor. Consolidated in a single pariah group, regardless of ancestry, language, religion, or native genius, they remained a small factor in Virginia's free society.

[69] Hening, III, 87. This provision originated in the council. *Legislative Journals of Council*, I, 149–51.

[70] Hening, IV, 132 (1723). The act requiring transportation of manumitted slaves was omitted from the comprehensive revision of laws in 1705. In 1713 the council, prompted by the manumission of sixteen slaves in the will of John Fulcher of Norfolk County, proposed that the assembly "provide by a law against such manumission of slaves, which may in time by their increase and correspondence with other slaves may [sic] endanger the peace of this Colony." *Executive Journals*, III, 332. But the assembly apparently did not enact the provision until 1723.

[71] Hening, III, 250–51, 298. Cf. Emory G. Evans, ed., "A Question of Complexion: Documents concerning the Franchise in Eighteenth-Century Virginia," *VMHB*, LXXI (1963), 411–15. John H. Russell, *The Free Negro in Virginia, 1619–1865* (Baltimore, 1913), is based on original sources and remains an excellent treatment of the subject.

17

TOWARD POPULISM

As Virginians nourished an increasing contempt for blacks and Indians, they began to raise the status of lower-class whites. The two movements were complementary. The status of poor whites rose not merely in relation to blacks but also in relation to their white superiors. Virginia had always been advertised as a place where the poor would be redeemed from poverty. And during the 1630s, 1640s, and 1650s it may actually have served that purpose, though more met death than success. With the decline in mortality and rise in population the numbers of poor freemen grew too large, and the scruff and scum of England became the rabble of Virginia. But as Indians and Africans began to man the large plantations and the annual increment of freedmen fell off, the economic prospects of the paleface poor began to improve.

This is not to say that poverty disappeared from white Virginia with the introduction of slavery. A class of homeless men continued to drift about the colony, cheating the tax collectors and worrying the authorities. They crop up from time to time in petitions against them from the proper people of different counties. Accomack, which had complained earlier, joined with Lancaster and Gloucester in 1699 to request "that a law may be made to punish Vagrant Vagabond and Idle Persons and to assess the Wages of Common Labourers." [1] In 1710 Henrico County proposed a workhouse for them.[2] But the assembly apparently did not consider the problem worth acting on

---

[1] *Journals of the House of Burgesses, 1695–1702,* 158.
[2] H. R. McIlwaine, ed., *Journals of the House of Burgesses of Virginia, 1702/3–1705, 1705–1706, 1710–1712* (Richmond, 1912), 270.

until 1723, when it passed an act modeled after the Elizabethan poor law. The preamble noted that "divers Idle and disorderly persons, having no visible Estates or Employments and who are able to work, frequently stroll from One County to another, neglecting to labour and, either failing altogether to List themselves as Tythables, or by their Idle and disorderly Life [render] themselves incapable of paying their Levies when listed." The act, which was renewed and enlarged from time to time thereafter, empowered county courts to convey vagrants to the parish they came from and to bind them out as servants on wages by the year. If the vagrant were "of such ill repute that no one will receive him or her into Service," then thirty-nine lashes took the place of servitude.[3]

The law was probably prompted by the immigration of convicts during the preceding five years. Parliament in 1717 had authorized English criminal courts to contract for transportation to the colonies of convicted felons, to serve for terms of seven or fourteen years, depending on the seriousness of their crime; and a year later the infamous Jonathan Forward began a long and profitable career of carrying convicts to Virginia and Maryland, collecting from the British government a fee of £5 sterling for each of them and from the planters as much as they would pay, usually averaging £8 to £10. Virginia tried to protect herself by an act requiring both the importer and the purchaser to give bonds for the good behavior of these dubious immigrants and to register with the county court their names and the crimes for which they were transported. But the Privy Council disallowed the law, and the demand for labor in Virginia insured a ready market.[4]

Though it can be estimated that some twenty thousand convicts were carried to Virginia and Maryland during the rest of the century, and though they undoubtedly included some habitual criminals,[5] the unredeemable were not so many but that they could be dealt with by traditional methods: the law that confined them to their parish and empowered the courts to put them to work was

[3] Waverly K. Winfree, *The Laws of Virginia: Being a Supplement to Hening's The Statutes at Large, 1700–1750* (Richmond, 1971), 253; Hening, IV, 208–14; VI, 29–33; Howard Mackey, "The Operation of the English Old Poor Law in Colonial Virginia," *VMHB*, LXXIII (1965), 29–40.

[4] Winfree, *Laws of Virginia*, 217–22; Jones, *Present State of Virginia*, 87, 210–12; Smith, *Colonists in Bondage*, 119–21.

[5] Smith, *Colonists in Bondage*, 116–17, 311, 325. Given the severity of English penal laws, it seems likely that many were not habitual criminals.

more effective in Virginia than in England because of Virginia's un-limited demand for labor and the close supervision of plantation la-bor by overseers. Those whom no one would venture to employ could be disposed of by that other traditional method, the military expedition. When recruits were needed to fight the French or the Spanish or the Indians, Virginians knew where to find them. In 1736 they shipped off a batch to Georgia to guard the frontiers; in 1741 they recruited several hundred for the English expedition against Cartagena.[6] And when George Washington began his military career in 1754 by attacking the French in the Ohio Valley, he was leading, by his own statement, a company composed of "those loose, Idle Persons that are quite destitute of House and Home." [7] Indeed, the Virginia assembly in ordering the troops raised had specified that military and naval officers could impress only such "able-bodied men as do not follow or exercise any lawful calling or employment, or have not some other lawfull and sufficient support and maintenance." And lest there be any doubt, the law added that no one was to be impressed who had a right to vote in elections to the House of Bur-gesses.[8]

Virginia parishes acknowledged the same responsibility that rested on English parishes to care for the destitute who were physi-cally incapable of supporting themselves. But the numbers involved in Virginia were minuscule by comparison with England, because the conversion to slave labor transferred from the parish to the plan-tation the responsibility for the unproductive and unemployable ele-ments of the laboring class: the aged, the disabled, and the young.[9] Though a master could extract as much labor from his slaves as he could drive them to, he must feed and clothe them whether they could work or not. And society did not allow him to shift the re-sponsibility. The laws against manumission had as an object not only

[6] *VMHB*, XXXVI (1928), 216–17; *WMQ*, 1st ser., XV (1907), 224; Jones, *Present State of Virginia*, 87, 210–12; Fairfax Harrison, "When the Convicts Came," *VMHB*, XXX (1922), 250–60; John W. Shy, "A New Look at Colonial Militia," *WMQ*, 3rd ser., XX (1963), 175–85. Another recourse was the royal navy. When warships in Virginia waters needed seamen, the council authorized the captains to impress "vagrant and idle persons and such as have no visible Estate nor Imployment." *Executive Journals*, III, 213, 215 (1709), 531 (1720). See also *ibid.*, I, 49.
[7] R. A. Brock, ed., *The Official Records of Robert Dinwiddie*, Virginia Historical Society, *Collections*, n.s., III and IV (Richmond, 1883–84), I, 92.
[8] Hening, V, 95, 96; VI, 438–39; *Executive Journals*, III, 213, 531.
[9] Mackey, "Operation of the English Old Poor Law," 30.

the limitation of the free black population but the restraint of masters who might be tempted to free a slave when he became too decrepit to work, whether the cause were age, accident, or abuse. Slavery, more effectively than the Elizabethan Statute of Artificers, made the master responsible for the workman and relieved society at large of most of its restive poor.

As the ranks of the free ceased to swell so rapidly, the number of losers among them declined; and in the eighteenth century as the rich grew richer, so did the poor. The most concrete evidence comes from the tithable records. As noted earlier, the most pronounced trend in these records during the third quarter of the seventeenth century was the increase in the number of one-man households, without servants or slaves. After leveling off in the last quarter of the century, the trend was in the opposite direction. In Lancaster (the only county for which both seventeenth- and eighteenth-century lists survive) 13 percent of the households had only one man in 1653, 32 percent in 1675, 38 percent in 1699, and 19 percent in 1745. If we compare surviving seventeenth-century records (see table in chapter 11) with surviving eighteenth-century records (see table below), it would appear that one-man households were decreasing, while large households with more than five tithables were increasing. The gap between the very rich and the not-so-rich had widened, but there were more of the rich and fewer of the not-so-rich.[10]

The same trend is observable in other figures. During the first half of the eighteenth century, while big planters were building the great mansions of tidewater Virginia and accumulating vast numbers of slaves, the moderately successful small farmer was also gaining a larger place even in this richest area of the colony. Property holdings in the tidewater declined in average size per owner from 417

[10] The figures are drawn from miscellaneous lists and records of tithables in the Virginia State Library and from *Tyler's Quarterly Historical and Genealogical Magazine*, VII (1926), 179–85. The counties are listed roughly from north to south. The decline in the number of one-man households may have resulted not only from the decrease in the annual numbers of new freedmen but also from an increase in native-born children over fifteen who remained with their parents on family farms. But native-born sons reaching adulthood and setting up on their own would also be responsible for many of the one-man households. And sons of small planters would probably have started from a somewhat more secure economic base than newly freed servants.

acres in 1704 to 336 acres in 1750, while the number of property owners increased by 66 percent.[11]

Tithables per Household

County and year	Average number of tithables per household	Percent of one-man households	Percent of households with 2 to 5 tithables	Percent of households with over 5 tithables
Loudoun 1760	2.67	45	44	11
Prince William (*Dilingen Parish*) 1747	2.7	38	53	9
Orange 1755	4.22	25	48	27
Lancaster 1745	4.34	19	54	26
York (*York-Hampton Parish*) 1763	6.03	22	45	33
Goochland 1754	3.46	31	53	16
Chesterfield 1756	3.17	41	43	16
Amelia 1753	3.31	39	45	16
Norfolk 1754	2.79	46	43	16
Lunenburg 1748	1.95	64	30	6
TOTALS	3.21	40	45	15

Wills proved in court also point to improved circumstances for the small man. A study covering the period 1660–1719 in four counties (Isle of Wight, Norfolk, Surry, and Westmoreland) divides

[11] D. Alan Williams, "The Small Farmer in Eighteenth-Century Virginia Politics," *Agricultural History*, XLIII (1969), 91–101.

the testators into lower, middle, and upper class on the basis of the value of property devised. In each county lower-class testators decreased, while middle- and upper-class testators increased.[12] A more detailed study embracing the whole Chesapeake region shows a similar growth in the value of testators' estates from 1720 to the 1760s. The number of persons with estates valued at £100 or less constituted 70 percent of those found around 1720. In the 1760s such persons accounted for only 41.4 percent, with a corresponding increase in those valued over £100.[13]

The figures of tithables, landholdings, and estate values do not mean that the small man was disappearing from Virginia. On the contrary, small planters continued to make up the great majority of the free population.[14] But the figures do suggest that the small man was not as small as he had been and that the chances of becoming bigger had increased since the seventeenth century.

The change did not come entirely from forces arising within the colony. During the second quarter of the eighteenth century a marked growth in the world market for tobacco lent stability to its price and improved the position of the small man at the same time that it improved the position of the large man. Tobacco production advanced in this period even more rapidly in the poorer regions on the south side of the James and in the piedmont than it did in the richer York River area.[15] But Virginia had enjoyed large economic opportunities during part of the seventeenth century without giving

[12] James W. Deen, Jr., "Patterns of Testation: Four Tidewater Counties in Colonial Virginia," *American Journal of Legal History*, XVI (1972), 154–76.

[13] Aubrey C. Land, "The Tobacco Staple and the Planter's Problems: Technology, Labor, and Crops," *Agricultural History*, XLIII (1969), 69–81, esp. 78–79. In 1766 John Wayles noted that in the preceding twenty-five years, "many Estates have increased more than tenfold." J. M. Hemphill, ed., "John Wayles Rates his Neighbours," *VMHB*, LXVI (1958), 302–6.

[14] Aubrey C. Land, "Economic Base and Social Structure: The Northern Chesapeake in the Eighteenth Century," *Journal of Economic History*, XXV (1965), 639–54; "Economic Behavior in a Planting Society: The Eighteenth-Century Chesapeake," *Journal of Southern History*, XXXIII (1967), 469–85, esp. 472–73; Brown and Brown, *Virginia, 1705–1786*, 32–62.

[15] Jacob M. Price, "The Economic Growth of the Chesapeake and the European Market, 1697–1775," *Journal of Economic History*, XXIV (1964), 496–511; Price, *France and the Chesapeake: A History of the French Tobacco Monopoly, 1674–1791, and of Its Relationships to the British and American Tobacco Trades* (Ann Arbor, Mich., 1973), I, 266; Brown and Brown, *Virginia, 1705–1786*, 7–31.

the small man a comparable benefit. The difference this time was slavery.

It would be difficult to argue that the introduction of slavery brought direct economic benefits to free labor in Virginia. Since the tobacco crop expanded along with the expansion of the slave population, slavery could scarcely have contributed to any improvement in the prices the small planter got for what he grew. And though the reduction in the annual increment of freedmen did reduce the competition among them for land and for whatever places society might have available, the avarice of their superiors could well have resulted in squeezing out small men as they were squeezed out of Barbados in the preceding century. Instead—and I believe partly because of slavery—they were allowed not only to prosper but also to acquire social, psychological, and political advantages that turned the thrust of exploitation away from them and aligned them with the exploiters.

The fear of a servile insurrection alone was sufficient to make slaveowners court the favor of all other whites in a common contempt for persons of dark complexion. But as men tend to believe their own propaganda, Virginia's ruling class, having proclaimed that all white men were superior to black, went on to offer their social (but white) inferiors a number of benefits previously denied them. To give the remaining white servants a better start in life, the assembly in 1705 required masters to provide servants, at the conclusion of their term, with ten bushels of Indian corn, thirty shillings in money, and "a well fixed musket or fuzee, of the value of twenty shillings, at least," a somewhat more useful, if not more generous, provision than the three barrels of corn and suit of clothes previously required by "the custom of the country." Women servants under the new act were to get fifteen bushels of corn and forty shillings in money. In addition, at the insistence of the English government, servants on becoming free were entitled to fifty acres of land, even though they had not paid for their own transportation.[16]

---

[16] Hening, III, 304, 451. The value of freedom clothes had probably amounted in most cases to somewhat less than the 40 shillings equivalent thus required, though the Norfolk County court in 1657 awarded 250 pounds of tobacco as a substitute for freedom clothes. Norfolk IV, 110. In similar cases the Northampton court in 1651 awarded 200 pounds in lieu of freedom clothes and in 1672, when the price of tobacco was down to a penny a pound or less, 400 pounds, and in 1675, 450 pounds in lieu of both corn and clothes. Northampton IV, 160a; X, 166; XII, 47. A York inventory of 1648 valued ten servants' suits at 1,000 pounds. York II, 390.

For men already free the assembly made what was probably its most welcome gesture by drastically reducing the poll tax. The annual levy paid by every free man in Virginia, for himself and his servants, was in three parts: public, county, and parish. The first and sharpest reduction came in the public levy, the amount collected for support of the colony government. From 1660 to 1686 the average annual public levy was 45 pounds of tobacco per person; from 1687 to 1700 it was 11 pounds; and from 1701 to 1750 it was 4.6 pounds.[17] The reduction was made possible in part by the increase (as tobacco production rose) in revenue from the two-shilling-per-hogshead export duty on tobacco and in part by the income from new duties imposed on the importation of liquors, servants, and slaves. Parish and county levies did not drop as dramatically as the public levy; but they too were reduced, especially in years when the public revenues yielded a large enough surplus to pay the burgesses, a major expense that had hitherto been paid by county levies. As the tables below indicate, the total burden of direct taxes borne by a Virginian in the eighteenth century seldom amounted to half that paid by his counterpart in the seventeenth century.[18] He may still have paid the difference indirectly through the customs duties, but he did not feel the pain as his forebears had.

As the small man's economic position improved, he was also enjoying the benefits of a shift in social and political attitudes that coincided with the rise of slavery. The shift seems to have begun with the efforts of the crown, after Bacon's Rebellion, to restrain the covetousness of Virginia's provincial magnates. Those efforts, as we have seen, were largely unsuccessful and initiated a power struggle between the royal governors of Virginia and the assembly. After Effingham's departure the struggle continued, as successive gov-

[17] Figures derived from Norfolk IV and VI; *Journals of the House of Burgesses, 1659/60–1963*; Hening, II–VI; Winfree, *Laws of Virginia*.

[18] Figures for county and public levies derived from Norfolk IV, VI, XI–XIV; Lancaster III, IV, VI, VII, XI, XII; Surry IV, V, VIII–X; Northumberland XIII, XIV; figures for parish levies from C. G. Chamberlayne, ed., *The Vestry Book of Christ Church Parish, Middlesex County, Virginia, 1663–1767* (Richmond, 1927); *The Vestry Book and Register of St. Peter's Parish, New Kent and James City Counties, Virginia, 1684–1786* (Richmond, 1937); *The Vestry Book of Petsworth Parish, Gloucester County, Virginia* (Richmond, 1933). George Mason in 1753 estimated that the total of public, county, and parish levies, one year with another, did not amount to more than eight shillings sterling per poll. Robert A. Rutland, ed., *The Papers of George Mason, 1725–1792* (Chapel Hill, N.C., 1970), I, 29.

ernors strove to effect royal policies, many of them designed to benefit both the crown and the ordinary planter at the expense of the big
men who continued to dominate the scene. But the 1690s saw a
radical change in the character of the conflict. New personalities
and new tactics on both sides combined with a crucial change in the
intellectual climate to transform Virginia politics in unexpected
ways. While the assembly was generating measures to align white

Average Annual Combined County and Public Levy in Four Counties in the 1660s, 1690s, and 1740s or 1750s

County	1660s	1690s	1740s or 1750s
Norfolk	81.4	53.5	18.5
Lancaster	59.2	45.8	10
Surry	?	35	5
Northumberland	?	45	10.5

Average Annual Parish Levy in Three Parishes in the 1690s and 1740s

Parish	1690s	1740s
Christ Church, Middlesex	41	31
St. Peters, New Kent	42.5	34
Petsworth, Gloucester	45	30

men of every rank against colored men of every tint, and while
magnates were tilting with governors, it became imperative for
everyone who aimed at power to court the good will of the small
freemen who made up the bulk of the voting population. The end
result was to bring the small man, not into political office, but into a
position that allowed him to affect politics as never before.

The change in intellectual climate originated in England. Effingham's departure from Virginia coincided with England's Revolution
of 1688, when James II was deposed because of his attempts to magnify the executive power and William of Orange was invited to take
his place. The result of that revolution, whatever else it did, was to

shift the balance of power between king and Parliament in the direction of Parliament. The king did not become a cipher. William did not accept the throne in order to sink it. And the philosopher of the revolution, John Locke, who did not fancy legislative tyranny more than any other kind, recommended for the executive a strong and independent role in the government. But Locke made it clear to Englishmen that the legislature must be supreme and that the executive must be limited by the laws that the legislative branch enacted.[19] In fact, the legislature had not only determined who should sit on the throne in 1688, but in 1701 it transferred the line of succession from the House of Stuart to the House of Hanover. Even affirmations of loyalty to King William or Queen Anne or King George could thus mean acknowledgment of the supremacy of Parliament, while Jacobitism, that is, loyalty to the Stuarts, meant rebellion against the lawful government.

The colonists readily gave their allegiance to the new king, presumably acquiescing thereby in the supremacy of Parliament over him. But Parliament made no attempt to exercise its new supremacy in America for many decades. English colonial policy after the Revolution of 1688, as before, emanated from the executive branch, and the precise relationship of the British legislature to the colonies was not defined. The primary impact of the revolution on England's relations with her colonies was not in the mechanics of government but in the frame of mind it induced in the Englishmen who directed colonial policy.[20] In the colonies, as we noted earlier, James II had attempted to tighten his hold by dismissing the representative assemblies of the northern colonies and consolidating them into a single province. During the revolution the colonists had tumbled this Dominion of New England, in which all powers were vested in the provincial executive, just as Englishmen had put an end to James's efforts to magnify the power of the executive in England. When William became king, he could scarcely have attempted to repudiate the revolution by restoring the Dominion or by subordinating the colonial legislatures to the colonial executive powers, even though the governors were the conduit through which British control of the colonies still flowed. Moreover, in 1696, to bring some order into the direction of colonial affairs, William established the Board of Trade

[19] John Locke, *Two Treatises of Government*, Peter Laslett, ed., (Cambridge, 1964), 375–87.

[20] The best study of the effects of the Revolution in the colonies is Lovejoy, *The Glorious Revolution in America*.

and appointed John Locke himself as one of the eight working members.[21] The revolution thus created in both England and the colonies a psychological environment in which legislative powers held a presumptive advantage over executive prerogatives.

It was not at first clear how the change would affect the distribution of power in Virginia, for legislative and executive powers were mingled there, as in other colonies. The council not only advised and consented to the governor's actions, including his vetoes of legislative measures, but also served as the upper house of the legislature and as the supreme court of the colony. For a governor to try to control his council, as all governors tried to do, might henceforth be interpreted as a sinister effort to subordinate the legislative to the executive power and to concentrate too much power in a single unchecked executive.

In this uncertain atmosphere there emerged on the political scene in Virginia a man who knew how to manipulate people and politics with a skill no previous Virginian had shown. James Blair had been a young Scottish clergyman in 1681 when, along with eighty others, he had refused to take an oath that would have acknowledged the Catholic James II, upon his accession, as head of the Scottish church. Blair was therefore ejected from his benefice and made his way to London, where he was befriended by Henry Compton, Bishop of London. In 1685 the bishop sent him to Virginia, recommended to the church of Varina Parish in Henrico County. Soon after establishing himself there, Blair displayed his prowess in social diplomacy. Virginia ministers did not rank high in the colony's social scale, partly because of the insecurity of their position. Since they could be dismissed at the whim of their vestries, planters of large means were reluctant to match their daughters with them. Blair had no estate of his own, and it thus suggests something of his native ability that within two years he won the hand of Sarah Harrison, daughter of the biggest man in Surry County and one of the biggest in the colony, despite the fact that she was already pledged to another. The marriage placed him at once in the top circle of Virginia gentry, the only clergyman who had ever attained such a place.[22]

Blair's superior, the Bishop of London, also recognized his talents and in 1689 appointed him as his commissary or agent in Virginia,

[21] Peter Laslett, "John Locke, the Great Recoinage, and the Origins of the Board of Trade: 1695–1698," *WMQ*, 3rd ser., XIV (1957), 370–402.

[22] Parke Rouse, Jr., *James Blair of Virginia* (Chapel Hill, N.C., 1971), 3–44.

with authority over the rest of the Virginia clergy. In this position Blair found that his efforts to raise the moral standards of his colleagues came to little, because the Virginia clergy at the time contained a high proportion of misfits, drunkards, and libertines who had come to the colonies because no parish in England would have them.[23] Perceiving that this situation might be remedied by educating native Virginians, whose families and reputations would be known in advance, Blair proposed the establishment of a college, went to England to secure backing, got it, and returned in 1693 to found the College of William and Mary.

There can be no doubt of Blair's abilities. His letters, written in support of whatever cause he argued, were always couched in convincing terms. And he generally got what he wanted, because he had the ability to make the most outrageous charges against his enemies seem plausible. His enemies included, successively, nearly every governor of Virginia for the fifty years that followed his return to the colony in 1693. That enmity, more than any other single factor, dictated the style of Virginia politics during those years.

Sir Edmund Andros, who became governor during Blair's absence, was the first to tangle with him. Blair had been on good terms with Andros' immediate predecessor, Francis Nicholson—probably because the two had had too brief a time to become acquainted—and he had carried to England Nicholson's recommendation that a clergymen be appointed to the council. There was not much doubt about which clergyman was meant, and in 1694 Andros received instructions from the king to swear the Scotsman in as a councillor.[24] By then Blair was already nettled because Andros was insufficiently zealous in support of the new college and of the clergy. Before long the council was treated to what the clerk recorded as "undecent reflections reiterated and asserted with passion by Mr. James Blair."[25] Andros responded by suspending Blair from the council. Blair wrote letters to England and was rewarded with an order from the king, restoring him to his seat.[26] For the next year he sat in it and found some reason to quarrel with the governor at nearly every meeting. At the same time he was building a coalition of supporters and feeling out the weak points of his adversary.

---

[23] William S. Perry, ed., *Historical Collections Relating to the American Colonial Church*. Vol. I: *Virginia* (Hartford 1870), 30, 38.

[24] Rouse, *Blair*, 83; *Executive Journals*, I, 315.

[25] *Ibid.*, I, 324.   [26] *Ibid.*, I, 352.

It was not difficult to devise a line of attack. Sir Edmund Andros, a military man whose sympathies lay entirely on the side of royal prerogative as opposed to Parliamentary power, had been James II's choice for governor of the Dominion of New England. He had angered the New Englanders by telling them that they had no more rights than slaves; and they had seized him and shipped him back to England when William took the throne. Although William had exonerated him and sent him to Virginia, he was nevertheless vulnerable, in the post-revolutionary atmosphere, to the charge of seeking excessive, arbitrary powers. In 1697 Blair took off for London again, ready with a convincing case against the governor. He not only enlisted the support of his patron, the Bishop of London, but went directly to the man who could speak most effectively against arbitrary government. Blair presented John Locke at the Board of Trade with a detailed criticism of the political structure that supplied Virginia's governors with dangerous, uncontrollable, arbitrary powers, powers that Andros in particular, he said, had been all too ready to use.[27]

Not surprisingly, a conspicuous example of arbitrary power in Blair's demonstration was the governor's ability to suspend from office a councillor who displeased him. But Blair did not confine himself to personal grievances. He mapped out the avenues by which all the most lucrative offices in Virginia accrued to a few big men. The governor's control of the council was almost absolute, as Blair put the case, because by his influence in the selection of the royally appointed councillors and his power of suspending them he could confer or deny access to the excessive rewards that lay open to the council.[28] There may have been something of the dog in the manger about Blair, for as the bishop's commissary he could scarcely have

---

[27] Some preliminary drafts and documents prepared by Blair are in Ms. Locke e 9 in the Bodleian Library, Oxford. One of these is printed in Michael Kammen, ed., "Virginia at the Close of the Seventeenth Century: An Appraisal by James Blair and John Locke," *VMHB*, LXXIV (1966), 141–69. A larger version, emended by Henry Hartwell (another disgruntled councillor) and Edward Chilton (formerly clerk of the council), was published as *The Present State of Virginia and the College*, cited several times above.

[28] In one of the documents in Ms. Locke e 9, Blair put the case more succinctly than in the published versions: "Sir: If you wud know how many places in Virginia are held by the same men, it is but proposeing the following Questions to anyone who knows the Country.

    1. What are tne names of the present Council of Virginia?

    2. Who make the house of peers in Virginia?

expected to hold many more offices beyond that of councillor. And those who supported him may have been moved by a feeling that they had not had a large enough share of the spoils. Nevertheless, whatever his motivation, Blair's analysis was not without merit; and with the assistance of Locke and the bishop, he persuaded the Board of Trade to arrange for the recall of Andros and the reappointment of his own presumably reliable friend, ex-Governor Francis Nicholson. Included in Nicholson's instructions, along with other provisions derived from Blair's indictment, was a prohibition against councillors' also holding office as collectors.[29] Stripped of their largest fringe benefit, councillors would have less incentive to dance to whatever tune a governor called. Henceforth governors would have to win their support in other ways—or look for support elsewhere.

Although Blair was not at once appointed to Nicholson's council, he probably expected to play the role of Richelieu in the new regime. And he was in an excellent position to manage it. The importance of family connections, which had never been negligible in Virginia politics, was magnified by the new independence of the council; and Blair had plenty of family. He had acquired a new set of political allies during his absence in England by the marriage of his wife's sister to Philip Ludwell II, the son of the man who had outwitted so many previous governors. The younger Ludwell had already stepped into his father's shoes, and the family had other marital connections that carried a heavy weight in politics. When Blair rejoined the council in 1701, his father-in-law, Benjamin Harrison II,

---

3. Who are the Lords Lieutenants of the severall Counties in Virginia?
4. Who are the Judges of the Court of Common Pleas?
   Who are the Judges in Chancery?
   Who are the Judges of the Court of Kings Bench?
   And soe for Exchequer Admiralty Spirituality.
5. Who are the Naval Officers in Virginia?
6. Who are the Collectors of the Revenue?
7. Who sell the Kings Quitrents?
8. Who buy the Kings Quitrents?
9. Who is Secretary of Virginia?
10. Who is Auditor of Virginia?
11. Who are the Escheators in Virginia?"

[29] *VMHB*, IV (1896–97), 52; *Executive Journals*, I, 440. The wording of the instructions is not altogether clear on this point, but the words were interpreted, and apparently intended, to convey such a prohibition.

was already a member, and Colonel Lewis Burwell of Gloucester, whose daughter was married to Benjamin Harrison III, was another member. So was Robert "King" Carter, whose daughter was married to Burwell's son. In the following year, when Burwell retired from the council, Philip Ludwell II and William Bassett, another Burwell relative, were appointed.[30] With this array of relatives beside him and with his consummate skill in manipulating people, Blair could count on a good deal of backing in any political dispute. And disputes were not long in coming, for Blair quickly began to see in Nicholson another Andros, an enemy of the college and of the clergy, and a tyrant in the making.

Nicholson, for his part, did not fancy Blair as an *éminence grise* in his administration. Nicholson had a forthright disposition and a violent temper that frequently crops up in the records. Like Andros he was a military man, with the military man's assumption that people ought to do what he told them to. When Blair crossed him, he fought back hard and effectively, by tactics that Andros had not attempted. He tried to forge a marital alliance of his own with Lucy Burwell, daughter of the councillor, with whom he fell genuinely in love. When she spurned him, Nicholson blamed Blair and the whole Blair connection.[31] Indeed, he apparently concluded that the first gentlemen of Virginia were all a parcel of rogues and that the councillors in particular "had got their estates by cheating the people," an opinion that may have held more than a grain of truth.[32] In this situation, with a hot-tempered governor tackling an alliance of Virginia's top families, the small planters were drawn into the fray by both sides and emerged as a force in Virginia politics.

Since most of the evidence that survives about the battle was written by Blair and his friends, it must be treated with caution. As they described him, Nicholson was a would-be despot, grasping for power by means of a standing army recruited from the lowest ranks. Nicholson, according to Blair, proposed to "take all the servants as Cromwell took the apprentices of London into his army, and indeed he has upon many occasions to my knowledge preached up the doctrine that all the servants are kidnapped and have a good action against their masters." Blair went on to claim that he had heard Nicholson say that once he had got "an army well fleshed in blood

[30] *Ibid.*, II, 274; Rouse, *Blair*, 133, 267–68.

[31] *Ibid.*, 135; Perry, *Historical Collections*, I, 102.

[32] Charges against Nicholson brought by members of the council, *VHMB*, III (1895–96), 373–82, esp. 376; Perry, *Historical Collections*, I, 98.

and accustomed to booty there would be no disbanding of them again if they were commanded by a man that understood his business. . . ." And in case anyone missed the point, Blair added, "Several persons have told me they have heard him say Bacon was a fool and understood not his business." [33] A rebellion against the ruling Virginians conducted by the governor himself, and a governor experienced in arms, with a legitimate army at his back, would be formidable indeed.

Actually Nicholson may only have been trying to carry out instructions from the Board of Trade directing him to see that all planters *and* all Christian servants be armed in preparation for attacks by the French and Indians in the impending war. The House of Burgesses explained why it would be dangerous to arm Virginia's servants, but Nicholson apparently kept trying, for the records show the council again demurring to the proposal two years later.[34] According to Blair, the governor was bent on arming the servants in order to forward his own sinister purposes.

Blair's suspicions of the governor seemed to be substantiated when Nicholson reorganized the militia so that it could better cope with the expected French attack. In order to build a more effective, disciplined force, he had the militia in every county select one-fifth of their number, "young, brisk, fit, and able," to form elite companies.[35] According to Blair, the men of these companies were not merely the "youngest and briskest" but also "the most indigent men of the Country," and Nicholson allowed them to pick their own officers. "Now I could not but think with terror," said Blair, "how quickly an indigent army under such indigent officers with the help of the Servants and Bankrupts and other men in uneasy and discontented circumstances (upon all which I have heard him reckon) so well arm'd and Countenanced by a shew of authority could make all the rest of Virginia submit." [36] When the governor held a giant festival at Williamsburg to celebrate the accession of Queen Anne, it looked like part of the same sinister strategy, for Nicholson brought his militia companies in for a free feast and as much liquor as they could hold—and this in June when industrious planters were busy with their crops.[37]

[33] Perry, *Historical Collections*, I, 107, 109–10.

[34] *Journals of the House of Burgesses, 1695–1702*, 188; *Executive Journals*, II, 184.

[35] *Ibid.*, II, 174.   [36] Perry, *Historical Collections*, I, 111.

[37] *Ibid.*, 71.

The question of who should and should not be armed in Virginia was only one issue in the struggle between the governor and the council. Behind the accusations against Nicholson seems to have been the conviction of the councillors that he intended to bypass them and rest his regime directly on his popularity with the people at large. In a petition for his recall the council charged that he not only sought to gain "the good opinion of the Comon people but allso to beget in them such jealousies and distrusts of the Council, as might render them incapable to withstand his arbitrary designs." [38] Nicholson was apparently appealing to the small planters for help against the barons who threatened to best him as they bested Andros. If he could win the small planters, Nicholson might get into the assembly a set of burgesses who would consistently support him in issues that the council opposed. With governor and burgesses aligned together, the councillors might find themselves taking a back seat. To keep that from happening, they had to discredit Nicholson with both the voters in Virginia and the government in England. And James Blair had found the way.

In crying up the threat of Nicholson's plans for an army, Blair had a point that would count strongly against the governor among the men in England who had supported the Revolution of 1688. John Locke's patron, the Earl of Shaftesbury, had been one of the first to expound the dangers of a standing army; and he had done so in defense of the House of Lords, a body corresponding in part at least to the council in Virginia. A monarch, Shaftesbury had argued, who did not rule through his nobility, must rule through an army. "If you will not have one," he told the peers in 1675, "you must have t'other." Rule through the Lords meant liberty; rule through an army meant tyranny. Hence "Your *Lordships* and the *People* have the same cause, and the same Enemies." The people must therefore recognize every attack on the Lords as a move toward military rule and tyranny. The argument was easily extended to include the House of Commons along with the House of Lords, and after 1688 opposition to a standing army became a hallmark of belief in the principles of the revolution. [39]

Thus Blair and his friends could win support in England by making it appear that Nicholson was seeking to subvert English

[38] *VMHB*, III (1895–96), 377.
[39] J. G. A. Pocock, "Machiavelli, Harrington, and English Political Ideologies in the Eighteenth Century," *WMQ*, 3rd. ser., XXII (1965), 549–83, esp. 558.

liberty (that is, the supremacy of the legislative branch) both by debasing the council and by building an elite corps—a standing army. The two obviously went together. If Virginians were not yet sufficiently versed in the principles that made this diagnosis plausible in England, they needed no instruction in the dangers of arming the indigent. If Nicholson did indeed seek to arm not only the indigent but also the Christian servants, he was being singularly obtuse about the colony's history and traditional psychology. And he had clearly overreached himself if he persisted (as the records seem to indicate) after the burgesses had explained their objections:

> The Christian Servants in this Country for the most part consists of the Worser Sort of the people of *Europe* And since the Peace [of Ryswick, 1697] hath been concluded Such Numbers of *Irish* and other Nations have been brought in of which a great many have been Soldiers in the late Warrs That according to our present Circumstances we can hardly governe them and if they were fitted with Armes and had the Opertunity of meeting together by Musters We have just reason to feare they may rise upon us.[40]

Whether or not Nicholson actually did threaten the planters with arming the servants, Blair and the council tried their best to fan suspicions. They knew that the small planters feared a servile insurrection as much as the large planters did, because the Christian servants whom Nicholson was supposed to arm belonged mainly to the small planters, who could not afford slaves.[41] And if Blair's suggestive description of Nicholson's "indigent army" under "indigent officers" brought to mind such men as the colony got rid of later by military expeditions—the shiftless, troublesome crowd of men traditionally feared by the rest of the population—then too the small planters as well as the large would feel uneasy about the new elite corps of militia. Nicholson's appeal to the common people for support would be demolished if his opponents could establish the idea that the governor wanted to rule them through his indigent army. Blair tried to get the idea across. He reported that Nicholson proposed to "Govern the Country without assemblies." The governor, said Blair, gave his opinion of English liberties with the expression, "Magna Charta, Magna F——a," and threatened to hang his opponents with Magna Charta about their necks.[42]

It was an accusation to shock Englishmen, but at the time it was

---

[40] *Journals of the House of Burgesses, 1695–1702,* 188.
[41] *Ibid.*   [42] Perry, *Historical Collections,* I, 106, 109.

probably more effective in England than in Virginia. A governor who courted the indigent masses was distinctly out of step with post-revolutionary thought and post-revolutionary politics in England, where the legislature was the center of power and legislators and the property owners who elected them were the men to court. If it could be shown that Nicholson's tactics had alienated the assembly, it would be prima facie evidence that he was unfit to govern. And in 1702 the assembly gave signs of alienation. When Nicholson, on orders from the king, asked the burgesses for money to assist New York against French invasion, they refused to comply. In England the refusal seemed to confirm the charges against the governor.[43]

One anonymous English friend chided him on his imprudence and suggested a more suitable strategy. It would not do, the writer said, to "speak so much of the Prerogative and so little of the law, and in truth the course must be steered now very evenly between Prerogative and Property, and with a due respect to the latter as well as the former, or our English Parliaments, such sure is the universal disposition of the nation, will vent their indignation." It was said, he heard, "that by your rough and Naballike Treatment of both Councill and Assemblies you have lost all interest in them, and that this has already appeared in that you could not get them to comply with the instructions about New York." And the writer went on to censure his friend for gathering so many common people in the extravagant celebration at Williamsburg, where one witness declared that "he saw 500 drunk for one sober." The common people, the writer advised, "are never more innocent and usefull than when asunder, and when assembled in a mob are wicked and mad." [44]

With the way prepared by letters detailing Nicholson's reckless appeal to the mob, Blair sailed for England in 1703, and by the spring of 1705 he had secured the governor's recall, just as he secured the recall of Andros seven years earlier.

It is not impossible that some of Blair's charges against Nicholson were valid. Nicholson's bluff manner, his violent temper, and his military cast of mind lent substance to them. But there was probably some justice also in the comment of one of the governor's friends that Blair and his crowd were simply disgruntled by the governor's

[43] *Journals of the House of Burgesses, 1695–1702*, 245–46, 259–60, 313–16; Perry, *Historical Collections*, I, 70–71.
[44] *Ibid.*

refusal to let them run the colony as they chose. When he would not, "they Left no stone unturned to perplex the affaires of Government, setting up for Liberty and property men but ware soone discovered." [45] "Liberty and property men" in contemporary political parlance meant champions of legislative supremacy, and on that, their own chosen ground, Nicholson proved able to best his opponents—at least in Virginia. Frustrated in the council by Blair, he had turned to the burgesses and competed with the council to influence elections to the House. In the election of 1703 he seems to have outdone them in lining up votes, for the burgesses elected that year for the most part supported him against the council in subsequent sessions. He was even able to get from them in the session of 1705 a resolution denying the allegations of the council against him. But his vindication came too late to save him from Blair's persuasive talents in England.[46]

It seems unlikely that the burgesses and voters would have backed the governor if they actually thought he had curried favor with the despised and feared part of the population. Although men in England may have believed the councillors' accusation, Virginians apparently knew better. Nicholson's success with the burgesses argues that his appeal was not to the shiftless and shifting indigents of Virginia but to small planters, men who expressed through their votes their satisfaction with a governor who was willing to court them instead of their lordly neighbors. Under Nicholson a new excitement had appeared in elections to the House of Burgesses. The governor had injected a new element into the political game. The ordinary planters had begun to sense their importance. If huge holdings of land were concentrated in the hands of a few, and if the colony still had a portion of landless rovers, there was still enough land to give the majority of men a little, enough to enable them to

[45] Robert Quary to William Blathwayt, Sept. 2, 1702. Alderman Library, Charlottesville.

[46] *Journals of the House of Burgesses*, 1702–1712, 107–8. D. Alan Williams, "Political Alignments in Colonial Virginia Politics, 1698–1750" (unpublished doctoral dissertation, Northwestern University, 1959), 48–76. This excellent dissertation is the most perceptive study of Virginia politics during these years. Many of the documents in the dispute between Nicholson and Blair have been printed in *VMHB*, VIII (1900–1901), 46–64, 126–46, 260–78, 366–85, and in Perry, *Historical Collections*, I, passim. They demonstrate that Nicholson's following in Virginia was not inconsiderable, even among the clergy.

vote. Suddenly they found that their votes mattered. The men who wished to rule Virginia could no longer do it without heed for them.

After Nicholson's departure and the death (within a year) of his successor, the council was able for a time to resume its dominance of the government, but Nicholson's struggle for the support of the assembly was a lesson not lost on Blair and his friends: control of Virginia would ultimately depend on control of the House of Burgesses. Not that the burgesses had been a negligible factor till now. The Ludwells and Beverleys had used them effectively on many occasions, as we have seen, in thwarting a Jeffreys or an Effingham. But henceforth it might be necessary to go beyond the burgesses to the voters who put them in office. Elections would have to be managed to see that the right people got in.

That a change was coming over Virginia politics was apparent as early as 1699, when the first assembly under Nicholson passed a law forbidding candidates to do what they had probably just been doing, to "give, present or allow, to any person or persons haveing voice or vote in such election any money, meat, drink or provision, or make any present, gift, reward, or entertainment . . . in order to procure the vote or votes of such person or persons for his or their election to be a burgess or burgesses." [47] It is, of course, no sign of democracy when candidates buy votes, whether with liquor, gold, or promises. But when people's votes are sought and bought, it is at least a sign that they matter.

They had probably begun to matter before Nicholson started his contest with the council for their votes. Before the end of the seventeenth century there were more big men than the council or the House of Burgesses had room for, and the law against treating suggests that the voters were already being courted by rival aspirants to public office. That in itself should have given them ideas. When the king's governor himself contended with local magnates for their votes, the small planters could scarcely fail to feel their stature rising. And they were reminded of it at every election. In spite of the law, which remained on the books throughout the colonial period, candidates continued to "swill the planters with bumbo" in hot pursuit of their votes. The election contests meant more than a few free drinks for the small planter. They sharpened his political intelligence and placed him closer than ever before to the seats of power.

The small man's new position was exhibited (and exaggerated)

[47] Hening, III, 173.

in the laments of the royal governor who succeeded Nicholson and continued to challenge the Virginia barons for control of the colony. Alexander Spotswood, another British military officer, who held the governor's chair from 1710 to 1723 (when James Blair again made a successful trip to England), had instructions that would have brought benefits to the small man, if successfully carried out, for they would have eliminated the accumulation of land by men who had no intention of cultivating it themselves. He was to see that all land grants required the owner of a tract to cultivate three acres for every fifty in it. Failure would result in its reversion to the crown.[48] Spotswood assumed that his principal opposition would come from the powerful gentlemen who sat on the council and who had been busy gobbling up land. He was not entirely mistaken, for he later found that Blair had a majority of the members in his camp, and any effort to change the situation was blocked by a clause in his instructions that required the consent of a majority of the council for dismissal of a member.[49] But Spotswood's greatest difficulty came from the burgesses. To his dismay, he discovered at the first election after his arrival "a new and unaccountable humour which hath obtained in several Countys of excluding the Gentlemen from being Burgesses, and choosing only persons of mean figure and character." [50]

Spotswood was right about the new humor of the voters but probably not about the quality of the men they elected. The new burgesses were, as usual, an affluent lot of landowners looking out for their own interests.[51] But they were also men who knew how to please the men who elected them.[52] It was a time of low tobacco prices, and as the burgesses gauged public opinion, taxes concerned the voters more than land. Accordingly these tribunes of the people could safely agree to a long and complicated law that seemed to

[48] Leonard W. Labaree, ed., *Royal Instructions to British Colonial Governors, 1670–1776* (New York, 1935), I, 589–90.

[49] *Ibid.*, I, 60; Spotswood, *Official Letters*, II, 154–55; Williams, "Political Alignments," 171; Rouse, *Blair*, 194–97. On the council's attitude to the instructions on land see *Executive Journals* III, 194–95, 221.

[50] Spotswood, *Official Letters*, I, 19. On the growth in power of the House of Burgesses during and after Spotswood's time see Jack P. Greene, *The Quest for Power: The Lower Houses of Assembly in the Southern Royal Colonies, 1689–1776* (Chapel Hill, N.C., 1963).

[51] Williams, "Political Alignments," 126–27.

[52] Cf. John C. Rainbolt, "The Alteration in the Relationship between Leadership and Constituents in Virginia, 1660 to 1720," *WMQ* 3rd ser., XXVII (1970), 411–34.

comply with the governor's instructions (but which put all existing grants beyond question, no matter what errors might have been committed in the surveying and patenting of them). But when he asked for money to raise troops against another impending French and Indian attack, they declined.[53] Spotswood blamed his failures on the ignorance and plebeian character of the assemblymen, who strove "to recommend themselves to the populace upon a received opinion among them, that he is the best Patriot that most violently opposes all Overtures for raising money." [54] At the next election in 1712 the new turn in politics was even more evident. "The Mob of this Country," wrote Spotswood, "finding themselves able to carry whom they please, have generally chosen representatives of their own Class, who as their principal Recommendation have declared their resolution to raise no Tax on the people, let the occasion be what it will." [55]

Although Spotswood underestimated the social quality of the men elected, he was not mistaken about the tenor of their politics. And he was ready with a solution. The trouble came, he believed, from "a defect in the Constitution, which allows to every one, tho' but just out of the Condition of a Servant, and that can but purchase half an acre of Land, an equal Vote with the Men of the best Estate in the Country." [56] As long as this situation prevailed, he was sure, "the meaner sort of People will ever carry the Elections, and the humour generally runs to choose such men as are their most familiar Companions, who very eagerly seek to be Burgesses merely for the lucre of the Salary, and who, for fear of not being chosen again, dare in Assembly do nothing that may be disrelished out of the House by the Comon People." [57] But when Spotswood proposed to the men of best estate, sitting on the council, that they remedy the evil by raising the qualifications for voting, some discreetly thought it was not a proper time for such a move, and others frankly declared themselves satisfied with the situation.[58]

When Spotswood tried to outwit the "vulgar mob" by tampering with their representatives after the election, he in effect cut himself out of the political game. In 1713 he inveigled the burgesses into passing a measure that was unpopular with the small planter. The act

[53] Hening, III, 517-35; IV, 37-42; Williams, "Political Alignments," 129-30, 144-45; *Journals of the House of Burgesses, 1702–1712*, 340-49.

[54] Spotswood, *Official Letters*, I, 140.

[55] *Ibid.*, II, 1-2.   [57] *Ibid.*, II, 124.

[56] *Ibid.*   [58] *Executive Journals*, III, 392.

provided for tobacco inspection and the destruction of tobacco that did not meet standards, and it created forty inspectors who were to receive fees that were estimated at £250 annually.[59] Twenty-five burgesses were rewarded with these plums, and Spotswood had already found other government offices for four more. A majority of the burgesses were thus in his debt, and during the rest of the session the measures he proposed went through easily.[60] But populist politics were already too strongly entrenched to be defeated by such crude tactics.

Queen Anne died in 1714, and the accession of a new monarch required new elections. The Virginia councillors, perceiving Spotswood's vulnerability with the people, campaigned for candidates who opposed him and the "court party" they accused him of forming. The result was not even close. Only seventeen members of the former House were reelected, and only two of them had accepted inspectorships.[61] It was nearly a clean sweep of Spotswood's supporters, a conclusive victory for the vulgar mob and for the councillors who had busied themselves in the campaign. Spotswood later complained that he had been "branded by Mr. Ludwell and his Adherents (who set themselves up for Patriots of the People,) for endeavouring to oppress the people by extending the Prerogative of the Crown." [62] But Spotswood and every other governor who tried to carry out British policy lent validity to the charge by wrapping themselves in the royal prerogative when challenging actions of the legislature. Prerogative after 1688 was a dubious weapon. For a dozen years Spotswood used it to no avail in the effort to free his administration from the grip that the Blairs, Burwells, and Ludwells held on Virginia politics. In 1722 he finally gave up trying to carry out his instructions from England and joined his opponents. It was too late to retrieve his career as governor, for they had already succeeded in arranging his recall. But before he left office he made up for lost opportunities by cultivating the men who had opposed him and by sealing their friendship in a flood of huge land grants in the west for them and for himself.[63] The requirement for cultivating three acres out of fifty was quietly ignored.

It will be evident, in spite of Spotswood's accusations, that the

[59] Winfree, *Laws of Virginia*, 75–90; Williams, "Political Alignments," 142–44; Spotswood, *Official Letters*, II, 49.

[60] Williams, "Political Alignments," 149–58.   [61] *Ibid.*, 159–63.

[62] Spotswood, *Official Letters*, II, 152.

[63] *Executive Journals*, III, 538–41, 546–48, 551.

new politics did not really constitute a surrender to the mob but a new triumph for the men who had dominated Virginia from the beginning. Some of the measures that Spotswood sponsored, on instruction from England, were designed to clip the wings of the Virginia barons and to favor the small man. But the burgesses would have none of them. In every popular contest Spotswood lost. How, then, did Virginia gentlemen persuade the voters to return the right kind of people to the House of Burgesses? How could patricians win in populist politics? The question can lead us again to the paradox which has underlain our story, the union of freedom and slavery in Virginia and America.

18

TOWARD
THE REPUBLIC

GOVERNOR Spotswood's explanation of the way Virginians gained office in the assembly was that they lowered themselves to the level of the mob, catering to the passions and prejudices of the louts whom they filled with drink.[1] At first sight this diagnosis seems to be supported in the classic portrayal of a Virginia election, Robert Munford's play, *The Candidates*, written in 1770.[2] The play opens with the hero, Wou'dbe, grumbling about the campaign he must undertake to please the voters.

> Must I again be subject to the humours of a fickle croud? Must I again resign my reason, and be nought but what each voter pleases? Must I cajole, fawn, and wheedle, for a place that brings so little profit?

The questions are rhetorical, and the play furnishes several vignettes of candidates cajoling, fawning on, and wheedling the freeholders. These very arts, we have already suggested, are testimony to the fact that the voters mattered, that they had to be won. But the larger lesson of the play is that cajoling, fawning, and wheedling did not win them. In spite of his opening speech, Wou'dbe does none of these things. When asked by the voters whether he will achieve this or that impossible goal for them, he says honestly that he cannot. He leaves it to his rivals to lie and flatter. For a time it looks as though he may lose, but then Worthy steps in. Worthy is evidently

[1] Spotswood, *Official Letters*, I, 140; II, 50, 128, 134–35.
[2] Jay D. Hubbell and Douglass Adair, eds., "Robert Munford's *The Candidates*," *WMQ*, 3rd ser., V (1948), 217–57.

a bigger man than any of the other candidates. He has sat in the House before but at first declined to stand in this election. He now changes his mind, at the same time declaring his support of Wou'dbe as a running mate (there are two seats to be filled). With his entry the voters have no hesitation in turning down the flatterers and elect Wou'dbe and Worthy forthwith.[3]

From this result we may perhaps conclude that Virginia politics was a compound of social deference and demagoguery. But demagoguery in this particular election failed; and the social prestige that succeeded could not have operated so powerfully unless the small planters, who made up the great majority of the voters, were persuaded that their interests would be well served by big men. Such a persuasion required that the two should perceive themselves as sharing interests that were more important, at least for political purposes, than those that divided them. Class consciousness was strong in Virginia. The weight carried by Worthy in the election testifies to the author's awareness of its strength. But Worthy's victory also testifies to the author's belief that Virginia's freeholders could be counted on to support worthy men in the end. The larger answer to the question of how patricians could win in populist politics is that Virginians, great and small, had begun to perceive a common identity.

This sense of common identity was based on common interests, some new, some old. The voters who elected the Worthies and Wou'dbes were not the drifting freedmen of Bacon's time. With the decline of immigrant free labor and the opening up of new areas, relatively free of Indian danger, the mass of white Virginians were becoming landowners. In any case only landowners could now be voters. The English government had itself insisted on that restric-

---

[3] For three scholarly accounts of eighteenth-century Virginia electoral politics see Charles Sydnor, *Gentlemen Freeholders* (Chapel Hill, N.C., 1952); Lucille Griffith, *The Virginia House of Burgesses, 1750–1774* (University, Ala., 1970), 45–127; and Brown and Brown, *Virginia, 1705–1786,* 169–214 and passim. The Browns have demonstrated the absence of class alignments in Virginia politics and have emphasized that membership in an upper class did not guarantee a candidate's election. My analysis of Virginia politics and of the absence of class alignments differs from that of the Browns but does not appear to me to be incompatible either with their findings or with those of Griffith and Sydnor. The Browns have been careful to point out (p. 227) that candidates were generally men of substance, a conclusion supported by both Griffith and Sydnor, who see Virginia politics as more dominated by such men than the Browns will allow.

tion. Though the amount of land was not at first specified,[4] Virginians could not be content with the small plots of a peasantry. Fifty acres per working hand was the standard ratio in Virginia's system of rotating tobacco, corn, and trees;[5] and few landowners had less than a hundred acres, especially in new counties on the frontier, where small men congregated to become rich in acres though poor in pocket. Even in an old county like Surry, the majority of new land grants in the 1690s were for tracts of more than 250 acres.[6] The owners of such grants had every reason to join forces with their more powerful neighbors against attempts from across the sea to regulate or adjust or restrict their titles. Small men could worry as much as large about losing their land for failure to pay quitrents or even for failure to cultivate the required three acres in fifty.[7]

Other common interests between large planter and small had existed from the beginning—for one, the fact that both depended on the same single crop. Whatever affected tobacco and its price

[4] The first specification of an amount seems to have been in 1736, when it was fixed at 100 acres of unimproved land or "twenty-five acres with a house and plantation." Hening, IV, 475.

[5] Carman, *American Husbandry*, 165.

[6] Kelly, "Economic and Social Development of Surry County," 130. In the 1704 rent roll of all Virginia landowners the average holding was 417 acres. Williams, "Small Farmer in Eighteenth-Century Virginia Politics," 93. In Prince William County on the upper Potomac in 1737 the majority of landowners held over 400 acres. Brown and Brown, *Virginia, 1705–1786*, 14.

[7] Not only large land speculators but many ordinary owners may have found it difficult to keep the legal three acres per fifty under cultivation; for while planters needed fifty acres per working hand, a man could tend no more than three or four acres in tobacco by himself, and two was probably a more common figure. He might tend another acre or two in corn, but probably the requirement of three acres out of fifty was stated in the law as about what one man could be expected to cultivate on a tobacco plantation. Yet most landowners probably had more than fifty acres for every tithable in their families. A comparison of the 1704 rent roll with the list of tithables for that year shows approximately one working hand per 100 acres of land owned. Fifty years later the working population of the tidewater was denser, but in the newer piedmont counties, where plantations averaged 375 acres, the workers were fewer, about one hand to 125 acres. (Williams, "Small Farmer in Eighteenth-Century Virginia Politics," 93.) The figures suggest that many Virginia voters would have felt as threatened as, say, members of the council by a strict enforcement of the land laws.

affected both. It was this that had made possible the plant-cutting riots in 1682. But common interests could not become bonds of common identity while the tensions that had surfaced in Bacon's Rebellion continued to agitate the colony. Once the small planter felt less exploited by taxation and began to prosper a little, he became less turbulent, less dangerous, more respectable. He could begin to see his big neighbor not as an extortionist but as a powerful protector of their common interests.

Their interests were not, to be sure, identical. The small man might be more hard pressed to pay taxes out of his small crop and therefore be particularly keen for low taxes; but since direct taxes were by poll and since the big man's tobacco was grown by slaves on whom he had to pay the tax, low taxes were a direct benefit to him too. The small man was frequently a debtor, but the large man, his creditor, was likely also to be in debt, either to London merchants or to other large men. The large man might make a profit from the small man by marketing tobacco for him, but both were sellers in the end. The very fact that the large man stood to lose along with the small man in a prolonged depression of tobacco prices made him seem all the more appropriate as a spokesman for the whole country.

What was more important for the future, the common interests that enabled the small planter to trust the large, also encouraged the large planter to trust the small. Large planters had been willing to follow Nicholson's lead in drawing the small planter into the political game, because they perceived that in a contest with higher authority they were likely to be on the same side. Spotswood complained that Virginians stuck together, that "He is the lover of this Country who in all Controversies justifies the Virginian and in all Dealings is ready to help him to overreach the Foreigner; He is the Patriot who will not yield to whatever the Government [i.e., the governor] proposes, and can remain deaf to all Arguments that are used for the raising of Money." [8]

By 1722 Spotswood himself had joined the company of Virginia patriots. When he gave up his contest with the leading planters, he inaugurated thirty years of harmony, during which royal governors seldom quarreled with their assemblies. The harmony was largely the result of England's willingness, for the time being, to let Virginians run the colony their own way. But the small planter did

[8] *Official Letters*, II, 50.

not thereby lose the position he had attained in Virginia politics. Even though he was no longer needed in contests with the royal governor, the big men continued to court his approval at election time in minor contests with each other. He continued to give them his votes, and they continued to instruct him and themselves in political principles that magnified his importance. They could afford to do so because he did have interests comparable with their own.

Put another way, they could afford it because their prosperity no longer depended on wringing the last possible penny from him. Although government office in Virginia continued to be more lucrative than in many other colonies, it was no longer a principal way to wealth. A new generation of magnates were multiplying the capital they inherited from their more aggressive parents, but they did not have to antagonize the lesser freemen in the process. They could be Virginians in a way that their predecessors never were. The difference lay not only in the prosperity that came to large men and small alike after the tobacco market began to rise. The difference lay in the new confidence that the two felt in each other and in their colony. As their fortunes rose, the most successful did not think so much of exchanging life in Virginia for life in the old country.

For seventeenth-century Virginians the security of high position had been associated with England and English ways of living. Some had tried to overcome the feeling. Governor Berkeley had dreamed of making the colony more deserving of patriotic devotion by making it more like England. But Berkeley's scheme never came close to success, and Virginians who reached the top in the seventeenth century went on feeling not quite satisfied, not quite settled. Many had in fact been immigrants who continued to think wistfully of the land they left behind. William Fitzhugh, for example, who cheered on other well-supplied immigrants with calculations of the comfortable income to be had from tobacco, nevertheless kept thinking of investing his Virginia winnings in some safe English country estate, where he would retire to live out his days in peace.[9] Few of those who made it in the seventeenth century, Fitzhugh included, became as committed to Virginia as Berkeley was, and they showed where they stood by the way they lived. They had too little confidence in the colony to sink their earnings in houses like the one Berkeley built at Green Spring or even like

[9] Davis, *Fitzhugh*, 175–176, 202–3, 218, 221, 253, 279–80.

those he arranged for in Jamestown (which Bacon burned to the ground). At the opening of the eighteenth century the typical planter, even though successful, still lived in something small and wooden. Permanent buildings were somehow inappropriate. Permanent buildings were for permanent places, like England.

Most of the successful nevertheless stayed on; and their children and grandchildren, born in the colony and borne up by its new labor force, discovered a commitment to Virginia that their forebears had never known. They became the patriots who thwarted Spotswood at every turn and finally thwarted George III. In the second quarter of the eighteenth century they built the great mansions, many of which still stand along the rivers of the tidewater and in the lower piedmont area above the falls or "freshes." Within the space of thirty years dozens of houses to equal or surpass Green Spring went up. It was at this time that the Pages built Rosewell, the Harrisons built Berkeley, the Lees built Stratford, the Carters built Sabine Hall, Nomini Hall, and Carter's Grove, and William Byrd II, after spending most of his life in London, built Westover. Far up the Potomac, Lawrence Washington started Mount Vernon, while his worshiping young brother George looked on; and Peter Jefferson, about the same time, moved his family, including three-year-old Thomas, into Tuckahoe, built above the falls of the James by his wife's parents, the Randolphs.[10]

The men who built the great houses and lived in them still thought of themselves as Englishmen and aped the style of the English country gentleman.[11] They read English newspapers and imported the latest English fashions; but with a few exceptions like Byrd they were content to be Englishmen in Virginia, without continually sighing for the security of the mother country. The commitment to Virginia that they expressed in bricks and mortar grew with the change in labor that made Virginia forever unlike England. The safe investment that a William Fitzhugh hoped for in an English estate would have come from the rents that other Englishmen would pay for land. Virginia's great planters too could count on getting some rent from their immense quantities of land, but their fortunes rested less on extracting rents from tenants or taxes from freemen

[10] Thomas T. Waterman, *The Mansions of Virginia, 1706–1776* (Chapel Hill, N.C., 1945), passim.

[11] Louis B. Wright, *The First Gentlemen of Virginia: Intellectual Qualities of the Early Colonial Ruling Class* (San Marino, Calif., 1940), passim.

than on the labor they extracted from African men and women permanently enslaved to them. They no longer needed to exploit other Englishmen in the ways their fathers had.

Thus by the second quarter of the eighteenth century Virginians had established the conditions for the mixture of slavery and freedom that was to prevail for at least another century: a slave labor force isolated from the rest of society by race and racism; a body of large planters, firmly committed to the country, who had become practiced in politics and political maneuvering; and a larger body of small planters who had been persuaded that their interests were well served by the leadership of their big neighbors. The way was now prepared for the final ingredient that locked these elements together in a vital combination and enabled Virginians large and small to join with other Americans in devotion to freedom and equality, in abhorrence of slavery—and in the preservation of slave-holding.

That ingredient was a conglomeration of republican ideas that had gained popularity in England at the time of the Commonwealth. In England the ideas had not in the end prevailed, but they continued to be studied and refined and proclaimed by men who have come to be known as the eighteenth-century commonwealthmen.[12] The commonwealthmen were not conspirators, hoping to overthrow the monarchy and restore the republic of the 1650s. But they were admirers of the Roman republic if not the English one, and caustic critics of the English monarchy. Along with other Englishmen they paid tribute to John Locke and the Revolution of 1688; but their favorite political philosophers were James Harrington and Algernon Sydney, who had championed the cause of republican government and suffered (the one imprisoned, the other executed) at the hands of Charles II.

The commonwealthmen believed that a monarch, if not curbed, would inevitably turn tyrant and reduce his subjects to slavery. In eighteenth-century England they saw in every exercise of executive power the signs of a drift toward tyranny and slavery, which they called on their countrymen to arrest. They suspected the army. They despised the churchmen who unflaggingly supported every infringement of liberty. They wanted to extend the suffrage and make representatives more responsive to the people. Above all, they

---

[12] From Caroline Robbins' study of them, *The Eighteenth-Century Commonwealthman* (Cambridge, Mass., 1959).

wanted a wide distribution of property to create an enlarged en-
franchised yeomanry who would see to it that government stuck to
its proper business of protecting liberty and property. Their countrymen paid them little heed, and their names have not survived
in fame: John Trenchard, Thomas Gordon, Robert Molesworth,
Francis Hutcheson, James Burgh—these are scarcely household
names today. But in the American colonies they were known and
admired. In Virginia their ideas gradually gathered strength in a
movement whose beginnings are difficult to discern but which became more and more palpable as the century advanced, until Virginians spoke in a language that would have astonished and disgusted
William Berkeley.

Governor Berkeley had rejoiced in 1671 that he had kept heresy
and sedition out of Virginia. When his people rose up against him
five years later, he must have been relieved at least that Bacon was
no Cromwell and that the rebellion bred no republican ideas of the
kind that had disfigured England for him in the 1650s. He wished,
as we have seen, that Virginia ministers would "pray oftener and
preach less." And he hoped that there would be no printing press
or free school "these hundreds years" to nourish the treasonous
learning that preachers, and schools, and printing presses fostered.[13]
He did not get his wish.

In 1730 William Parks, a printer who had already started a
press in Maryland, established one in Williamsburg, now the capital
of Virginia. Two years later the burgesses authorized him to publish
their votes and proceedings.[14] And in 1736 he started Virginia's first
newspaper, the *Virginia Gazette*. He filled it mainly with news
taken from the London papers and from other colonial ones, along
with those tedious essays in which eighteenth-century authors tried
to imitate the *Spectator*. But he also made it a forum to which legislators and would-be legislators could carry the debate on public
policies outside the doors of the House of Burgesses. Although only
scattered issues of the *Gazette* are extant from before the 1770s, they
do reveal appeals to the public for and against an ingenious scheme
to let the French buy tobacco in Virginia (February–April, 1738),
for and against a tobacco-inspection law (August–December, 1738),
and for and against the relief of dissenters from parish levies (March–

[13] Hening, II, 517.
[14] H. R. McIlwaine, ed., *Journals of the House of Burgesses of Virginia, 1727–1734, 1736–1740* (Richmond, 1910), 121.

April, 1752). There was nothing seditious about any of these discussions, and it is difficult even to know who the readers of the *Gazette* may have been. But to publish the proceedings of the assembly and to carry arguments over public policy to the press could scarcely diminish the expectation of popular participation in politics.

Popular participation in politics did not necessarily indicate the presence of republican ideas in Virginia, but it did carry that implication for many eighteenth-century Englishmen; and governors who were vexed by it did make the connection. Nicholson, who had tried some appeals to the people himself, allegedly called the Virginians "a rich, populous, and obstinate People of Commonwealth Principles." [15] And in some of the products of William Parks' press Nicholson, had he still been around, would have seen justification both for his accusation and for William Berkeley's denunciation of printing. In 1745, for example, the rising in Scotland led by the young Stuart pretender to the throne offered republican-minded Virginians an opportunity to oppose rebellion and yet safely support revolution. Loyalty to the Hanovers against the deposed House of Stuart meant acceptance of the right of the people to replace a monarch who failed to protect their liberty and property. The *Gazette* accordingly reported how the people of Norfolk, Virginia, celebrated news of the Pretender's defeat in a parade with banners bearing the slogan "Liberty and Property." And on the same occasion a writer for the *Gazette* taught republican principles to his readers with two appropriate lessons from Scripture. In the disobedience of the people of Israel to Saul he found "an early Instance against passive Obedience"; and in their choice of David as king, despite the fact that Saul had lawful heirs, he found "an early Instance against hereditary Succession to the Crown when 'tis against the Good of the People to permit it." Thus he celebrated the defeat of a rebellion by urging the right of revolution whenever the "good of the people" called for it.[16]

It is not unlikely that the author of this bit of exegesis was a young Virginia-born clergyman, who preached more than he prayed. William Stith, rector of Henrico Parish and chaplain to the House of Burgesses, had stepped into James Blair's place, not as com-

[15] *Executive Journals*, II, 393; Perry, *Historical Collections*, I, 106-7; Beverley, *History and Present State of Virginia*, 112, 113. Cf. Burk, *History*, II, 326.

[16] *Virginia Gazette*, June 23–July 26, July 24–31, 1746.

missary or councillor but as self-appointed political docent to Virginia. In a sermon to the burgesses, which Parks printed as a pamphlet, Stith had already denounced the rebellion of the Pretender by extolling the Revolution of 1688 as "the wisest, best-conducted, and most happy Event, that any where appears upon the British Annals." The British Constitution, as Stith explained it, was distinguished by the limits it placed on the executive. And he added a novel explanation of the maxim "The King can do no wrong." What was meant here was that the Constitution prevented the king from wrongdoing: "This is to say, his Prerogative can never extend so far, as to injure and oppress his People." [17] If their king was so limited, Virginians could draw their own conclusions about the powers he was entitled to delegate to his colonial governors.

Stith continued his indoctrination of Virginians in 1747 by writing a history of the colony under the Virginia Company (1606–24), which again William Parks printed for him. Although the period was remote, Stith discovered in it relevant lessons about the dangers of prerogative power and the blessings of liberty. He announced in the preface that his purpose was to "un-solomonize that silly Monarch," James I. He displayed the hardships of Virginians under the tyranny of Governor Argall and exulted when "the People were again restored to their Birthright, the Enjoyment of British Liberty," by the calling of the first representative assembly. And he offered other hints of the defects of absolute monarchy in his account of the different Indian tribes. The Chickahominies, he reported, were "a stout, daring and free People," who "were governed in a Republican Form" and consequently "took all Opportunities of shaking off Powhatan's Yoke, whom they looked upon and hated, as a Tyrant." The superiority of republican government was evident in their prosperity, for though their land was poor they made more plentiful crops and had greater abundance of provisions than any other tribe. "Such a happy Influence," concluded Stith, "had Liberty, and such visible Incitement did firm Property give to the Industry of even that lazy and improvident People." [18]

When the harmony between Virginia's burgesses and governors was finally disrupted in 1753 by Governor Robert Dinwiddie's at-

---

[17] William Stith, *A Sermon Preached before the General Assembly at Williamsburg, March 2, 1745/6* (Williamsburg, 1745/6), 19–20.

[18] William Stith, *The History of the First Discovery and Settlement of Virginia* (Williamsburg, 1747), vi, 130–31, 160–61.

tempt to exact a fee of a pistole (about 17 shillings) for every land patent, Stith took a hand in arousing popular opposition to the governor. "Liberty and property and no pistole" was Stith's slogan.[19] And Dinwiddie reported to his superiors that the House of Burgesses in opposing him showed themselves to be "very much in a Republican way of thinking." [20]

How widely republican ideas were disseminated in the years between Nicholson and Dinwiddie we can only guess. If it were not for Stith and the *Gazette*, we might even dismiss Dinwiddie's report as the kind of exaggeration that political contests often generate. But the governor's diagnosis gains credence by the fact that many who stood against him in the pistole-fee dispute also stood against the British Parliament a dozen years later when the colonies' ultimate quarrel with England began. The Virginia House of Burgesses then took the lead in arousing colonial opposition to the Stamp Act; and in the years that followed Virginians stayed at the forefront of resistance to England and took the leading roles in creation of the American republic. By 1776 there could be no doubt that Virginians were "very much in a republican way of thinking."

Who taught them, besides Parks and Stith, will remain something of a mystery. In spite of Governor Berkeley's fulminations against printing presses and preachers, we can scarcely give Parks and Stith the whole credit. Nor can we lay the charge to that other instrument of sedition condemned by Berkeley, the school. Although a number of Virginians, more charitably inclined to education than the governor, left bequests for the founding of schools, and though some were opened, Virginia by 1776 was still short of them, and a large proportion of the small planters remained illiterate.[21] The wealthiest families sometimes sent their children to England for education, where a few may have attended the popular academies run by dissenters from the Anglican establishment. There they could have imbibed some of the notions of the eighteenth-century commonwealthmen. But most attended the "public" schools or, if old enough, Oxford or Cambridge, or more likely studied law at the Inns of Court, where their teachers would not have been selected

[19] Morton, *Colonial Virginia*, II, 625; Griffith, *Virginia House of Burgesses*, 25.

[20] Brock, *Official Records of Robert Dinwiddie*, I, 100, 103, 236.

[21] Kenneth A. Lockridge, *Literacy in Colonial New England: An Enquiry into the Social Context of Literacy in the Early Modern West* (New York, 1974), 72–93.

for republican sympathies. In any case, the number who went to England was small; and parents generally complained that the principal lesson learned there was extravagance. Most Virginians got whatever schooling they received at home, from their parents or, if their parents were wealthy enough, from a private tutor. Some went on to William and Mary (where from 1752 until his death in 1755 William Stith was president) or to the northern colleges. There the young Virginians may have met the writings of the English commonwealthmen and a sympathetic presentation of the classical republicans of Greece and Rome.[22]

Those who went north could have returned with some of the leaven of dissent. But those who stayed behind could also have been infected with it by the Scotch-Irish Presbyterians who descended on Virginia's back-country counties in the eighteenth century. Or they could have got it from other puritanical immigrants. Because of the scarcity of reputable Anglican ministers, Virginia had always been prone to invasion by dissenting missionaries of higher character and more democratic political philosophy. The Quakers had attracted men of all classes, including county commissioners, in the seventeenth century; and in the eighteenth the Baptists made inroads everywhere. Quakers, Baptists, and Presbyterians all sought souls, not political converts; but James I's maxim, "No bishop, no king," still held true. Dissenters from the Church of England had a proclivity for preaching rather than praying, and for books, schools, and colleges. In 1776 they founded the first college in Virginia after William and Mary, and they named it Hampden-Sydney, for two republican heroes.[23]

But most of the men who ran Virginia were not dissenters, and neither were those who ran the American republic in its first years. They may have learned something from the dissenters, but they probably learned more from their own libraries, which were not confined to the volumes that William Parks could supply. Although all Virginia planters were likely to spend more time in the saddle than in the study, they did have books and some read widely.[24] William Byrd recorded his daily sessions with Latin and Greek au-

[22] E. S. Morgan, *Virginians at Home* (Williamsburg, 1952), 5–28.

[23] Chap. 7, note 48; W. M. Gewehr, *The Great Awakening in Virginia, 1740–1790* (Durham, N.C., 1930). Cf. Rhys Isaac, "Evangelical Revolt: The Nature of the Baptists' Challenge to the Traditional Order in Virginia, 1765 to 1775," *WMQ*, 3rd ser., XXI (1974), 345–68.

[24] See again Wright, *First Gentlemen of Virginia*.

thors. Thomas Jefferson, whose copy of Harrington's *Oceana* came from Byrd's library, was the most bookish of the lot and left us some clues about his reading, in comments on different authors. For example, he called Sydney's *Discourses concerning Government* "the best elementary book of the principles of government . . . in any language." [25] Yet we would hardly know of his familiarity with John Locke's *Two Treatises of Government* if he had not incorporated passages almost word for word in the Declaration of Independence, apparently unaware that he was doing so. Perhaps other children who grew up in eighteenth-century Virginia also read themselves into republicanism without leaving us a record of their progress.

In Jefferson's own view the education of young Virginians was unlikely to make anything but tyrants of them, especially those who spent their early years, as he did, on one of the great plantations. The children of the planters mingled freely with the children of slaves, and the result, in Jefferson's opinion, was to train them in tyranny. "The whole commerce between master and slave," he wrote in a famous passage, "is a perpetual exercise of the most boisterous passions, the most unremitting despotism on the one part, and degrading submissions on the other. Our children see this, and learn to imitate it. . . . The parent storms, the child looks on, catches the lineaments of wrath, puts on the same airs in the circle of smaller slaves, gives a loose to his worst of passions, and thus nursed, educated, and daily exercised in tyranny, cannot but be stamped by it with odious peculiarities." Virginia not only had too few schools, but her great plantations were thus themselves schools of vice and tyranny. "The man must be a prodigy," Jefferson concluded, "who can retain his manners and morals undepraved by such circumstances." [26]

If Jefferson was right, he was a prodigy. And so were his friends George Mason, George Washington, James Madison, James Monroe, and a host of other revolutionary Virginians who, whatever their complicity in the preservation of slavery, cannot otherwise by any stretch of the imagination be called depraved. They grew up under the conditions that Jefferson described, yet they displayed none of the boisterous passions, none of the lineaments of wrath, and certainly none of the disposition for tyranny that those con-

[25] E. Millicent Sowerby, *Catalogue of the Library of Thomas Jefferson* (Washington, D.C., 1952–59), III, 13.

[26] Thomas Jefferson, *Notes on the State of Virginia*, William Peden, ed. (Chapel Hill, N.C., 1955), 162.

ditions were supposed to induce. Washington, to be sure, had a hot temper, and his manner was sufficiently monarchical to make some of his admirers wish to award him a crown; but no man ever had his temper better under control, and anyone who reads his correspondence cannot fail to be impressed by his meekness in submitting to the popular will, even when he thought it mistaken. Jefferson himself, whatever his shortcomings, was the greatest champion of liberty this country has ever had. As for giving loose to his passions, it has indeed been suggested that he carried on a passionate affair with one of his slaves; but if he did, so little did he show his passion that the evidence for it is entirely circumstantial. And Madison, who was to make the most original contributions to republican political thinking of any of the American revolutionists, was at the same time an adroit politician, who organized the first opposition party in the new nation, an accomplishment that could scarcely accord either with ungoverned passions or a predilection for despotism.

It may be coincidence that so many Virginians who grew up after the advent of slavery turned out to be ardent republicans. And it may be coincidence that among their predecessors who lived before slavery became prevalent, so many were unrepublican, unattractive, and unscrupulous, not to say depraved. On the other hand, there may have been more than coincidence involved. Although it seems unlikely that slavery had any tendency to improve the character of masters, it may have had affinities with republicanism that escaped Jefferson's analysis. The presence of men and women who were, in law at least, almost totally subject to the will of other men gave to those in control of them an immediate experience of what it could mean to be at the mercy of a tyrant. Virginians may have had a special appreciation of the freedom dear to republicans, because they saw every day what life without it could be like.

There were other affinities between slavery and republicanism, as we shall see. But, whatever the reason, it is clear that Virginia's great planters were extraordinarily receptive to the "republican way of thinking." And it was that way of thinking which completed the elevation of the small planter and solidified the identity of interest among planters, large and small. Republicanism had always been associated with men who worked in the ground. Aristotle had laid down the axiom that "the best material of democracy is an agricultural population," and that people engaged in other occupations had "no room" for the virtues that were necessary to a republic.[27] Har-

[27] Aristotle, *Politics*, Book VI.

rington and Sydney had elaborated Aristotle's views. In their pages Virginians could read that the liberty of a people depended not merely on constant vigilance against monarchical encroachments but on the wide diffusion of land and virtue and arms. Men who labored on their own land grew not only food but independence. No would-be tyrant could starve them into submission or win their votes with paltry promises. If they were armed with guns as well as land, they would have both the will and the means to defend their country's freedom against usurpation from within and invasion from without. The yeoman farmer, standing foursquare on his own plot of land, gun in hand and virtue in his heart, was thus the ideal citizen of a republic. Thomas Jefferson was echoing an old republican tradition when he argued that "Those who labour in the earth are the chosen people of God," that "the proportion which the aggregate of the other classes of citizens bears in any state to that of its husbandmen, is the proportion of its unsound to its healthy parts." [28]

To be sure, Virginia's husbandmen did not all fit the picture that Jefferson drew. In particular they did not seem to many observers to exhibit the virtue that their labors in the soil should have generated.[29] Nor did they all qualify as yeoman farmers by owning their own land. There had always been tenancy in Virginia, and it seems to have grown in the last part of the eighteenth century,[30] so that many of Virginia's small men did not have the independence that came from being able to bid defiance to landlords. Nevertheless, during the colonial period there were enough who did own land to make Virginia, in the eyes of Virginians at least, a land to fit the

[28] Jefferson, *Notes on Virginia*, 164–65. A classic work, much read but still unpublished, is Douglass Adair, "The Intellectual Origins of Jeffersonian Democracy: Republicanism, the Class Struggle, and the Virtuous Farmer" (doctoral dissertation, Yale University, 1943).

[29] Marvin L. Brown, ed., *Baroness von Riedesel and the American Revolution* (Chapel Hill, N.C., 1965), 85–86; Newton D. Mereness, ed., *Travels in the American Colonies* (New York, 1916), 591–92; Ferdinand-Marie Bayard, *Travels of a Frenchman in Maryland and Virginia*, Ben C. McCary, ed. and trans. (Williamsburg, 1950), 42; Thomas Anburey, *Travels through the Interior Parts of America* (London, 1791), II, 309–11; Elkanah Watson, *Men and Times of the Revolution* (2nd ed., New York, 1856), 71–72; Samuel Kercheval, *A History of the Valley of Virginia* (3rd ed., Woodstock, Va., 1902), 294, 297.

[30] Willard F. Bliss, "The Rise of Tenancy in Virginia," *VMHB*, LVIII (1950), 427–41; Jackson T. Main, "The Distribution of Property in Post-Revolutionary Virginia," *Mississippi Valley Historical Review*, XLI (1954), 241–58. Cf. Williams, "Small Farmer in Eighteenth-Century Virginia Politics," 93.

picture in the republican textbooks. Even the small farmers themselves seem to have shared the vision. Although few would have gained it from reading, they were willing to be taught by their literate neighbors. A half century or more of populist politics, of being called out to defeat with their votes the designs of royal governors or of rival politicians, had given them an understanding of the political role that yeomen were supposed to play in a republic. Edmund Randolph, remarking on their willingness to stand with their larger neighbors in the contest with England, observed that they "seemed to catch the full spirit of the theories which at the fountainhead were known only to men of studious retirement." [31]

An easy familiarity between large men and small had grown up over the years. A young English minister who came to Virginia at the end of the eighteenth century was surprised to find that "Those European prejudices are not known which insulate the man of rank and property and make him solitary in the midst of society. The man who made such pretensions to superiority would be despised." [32] Another Englishman, who had lived long in Virginia, noted that the rude manners of the lower class frightened the European "who expects to find in all men those gradations of humble distance to which he may happen to have been accustomed." But he advised the foreign traveler to put off his haughty airs: let him "accost them like fellow mortals of the same species, and they will be the first to do him a real service." [33] Thomas Anburey, a captured British officer, on parole during the Revolutionary War, remarked on the way in which the "levelling principle" animated the colony, especially during the war. He cited an episode at Tuckahoe, the plantation of Colonel Thomas Mann Randolph near Richmond. Anburey was enjoying an evening with the colonel when three "peasants" (a word which no native Virginian would have used)

> entered the room where the Colonel and his company were sitting, took themselves chairs, drew near the fire, began spitting, pulling off their country boots all over mud, and then opened their business, which was simply about some continental flour to be ground

[31] Edmund Randolph, *History of Virginia*, Arthur H. Shaffer, ed. (Charlottesville, 1970), 193.

[32] Harry Toulmin, *The Western Country in 1783: Reports on Kentucky and Virginia*, Marion Tinling and Godfrey Davies, eds. (San Marino, Calif., 1948), 40. Cf. William Eddis, *Letters from America*, Aubrey C. Land, ed. (Cambridge, Mass., 1969), 65.

[33] Tatham, *Historical and Practical Essay on Tobacco*, 60.

at the Colonel's mill: when they were gone, some one observed what great liberties they took: he replied, it was unavoidable, the spirit of independency was converted into equality, and every one who bore arms, esteemed himself upon a footing with his neighbour, and concluded with saying, "No doubt, each of these men conceives himself, in every respect, my equal." [34]

Firearms were great levelers, and the use of them by ordinary men against established authority was in itself enough to generate leveling thoughts. Republican ideology encouraged such thoughts, and those who drew their ideas from the fountainhead expressed them continually. The wartime phase of republican exaltation of the farmer was an exaltation of the militia, an insistence on an organized armed populace. George Mason was expressing the standard republican view when he drafted for the Fairfax County Committee of Safety a resolution declaring that "a well regulated Militia, composed of Gentlemen Freeholders, and other freemen, is the natural strength and only stable security of a free Government." Mason doubtless expected the "other freemen" to be led by officers drawn from the "gentlemen freeholders." But his own prescription for a well-regulated militia included annual election of officers by the men they commanded, and his argument for such elections was premised on the fact that "We came equals into this world, and equals shall we go out of it. All men are by nature born equally free and independent." [35]

Other Virginia patricians expressed a similar devotion to equality. One, who cast himself in the columns of the *Gazette* as "the Independent Whig," warned Virginians, after the winning of independence, that their new government could thrive only as long as it suppressed any aristocratic tendencies. "Without *equality*," he explained, "the attachment to the Commonwealth grows weak . . . the people lose sight of their original institutions, and sink into slavery." The Independent Whig wanted none of England's mixed government: "He who talks of *Kings, Lords* and *Commons,* and is in love with the *constitution* of Britain, is either a fool or a knave." And looking about him, he could announce, "We have no such materials here to build with." [36]

It speaks volumes about the prevailing sentiments that an ardent

---

[34] Anburey, *Travels,* II, 329–30.   [35] Mason, *Papers,* I, 212, 229.
[36] *Virginia Gazette; or, The American Advertiser,* Jan. 4, 1783. Cf. Brown and Brown, *Virginia, 1705–1786,* 32–34.

advocate of equality could see neither aristocracy nor materials for aristocracy in Virginia. What blindness affected him and Virginia's other advocates of equality? Surely they could not have wished to make equality a literal fact, to pull down Westover and Mt. Vernon and Carter's Grove, not to mention Monticello, and replace them with farmhouses? It was one thing to be on familiar terms with the lower classes, but did Virginia's patricians wish to promote their own demise? Did not the exhortations to equality invite slaves, servants, and small farmers to turn them out?

The question occurred later to an astute English diplomat, who served in Washington during Jefferson's presidency. During his tour of duty Sir Augustus John Foster visited both the northern and the southern states and was surprised to find in the North a greater attention to social distinctions than in the South. Virginians above all others seemed bent on reducing all men to an equal footing. "Owners of slaves," he observed, "among themselves, are all for keeping down every kind of superiority"; and he attributed this affectation in part to their "being rivals in their own states for the voice of the people, whom they court by dressing and looking like them as much as they can." But he had a further explanation why the South could outdo the North in its zeal for equality. The Virginians, he said, "can profess an unbounded love of liberty and of democracy in consequence of the mass of the people, who in other countries might become mobs, being there nearly altogether composed of their own Negro slaves. . . ."[37]

There it was. Aristocrats could more safely preach equality in a slave society than in a free one. Slaves did not become leveling mobs, because their owners would see to it that they had no chance to. The apostrophes to equality were not addressed to them. And because Virginia's labor force was composed mainly of slaves, who had been isolated by race and removed from the political equation, the remaining free laborers and tenant farmers were too few in number to constitute a serious threat to the superiority of the men who assured them of their equality. Moreover, the small farmers had been given a reason to see themselves as already the equals of the large. The majority of households in Virginia, as we have seen, contained more than one tithable, and in such cases the working members of

[37] Richard B. Davis, ed., *Jeffersonian America: Notes on the United States of America Collected in the Years 1805-6-7 and 11-12 by Sir Augustus John Foster, Bart.* (San Marino, Calif., 1954), 163, 307.

the household, other than the head, were probably by this time slaves. The small planter's small stake in human property placed him on the same side of the fence as the large man, whom he regularly elected to protect his interests. Virginia's small farmers could perceive a common identity with the large, because there was one, even more compelling than those we have already noticed. Neither was a slave. And both were equal in not being slaves.

This is not to say that a belief in republican equality had to rest on slavery, but only that in Virginia (and probably in other southern colonies) it did. The most ardent American republicans were Virginians, and their ardor was not unrelated to their power over the men and women they held in bondage. In the republican way of thinking as Americans inherited it from England, slavery occupied a critical, if ambiguous, position: it was the primary evil that men sought to avoid for society as a whole by curbing monarchs and establishing republics. But it was also the solution to one of society's most serious problems, the problem of the poor. Virginians could outdo English republicans as well as New England ones, partly because they had solved the problem: they had achieved a society in which most of the poor were enslaved.

The poor had figured largely in the thinking of the men who promoted the founding of Virginia, both the poor who fed the gallows in England and the poor whom the Spanish oppressed in America. In spite of the severe laws by which England dealt with beggars in the sixteenth and early seventeenth centuries, there had been compassion (and no zeal for equality) in the plans of a Richard Hakluyt for redeeming the wretched in the New World. But the seventeenth century had seen the simultaneous rise of republican thinking and of that contempt for the poor which we have already noticed. The two were closely connected. The calls for enslavement of poor and disorderly Englishmen and Scotsmen came not so much from royalists as from the men who drew their inspiration out of Oliver Cromwell's Commonwealth and out of the revolution that sent James II packing.

John Locke, who wrote the classic defense of the right of revolution, does not seem to have thought of extending that right to the poor. His proposals for working schools where the children of the poor would learn labor—and nothing but labor—from the age of three stopped a little short of enslavement, though it may require a certain refinement of mind to discern the difference. Locke was no republican; but the most admired among England's eighteenth-century commonwealthmen, admired at least in America, held similarly dichotomous views. John Trenchard and Thomas Gordon, the authors of *Cato's Letters*, were probably the most eloquent English advocates of equality. "Equality," they insisted, "is the Soul of liberty." And because "Liberty can never subsist without Equality," they wanted government to limit the acquisition of property. The superiority of one man over another, they proclaimed, was the result either of force or folly. But like Locke defending revolution, Trenchard and Gordon seem to have been talking about men who were not poor, for one of their harshest diatribes was against the charity schools that "were breeding up Beggars to be what are called Scholars. . . . putting Chimera's and airy Notions into the Heads of those who ought to have Pickaxes in their Hands." [38]

Trenchard and Gordon did not propose enslaving beggars, but some of the people we have seen proposing it were equally ardent commonwealthmen, like James Burgh, who wanted to enslave "idle and disorderly persons," and Andrew Fletcher of Saltoun, who wanted to enslave 200,000 Scotsmen, roughly the number of slaves in Virginia. Burgh and Fletcher both ranked high in the esteem of American republicans, and especially in the esteem of Virginia's and America's arch-republican, Thomas Jefferson. Jefferson encouraged a Philadelphia printer to bring out an American edition of Burgh's *Political Disquisitions* in 1775; and he later hailed in Fletcher a patriot whose political principles were those "in vigour at the epoch of the American emigration [from England]. Our ancestors brought them here, and they needed little strengthening to make us what we are. . . ." [39] In the republican way of thinking, zeal for liberty and equality could go hand in hand with contempt for the poor and plans for enslaving them.

The combination, which to us seems bizarre and unnatural, may become more comprehensible if we take a closer look at the role of the independent yeoman farmer and at the role of the not-so-independent poor in republican thought. We have seen that the commonwealthmen elevated the yeoman farmer and insisted on his independence to resist the encroachments of tyranny. By the same token they distrusted anyone who could be bent to the will of another.

[38] John Trenchard and Thomas Gordon, *Cato's Letters; or Essays on Liberty, Civil and Religious, and Other important Subjects* (3rd ed., London, 1733), I, 101; II, 16, 86, IV, 243.
[39] Sowerby, *Catalogue of the Library of Thomas Jefferson*, I, 192; III, 125.

They knew, of course, that society always contained a body of people who remained dependent, women and children, for example. But women and children posed no threat if joined to independent men. Neither did the impotent and aged. And neither did slaves. It was the able-bodied poor, nominally but not actually independent, who spelled danger to liberty. Not only did they contribute nothing to the common welfare, but they sapped the independence of those who had to succor them. What was worse, an ambitious adventurer could buy them with bread, and arm them to attack the liberty of the rest. When Andrew Fletcher proposed enslaving them, it was not to make them wards of the state, which would have aggravated the danger, but to spread them among the independent landholders, whose strength they would thereby increase instead of diminish.

Fletcher did not consider the possibility of transforming the poor into independent yeomen. There were far too many of them and too little land. Fletcher's Scotland already contained many landowners whose holdings were too small to give them the independence they needed in order to play their republican role, and it also contained some large holders who had more than they cultivated. At the same time that he proposed enslaving beggars, Fletcher proposed a complex scheme the effect of which would be to confiscate and consolidate into viable, productive tracts both the excess lands of the over-rich and the too small patches of the inadequate yeomen. In this way everyone who had land would have enough to be a prosperous, independent defender of freedom, bolstered by the labors of the former scruff and scum of Scotland.[40]

Poverty, then, in republican thought, was as much a threat to liberty as the ambition of monarchs and of over-rich landlords. And some British republicans thought it better to enslave the poor than be enslaved by them or by the demagogic leaders that their condition invited. The solution was drastic—there is no reason to suppose that Jefferson, in praising Fletcher, was endorsing it—but the problem it dealt with loomed large among men who thought about freedom, even in America, where the poor appeared to be few. Concern about the dependent poor lay behind two of Jefferson's seemingly irrational phobias that appear at first sight to be unrelated to his views on slavery: his obsessive aversions to debt and to manufacturing. The trouble with debt was that it undermined the independence of the debtor. It opened him to pressure from his creditors

---

[40] Fletcher, *Second Discourse on the Affairs of Scotland*, 102–19.

and thereby limited his freedom and his capacity to defend freedom. A nation of men each of whom owned enough property to support his family could be a republic, but a nation of debtors, who had lost their property or mortgaged it to creditors, was ripe for tyranny.[41]

Manufacturers—the landless artisans who had only their labor to support them—were even more dangerous than debtors. They were dependent on "the casualties and caprice of customers." If work was scarce, they had no land to fall back on for a living. They were likely to be, at least periodically, poor and dependent. In their dependence lay the danger. "Dependance," Jefferson argued, "begets subservience and venality, suffocates the germ of virtue, and prepares fit tools for the designs of ambition." Because artisans could lay claim to freedom though they did not have the land-based independence that should go with it, they were "the instruments by which the liberties of a country are generally overturned." [42]

Jefferson would have liked the United States to be a country without manufacturers and without poor, without the instruments by which its liberties could be overturned. There seemed at the time to be enough land in America to support an unlimited population of pure yeomen farmers. And yet—would it be possible in the long run to have a society without a body of dependent poor? Jefferson's friend James Madison did not think so. When Jefferson saw the masses of poor in France, he suggested to Madison that they had a natural right to appropriate the surplus lands held by the French nobility.[43] Madison in reply doubted that there would be enough land to give all the people independence in any country as populous as France. "A certain degree of misery," he concluded, "seems inseparable from a high degree of populousness." [44] In other words, the poor ye have always with you, whether in a monarchy or a republic.

Jefferson and Madison differed from their contemporaries in possessing an extraordinarily acute perception both of the perils that beset republican liberty and of the strengths it possessed for meeting those perils. But they were not ahead of their fellow Virginians in perceiving the dangers that lurked in the freedom of the dependent poor. It did not necessarily follow that because of those

[41] For examples of Jefferson's aversion to debt and corresponding distrust of credit see his *Papers*, Julian P. Boyd, ed. (Princeton, 1950–   ), II, 275–76; VIII, 398–99, 632–33; IX, 217–18, 472–73; X, 304–5, 615; XI, 472, 633, 636, 640; XII, 385–86.

[42] *Ibid.*, VIII, 426; *Notes on Virginia*, 165.

[43] Jefferson, *Papers*, VIII, 681–83.   [44] *Ibid.*, IX, 659–60.

dangers the poor must be enslaved. But it did follow that the keepers of republican liberty must be wary of extending a share of it to men who were incapable of defending it and might become a means of destroying it. If the poor were already enslaved, would it not be wise to keep them so? Virginia, in spite of her abundant lands, had already encountered a rebellion of the unenslaved poor in 1676. Since then she had gradually replaced her free labor force with slaves, and by 1776 she enjoyed the situation that Andrew Fletcher had wished to achieve in Scotland. Two-fifths of Virginia's people were as poor as it is possible to get; but they were all enslaved, and all worked productively for private masters, who were thereby strengthened in their independence and able to take the lead in resisting British tyranny. As if to underline the connection, the Virginia assembly voted in 1780 to reward its soldiers in the fight for freedom with a bounty of 300 acres of land *and* a slave.[45]

Virginia's republicans had the decency to be disturbed by the apparent inconsistency of what they were doing. But they were far more disturbed by the prospect of turning 200,000 slaves loose to find a place in their free society. "If you free the slaves," wrote Landon Carter, two days after the Declaration of Independence, "you must send them out of the country or they must steal for their support."[46] They would be, after all, what they were, poor, and they would exhibit the congenital laziness and immorality of the poor. Jefferson himself thought that slaves could not safely be freed unless they were exiled. And the only serious plan for their emancipation, proposed by St. George Tucker in 1796, would have transformed their slavery into a kind of serfdom, under which they would still be compelled to labor, lest they become "idle, dissipated, and finally a numerous banditti."[47] But even Tucker's plan seemed too dangerous to receive serious consideration.

One wonders if it might not have been taken more seriously if Virginia's slaves had belonged to the same race as their masters. The fact that they did not made it easier for Virginians to use slavery as a flying buttress to freedom. The English had come to view their poor almost as an alien race, with inbred traits of character that justified plans for their enslavement or incarceration in workhouses.

---

[45] Hening, X, 331.　　[46] Carter, *Diary*, II, 1055.
[47] St. George Tucker, *A Dissertation on Slavery with a Proposal for the Gradual Abolition of It, in the State of Virginia* (Philadelphia, 1796). See also Jordan, *White over Black*, 555–60.

Almost, but not quite. It required continual denunciations from a battery of philosophers and reformers; it even required special badges, to proclaim the differentness of the poor to the undiscerning, who might otherwise mistake them for ordinary men.

In Virginia neither badges nor philosophers were needed. It was not necessary to pretend or to prove that the enslaved were a different race, because they were. Anyone could tell black from white, even if black was actually brown or red. And as the number of poor white Virginians diminished, the vicious traits of character attributed by Englishmen to their poor could in Virginia increasingly appear to be the exclusive heritage of blacks. They were ungrateful, irresponsible, lazy, and dishonest. "A Negroe can't be honest," said Landon Carter and filled his diary with complaints of the congenital laziness and ingratitude of black men.[48]

Racism thus absorbed in Virginia the fear and contempt that men in England, whether Whig or Tory, monarchist or republican, felt for the inarticulate lower classes. Racism made it possible for white Virginians to develop a devotion to the equality that English republicans had declared to be the soul of liberty. There were too few free poor on hand to matter. And by lumping Indians, mulattoes, and Negroes in a single pariah class, Virginians had paved the way for a similar lumping of small and large planters in a single master class.

Virginians knew that the members of this class were not in fact equal, either in property or in virtue, just as they knew that Negroes, mulattoes, and Indians were not one and the same. But the forces which dictated that Virginians see Negroes, mulattoes, and Indians as one also dictated that they see large and small planters as one. Racism became an essential, if unacknowledged, ingredient of the republican ideology that enabled Virginians to lead the nation.

How Virginian, then, was America? How heavily did American economic opportunity and political freedom rest on Virginia's slaves? If Virginia had continued to rely on the importation of white servants, would they have headed north when they turned free and brought insoluble problems of poverty with them? Would they have threatened the peace and prosperity of Philadelphia and New York and Boston, where the poor were steadily growing in numbers anyhow? Would Northerners have embraced republican ideas of equality so readily if they had been surrounded by men in "a certain

[48] Carter, *Diary*, I, 254, 290–92, 295, 300, 301, 303, 316, 429–30, 576.

degree of misery"? And could the new United States have made a go of it in the world of nations without Virginia and without the products of slave labor? Northern republicans apparently thought not. Some could not condone slavery and talked of breaking loose from the South in their own independent confederation. But the fact is that they did not. They allowed Virginians to compose the documents that founded their republic, and they chose Virginians to chart its course for a generation.

Eventually, to be sure, the course the Virginians charted for the United States proved the undoing of slavery. And a Virginia general gave up at Appomattox the attempt to support freedom with slavery. But were the two more closely linked than his conquerors could admit? Was the vision of a nation of equals flawed at the source by contempt for both the poor and the black? Is America still colonial Virginia writ large? More than a century after Appomattox the questions linger.

Footnote Abbreviations

Four works have been cited so often that I have abbreviated references to them throughout as follows:

Hening William W. Hening, ed., *The Statutes at Large: Being a Collection of All the Laws of Virginia* (Richmond, 1809–23).

RVC Susan M. Kingsbury, ed., *The Records of the Virginia Company of London* (Washington, 1906–35)

VMHB *Virginia Magazine of History and Biography*

WMQ *William and Mary Quarterly*

I have also used the standard abbreviation for documents in the British Public Record Office, in which the initial letters indicate the group (C.O. for Colonial Office, T. for Treasury, H.C.A. for High Court of Admiralty, etc.). The first number, followed by a slash, indicates the class, the next number the piece, and the final number, preceded by f or ff., the folio number. I have examined most British documents in microfilm, some in the films made by the Virginia Colonial Records Survey, and some in films at the Library of Congress. For the C.O. 5 group, however, I have used the Library of Congress transcripts, made before the present numbering of the folios. Citations to the C.O. 5 series are therefore, in most cases, to the number of the document.

I have cited Virginia county court records by the name of the county and a volume number in Roman numerals. I have used the photostats and microfilms of these records in the Virginia State Library. The volumes as filmed are designated with various titles and sometimes with volume numbers, but the titles and numbers frequently bear no close relationship to the contents or to chronological order. For example, the Norfolk volumes labeled "Wills and Deeds" contain orders, and the Lancaster volume labeled "Orders, No. 1" is not the first extant order book of the county. For convenience I have arbitrarily assigned my own numbers to the volumes I have used, so far as possible placing them in chronological order. These are *not* all the extant volumes, for I have concentrated on the records of orders rather than on deeds and wills. The numbers I have assigned, it will be noted, do not necessarily correspond to the numbers on the volumes (some of which are numbered and some not).

The following list is of the volumes I have used and the numbers I have assigned them, together with the titles by which they are designated at the State Library. Two of the volumes, Northampton I and Northampton II have been published, and in these two cases my citations are to the published version. Some of the volumes were transcribed in the nineteenth or early twentieth century, and where the original is now illegible my citations are to the transcript.

Accomack

ACCOMACK I	Deeds and Wills, 1663–66
ACCOMACK II	Deeds and Wills, 1664–71
ACCOMACK III	Orders, 1666–70
ACCOMACK IV	Orders and Wills, etc., 1671–73
ACCOMACK V	Wills, 1673–76
ACCOMACK VI	Wills and Deeds, 1676–90
ACCOMACK VII	Orders, 1676–78
ACCOMACK VIII	Wills, Deeds and Orders, 1678–82
ACCOMACK IX	Wills and Orders, 1682–97
ACCOMACK X	Orders, 1690–97
ACCOMACK XI	Wills, etc., 1692–1715
ACCOMACK XII	Orders, 1697–1703

Henrico

HENRICO I	Deeds and Wills, 1677–92
HENRICO II	Order Book, 1678–93 (Page references are to the transcript of this volume. The original is too faint to read in microfilm.)

Lancaster

LANCASTER I	Deeds, Wills, and Settlements of Estates, No. 1, 1652–57
LANCASTER II	Deeds, Wills, and Settlements of Estates, 1654–1702

LANCASTER III	Orders, 1655–66
LANCASTER IV	Orders, No. 1, 1666–80
LANCASTER V	Orders, No. 2, 1680–86
LANCASTER VI	Orders, No. 3, 1686–96
LANCASTER VII	Orders, No. 4, 1696–1702
LANCASTER VIII	Orders, No. 5, 1702–12
LANCASTER IX	Orders, No. 6, 1712–21
LANCASTER X	Orders, No. 7, 1721–29
LANCASTER XI	Orders, No. 8, 1729–43
LANCASTER XII	Orders, No. 9, 1743–52

Norfolk

NORFOLK I	Deed Book A, 1637–46
NORFOLK II	Wills and Deeds B, 1646–51
NORFOLK III	Wills and Deeds C, 1651–56
NORFOLK IV	Wills and Deeds D, 1656–66
NORFOLK V	Wills and Deeds E, 1666–75
NORFOLK VI	Order Book, 1666–75 (in the same volume as Norfolk V, but beginning at the other end, with separate pagination)
NORFOLK VII	Order Book, 1675–86
NORFOLK VIII	Deed Book 5, part 1, 1686–95
NORFOLK IX	Deed Book 5, part 2, 1686–95 (actually an order book)
NORFOLK X	Deed Book 6, 1695–1703
NORFOLK XI	Order Book, 1742–46
NORFOLK XII	Order Book, 1746–50
NORFOLK XIII	Order Book, 1750–53
NORFOLK XIV	Order Book, 1753–55

Northampton

NORTHAMPTON I	Orders, Wills, Deeds, etc., vol. I, 1632–40 (Susie M. Ames, ed., *County Court Records of Accomack–Northampton, Virginia, 1632–1640*. American Legal Records, VII. Washington, D.C., 1954.)
NORTHAMPTON II	Orders, Deeds, Wills, etc., vol. II, 1640–45 (Susie M. Ames, ed., *County Court Records of Accomack–Northampton, Virginia, 1640–1645*. Charlottesville, 1973.)
NORTHAMPTON III	Orders, Deeds, Wills, etc., 1645–51
NORTHAMPTON IV	Deeds, Wills, etc., 1651–54
NORTHAMPTON V	Deeds, Wills, etc., 1654–55
NORTHAMPTON VI	Orders, 1655–56
NORTHAMPTON VII	Deeds, Wills, etc., 1655–68
NORTHAMPTON VIII	Order Book, 1657–64

NORTHAMPTON IX   Deeds, Wills, etc., 1657–66
NORTHAMPTON X   Order Book, 1664–74
NORTHAMPTON XI   Deeds, etc., 1668–80
NORTHAMPTON XII   Order Book, Wills, etc., 1674–79
NORTHAMPTON XIII   Order Book, 1678–83

Northumberland

NORTHUMBERLAND I   Order Book, 1652–65
NORTHUMBERLAND II   Order Book, 1666–78
NORTHUMBERLAND III   Order Book, 1678–98
NORTHUMBERLAND IV   Order Book, 1699–1713
NORTHUMBERLAND XII   Order Book, 1753–56
NORTHUMBERLAND XIII   Order Book, 1756–58
NORTHUMBERLAND XIV   Order Book, 1758–62

Surry

SURRY I   Deeds, etc., No. 1, 1652–72
SURRY II   Deeds, Wills, etc., No. 2, 1671–84
SURRY III   Deeds, Wills, etc., No. 3, 1684–87
SURRY IV   Deeds, Wills, etc., No. 4, 1687–94
SURRY V   Deeds, Wills, etc., No. 5, 1699–1709
SURRY VI   Orders, 1671–91
SURRY VII   Orders, 1691–1713
SURRY VIII   Orders, 1713–18
SURRY IX   Orders, 1741–44
SURRY X   Orders, 1744–49
SURRY XI   Orders, 1749–51

Westmoreland

WESTMORELAND I   Deeds, Wills, Patents, 1653–59
WESTMORELAND II   Deeds, Wills, etc., 1661–62
WESTMORELAND III   Orders, 1662–69
WESTMORELAND IV   Deeds, Patents, Wills, 1665–77
WESTMORELAND V   Orders, 1675–89
WESTMORELAND VI   Orders, 1690–98

York

YORK I   Deeds, Orders, Wills, etc., No. 1, 1633–94
YORK II   Wills and Deeds, No. 2, 1645–49
YORK III   Deeds, Orders, Wills, etc., No. 3, 1657–62
YORK IV   Deeds, Orders, Wills, etc., No. 4, 1665–72
YORK V   Deeds, Orders, Wills, etc., No. 5, 1672–76
YORK VI   Deeds, Orders, Wills, etc., No. 6, 1677–84

YORK VII	Deeds, Orders, Wills, etc., No. 7, 1684–87
YORK VIII	Deeds, Orders, Wills, etc., No. 8, 1687–91
YORK IX	Deeds, Orders, Wills, etc., No. 9, 1691–94
YORK X	Deeds, Orders, Wills, etc., No. 10, 1694–97
YORK XI	Deeds, Orders, Wills, etc., No. 11, 1698–1702

APPENDIX
Population Growth
in Seventeenth-Century Virginia

I<small>T</small> is impossible to perform for seventeenth-century Virginia what historical demographers have been doing for contemporary England and France and even for New England. The necessary data, if ever recorded, have been lost or destroyed, and only sporadic and inconclusive vital statistics from a few isolated locations survive. The records of headrights, which have been preserved, have limitations which I have discussed elsewhere.[1] Nevertheless, records of other kinds survive, especially county court records from the second half of the century and reports from governors and other officers to their superiors in England. From a variety of sources, though we cannot reconstruct the population of seventeenth-century Virginia in detail, we can at least perceive some of the larger outlines and trends.

Much of the initial work was done forty years ago by Evarts Greene and Virginia Harrington in their monumental and indispensable collection of contemporary estimates and censuses for all the colonies.[2] Since they made no attempt to interpret or evaluate what

[1] E. S. Morgan, "Headrights and Head Counts: A Review Article," *VMHB*, LXXX (1972), 361–71.

[2] Evarts B. Greene and Virginia Harrington, *American Population before the Federal Census of 1790* (New York, 1932), 134–55. Where not otherwise indicated, the lists of tithables and inhabitants in the whole colony have been taken from this volume. Lists of tithables for particular counties have been taken from the microfilms of county court records in the Virginia State Library at Richmond. In order to avoid excessive citations, I have not ordinarily cited the volume and page of county records, since the finding aids at the State Library make it possible to locate easily most of the lists of tithables. Though the lists were made in June of each year, they nor-

they presented and since there were gaps in their materials which can now be filled, it seems worthwhile to assemble the available information and to offer some educated guesses about what remains unavailable.

There are three points at which we can fix the total population of seventeenth-century Virginia with a fair degree of certainty: 1625, 1634, and 1699. For 1625, a list gives the name of every person in the colony, his location, and often his age and the date of his arrival. For most locations, the names of persons who have died in the preceding year are also given. The 1625 list is supported by another, taken a year earlier, which gives the names and locations of the living and of those who had died in the preceding ten months.[3] In 1634, when the colony was divided into counties, Governor John Harvey reported the total number of inhabitants in each county.[4] For 1699, a list tabulates the number of tithables and the number of untithables in each county. Tithables were the people supposed to be income-producing and for whom a poll tax or tithe was payable (how they were defined is, as we shall see, a complex matter).

---

mally appear in the records, when they appear at all, at the time the county levy was laid, in October, November, or December.

[3] The two lists are in the Colonial Office group, class I, piece 3, Public Record Office. (Hereafter Public Record Office documents will be cited in the standard abbreviated form: C.O. 1/3, etc.) Both are printed in John C. Hotten, *The Original Lists of Persons of Quality . . . and Others Who Went from Great Britain to the American Plantations, 1600–1700*, (London, 1874), 169–95, 201–65. The 1625 list is also printed in Annie L. Jester and Martha W. Hiden, *Adventurers of Purse and Person, 1607–1625* (Princeton, 1956), 5–69. The 1625 list is analyzed in Irene W. D. Hecht, "The Virginia Muster of 1624/5 as a Source for Demographic History," *WMQ*, 3rd ser., XXX (1973), 65–92. The figures she has obtained from the list are not quite the same as mine. For example, she counts at one point 1,218 persons living, but reduces this to 1,216 on the grounds that Edward Bennett and Daniel Gookin were probably not present. I believe she has overcounted, however, by failing to notice that six persons (William Hampton, Joan Hampton, Oliver Jenkins, Joan Jenkins, John Washborne, and William Stafford) are listed twice. My own count is 1,210, and this includes at least one possible duplication, namely, Thomas Spillman. Since a person of that name is listed once as having arrived in 1616 and in another place as having arrived in 1623, I have assumed that there were two Thomas Spillmans. Mrs. Hecht's count of the ages of men and women also differs from mine (see table 2). She finds 63 men over 39 while I can find only 53, and she finds no women over 39, while I count 8.

[4] C.O. 1/8, f.155; *VMHB*, VIII (1900–1901), 302.

All these lists are imperfect. For example, the 1625 list gives the dates of arrival of 740 persons (out of the total of 1,210 living), of whom 697 had arrived before 1624; but at least 150 of the 697 are missing from the 1624 list.[5] The 1625 list is also demonstrably incomplete. In the surviving records of the governor and council for January and February, 1625, the months when the list was being compiled, 66 persons are mentioned in such a way as to indicate that they were alive and in Virginia.[6] Of these, only 55 are to be found in the list. Of the missing 11, 5 can be accounted for as transient sailors or shipmasters. But Francis Bolton, Edward Grundon or Grindon, William Cowse, William English, Christopher Barker, Gilbert Peppett, and John Rowe were clearly resident and not listed. It seems likely from these samples that the 1624 list is short by at least 20 percent and the 1625 list by about 10 percent. Since the 1634 and 1699 lists contain no names, it is impossible to check them in the same way, but from other surviving records (see below) it appears that the 1699 list omitted the entire population of Bruton Parish in York County and probably about 6 percent of the tithables in other counties. Nevertheless, whatever their deficiencies, the population counts for 1625, 1634, and 1699 are the frame of reference from which we must proceed and into which we must fit all estimates of population that we dare postulate for intervening years.

Although 1699 is the only year during the century in which we have an enumeration of both tithables and untithables,[7] there are

---

[5] In comparing the two lists I have not included women, whose names could have changed by marriage between 1624 and 1625, but I have made allowance for the vagaries of seventeenth-century spelling and have assumed, for example, that George Bailife is George Bayley, William Cooksey is William Coxe, and Pharrow Phlinton is Farrar Flinton.

[6] H. R. McIlwaine, ed., *Minutes of the Council and General Court of Colonial Virginia* (Richmond, 1924), 43–47.

[7] There is also a list of tithables and untithables for 1701, the only other year during the colonial period for which such a list exists. It is similar to the 1699 list, and for some counties identical. For the sake of simplicity, I will confine attention to the 1699 list, which is located in C.O. 5/1312, f.135. This single sheet is apparently all that survives of a much more detailed enumeration. The instructions for making the enumeration, in C.O. 5/1310, f.177, call for a record of the names of the master and mistress of the household; free Christian men and women, free Christian boys and girls, Christian men and women servants, men and women slaves, and boy and girl slaves. If such an enumeration for any county should turn up, it would make possible a much closer analysis of Virginia's population structure at the end of the century than can now be attempted.

other years for which records of the total number of tithables survive. If we can estimate the proportion between tithables and total population in those years, we can derive a figure for total population. Surviving colony records provide us with the total number of tithables in 1662, 1674, 1682, 1698, and 1699. The colony records also list the number of tithables in seven out of ten counties in 1644 and seven out of fourteen counties in 1653.[8] For these years we can estimate the missing tithables by drawing on surviving county records and by extrapolation. Accounts of public expenses in 1629 and 1632, with the amount to be levied per tithable in order to meet them, enable us to calculate the number of tithables for those years; and from legislation attempting to limit tobacco production (see below) we can calculate both tithables and total population in January, 1640.[9] We also have Governor Edmund Andros' precise statement in 1696 that sets the tithables for that year at 19,566.[10] We thus have, or can calculate, the number of tithables in 1629, 1632, 1640, 1644, 1653, 1662, 1674, 1682, 1696, 1698, and 1699.

Before attempting to determine the proportion of tithables to total population in these years, we should ask how reliable the tithable figures are. The lists of tithables from which they originally derived were tax lists, and since dodging taxes is surely as ancient an art as collecting them, we should know what steps the government took to insure the integrity of its lists.

In every county, the master of every household was annually required to report the number of tithables in it. Failure to report a tithable was punishable by an act of 1658 with a treble tax and by an act of 1663 with forfeiture of the person concealed or a fine of 1,000 pounds of tobacco. A sheriff or clerk or collector who turned in a deficient list of tithables was also subject to fines. After 1670 the whole county list was supposed to be posted annually on the court-

[8] The list for 1662 is in Clarendon Mss. 82, Bodleian Library, Oxford; that for 1674 is in Blathwayt Papers, XVII, Colonial Williamsburg; that for 1644 is in Hening, I, 287–88. These three are the only ones not given in Greene and Harrington, *American Population*, 134–55.

[9] Hening, I, 142–43, 196–97, 224–25, 228; *WMQ*, 2nd ser., IV (1924), 159–62.

[10] C.O. 5/1309, f.33. Andros also stated that in the preceding four years the number had been "above 19,000 and never came to 20,000." We also have estimates by Philip Ludwell in 1679 that the total number of tithables was "not 14,000" and by Governor Thomas Culpeper in 1681 that it was "about 14,000." Coventry Papers, LXXVIII, 444; C.O. 1/47, f.260.

house door. Since concealment meant a larger tax for everyone else in the community, there must have been a certain amount of local vigilance against delinquent masters and against officials who submitted a short count in order to pocket part of the proceeds.[11] Nevertheless, some concealment was doubtless successful, especially of boys who had recently reached tithable age.

An additional problem in trying to assess the tithable lists is the discrepancy between colony records and county records. Where figures for a particular county in a particular year survive in both colony and county records, the two are seldom identical. Occasionally the figure in the county records is lower than that in the colony records, but in the majority of cases it is higher, sometimes by a substantial amount.[12] Where the discrepancy is small, the reason probably lies in the fact that certain individuals (aged and impotent) were excused from public (colony) levies, but not from parish levies. Discrepancies may also represent numbers of people bankrupt or insolvent, from whom the levy could not be collected. The Northampton records list 20 persons in these categories in 1661.[13] In a few cases it is clear that the colony figure is simply out of date, based on an earlier enumeration. Other discrepancies may

---

[11] Hening, I, 376, 455; II, 83, 187, 412; Henry Hartwell, James Blair, and Edward Chilton, *The Present State of Virginia and the College* (1697), 53.

[12] The widest discrepancies occur in 1682, when we find the following figures:

	Colony List	County List
Henrico	471	477
Surry	486	494
Norfolk	694	850
York	1041	1041
Lancaster	421	531
Middlesex	546	611
Northumberland	624	774
Stafford	407	499
Accomack	583	628

In the case of Stafford it came out in the House of Burgesses three years later that the list presented to the colony was 92 persons short, and Stafford was required to make up the difference at the next levy. (See the journal for this meeting of the House, pp. 29, 48, in the Effingham Papers.) But nothing was said about the other counties.

[13] Northampton VIII, 102–4.

represent an increase in the county's population between the time when the levy was apportioned and the time when the county collected it.[14] Whatever the reasons for the differences, the county figures, where available, are probably the more reliable. Although they survive only for a minority of counties, there are enough to enable us to make some rough adjustments in the population figures that we project from the colony lists of tithables.

There remains the problem of making those projections by determining the proportion of tithables to total population. That proportion can be ascertained with a fair degree of confidence at three points, 1625, 1640, and 1699. The different figures for these years will show, what we would expect, that the untithable portion of the population, consisting largely of women and children, rose as the century progressed. But because so many varying factors affected the rate of rise, it can hardly have been a steady one.

An important variable was the changing legal definition of who was tithable. Until 1649 the term apparently included only males over fifteen (who remained tithable throughout the colonial period), but in that year the assembly decreed that all imported male servants of whatever age were tithable. In 1658 a law, ambiguously phrased, seemed to add imported Negro and Indian females over 15; in 1662 this was emended to make plain that all imported Negroes, male or female, were tithable, but Indians, however procured, were tithable only when they were over fifteen. At the same time any women servants of whatever color who worked in the ground were made tithable. In 1672 a law prescribed that Virginia-born Negro women became tithable at the age of sixteen. In 1680 the laws were changed again to make imported Negro children tithable only after they reached the age of twelve and imported Christian servants tithable only after they reached fourteen. In 1705 the law was changed once

[14] This is suggested by the fact that in several instances the county records themselves record two widely differing tithable figures, one being the number actually in the county and the other being the number on which the assembly calculated the county's contribution to public (colony) expenses. In Norfolk in 1660 the county's contribution to the public was calculated at 19,600 pounds of tobacco on the basis of 56 per poll for 350 tithables, but the 19,600 was actually divided among 402 tithables then in the county. In 1662 the corresponding figures were 400 tithables in the public calculation and 488 actually in the county. But in 1664 the figures were 589 and 590. Norfolk IV, 268, 355, 412. There are similar disparities in several other counties.

more to make sixteen the age of tithability for all males and all Negro, mulatto, and Indian women.[15]

The changing definitions, combined with the changing but unknowable age and sex ratios and rates of birth, death, and immigration, make it highly problematic to estimate the multiplier by which we may transform tithables to total population in any given year. How to weigh each of the variables is an enterprise that I will leave to someone with greater numerical skill and greater powers of divination than I can muster. Instead, I will assume that the figure by which we must multiply tithables in order to obtain total population rose at a steady rate between the points at which it can be ascertained, i.e., 1625, 1640, and 1699. The results will be necessarily imperfect, but I hope a good deal closer to reality than the estimates of Virginia population on which historians have hitherto had to rely.[16]

The most precise ratio on which to hinge our calculations is that for 1699. The list of tithables and untithables reported to England in that year reveals that in different counties the total popula-

[15] Hening, I, 361, 454; II, 84, 170, 296, 479–80; III, 258. The provisions of the 1705 law may have been enacted earlier. They are substantially the same as those of a Maryland law of 1692 (*Archives of Maryland*, XIII [Baltimore, 1894], 538–39), and it is unlikely that the Virginia assembly would have given such an advantage in taxes to Maryland planters over Virginia planters. Hartwell, Blair, and Chilton in 1697 also defined tithables in the same way as the 1705 law (*Present State of Virginia*, 53).

[16] The multiplier that has usually been used for converting tithables to total population for the whole colonial period has been that furnished by Governor William Gooch in 1730: "The Rule for computing the number of Inhabitants is by the List of Tithables on which the publick Tobacco Taxes are laid; These are all white male Persons above sixteen years of age, and all Blacke male and Female above the same Age. Of these there are now about 51,000 and of them about 30,000 may be reckoned Blacks. Accounting therefore the white women married and unmarried and the white and black children under sixteen years to be treble the number of the white tithables, the number of souls in Virginia will amount to 114,000 at least. i.e. take 30,000 out of 51,000 and there remains 21,000. Treble the number makes 63,000, to which add the 51,000 and that makes 114,000." Gooch to Board of Trade, July 23, 1730, C.O. 5/1322, f.71; Greene and Harrington, *American Population*, 145n. (Gooch, like other Virginians, is ambiguous about the exact age when a person became tithable, that is, whether it was at sixteen or over sixteen. The law said at sixteen.) No formula based on the relative proportion of blacks and whites in the eighteenth century can be of any use for the seventeenth century. It is impossible from the lists of tithables to determine the proportion of blacks to whites during any part of the seventeenth century except in Surry and Northampton counties (see below).

tion varied from 1.86 to 3.54 times the number of tithables. The figure for the colony as a whole was 2.69 (see table 3). This figure is probably not seriously distorted by the fact that the number of tithables for 1699 needs increasing (according to surviving county records), because the number of untithables is probably also low. There would have been no immediate motive for undercounting women and children,[17] but on the other hand there was no motive for being careful in the count either, and census counts tend to underrecord. Therefore I will assume that both tithable and untithable figures are low by the same amount and use 2.69 as the number by which to multiply tithables in order to arrive at total population for the colony at the end of the seventeenth century.

At the other end of our time span in 1625 the categories tithable and untithable did not exist, but it is possible to formulate a hypothetical group of tithables for that year by estimating the number of men who were over fifteen years old (the definition of tithable before 1649). The 1625 list gives the ages for 750 persons out of the 1,210 who were then living in the colony (see table 2). For some locations, the ages of all persons are given; for others, where a different man was probably taking the census, no ages are given. In a few places, ages are given for some and not for others. On the whole, it seems likely that age distribution was roughly the same among those whose ages we do not know as among those we do. Of the 634 males whose age is given, 558 were over fifteen. If we assume the same proportion among the 291 men of unknown age, then there were altogether about 814 men over fifteen. The multiplier for transforming this hypothetical group of tithables into the colony's total of 1,210 inhabitants in 1625 is 1.49.

In the seventy-five years between 1625 and 1699, then, the number by which tithables must be multiplied in order to obtain total population rose from 1.49 to 2.69. We may pinpoint the progress of that rise in January, 1640. In that month, when the definition of tithable still embraced only men over 15, the Virginia House of Burgesses decided to limit tobacco production to 170 pounds per person and evidently intended "person" to mean untithables as well as tithables. The yield from 170 pounds per person was expected to

[17] But Virginians, like other peoples, may have been reluctant to give the numbers of their families, for fear of a later capitation tax. Governor Spotswood maintained that such was the case in 1712. R. A. Brock, ed., *The Official Letters of Alexander Spotswood*, Virginia Historical Society, *Collections*, n.s. (Richmond, 1882–85), I, 165–66.

be 1,300,000 pounds, thus implying a population of 7,647.[18] In January, 1640, the assembly also calculated that a levy of 4 pounds per tithable throughout the colony would yield 18,584 pounds, thus implying 4,646 tithables.[19] If the assembly's figures were correct, the multiplier for transforming tithables to whole population had gone up to 1.65, a little below where it would have been (1.73) if it had risen steadily from 1625 to 1699. We shall assume that the multiplier rose steadily from 1.49 to 1.65 between 1625 and 1640 and from 1.65 to 2.69 between 1640 and 1699. If we do so, we obtain the other figures given in table 1 (I have omitted the year 1698 because of its proximity to 1699).

Since the enumeration of both tithables and (in 1625, 1634, and 1699) total population is almost certainly low, the figures thus obtained must also be low. In the bottom line of the table, I have adjusted them upward in the following ways. For 1625 I have added roughly 10 percent to the total for the reasons explained on p. 397. For 1674 and 1699 I have added 6 percent, and for 1682, 12 percent. These are the average amounts by which the enumerations of tithables in extant county records for these years differ from the figures for the same counties in the colony list. I have also added 900 persons to the 1699 list to make up for the absence from the list (for reasons unknown) of Bruton Parish, York County, which seems to have had about 350 tithables that year.[20] For the other years there is no way of determining the deficiency, but I have arbitrarily added 6 percent, as the probable minimum by which the colony's enumeration of tithables or total population is likely to have been low. I have rounded off the figures to emphasize that they are estimates.[21]

Although most of the figures are considerably lower than those that historians have previously accepted, they suggest a spectacular rate of growth, for they show Virginians quadrupling in number in the ten years from 1625 to 1634, almost tripling in the twenty years from 1634 to 1653, and almost tripling again in the thirty years from 1653 to 1682. Taken by themselves, however, the figures tell us little about the society that was growing so rapidly. They do not tell

[18] *WMQ*, 2nd ser., IV (1924), 31. That the limitation was per person, not per tithable, is indicated by a supplementary act (*ibid.*, 156–57) allowing planters with wives and children in England to include them in calculating the allowed crop.

[19] *Ibid.*, 160.   [20] C.O. 5/1312, ff.134, 135.

[21] For the detailed figures on which this table is based, see table 3 and notes 2, 3, 7, 8, 10, and 42.

TABLE 1 *Population Growth*

Year	1625	1629	1632	1634	1640	1644	1653	1662	1674	1682	1696	1699
Tithables (from colony records)	814 *	1,604	1,943		4,646	4,370	7,190	11,838	13,392	15,162	19,566	21,606
Probable ratio of total population to tithables	1.49	1.53	1.56		1.65	1.72	1.88	2.04	2.25	2.39	2.64	2.69
Total population by contemporary count	1,210			4,914	7,647							58,040
Total population by computation from tithables		2,454	3,031			7,516	13,517	24,149	30,132	36,237	51,654	
Adjusted probable total population	1,300	2,600	3,200	5,200	8,100	8,000	14,300	25,600	31,900	40,600	54,750	62,800

404

* See p. 402.

us how it grew, whether by immigration, natural increase, increased longevity, or by some combination of these or other factors. They do not tell us where it grew fastest, whether in one region or another, among one age group or another, among men or women, among blacks or whites. They do not tell us how many died while the number of living was rising so rapidly.

The dearth of vital statistics for seventeenth-century Virginia guarantees that the answers to such questions must remain even more uncertain than the estimates of total population. There are nevertheless enough hints in a variety of surviving sources to enable us to make a stab at a few of the answers.

Sources of Increase

The evidence has been presented in the text that mortality rates were extremely heavy in Virginia in the early years and probably continued to be so until sometime in the 1640s. It is likely that the big jump in population from 1644 to 1653 was due in some measure to a decline in mortality. If other factors remained constant, a decline in mortality would naturally result in a corresponding increase in population. In the long run, however, continued growth, indeed the continuation of any population at all, had to come from births and from immigration. Of the two, immigration probably continued to be the larger source of Virginia's population during most of the century, perhaps throughout it. Records of immigration may have been kept from as early as 1643, but none survive.[22]

We can, however, gain some idea of the number of immigrants from the patents for land issued by the secretary of the colony, a nearly complete record of which survives. A man was entitled to fifty acres of land for every person, including himself, whom he transported to the colony. The "headright" thus earned could be sold, and it did not have to be used within a given time. The date of a land patent is therefore no clue to the date of arrival of the person or persons for whose passage it was issued. People were still getting land in the 1640s with the headrights of persons transported in the 1620s. Later in the century, when the population increased and land became more valuable, rights were probably exercised more promptly. On the other hand, the county courts and the secretary of the

[22] Hening, I, 27; II, 135.

colony may have become increasingly indifferent to the validity of
the claims men submitted to obtain the headright certificates that
would entitle them to a land patent. According to Henry Hartwell,
James Blair, and Edward Chilton, writing in 1697, several headrights were frequently issued for the same immigrant, and in the
absence of any genuine claim, the clerk in the secretary's office
would manufacture one for anywhere from a shilling to five shillings.[23] One must therefore treat with some suspicion the figures
derived from these patents. On the basis of them T. J. Wertenbaker
estimated that immigrants came to Virginia in the seventeenth cen-
ury at an average of 1,500 to 2,000 a year. More recently, W. F.
Craven has counted 82,000 headrights in the patents issued from
1635 to 1700, an average of about 1,250 a year.[24]

Another rough estimate of immigration can be derived from
the records of quitrents claimed by the king. For every fifty acres of
land that passed from the king's Virginian domain into private
ownership, an annual quitrent of a shilling was owed to the king. It
was common knowledge that men reported fewer acres than they
actually held. The rent rolls (of which none survives from the seventeenth century) were probably much more deficient than the lists of
tithables. Moreover, when land was not occupied or when the owner
died intestate, it could revert to the king and thus be removed from
the rent rolls. Any estimate of immigration based on the amounts
owed the king in quitrents is therefore likely to be low. In 1663
quitrents were owed on 973,794 acres, equivalent to 19,476 immigrants (at the headright rate of fifty acres per immigrant).[25] By 1702
the figure was 2,164,232 acres exclusive of the Northern Neck (be-

[23] *Present State of Virginia*, 16–18. Instances of more than one headright issued for the transportation of a single individual are discernible in
both the patent books (Virginia State Library) and the county court records long before 1697. Fraud or failure to verify claims is also suggested by
the fact that many patents simply give the number of persons transported
without specifying their names.

[24] Thomas J. Wertenbaker, *The Planters of Colonial Virginia* (Princeton, 1922), 35; W. F. Craven, *White, Red, and Black: The Seventeenth-
Century Virginian* (Charlottesville, 1971), 10–17. For a more extended discussion of the land patents as an index of immigration, see my review cited
in note 1. For a discussion of the relation of immigration to tobacco prices,
see Russell R. Menard, "Immigration to the Chesapeake Colonies in the
Seventeenth Century," *Maryland Historical Magazine*, LXVIII (1973), 323–
29.

[25] William Byrd I, Letter Book, Virginia Historical Society; *VMHB*,
III (1895–96), 42–47; LI (1943), 173–85.

tween the Rappahannock and the Potomac, which paid quitrents to Lord Fairfax).[26] If we allow 400,000 acres for the Northern Neck, a minimum figure, we can calculate that at least 51,285 immigrants had arrived by 1702.

Estimates based on headrights or quitrents would thus place immigration to Virginia during the seventeenth century somewhere between 50,000 and 100,000 (if we allow 18,000 before the 82,000 headrights counted by Professor Craven between 1635 and 1700). The annual average would have been roughly between 500 and 1,000. Whether immigration averaged 500 a year, 1,000 a year, or even 1,500, it was obviously very substantial.

Because immigration in the seventeenth century was predominantly male, it is unlikely that births contributed nearly as much to Virginia's growth as did immigration. In the census of 1625 Virginia had a sex ratio of 333 men to 100 women, and miscellaneous evidence argues that immigration tended to sustain the imbalance. Among 2,010 passengers embarking from London for Virginia in 1635, female names constituted less than 14 percent of the total.[27] A few passenger lists that have survived from later years show higher proportions, such as the 73 men and 37 women aboard the *Unity* in 1643.[28] Indentures of servants bound for Virginia from Middlesex County, England, in 1683–84 show 145 men and 37 women.[29] Among the records of Bristol are two books containing the names and destinations of some 10,000 servants embarking at that port for the colonies during the years from 1654 to 1679.[30] These list 1,168 women and 3,534 men bound for Virginia. If the names of persons for whom headrights were awarded are reliable, they tell much the same story. In the patent book covering the years from 1644 to 1651, headrights were claimed for 3,240 men as against 879 women, or about 370 men to 100 women. Samplings of the headrights claimed in later decades of the century show about the same ratio, ranging between 330 and 410 men to 100 women.[31]

[26] C.O. 5/1313, f.196.   [27] Hotten, *Original Lists*, 35–145.

[28] Additional Mss. 5489, f.85, British Museum.

[29] Middlesex County Record Office, London.

[30] N. D. Harding, W. D. Bowman, and R. Hargreaves-Mawdesley, *Bristol and America: A Record of the First Settlers in the Colonies of North America, 1654–1685* (London, n.d.). I have not counted persons with ambiguous names like "Francis" or persons bound for "Virginia or Maryland" and "Virginia or Barbados."

[31] Patent books, Virginia State Library. Again, I have not counted persons whose names do not clearly indicate sex. W. B. Blanton found

In spite of the small number of female immigrants, the colony's birth rate may have been somewhat greater than the sex ratio would lead us to expect. According to the census of 1625, the population was concentrated in age between 16 and 35, years when women bear children (see table 2). Later on, too, most female immigrants were probably of childbearing age, because the majority came as servants. Moreover, the sex ratio in the colony itself may have been less un-

TABLE 2   *Ages Given for 750 Persons out of 1,210 Living in January and February, 1625*
(*Figures in parentheses are percentages*)

Age	Male	Female	All
1–5	30 (4.7)	23 (19.8)	53 (7.1)
6–9	5 (0.8)	9 (7.8)	14 (1.9)
10–15	41 (6.5)	10 (8.6)	51 (6.8)
16–19	81 (12.8)	4 (3.4)	85 (11.3)
20–24	212 (33.4)	32 (27.6)	244 (32.6)
25–29	106 (16.7)	14 (12.1)	120 (16.0)
30–34	65 (10.3)	11 (9.5)	76 (10.1)
35–39	41 (6.5)	5 (4.3)	46 (6.1)
Over 39	53 (8.4)	8 (6.9)	61 (8.1)
TOTAL	634 (100)	116 (100)	750 (100)

17,350 women and 75,884 men in "a prolonged search of the patent books and other records of the times" (presumably not limited to immigrants), a ratio of 440 men to 100 women. "Epidemics, Real and Imaginary, and Other Factors Influencing Seventeenth-Century Virginia's Population," *Bulletin of the History of Medicine*, XXXI (1957), 454–62, at p. 462.

balanced than the immigration figures suggest, because in the first part of the century at least, as we have already suggested, women were probably better able to survive the diseases of the country than were men.[32]

It is likely, then, that Virginia had a higher birth rate than the initial small numbers of women and the high death rate would suggest.[33] We have no statistics to show that after the decline in mortality began, more female immigrants survived, more female children reached maturity, or that increased longevity enabled women to produce larger families. But there can be little doubt that the birth rate did rise. The increasing ratio of total population to tithables, from 1.49 in 1625 to 2.69 in 1699, indicates a growing number of women and children and consequently of births.

It is unlikely that women reached anything like a parity with men as long as immigration continued to be heavily masculine, but by the end of the century they may well have been sufficiently numerous to make the birth rate match the death rate. In the register of Charles Parish, York County, which appears to have been kept more regularly than any other that remains from the seventeenth century, 746 births were recorded in the period 1665–1700, as against 650 deaths.[34] Although it is safe to assume that deaths were less conscien-

---

[32] See above, chap. 8.

[33] The greater capacity of women to survive a heavy death rate is also suggested by the sex ratio in West Indian slave populations. Though slaves were imported in a ratio of sixty men to forty women, the sex ratio of slaves in all the English islands in the late seventeenth century was about even, because the men died more rapidly. See Richard S. Dunn, *Sugar and Slaves: The Rise of the Planter Class in the English West Indies, 1624–1713* (Chapel Hill, N.C., 1972), 314–17. Richard Ligon observed that in an epidemic in the 1640s ten men died for every woman. Ligon, *A True and Exact History of the Island of Barbados* (London, 1657), 21.

[34] Photostat in Virginia State Library. The only other seventeenth-century register that appears at all regular is that of Christ Church Parish, Middlesex County (Sally N. Robins, ed., *The Parish Register of Christ Church, Middlesex County, Virginia, from 1653 to 1812* [Richmond, 1897]). The seventeenth-century portions of it seem to have been kept with any regularity only during the years 1678–87. In that period the recorded births greatly exceeded the recorded deaths. Russell R. Menard, in an unpublished paper, "Immigrants and Their Increase: The Process of Population Growth in Early Colonial Maryland," has calculated from a study of wills that the Maryland population became capable of sustaining itself without immigration by the end of the seventeenth century. I am indebted to Dr. Menard for a copy of his paper.

tiously recorded than births, this looks like a population able to sustain itself. In only two five-year periods, 1675–79 and 1685–89, did the recorded deaths outnumber the recorded births.

In sum, Virginia's extraordinary population growth in the seventeenth century was probably due primarily to immigration, but the addition to the population through births may have been greater than a low proportion of women in the population would suggest.

Population Distribution

Tidewater Virginia, as all Virginians know, is naturally divided by its rivers and bays into five areas: the south side of the James River, and four peninsulas, "the Peninsula" between the James and the York, the "Middle Peninsula" between the York and the Rappahannock, the "Northern Neck" between the Rappanhannock and the Potomac, and the "Eastern Shore" of Chesapeake Bay. By the end of the seventeenth century, these areas had begun to emerge as distinctive, but during most of the century, because settlement was spreading along the navigable waterways, each river with the lands on either side of it formed more of a regional unit than any peninsula other than the Eastern Shore. Because five of the eight counties designated in 1634 spanned a river and only later were divided by it into two or more counties, and because each river was a separate customs district, both county and customs records are river-oriented. In tracing the growth of population in different parts of the colony, then, it is revealing to look beyond the county units and examine also the James, the York, the Rappahannock, the Potomac, and the Eastern Shore as regional units.

Table 3 shows the population distribution in seventeenth-century Virginia by counties (arranged roughly from south to north, with the two Eastern Shore counties last). The figure immediately following the name of each county is the date of its founding. The figures in italics (for 1624, 1625, 1634, and 1699) are total population; those in roman are tithables; those in parentheses are estimates obtained by extrapolation or figures taken from county records.[35]

---

[35] The sources for table 3 are indicated in notes 2, 3, 7, 8, and 10. The 1644 estimate for Nansemond (then known as Upper Norfolk) is based on the fact that in 1645 the sum of 38,414 pounds of tobacco was to be raised by a levy of 31 pounds per tithable in Upper Norfolk and Isle of

The unestimated tithable figures have been taken from colony records, except those for 1662 and those for Norfolk and Lancaster in 1653, which survive only in county records. In using the table, it should be remembered that the county records frequently show a considerably higher number. The final column shows the ratio of total population to tithables in 1699. Each county that is indented was formed wholly or partly from the county above it on the list. Although there were no counties in 1624 and 1625, the locations of settlers are known, and they have been distributed according to the county boundaries of 1634.[36]

Table 4 contains the same information as table 3, arranged by region. The population statistics in table 4 may be compared with the figures in tables 5 and 6, which offer a rough index of relative productivity of the different regions. After 1662, Virginia collected a duty of two shillings per hogshead on tobacco exported.[37] Surviving records of this duty for 1664, 1674, 1675, 1676, 1687 and 1698–99 tell the number of hogsheads exported from each of the rivers and from the Eastern Shore (see table 5).[38] For the years from July 24,

---

Wight and 28 pounds per tithable in Lower Norfolk (later known as Norfolk). See Norfolk I, 286. Lower Norfolk had 305 tithables and thus raised 8,540 pounds. This left 29,874 to be raised by the 31-pound levy in Isle of Wight and Upper Norfolk. Isle of Wight had 463 tithables in 1644 and thus raised about 14,353. This left 15,521 to be raised by Upper Norfolk. At 31 pounds per tithable, this would have required 501 tithables.

The other estimated figures for 1644 and 1653 are extrapolations from the numbers reported in other years. The total figure for 1644 is not far from the estimates given by the assembly in a letter to the king in October, 1644, stating that there were 4,000 planters of tobacco. Ms. Clarendon 24, f.52, Bodleian Library, Oxford. The low figure of 738 for York in 1699 arises from the fact that it does not include Bruton Parish (see above). Some of the other irregularities in the growth and decline of particular counties may be explained by the formation of new counties from old ones; but some, like the sharp drop in Surry from 1653 to 1674, are difficult to account for.

[36] It is impossible to be certain of the exact location of many settlements, and my assignments differ a little from earlier ones. It should be noted that the boundaries of the corporations existing in the early years were not necessarily the same as those of later counties that carried the same name.

[37] Hening, I, 491, 523; II, 130–32.

[38] For 1664: Clarendon Mss. 82, Bodleian Library, Oxford; for 1674: Coventry Papers, LXXVI, 319, ACLS British Mss. Project, reel 63, Library of Congress; for 1675 and 1676; H. R. McIlwaine, ed., *Journals of the House*

TABLE 3 *Population Growth by County*
*(Figures in italics are total population; figures in roman
are tithables; figures in parentheses are estimates)*

County	1624	1625	1634	1644	1653
Henrico 1634	*139*	*127*	*419*	(300)	(300)
Charles City 1634	*129*	*130*	*511*	*(500)*	532
James City 1634	*494*	*451*	*886*	687	(750)
Surry 1652					518
Warwick 1634	*24*	*56*	*811*	328	(350)
Isle of Wight 1634	*53*	*31*	*522*	463	673
Elizabeth City 1634	*360*	*364*	*859*	341	395
Nansemond 1637				(500)	(600)
Norfolk 1637				(296)	(471)
Princess Ann 1691					
York 1634			*510*	609	(900)
Gloucester 1651					367
New Kent 1654					
King and Queen 1691					
Lancaster 1651					384
Middlesex 1669					
Rappahannock 1656					
Richmond 1692					
Essex 1692					
Northumberland 1645					450
Westmoreland 1653					
Stafford 1664					
Northampton 1634	*76*	*51*	*396*	346	500
Accomack 1663					
TOTAL	*1,275*	*1,210*	*4,914*	(4,370)	(7,190)

1662	1674	1682	1699	1699	Ratio of total population to tithables, 1699
	372	471	724	2,222	3.07
569	649	714	1,260	3,899	3.09
	819	982	1,059	2,760	2.61
	383	486	664	2,014	3.03
	412	306	474	1,362	2.87
	601	735	781	2,766	3.54
	311	287	453	1,188	2.62
	802	755	781	2,571	3.29
488	652	694	684	2,256	3.3
			620	1,971	3.18
1,140	957	1,041	738	1,909	2.57
	1,687	2,005	2,514	5,730	2.28
	1,299	1,802	1,116	3,172	2.84
			1,664	4,306	2.59
842	414	421	869	2,093	2.41
	435	546	658	1,541	2.34
	1,020	1,053			
			1,262	2,540	2.01
			1,018	2,602	2.56
700	587	624	1,088	2,019	1.86
	538	695	936	2,541	2.71
	436	407	708	1,860	2.63
707	400	555	681	2,050	3.01
	618	583	854	2,668	3.11
11,838	13,392	15,162	21,606	58,040	2.69

TABLE 4   *Population Distribution by Region*
(Figures for total population in italics, for tithables in roman; figures in parentheses are percentages)

Region	1625	1634	1644	1653	1674	1682	1699	1699	Ratio of total population to tithables, 1699
James R.	1,159 (95.8)	4,008 (81.6)	3,415 (78)	4,589 (63.8)	5,001 (37.3)	5,430 (35.8)	7,500 (34.7)	23,009 (39.6)	3.07
York R.		510 (10.4)	609 (14)	1,267 (17.6)	3,943 (29.4)	4,848 (32)	6,032 (27.9)	15,117 (26.1)	2.56
Rappahannock R.				384 (5.3)	1,869 (14)	2,020 (13.3)	3,807 (17.6)	8,776 (15.1)	2.31
Potomac R.				450 (6.3)	1,561 (11.7)	1,726 (11.4)	2,732 (12.6)	6,420 (11.1)	2.35
Eastern Shore	51 (4.2)	396 (8)	346 (8)	500 (7)	1,018 (7.6)	1,138 (7.5)	1,535 (7.1)	4,718 (8.1)	3.06
TOTAL	1,210 (100)	4,914 (100)	4,370 (100)	7,190 (100)	13,392 (100)	15,162 (100)	21,606 (100)	58,040 (100)	2.69

TABLE 5   *Number of Hogsheads Exported*

River	1664		1674–76		1687		1698–99	
James	9,644	(46.8%)	21,520	(30.8%)	13,444	(37.5%)	19,827	(35.3%)
York	4,123	(20 %)	20,305	(29.1%)	8,719	(24.3%)	16,190	(28.8%)
Rappahannock	2,606	(12.7%)	13,230	(19 %)	7,189	(20 %)	13,542	(24.1%)
Potomac	2,596	(12.6%)	10,715	(15.3%)	5,037	(14 %)	4,523+	(8 %)
Eastern Shore	1,622	(7.9%)	4,041	(5.8%)	1,495	(4.2%)	2,116	(5.8%)
TOTAL	20,591	(100%)	69,811	(100%)	35,884	(100%)	56,198	(100%)

1688, to July 24, 1689, and from October 25, 1704, to July 20, 1711, we have records not of the number of hogsheads but of the total revenue produced by three duties: 2 shillings per hogshead of tobacco, 6d. per immigrant, and 15d. per ton of shipping, the three of which were reckoned together in a single account (see table 6).[39] While it is impossible to differentiate the exact proportion derived from each duty, the two shillings per hogshead duty probably accounted for about 80 percent of the total.[40] But whether the proportion of hogsheads was somewhat smaller and the proportion of immigrants higher matters little, for both signify manpower and are hence clues to population distribution.[41]

---

of *Burgesses of Virginia, 1659–1693* (Richmond, 1914), 501; for 1687: Blathwayt Papers, BL89, Huntington Library; for 1698–99: *VMHB*, XXIV (1916), 304, 403. The early records give only the name of the collector, but the river for which each was responsible can be inferred from a variety of evidence, and directly, for 1676, from *Calendar of Treasury Books*, V, 347, and for 1687 from Lord Howard of Effingham's letters to the Commissioners of Customs, Aug. 1, 1686, and to the Lords of Trade, Feb. 22, 1686/7, Effingham Papers.

[39] The records for 1688–89 are from a volume of William Byrd I that was on deposit in the Virginia Historical Society in 1850 but is no longer there. It contained the accounts from 1688 to 1704. From it the *Virginia Historical Register*, III (1850), 187, printed the first and last entries. The records for 1704 to 1711 are in C.O. 5/1317, ff.25–30. One report out of nine is missing for Rappahannock and three out of nine for the Eastern Shore, so the figures for these areas are a little low.

[40] This was the case in 1698–99, when we have a breakdown of the amount received from the two shillings per hogshead and from the other two duties. *VMHB*, XXIV (1916), 304, 403.

[41] None of these figures should be used as an index of Virginia's total tobacco exports. Those for the seventeenth century are too isolated to show what the average annual crop may have been, for tobacco harvests varied enormously from year to year. Moreover, the amounts packed in a hogshead varied almost as much as the harvests, in spite of legislation regulating the dimensions. The number of pounds in a hogshead tended to increase throughout the century, because regardless of weight four hogsheads were accounted a ton in the freight charges (H.C.A. 13/71, deposition of John Jeffreys, June 5, 1656), and regardless of weight each hogshead was subject to the two shillings duty. Records of shipments of 534 hogsheads by Thomas Stegge in 1666 and 1669 show a range in weight from 352 to 670 pounds, with an average of 456 (Letter Book of William Byrd I, 1683–91, Virginia Historical Society). There were numerous allegations that the number of hogsheads which paid the duty was considerably smaller than the number shipped (C.O. 1/20, f.11), and that a good deal was shipped in bulk, fitted

TABLE 6 *Proceeds from Duty of 2 Shillings per Hogshead, 15 Pence per Ton, and 6 Pence per Immigrant*

River	1689		1704–11	
James	£1,136	(31.3%)	£4,905	(20.9%)
York	£1,154	(31.7%)	£9,359	(39.8%)
Rappahannock	£747	(20.6%)	£5,600	(23.8%)
Potomac	£458	(12.6%)	£3,216	(13.7%)
Eastern Shore	£138	(3.8%)	£436	(1.8%)
TOTAL	£3,633	(100%)	£23,516	(100%)

From tables 4 through 6 a few clear trends emerge. The Eastern Shore retained 7 to 8 percent of the tithables and of the population throughout the century. The James River, which originally held the mass of the population, was gradually outweighed by the growth of settlement on the northern rivers. As late as 1653, the James River counties held more than 60 percent of the recorded tithables, but in the succeeding thirty years the number of tithables increased in this area by less than 1,000, while the York, Rappahannock, and Potomac regions gained over 6,000. In 1682 they held, together, over 8,500 tithables. After 1682 the distribution of population seems not to have changed appreciably, but the northern rivers maintained their dominant position, and in the early eighteenth century were producing the lion's share of Virginia tobacco.[42]

More interesting than these obvious and perhaps expectable trends is the fact that the areas of most rapid growth, the York, Rappahannock, and Potomac counties, were also the areas with the heaviest concentration of tithables in relation to total population. The Rappahannock and Potomac had 30.3 percent of the colony's tithables in 1699 but only 26.2 percent of the total population,

---

in by the sailors in the spaces between hogsheads. The figures are therefore too fragmentary to be more than a rough index of the differing productivity of the different areas.

[42] The James was to recover its preeminence later in the century. By the early 1760s the tonnage of shipping entering and clearing in the James surpassed that in all other districts put together. Add. Mss. 38,335, f.210, British Museum.

whereas the James, with 34.7 percent of the tithables, had 39.6 percent of the total population. On the York one in every 2.56 persons was tithable, on the Rappahannock, one in 2.31 and on the Potomac, one in 2.35. But on the James only one in 3.07 persons was tithable, and on the Eastern Shore, one in 3.06. For the south bank of the James (below Charles City and Henrico, which still covered both sides in 1699) the proportion of tithables was even smaller, one in 3.27. The Southside counties held only 13.3 percent of the colony's tithables, but 16.2 percent of the total population, while the Rappahannock held 17.6 percent of the tithables, but only 15 percent of the population.

It seems probable that the York, Rappahannock, and Potomac areas gained their high proportion of tithables by gaining the majority of immigrants. These northern areas attracted the colony's wealthiest planters, especially newcomers arriving with substantial amounts of capital. They could afford to buy the tithable servants and slaves, who made up the majority of immigrants. That at least one of the northern counties was servant-rich is confirmed by the records of Lancaster, the only county in the area for which the size of households can be ascertained. Most surviving county records give only the annual total of tithables, but for a few years Lancaster in the Northern Neck and Surry on the south side of the James (as well as Accomack and Northampton on the Eastern Shore) give the names of the heads of households with the number of tithables that each is responsible for. Table 7 compares the number of households in Lancaster and Surry in 1699, showing the average number of tithables per household, the average number of untithables, the overall average household size, and a breakdown of households by the number of tithables each was listed for. It will be seen that Lancaster, with far fewer households than Surry, had far more tithables, and thus far more servants per household.[43]

There may be another hint in table 7 about Lancaster's growth from immigrants. That is the seemingly incongruous fact that while Lancaster had a smaller proportion of untithables in its population, it had a larger number of untithables as well as tithables per house-

[43] The same was true throughout the period when figures are available. For example, in 1675, when 140 of Surry's 245 households had only one tithable, the number for Lancaster was 46 out of 146. The figures in table 7, except those for untithables, are taken from county records (Lancaster VII, 92–95; Surry V, 189–94) and thus differ from those in table 3, taken from colony records.

TABLE 7 *Lancaster and Surry in 1699*
(*Figures in parentheses are percentages*)

	Lancaster	Surry
Total households	243	361
Total tithables	865	683
Average number of tithables per household	3.56	1.9
One-man households	92 (38)	206 (57)
Households with 2–5 tithables	119 (49)	142 (39)
Households with 6–10 tithables	25 (10)	10 (3)
Households with 11–20 tithables	5 (2)	3 (1)
Households with over 20 tithables	3 (1)	0
Total untithables	1,224	1,350
Average number of untithables per household	5.04	3.74
Average number of total persons per household	8.56	5.64

hold. Such a situation could have developed if Lancaster men acquired substantially larger numbers of slaves of both sexes than Surry men did. During the last quarter of the seventeenth century the importation of slaves, both male and female, rose; and any county that invested heavily in these expensive immigrants might have gained a significant pool of native-born black children by 1699. As will be shown, there was a closer balance between slave women and slave men than between servant women and servant men. The children born to slave women could have raised the number of untithables per household while their mothers added to the number of tithables.

Another reason for the smaller number of untithables per household in Surry than in Lancaster may be that the number of households in Surry was swelled—and the average number of untithables per household lowered—by unmarried freedmen moving in from other parts of Virginia after their terms of service were up. With nothing but three barrels of corn and a suit of freedom clothes to start with, an ex-servant would have had difficulty competing for either women or land in a county of affluent planters like Lancaster.[44] He may have found a better chance south of the James to squat, sharecrop, or work for wages, to rent a house and land in partnership with another man or two, and eventually to acquire a plot of his own, a wife, and children.

Whether or not the population picture suggested by table 7 can be attributed to the migration of freedmen within the colony, to immigration, or to different rates of natural increase, it is clear that the majority of householders in Surry had no servants or slaves in 1699, and those who did have them had fewer than was the case in Lancaster. There were no big men in Surry to compare with Robert Carter, listed in Lancaster for 81 tithables in 1699. In Surry that year the largest household had 17 tithables.

The Black Population

In two counties, Northampton and Surry, it is possible to ascertain the number of black tithables for certain periods during the seventeenth century, in Northampton for most years from 1664 to 1677 and in Surry from 1674 to 1703. In Northampton, black tithables increased from 62 in 1664 to 75 in 1677, while total tithables increased from 438 to 469. Thus in 1664, 14 percent of the tithables were black and in 1677, 16 percent, a gain of only 2 percent in thirteen years. In Surry the figures begin just before Virginia began converting to slave labor, and they reflect the change even in a poor southside county. In Surry black tithables rose from 40 in 1674 to 67 in 1682 to 155 in 1699, while total tithables rose from 420 to 494 to 683. Thus 9.5 percent of Surry's tithables were black in 1674, 13.6 percent in 1682, and 22.7 percent in 1699.[45]

[44] See chap. 11.

[45] All these figures are from county records, not colony records, and thus differ from the figures in table 3. The Surry lists start in 1668, but give the names only of householders until 1674. Beginning in that year they give the names of most other tithables as well, and after 1677 they give the names of all tithables. It is possible from later lists and other county records to

From the black tithable figures for Northampton and Surry we may make some rough estimates of the black population of Virginia in 1674, 1682, and 1699, the years for which we have a figure for the total tithables in the colony. Because of deficiencies in the colony records explained in connection with table 1, we will add to the total tithable figures 6 percent for 1674 and 1699 and 12 percent for 1682 (thus estimating the total tithables of the colony as 14,196 in 1674, 16,981 in 1682, and 22,902 in 1699). In 1674 Northampton had 479 tithables, of whom 72 were black. If the rest of the colony had the same proportion, the total number of black tithables in Virginia would have been about 2,130 in 1674. If we extrapolate from the Surry returns for the same year, we get a figure for the colony as a whole of about 1,350 black tithables.

An estimate of how many black untithables there may have been must be even more tentative. In 1674 the only untithable blacks were those under sixteen who had been born in Virginia. But how many of these there were in the whole colony depended on the size and sex ratio of the black population in each county. Surry, with only 40 black tithables in 1674 and fewer women than men, may not have had many native-born black children. Northampton, which in 1664 already had 62 black tithables and an almost even sex ratio, may have acquired a greater number of native-born black children by 1674. But if so, they had apparently not yet reached the age of sixteen, since there was no rise in Northampton's black tithables as a result of the act of 1672 which made native-born black females tithable at that age. Northampton's adult sex ratio for blacks continued to be about even during the years for which records survive (28 male, 29 female, and 5 unknown in 1664; 31 male, 28 female, and 13 unknown in 1674; 36 male, 38 female, and 1 unknown in 1677). Surry's black sex ratio remained uneven throughout the century (18 male, 10 female, and 12 unknown in 1674; 36 male, 28 female, and 3 unknown in 1682; 104 male, 47 female, and 4 unknown in 1699).

Since we do not have data to establish a ratio between tithable and untithable blacks, I shall assume that Virginia's black untithables in 1674 amounted to 15 percent of the colony's black population, which seems a generous number (see footnote 46). Then if the proportion of blacks in the colony as a whole was the same as their proportion in Northampton, the total black population of Virginia

---

identify 12 Negroes not named as such in the 1674 list. These have been included in the number (40) for that year.

in 1674 could have been about 2,510. Or, if we extrapolate from Surry figures, the total black population could have been 1,550.

If we extrapolate in the same way from Surry figures for 1682, the total black population in that year would have been about 2,650. It seems probable, however, that the percentage of black untithables in the colony had risen as a result of the law of 1680 which defined black untithables as imported children under twelve (Virginia-born black children under sixteen presumably remained untithable also). If, as seems likely, the new law reflected an increase of children, perhaps to 20 percent, the total black population in 1682 would have been about 2,760.[46]

Similar extrapolation from Surry figures for 1699 gives us a total black population of about 5,975 if we use 15 percent as the proportion of untithables in the black population, and about 6,240 if we use 20 percent.

Because of the disparity in number and in sex ratio between the black tithables of Surry and Northampton and because the composition of the population varied so widely from county to county in Virginia, it may well be that the figures derived from Northampton and Surry are unrepresentative. And since the over-all ratio of total population to tithables was about the same in Virginia as in Maryland, it may be that the over-all percentage of blacks in the population was about the same. In that case, we might more safely extrapolate from Maryland figures than from those for Northampton and Surry. If blacks constituted 15.5 percent of Virginia's population in 1704, as slaves did in Maryland,[47] then Virginia, with a total popula-

[46] Gregory King placed 27.6 percent of the population of England and Wales at under eleven years old (D. V. Glass, "Two Papers on Gregory King," in D. V. Glass and D. E. C. Eversley, eds., *Population in History* [London, 1965], 159–220, at p. 214). It is likely that the black population of Virginia at this time was heavily weighted toward persons over twelve, but it is clear that the slavers brought in and sold small children as well as adults. By the law of 1680 a master had to register the age of a black child in the county court within three months of arrival; and the court records regularly show such registrations. For example, in Norfolk IX there are 13 registrations between March, 1687, and July, 1691, with ages varying from four to twelve. It seems likely that children under twelve, either immigrant or native-born, would have amounted to no more than 20 percent of the total black population in 1682. But the figure is merely a guess.

[47] Russell Menard, in "Economy and Society in Early Colonial Maryland" (unpublished doctoral dissertation, University of Iowa, 1974), has shown that the tables in *Archives of Maryland*, XXV (Baltimore, 1905),

tion of about 75,600,[48] would have had a black population of about 11,718 in 1704. We may subtract from this figure a recorded number of 1,892 slaves imported from June, 1699, through June, 1704,[49] and arrive at a black population of 9,826, or roughly 10,000.

However obtained, these estimates for 1699 are considerably below the figure (16,390) given in the *Historical Statistics of the United States* for the year 1700, but closer to the estimate of 6,000 offered by Bruce and the "somewhat larger but not greatly in excess of six thousand" obtained by Craven.[50] All are conjectural. Perhaps the safest conclusion to draw from the few statistics that survive from the seventeenth century would be that the black population of Virginia in 1674 was not less than 1,000 and not much more than 3,000. By the end of the century the number was not much less than 6,000 and not much more than 10,000, but about to expand rapidly.

Northampton County, 1664–77

In Northampton from 1664 to 1677 and in Surry from 1674 to 1703, surviving lists give the names not only of household heads but also of the tithables in their households. Although these are scarcely substitutes for vital statistics and tell us nothing about sex ratios (except for blacks), life expectancy, age structure, age at marriage, and the other usual data of demography, they can tell us a little about social and geographic mobility.

255–56, which make the black population about 12.8 percent of the total, have omitted black children in most counties. He calculates slaves as 5,609 out of a total Maryland population of 36,213 in 1704, or 15.5 percent. I am indebted to Dr. Menard for showing me this section of his dissertation.

[48] The total listed number of tithables in that year was 26,928. If we add 6 percent for undercounting in the list, the number is 28,544. The ratio of total population to tithables in 1701 had gone down from 2.69 to 2.65, probably as a result of the importation of large numbers of Negro tithables. The importation was continuing, and in order to arrive at total population we should multiply by a figure no larger than 2.65. This would give us a total of about 75,600, which may still be too large.

[49] Elizabeth Donnan, *Documents Illustrative of the History of the Slave Trade to America* (Washington, D.C., 1930–35), IV, 67, 172–73.

[50] U.S. Bureau of Census, *Historical Statistics of the United States: Colonial Times to 1957* (Washington, D.C., 1960), 756; Philip A. Bruce, *Economic History of Virginia in the Seventeenth Century* (New York, 1895), II, 108; Craven, *White, Red, and Black*, 103.

To extract the information from them is an arduous process, and it is attempted here only for Northampton.[51] Although Northampton, located on the Eastern Shore, may have been out of the main currents of Virginia life, its household structure, so far as we can compare it with other counties, was not idiosyncratic (see table in chapter 11). The Northampton tithable lists are extant for ten of the fourteen years from 1664 to 1677, those for 1669, 1670, 1672, and 1673 being missing. In order to compare the names on the various lists it was necessary to standardize the spellings, which vary a great deal from list to list. Once the "linkages" had been made between a name on one list and the same name, spelled differently, on other lists, it was possible by computer to trace each individual from one list to the next and thereby to tabulate changes of an individual's status and location from household to household, and also to determine the duration of households, and their growth and decline in numbers of tithables. Some of the results have been given in the text, but it seems worthwhile to support these with a more detailed analysis.

First, a few over-all figures. The total number of persons named on the ten lists is 1,043. Of these, 205 appear only as householders (heads of households), and 578 appear only as non-householders. The remaining 260 appear as householders in some years and non-householders in others. Of those who changed status 246 appear at some time as non-householders and later as householders; 88 appear at some time as householders and later as non-householders; 74 shuttled back and forth more than once from one status to the other (and thus are included both among the 88 and the 246).

Table 8 shows the annual distribution of tithables among households, together with the total number of tithables, the total number of households, and the average number of tithables per household. It will be seen that the average number of tithables per household declined over the period covered, and that the decline is mainly, though not entirely, the result of an increase in the number of households with only one tithable—in other words, an increase of house-

---

[51] The Surry lists (see note 45) have been analyzed, in different ways, in Kevin P. Kelly, "Economic and Social Development of Seventeenth-Century Surry County, Virginia" (unpublished doctoral dissertation, University of Washington, 1972). The Northampton lists are in Northampton VIII, 197–98; X, 14–15, 28–29, 41–42, 54–55, 114–15, 272–73; XII, 73–75, 148–49, 189–91.

holds that contained no worker (slave, male servant, or grown son) except the head of the house.[52]

Some impression of the transience of the population can be gained from table 9, giving the number of lists on which people ap-

TABLE 8 *Size of Northampton Households, 1664–77*
(*In number of tithables*)

Number of tithables per household	1664	1665	1666	1667	1668	1671	1674	1675	1676	1677
1	43	52	57	67	73	86	104	109	116	110
2	58	47	49	47	57	47	43	44	35	41
3	12	19	15	24	23	14	23	23	24	24
4	14	9	12	13	7	9	15	10	11	9
5	6	8	7	8	3	6	5	8	9	6
6	3	5	7	6	4	8	5	3	2	3
7	4	5	2	–	4	1	3	1	4	2
8	3	1	3	1	3	3	–	–	–	3
9	2	2	1	–	–	–	–	1	2	4
10	2	1	1	1	2	1	–	1	–	–
11–15	1	4	4	3	1	3	3	3	4	2
16–20	2	2	–	1	–	1	–	–	1	1
21–25	–	–	–	–	–	–	2	2	–	–
Total households	150	155	158	171	177	179	203	205	208	205
Total tithables	438	462	434	439	406	436	479	473	471	469
Average number of tithables per household	2.92	2.98	2.75	2.57	2.29	2.44	2.36	2.31	2.26	2.29

[52] The total number of households in table 8 includes households headed by a widow (of which in most years there were three or four), but widows are not included in the number of tithables.

peared. It should be noted that since the ten lists cover fourteen years, the number of years a person appears on the surviving lists does not necessarily correspond exactly with the number of years he may have remained in the county. Moreover, persons appearing on more than one list were not necessarily in the county continuously: 134 persons are listed more than once but not in consecutive lists.

TABLE 9   *Duration of Stay in Northampton County*

Number of persons	Number of years listed
248	1
129	2
101	3
136	4
117	5
60	6
41	7
45	8
57	9
109	10

Tables 10 and 11 offer other ways of looking at the transience or continuity of the county's population. Table 10 gives the number of tithable persons who were present in each of the first four lists and also present ten years later, together with the percentages they formed of the total tithables. For example, 183 persons who were present in 1667 were also present in 1677. They constituted 41.7 percent of the total tithables in 1667 and 39 percent of the larger total in 1677.

Because of the tendency of people to disappear from the lists and then reappear later, a fairer indication of the degree of continuity may be the fact that 207 tithables in 1677 had also been on one of the first four lists (1664–67). In other words, 44.1 percent of 1677's 469 tithables had been in the county ten to fourteen years before. Of the 207, 85 had been householders, and 82 of these (including 4 blacks) had retained that status. The other 122 (including 42 blacks) had been non-householders, and 73 of them (including 40 blacks) were still in that position, but 49 (including 2 blacks) had made it into the ranks of householders.

Table 11, using the tithable figures in a different way, registers

TABLE 10 *Tithable Persons Persisting for a Decade in Northampton*

Decade	Number persisting	Percent of total tithables at beginning of decade	Percent of total tithables at end of decade
1664–74	195	44.5	40.7
1665–75	200	43.3	42.3
1666–76	198	45.6	42.0
1667–77	183	41.7	39.0
AVERAGE	194	43.8	41.0

the growth, decline, and continuity of households from year to year. The table shows a substantial body of households continuing at about the same size each year, but the number that decreased in size generally exceeded the number that increased. In this table the percentage of households decreasing, increasing, and at the same size is compared with the households of the preceding year, so that no figure could be given for the first year, 1664. It should be noted that the figures for 1671 are compared with those for 1668, and those for 1674 are compared with those for 1671, because the intervening years are missing.

Since the most noticeable development during the years covered by the lists was the increase of households with a single tithable, it may be of interest to trace the rise of persons who started as non-householders. Of the 230 who eventually became householders, 121 remained as the sole tithable in the house they headed during the time they headed it (26 of the 121 reverted and ended as non-householders). But 60 at some point obtained another tithable (11 of the 60 ended as non-householders); 28 obtained 2 more (2 of the 28 ended as non-householders); 9 obtained 3 more; 8 obtained 4 more (2 of the 8 ended as non-householders); 2 obtained 5; 1 obtained 6; and 1 obtained 7 (the last two were sons of prominent men who set up households of their own during the period, and several others were apparently men of some means who had lived for a while in the household of another man before becoming householders them-

TABLE 11 *Household Stability in Northampton*

	1665	1666	1667	1668	1671	1674	1675	1676	1677
Number of new households	27	23	28	23	48	69	34	39	32
Number of households remaining from preceding list	128	135	143	154	131	134	171	169	173
Percentage of remaining households at same size as in preceding list	49	40	44	55	38	40	60	57	56
Percentage of remaining households decreasing in size	27	39	31	28	29	32	23	27	24
Percentage of remaining households increasing in size	24	21	25	18	33	28	17	16	20

TABLE 12 *Mobility of Non-Householders in Northampton*

	1665	1666	1667	1668	1671	1674	1675	1676	1677
Number of whites	260	236	221	183	193	213	207	195	197
Percentage present in preceding list	67	75	78	80	47	47	72	76	69
Percentage in same household as in preceding list	48	50	47	52	23	26	57	53	46
Number of blacks	49	45	49	49	68	69	68	72	71
Percentage present in preceding list	98	96	90	98	66	84	97	92	96
Percentage in same household as in preceding list	73	78	76	84	41	68	82	72	76

selves). Of 92 persons who first appear in the lists as the head of a house in which they were the only tithable, 21 at some point became non-householders; 42 clung to their position without increasing it; 20 gained another tithable; 7 gained 2 more; and 2 gained 3 more.

The number of Negro householders in these years was not large, but neither was it as small as might be expected. Of the 1,043 persons named on any list, 101 were Negroes; and of these, 13 were or became householders, as compared with 45 percent of whites. But this comparison is distorted by the fact that Negro women were tithable while white women ordinarily were not. The 101 Negroes on the lists included 48 women, of whom 3 became householders (as widows). If we confine the comparison to men, 10 out of 53 Negroes named, or 19 percent, were or became householders.

Table 12 shows the percentages of non-householders moving and static each year. Tables 13 and 14 show the movements of individual non-householders. The top figure in each vertical column of tables 13 and 14 shows the number of people who made the maximum possible number of household changes for the length of time that they were non-householders (some were householders in other years and movement from non-householder to householder or vice

TABLE 13   *Mobility of White Non-Householders in Northampton*

Number of years listed as non-house holders	1	247									
	2	78	63								
	3	61	34	16							
	4	52	29	14	10						
	5	17	22	13	7	3					
	6	4	6	8	8	3	1				
	7	3	2	3	4	2	2	0			
	8	4	3	0	3	4	1	1	0		
	9	2	0	2	1	3	2	1	0	0	
	10	0	1	1	1	0	0	0	0	0	0
		1	2	3	4	5	6	7	8	9	10

Number of households

TABLE 14 *Mobility of Black Non-Householders in Northampton*

		1	2	3	4	5	6	7	8	9	10
Number of years listed as non-house holders	1	10									
	2	3	3								
	3	0	0	1							
	4	2	6	2	0						
	5	9	10	2	0	1					
	6	2	4	0	0	0	0				
	7	0	0	3	0	0	0	0			
	8	1	2	1	0	0	0	0	0		
	9	0	5	2	1	0	0	0	0	0	
	10	10	8	4	1	3	0	0	0	0	0

Number of households

versa is not recorded in these two tables). Thus, for example, in table 13 there are 16 white non-householders who appear on four lists in four different households, and so forth. The figures show that there was a large movement of white non-householders from household to household. Since most non-householders were probably servants, either indentured or hired, tables 12 and 13 suggest that each year many servants moved or were moved from one master to another.

The figures for black non-householders in tables 12 and 14 should be treated as approximations. Blacks are much more difficult to identify than whites, because most are listed with no surname, and sometimes they are listed simply as Negro, Negro man, or Negro woman. In these cases they have been identified by inference from their location in preceding or succeeding years. The result may be to exaggerate the stability of the black population. It nevertheless seems highly probable that blacks moved from household to household much less than did white non-householders.

The figures in all these tables, not only for Northampton but for all Virginia, are probably less solid than they may appear to be to one who has not struggled with the records from which they are derived. I have striven to eliminate errors both in counting and in computation, but it is not unlikely that many remain. It should be remembered, moreover, that people in the seventeenth century had less respect for numbers than their modern counterparts. Figures derived from seventeenth-century sources are apt to be shaky at best, and those from seventeenth-century Virginia are shakier than most. What I hope can be discerned from all the tables is simply the broad outline of developments taking place in a society that was later to contribute so heavily to the making of the United States.

A Note on the Sources

Every historian builds on the work of those who precede him. My study has depended, probably more than I realize, on the work of Alexander Brown, Philip A. Bruce, Thomas J. Wertenbaker, Wesley Frank Craven, Richard L. Morton, and Wilcomb E. Washburn. But my story is different from theirs, and probably none of them would or will find it wholly acceptable. I have tried to acknowledge particular debts in footnotes, which I hope may serve in lieu of a formal bibliography of secondary works. But since I have relied primarily on original sources, and since a book is generally shaped by the nature of the sources available, a note about them may be appropriate.

Printed Sources

The printed sources for study of colonial Virginia are voluminous. England's first approaches to colonization can be viewed not only in Richard Hakluyt's *Divers Voyages Touching the Discoverie of America* (London, 1582) and *Principall Navigations, Voiages, and Discoveries of the English Nation* (London, 1589, 1598–1600), but also in the many *Works* issued by the Hakluyt Society, especially E. G. R. Taylor, ed., *The Original Writings and Correspondence of the Two Richard Hakluyts* (London, 1935, 2nd ser., LXXVI, LXXVII); Clements R. Markham, ed., *The Hawkins Voyages* (London, 1878, 1st ser., LVII); R. Collinson, ed., *The Three Voyages of Martin Frobisher* (London, 1867, 1st ser., XXXVIII); David B. Quinn, *Voyages and Colonizing Enterprises of Sir Humphrey Gilbert* (London, 1940, 2nd ser., LXXXIII, LXXXIV), and the same editor's great collection of *The Roanoke Voyages, 1584–1590* (London, 1955, 2nd ser., CIV, CV). Many of the

English voyages, as reported by Spanish officials in the Caribbean, can be followed in Irene A. Wright, ed., *Documents concerning English Voyages to the Spanish Main, 1569–1580* (London, 1932, 2nd ser., LXXI); *Further English Voyages to Spanish America, 1583–1594* (London, 1951, 2nd ser., XCIX); and Kenneth R. Andrews, ed., *English Privateering Voyages to the West Indies, 1588–1595* (Cambridge, 1959, 2nd ser., CXI). A further perspective on the Roanoke venture can be gained from Raleigh's later enterprises in Guiana, in Vincent T. Harlow, ed., *The Discoverie of the Large and Bewtiful Empire of Guiana* (London, 1928) and *Ralegh's Last Voyage* (London, 1932).

The largest collection of documents for the early years of the James-town settlement is Alexander Brown's monumental work *The Genesis of the United States* (Boston, 1890), which is only partially replaced by Philip Barbour's more limited selection in *The Jamestown Voyages under the First Charter, 1606–1609* (Cambridge, 1969, Works issued by the Hakluyt Society, 2nd ser., CXXXVI, CXXXVII). The single most important contemporary account of these years lies in the *Travels and Works* of Captain John Smith, Edward Arber and A. G. Bradley, eds. (Edinburgh, 1910). A critical edition of all of Smith's writings is much needed, for in some passages he writes from his own experience, while in others he copies or paraphrases other writers, often without indicating that he is doing so. The segments of Smith's writing contained in Barbour's *Jamestown Voyages* are more accurately transcribed from the original than in the Arber-Bradley edition; but the annotation falls short of what is needed.

As Smith copied from others, William Strachey in his *Historie of Travell into Virginia Britania*, Louis B. Wright and Virginia Freund, eds. (London, 1953, Works issued by the Hakluyt Society, 2nd ser., CIII), seems to have copied mainly from Smith, though Strachey him-self had been in Virginia and supplied some details of his own. Strachey was responsible for publishing *For the Colony in Virginea Britannia: Lawes Divine, Morall and Martiall* (London, 1612; David H. Flaherty, ed., Charlottesville, 1969). And he also wrote "A True Repertory of the Wreck and Redemption of Sir Thomas Gates, Knight," Louis B. Wright, ed., *A Voyage to Virginia in 1609* (Charlottesville, 1964).

Other participants in the Jamestown venture who recorded their experiences or their impressions included Gabriel Archer, John Pory, John Rolfe, Henry Spelman, Lord De la Warr, and Edward Wingfield, whose accounts are included along with other documents, in the intro-duction by Arber and Bradley to Smith, *Travels and Works*, or in L. G. Tyler, ed., *Narratives of Early Virginia, 1606–1625* (New York, 1907). Not included in these two convenient collections are Ralph Hamor, *A True Discourse of the Present Estate of Virginia* (London, 1615); George Percy, "A Trewe Relacyon of the Procedeinges and

Occurrentes of Momente . . . ," *Tyler's Quarterly Historical and Genealogical Magazine*, III (1922), 260–82; and Alexander Whitaker, *Good Newes from Virginia* (London, 1613). A valuable tract by a non-participant that is not fully reprinted in any collection is Robert Gray, *A Good Speed to Virginia* (London, 1609).

The earliest records of the Virginia Company are missing, but those for its last years, 1619–24, along with various miscellaneous papers and correspondence, including the journals of the first two meetings of the House of Burgesses, have been published (without annotation) in Susan Kingsbury, ed., *The Records of the Virginia Company of London* (Washington, D.C., 1906–35). The decades that followed the demise of the company are less well documented in printed works than the early years. Since the crown was responsible for administration of the colony after 1624, the great bulk of available documents are those in the Public Record Office of Great Britain. Many of these were printed or summarized in early issues of the *Virginia Magazine of History and Biography* abstracted by W. Noel Sainsbury, with fuller extracts than he printed in the *Calendar of State Papers, Colonial*. A number of others may be found in Edward Neill, *Virginia Carolorum* (Albany, N.Y., 1886). Many previously unpublished early manuscripts, both from Virginia sources and from English archives, are scattered through the volumes of the *Virginia Magazine of History and Biography*, the *William and Mary Quarterly, Tyler's Quarterly Historical and Genealogical Magazine*, and the *Virginia Historical Register* (a convenient aid in using these is Earl G. Swem, *Virginia Historical Index*, Roanoke, 1934–36). And many early published tracts relating to the colony were reprinted by Peter Force in his *Tracts and Other Papers Relating Principally to the Origin, Settlement, and Progress of the Colonies in North America* (Washington, D.C., 1836–46). The "Aspinwall Papers," Massachusetts Historical Society, *Collections*, 4th ser., IX (1871), contains documents from the 1620s and 1630s as well as from the time of Bacon's Rebellion. David Peter de Vries, "Voyages from Holland to America, A.D. 1632 to 1644," New-York Historical Society, *Collections*, 2nd, ser., III (1857), 9–136, gives a Dutchman's impressions.

Virginians did not write about themselves or their colony with anything like the zeal shown by New Englanders, but a number of them at different times did attempt to describe the "present state" of the colony, usually with some political end in view. William Bullock, *Virginia Impartially Examined* (London, 1649) is not quite of this sort, since the author seems never to have been to Virginia, but he thought he knew enough to denounce its governing class. Lionel Gatford, *Publick Good without Private Interest* (London, 1657) is another denunciation, not merely of the governors but of the people they governed. William Berkeley, *A Discourse and View of Virginia* (London, 1663) was

written to promote his plans for diversification. The tracts relating to
Bacon's Rebellion, most of which are reprinted either in Force, *Tracts*,
or in C. M. Andrews, ed., *Narratives of the Insurrections* (New York,
1915), are expectably partisan, in one direction or the other. Henry
Hartwell, James Blair, and Edward Chilton, *The Present State of
Virginia and the College* (London, 1727) is a report submitted to the
Board of Trade thirty years earlier, in order to discredit Governor
Francis Nicholson. Robert Beverley also filled his *History and Present
State of Virginia* (London, 1705; L. B. Wright, ed., Chapel Hill, N.C.,
1947) with diatribes against Nicholson. Hugh Jones, *The Present State
of Virginia* (London, 1724) is much less partisan, though Jones, a
clergyman, was a friend of Governor Spotswood and an opponent of
James Blair. William Stith, another clergyman, in his *History of the
First Discovery and Settlement of Virginia* (Williamsburg, 1747),
managed to express a contemporary political position in recounting the
history of the colony under the company. Stith's was the first book about
Virginia to be printed in the colony itself. Subsequent political controversies, including the quarrel with England, elicited a good many more
publications from the colony's presses as well as filling many of the
pages of the *Virginia Gazette*, but most of these lie beyond the scope of
the present work. Edmund Randolph's *History of Virginia*, written in
the early years of the nineteenth century, was not published until 1970
(Charlottesville, Arthur H. Shaffer, ed.). This and John Daly Burk's
History of Virginia (Petersburg, 1804–16) are still valuable, because the
authors had access to documents that have since been lost or destroyed.

Most of the official records of seventeenth-century Virginia subsequent to the dissolution of the company have been lost, many of them in
the burning of Richmond. But the records of the governor and council
covering the period 1622–32 and 1670–76 survived and are printed,
along with notes on the missing years by Conway Robinson (made before the fire), in H. R. McIlwaine, ed., *Minutes of the Council and
General Court of Colonial Virginia* . . . (Richmond, 1924). William
Waller Hening printed all the statutes and orders passed by the assembly, so far as he could find copies, in *The Statutes at Large: Being a
Collection of All the Laws of Virginia* . . . (Richmond, 1809–23). One
set of records that survives nearly intact is that of the patent books, in
which were copied the patents granting lands to individuals. Abstracts
of Books 1–5, containing patents issued from 1623 to 1666, have been
published in Nell M. Nugent, *Cavaliers and Pioneers* (Richmond, 1934).
Miss Nugent also prepared abstracts of Books 6–9, which have not been
published but are available at the State Library.

Copies of Virginia legislative acts and proceedings were regularly
sent to England and to the county courts; and copies and notes were also
made of some of them in the eighteenth century for Sir John Randolph

(the so-called Bland Manuscript now in the Library of Congress). It is from such copies and notes that it' has been possible to recover much of the early legislative record of seventeenth-century Virginia, as printed in Hening and in J. P. Kennedy and H. R. McIlwaine, eds., *Journal of the House of Burgesses*. There are twelve volumes of this work, covering the years from 1619 to 1776, each distinguished, not by a volume number, but by an indication on the title page of the years covered. The volumes were published at Richmond from 1905 to 1915, in an edition more noteworthy for typographical than for editorial care. The text has often been taken from Hening or from other reprintings even when the original manuscript was available; and although a number of legislative papers and documents from the British Public Record Office have been included in the early volumes in order to fill gaps in the record, the selection of these seems capricious.

Some of the gaps in Hening and in the printed *Journals* have been filled in other publications. The acts of the assembly for the session beginning January 6, 1639/40, are in *William and Mary Quarterly*, 2nd ser., IV (1924), 16–35, 145–62. The acts for the session beginning January 12, 1641/2, are in *Virginia Magazine of History and Biography*, IX (1901–2), 51–59. Those for the sessions in 1643–46 are in *ibid.*, XXIII (1915), 225–55. Other missing seventeenth-century acts and proceedings must be sought in manuscript sources (see below), but for the period 1700–1750 acts missing from Hening have been gathered and printed in Waverly K. Winfree, *The Laws of Virginia: Being a Supplement to Hening's The Statutes at Large* (Richmond, 1971).

The legislative and executive journals of the governor's council from 1680 onward have survived (though not the records of the council acting in its judicial capacity as the General Court). The council evidently kept separate journals in its different capacities, at least from 1680 on and probably earlier. The existing journals have been published: H. R. McIlwaine, ed., *Legislative Journals of the Council of Colonial Virginia* (Richmond, 1918–19); and H. R. McIlwaine et al. eds., *Executive Journals of the Council of Colonial Virginia* (Richmond, 1925–66).

The *Journals* are often disappointingly silent about substantive issues discussed by the council and the burgesses, and the formal record should be read in conjunction with official and unofficial correspondence and reports. The most valuable single body of material of this kind is in the British Public Record Office, and abstracts have been published, as noted above, in the *Calendar of State Papers, Colonial* and the *Virginia Magazine of History and Biography*, but any intensive study requires use of the full originals, which are readily available on microfilm (see below). Other surviving papers and documents are abstracted in W. F. Palmer, ed., *Calendar of Virginia State Papers and Other Manu-*

scripts . . . Preserved in the Capitol at Richmond (Richmond, 1875–93). The most valuable printed collections of letters by governors are those of Spotswood and Dinwiddie: R. A. Brock, ed., *The Official Letters of Alexander Spotswood* (Richmond, 1882–85, Virginia Historical Society, *Collections*, n.s., I–II); R. A. Brock, ed., *The Official Records of Robert Dinwiddie* (Richmond, 1883–84, Virginia Historical Society, *Collections*, n.s., III–IV). For a much earlier date there are official papers of Governor Sir Francis Wyatt, in *William and Mary Quarterly*, 2nd ser., VI (1926), 114–23; VII (1927), 42–47, 125–31, 204–14, 246–54; VIII (1928), 48–57, 157–67. William Stevens Perry, ed., *Historical Collections Relating to the American Colonial Church*, vol. I: *Virginia* (Hartford, 1870) contains many documents bearing on the activities of James Blair and his dispute with Governor Nicholson. Other papers relating to this dispute are published in the *Virginia Magazine of History and Biography*, III (1895–96), 373–82; VII (1899–1900), 153–72, 275–86, 386–401; VIII (1900–1901), 46–64, 126–46, 260–78, 366–85; IX (1901–2), 18–29, 152–62, 251–62. Another convenient collection on a topic of particular importance for the present study is Elizabeth Donnan, ed., *Documents Illustrative of the History of the Slave Trade to America*, vol. IV: *The Border Colonies and the Southern Colonies* (Washington, D.C., 1935), 49–234.

The only extensive private correspondence surviving from the seventeenth century is that of William Fitzhugh, edited by Richard B. Davis in *William Fitzhugh and his Chesapeake World* (Chapel Hill, N.C., 1963). Letters of William Byrd I, from 1684 to 1691, are in *Virginia Magazine of History and Biography* XXIV (1916), 225–35; XXVI (1918), 17–31, 124–34, 247–59, 380–92; XXVII (1919), 167–68, 273–78; XXVIII (1920), 11–25. For the eighteenth century private records are much more numerous. The letters of William Byrd II are in *Virginia Magazine of History and Biography*, IX (1901–2), 113–30, 225–51; XXXV (1927), 221–45, 371–89; XXXVI (1928), 36–44, 113–23, 209–22, 353–62; XXXVII (1929), 28–33; 101–18. Byrd's other writings and diaries have been edited by Louis B. Wright and others in a succession of volumes: L. B. Wright and Marion Tinling, eds., *The Secret Diary of William Byrd of Westover, 1709–1712* (Richmond, 1941); Maude H. Woodfin and Marion Tinling, eds., *Another Secret Diary of William Byrd of Westover, 1739–1741, with Letters and Literary Exercises, 1696–1726* (Richmond, 1942); Louis B. Wright and Marion Tinling, eds., *The London Diary (1717–1721) and Other Writings* (New York, 1958); L. B. Wright, ed., *The Prose Works of William Byrd of Westover* (Cambridge, Mass., 1966).

The Byrd diaries reveal less than one could wish about plantation life, but the *Diary of Colonel Landon Carter*, Jack P. Greene, ed. (Charlottesville, 1965), is full of the details of plantation management.

Louis B. Wright has edited the letters of Landon's father, *Letters of Robert Carter, 1720–1727* (San Marino, Calif., 1940), most of them to business correspondents in England. Two diaries kept by newcomers to Virginia give a perspective not to be found in either Byrd or the Carters. Edward M. Riley, ed., *The Journal of John Harrower* (Williamsburg and New York, 1963) is that of a Scottish indentured servant employed as a tutor on the plantation of Colonel William Daingerfield. Hunter D. Farish, ed., *Journal and Letters of Philip Vickers Fithian* (Williamsburg, 1957; Charlottesville, 1968) is that of a young Princeton graduate employed as a tutor by Robert Carter of Nomini Hall (nephew of Landon Carter and grandson of the Robert Carter mentioned above).

A number of foreign travelers in Virginia also recorded their impressions. The most notable such record from the seventeenth century is that of one Durand, in Gilbert Chinard, ed., *A Huguenot Exile in Virginia* (New York, 1934). Another Huguenot's journal is Edward P. Alexander, ed., *The Journal of John Fontaine: An Irish Huguenot Son in Spain and Virginia, 1710–1719* (Charlottesville, 1972). A few more early visits are in Newton D. Mereness, ed., *Travels in the American Colonies* (New York, 1916), but far more travel accounts exist from the revolutionary period and after. Among the keener observers of Virginia society in those years were the Marquis de Chastellux (*Travels in North America in the Years 1780, 1781, and 1782*, Howard C. Rice, ed., Chapel Hill, N.C., 1963); J. P. Brissot de Warville (*New Travels in the United States of America, 1788*, Durand Echeverria, ed., Cambridge, Mass., 1964); the Baroness von Riedesel (*Baroness von Riedesel and the American Revolution*, Marvin L. Brown, Jr., ed., Chapel Hill, N.C., 1965); and Sir Augustus John Foster (*Jeffersonian America*, Richard B. Davis, ed., San Marino, Calif., 1954).

Manuscript Sources

The manuscript sources for Virginia's colonial period are even richer than those which have been published. On the occasion of the 350th anniversary of the first settlement at Jamestown the state undertook an extensive search for documents in England and France relating to Virginia. The Virginia Colonial Records Survey compiled reports on nearly 10,000 documents and collections of documents in the British Public Record Office, the British Museum, the Bodleian Library, and other English and European repositories. On the basis of the reports nearly 1,000 reels of microfilms were made of the most important collections, and copies were deposited, along with a complete set of the reports, at the Alderman Library in Charlottesville, the State Library, and the Research Library of Colonial Williamsburg. The collection constitutes the basic resource for study of Virginia history, especially political history, and the reports are the basic guide to that resource. But the films and reports are so voluminous that further indexes and finding aids are now much needed. The staff of the Colonial Williamsburg Research Library have prepared several of these already and thereby greatly facilitated the use of the collection.

The most valuable papers for this study were the familiar Colonial Office group in the Public Record Office, especially classes 1 and 5, which are also available in transcripts and films at the Library of Congress. But a number of collections outside the Public Record Office contain materials of the first importance for seventeenth-century Virginia history. At the Bodleian Library in Oxford the Locke Mss. contain some of James Blair's lengthy strictures on the administration of Governor Nicholson. The Rawlinson Mss. and the Clarendon Mss. contain a variety of letters and reports from Virginia. Of particular importance is Clarendon Ms. 82, the record of expenditures authorized by the assembly in 1662 and also the number of tithables in the colony that year. It is comparable to the records for 1677, 1682, and 1684 printed in McIlwaine's *Journals of the House of Burgesses, 1659/60–1693*, which McIlwaine assumed to be the only such document surviving. Similar records for 1673 and 1674 are in another collection, the Coventry Papers of the Marquess of Bath at Longleat House (microfilm in the Library of Congress). This collection also contains the most valuable papers relating to Bacon's Rebellion outside the Public Record Office. Another special collection, the Baron Howard of Effingham Papers in the Library of Congress, contains not only the reports made by Governor Howard to his superiors but also the journals of the assembly for the sessions of November, 1682; April, 1684; November, 1685; October, 1686; and April, 1688, along with acts passed. Those for 1682, 1685, and parts of 1684 are missing from McIlwaine's edition and available only here.

The Research Library at Colonial Williamsburg has the largest body of Blathwayt Papers. William Blathwayt became involved in the administration of the colonies in 1675 and remained so for the rest of the century, from 1680 on as auditor general and after 1696 as a member of the Board of Trade. The papers contain many reports to him by colonial officials. Among them is the list of Virginia tithables for 1674. Blathwayt's own journals are in the Public Record Office and more of his papers are in the Henry E. Huntington Library in San Marino, California, which also has various other papers relating to colonial Virginia.

The Virginia State Library has a great variety of manuscript materials, including the "Colonial Papers" which are abstracted in the *Calendar of Virginia State Papers*. But its most valuable holding, apart from the microfilms from the Virginia Colonial Records Survey (which unaccountably are not at present available to readers at the Library), is the great collection of microfilms and photostats of Virginia county court records, some made by the Library, others by the Genealogical Society of Utah. The court records are the principal source available for the study of Virginia social history in the colonial period. Unfortunately, few of the earliest records survive, especially in the counties on the peninsula between the James and the York. The most complete records for the seventeenth century are those for Northampton and Accomack counties on the Eastern Shore and those for Norfolk on the south side of the James. But there are extensive records for several other counties from the second half of the century. Those used for the present study are indicated in the explanation of footnote abbreviations on pp. 389–93. As explained there, only two volumes of these records have been published. Selected abstracts from several more are scattered through the pages of the *Virginia Magazine of History and Biography* and the *William and Mary Quarterly* and in Beverly Fleet, ed., *Virginia Colonial Abstracts* (Richmond, 1937–48). But the latter were selected with an eye more to their genealogical than to their historical interest.

The Alderman Library at Charlottesville has extensive manuscript collections relating to Virginia, but few date from the seventeenth century. Those from the early eighteenth century that proved of greatest use for this study were the Carter Family Papers, the Journal of William Hugh Grove and the Letter Book of Robert Anderson. The only other important repository of Virginia manuscripts is the Virginia Historical Society in Richmond. Its most valuable seventeenth-century holdings for this study, including many of the colony's officials records and private papers of the Byrd family, have been published, but it contains a wealth of other materials.

Index

Abbott, Elizabeth, 127

Accomack County, land speculation in, 220; households in, 226, 228; vagrants in, 238, 338; Indian slaves in, 330; population of, 412–13

Adair, James, 48

Agriculture, at Roanoke, 39–40; in England, 63–65, 67; among Indians, 52–56; shifting, 52–56, 141–42; methods of, 141–42, 172–73. *See also* Corn, Tobacco

Alexandria, 219

Allen, Thomas, 199

Allerton, Isaac, 251, 261

Amadas, Philip, 26–27, 38

Amelia County, households in, 342

Anburey, Thomas, 378–79

Andros, Edmund, 349–51, 398n

Anne, queen of England, 353, 361

Apprentices, in England, 65–66, 126, 128, 352; and Virginia Co., 98, 116; and Dr. Pott, 126; mulatto, 334

Aquascogoc, 38

Arawaks, 7, 18, 24

Argall, Samuel, 83, 84, 139

Aristotle, 375, 376

Arlington, Henry Bennet, Earl of, 245

Army, 59, 279, 354–55. *See also* Impressment, Militia

Arondelle, Peter, 103

Arthur, king of England, 16

Artisans, in England, 65–67, 69; and Jamestown settlement, 85–86, 89; and Sandys program, 95; wages of, 106; encouragement of, 140–41, 190–92

Assembly, origin of, 96; and servants, 123n, 216–17, 276, 344; and first royal governors, 143–46; and English Civil Wars, 146–48; and immigrants, 183–84; and diversification, 189–90; and tobacco restriction, 192–93; cost of, 208; of March, 1676, 253–54; of June, 1676, 261–65; of Feb., 1677, 273–74, 276; and judicial appeals, 281, 289; and Lords of Trade, 281–82; and export duty, 283; of April, 1682, 285–86; and Effingham, 287–89; and slavery, 311–13; and race, 330–37; and poor, 338–39; and reduction of taxes, 345; and Nicholson, 354–57; and Spotswood, 359–62. *See also* Burgesses, Council,

House of Burgesses

Ayleway, Robert, 210–11

Bachelors, 163, 221, 235–42

Bacon, Nathaniel, 254–70; appointed to council, 254; at Jordan's Point, 256; in New Kent, 258; dismissed from council, 259; and Occaneechees, 259; in May assembly, 261–62; gets commission, 264; issues Declaration, 266; marches against Pamunkeys, 268; burns Jamestown, 258; dies, 269; and racism, 328–29; mentioned, 353

Bacon's Rebellion, 250–70; royal commission on, 271–79; lawsuits arising from, 272–75; acts of indemnity for, 274, 283; servants and slaves in, 327

Baffin Land, 19

Baker, Daniel, 157

Ballard, Thomas, 203

Baltimore, Lord, 193–95, 272n, 286

Baptism, and slavery, 331–32

Baptists, 374

Barbados, slavery in, 133, 298–301, 314; exports to, 139, 139n, 192; servants in, 298–99; mortality in, 298; slave trade from, 327; mentioned, 344

Barlowe, Arthur, 26–27, 33, 37, 55–56

Barnes, Richard, 124

Barry, William, 119

Bass, Nathaniel, 125

Bassett, William, 352

Beckford, Peter, 309

Bellamy, John, 203

Bennett, Edward, 119

Bennett, Richard, 148

Bennett, Robert, 119n

Berkeley, Frances, 254, 275

Berkeley, George, 324

Berkeley, Richard, 107

Berkeley, William, first term as governor, 146–47; and Indians, 149, 230–33, 251–57, 260, 263; on mortality, 182; and diversification, 186–95; on New England, 187; and *Phoenix*, 203; income of, 204–6; and Dutch wars, 241–43; and Northern Neck, 244–45; and discontent, 246–47; and Bacon's Rebellion, 250–70; and royal commis-